PORRIDGE: THE SCRIPTS

DICK CLEMENT AND IAN LA FRENAIS

EDITED BY RICHARD WEBBER

headline

First published in 2002
by HEADLINE BOOK PUBLISHING

First published in paperback in 2004
by HEADLINE BOOK PUBLISHING

10 9 8 7 6 5 4 3 2 1

ISBN 0 7472 5862 7

Printed and bound in Great Britain by
Mackays of Chatham Plc, Chatham, Kent

Headline's policy is to use papers that are natural, renewable and recyclable
products and made from wood grown from sustainable forests. The logging and
manufacturing processes are expected to conform to the environmental regulations
of the country of origin.

Typeset in Sabon, Helvetica Light and American Typewriter by Letterpart Ltd
16 Bell Street, Reigate, Surrey

Text design by designsection, Frome, Somerset

HEADLINE BOOK PUBLISHING
A division of Hodder Headline
338 Euston Road
London NW1 3BH

www.headline.co.uk
www.hodderheadline.com

CONTENTS

PILOT

SERIES ONE

SERIES TWO

3 SERIES THREE

CHRISTMAS SPECIALS

FOREWORD

Fletcher was an easy character to play and I didn't have to think too much about it, which is fortunate. I think much of that is because there was a lot of me in Fletch; there was also plenty of my father, too. Although the character was a Cockney and I was born in Oxford, he was working class and I could relate to him.

Although he was out for everything he could get, being a wide-boy, he was a likeable chap. You always need charm in a character, even if you're playing an old tramp, and I think Fletcher possessed a lot of that.

Working on the show was such a delight, particularly as everyone worked so well together. When it came to rehearsals we'd race through them with ease. We'd often start at ten and be finished by one, simply because we all knew what we were doing. Obviously I was carrying a lot of the responsibility on my shoulders but I never received anything but total support from the rest of the team; you knew no one was going to let you down, ruin a gag or bit of timing.

I feel I owe much to *Porridge*. It was probably the best and most important show I did.

RONNIE BARKER 2002

INTRODUCTION

The first time Ian and I ever sat down to write together was in a pub in the Old Brompton Road. I don't remember any discussion about who should do the actual scribbling, but it was me. This tradition continued and when asked about it we used to answer that it was because my calligraphy was more legible than Ian's. It is, but I don't think that is the entire reason.

The essentials haven't varied much over the years. We write *together*. Other collaborators work by e-mail or split the script up and say, 'You do that scene, I'll do this one.' If it works, fine, but it's not the way we do it. We discuss everything. It starts with the story. What's the main thrust and where are the juicy scenes? Inevitably, while we're kicking ideas around, some dialogue occurs to us. I suppose we're doing a form of actors' improvisation. So we step into character and throw out a line and a response may occur and if it's any good we incorporate it when we do the actual writing.

A tape recorder might sound like a good idea for this stage of the process. I think we even bought a couple over the years but the batteries ran out, or we forgot to switch them on and then the thought of wading through all the discarded drivel in search of a forgotten gem was too daunting and time-consuming. We jot down anything we really like and then it's time to write 'Fade In'.

Everything is debated, alternatives considered, choices made. And as I'm always the one with the pen in my hand – here's the hidden agenda – I have the power to choose my version over Ian's if it is a split vote. But if he doesn't like it when he sees it on the page and raises the red flag, back it goes. Or maybe we find a compromise, another line, another word.

We switched to a computer a few years ago. Ian stared at the grey cube on the table with deep suspicion. When I started to tap the keys he was appalled. 'You're not going to do that *while we're writing*?' I certainly was, because the alternative was transcribing everything at the end of the day after he'd gone home. He grudgingly got used to it after a while, won over by the obvious advantages of instant print-outs and corrections, though it was a year before he walked round to my side of the table to take a look at the text on the screen.

Somebody once said that writing is all about re-writing. It's certainly true in our case. Bang the words down on paper then polish, edit, tighten and improve. With an original screenplay everything is carved as if from a new block of granite. Every character, every setting needs to be discovered. It's different with a television series. Once the actors have played the characters a few times, their voices are in your head.

If I wanted to conjure up Fletcher, I imagined him sitting in his cell and somebody bursting in to tell him that an asteroid was due to hit the earth in three days. I can hear his response now: 'Oh yes?'

Just two words. But spoken with the infinite scepticism of a man who believes nothing until he sees it with his own eyes. A small thing in itself but a great clue to character. He's wary, protective of what's his and determined to let no man make a sucker of him.

We wrote the first series of *Porridge* when we were rehearsing the stage musical *Billy*. It was a very happy time. One show was written on our knees in the Midland Hotel, Manchester. I'm pretty certain it was 'A Night In'. We felt it was important to do one show entirely in the cell, since prison is, after all, about being locked in. We also felt it should touch on how tough it is, especially for a young prisoner. It ended up as one of our favourite episodes, a 'two-hander' between Ronnie Barker and Richard Beckinsale, who wonderfully captured all of Lennie's fear and vulnerability.

The last series was written in California, where we were already doing the American version of the show. The writing process for Network TV was totally different, quite horrible and we never ever wanted to do it again. However, we kept it on the air for an entire season – twenty-two shows – and had run out of the original scripts. So as a matter of record, the story of the judge who sent Fletcher down turning up in Slade was originally done in America and then 'translated' back into English. It was sometimes difficult to remember if a line had originated in the American version or had already been used.

We're often asked about the differences between American humour and the English variety. The truth is, a good joke is a good joke. The real difference is to do with sociology and class in particular. Think of Shaw's *Pygmalion* or anything by Alan Ayckbourn. But when you mine for the American equivalent you run into race, a subject on which people are far more sensitive.

The last thing to say about writing *Porridge* is how painless it was. From the outset we knew we were writing for Ronnie Barker, in our view a comic genius.

Syd Lotterby did us an enormous favour when he cast Fulton Mackay and Brian Wilde for the pilot – though at the time we had no idea that it would become a series. But all three performances were firmly in our mind's eye – and ear – when we sat down to begin the series.

True, the research set us back, when we went round Wormwood Scrubs and Brixton, because we were hit by the harsh reality of life inside and how very unfunny it is. Even more reassuring, then, to picture Ronnie as Fletcher. The key was his attitude, his ability to make the very best of a bad situation and find little victories that get him through each day. He is a survivor, in the tradition of Falstaff or the Good Soldier Schweik. What would he say to that?

'Oh yes?'

DICK CLEMENT 2002

EPISODE GUIDE

THE PILOT

PRISONER AND ESCORT

Original transmission: Sunday 1 April 1973, BBC2, 8.15 p.m.

First repeat: Tuesday 7 August 1973, BBC1, 8.30 p.m.

Cast: Norman Fletcher Ronnie Barker **Mr Barrowclough** Brian Wilde

Mr Mackay Fulton Mackay **Prison Constable** Hamish Roughead

SERIES ONE

1. NEW FACES, OLD HANDS

Original transmission: Thursday 5 September 1974, BBC1, 8.30 p.m.

First repeat: Friday 21 February 1975, BBC1, 8.30 p.m.

Cast: Norman Fletcher Ronnie Barker **Mr Barrowclough** Brian Wilde

Mr Mackay Fulton Mackay **Lennie Godber** Richard Beckinsale **Cyril Heslop**

Brian Glover **Medical Officer** John Bennett **The Governor** Michael Barrington

Other prison officers Ronald Musgrove, Edward Cogdale and Keith Norrish

2. THE HUSTLER

Original transmission: Thursday 12 September 1974, BBC1, 8.30 p.m.

First repeat: Friday 28 February 1975, BBC1, 8.30 p.m.

Cast: Norman Fletcher Ronnie Barker **Mr Barrowclough** Brian Wilde

Mr Mackay Fulton Mackay **Lennie Godber** Richard Beckinsale **Heslop**

Brian Glover **Ives** Ken Jones **Lukewarm** Christopher Biggins **Evans** Ray

Dunbobbin **Mr Appleton** Graham Ashley **Prison Officer** John Quarmby

3. A NIGHT IN

Original transmission: Thursday 19 September 1974, BBC1, 8.30 p.m.

First repeat: Friday 7 March 1975, BBC1, 8.30 p.m.

Cast: Norman Fletcher Ronnie Barker **Lennie Godber** Richard Beckinsale

Prison Officer Paul McDowell

4. A DAY OUT

Original transmission: Thursday 26 September 1974, BBC1, 8.30 p.m.
First repeat: Friday 14 March 1975, BBC1, 8.30 p.m.
Cast: Norman Fletcher Ronnie Barker **Mr Mackay** Fulton Mackay
Lennie Godber Richard Beckinsale **Ives** Ken Jones **Navyrum** Paul Angelis
Dylan Philip Jackson **Scrounger** Johnny Wade **Vicar** Robert Gillespie
Verger John Rutland **Chief Prison Officer** Arnold Peters **Landlord**
Ralph Watson **Nurse** Peggy Mason

5. WAYS AND MEANS

Original transmission: Thursday 3 October 1974, BBC1, 8.30 p.m.
First repeat: Friday 21 March 1975, BBC1, 8.30 p.m.
Cast: Norman Fletcher Ronnie Barker **Mr Barrowclough** Brian Wilde
Mr Mackay Fulton Mackay **Ives** Ken Jones **The Governor** Michael
Barrington **McLaren** Tony Osoba

6. MEN WITHOUT WOMEN

Original transmission: Thursday 10 October 1974, BBC1, 8.30 p.m.
First repeat: Friday 28 March 1975, BBC1, 9.05 p.m.
Cast: Norman Fletcher Ronnie Barker **Mr Barrowclough** Brian Wilde
Mr Mackay Fulton Mackay **Warren** Sam Kelly **Cyril Heslop** Brian Glover
The Governor Michael Barrington **Lukewarm** Christopher Biggins
Sergeant Norris Royston Tickner **Tolly** Emlyn Price **Isobel** June Ellis
Ingrid Fletcher Patricia Brake **Norma** Susan Littler **Iris** Andonia Katsaros
Elaine Rosalind Elliot **Trevor** Donald Groves

SERIES TWO

1. JUST DESSERTS

Original transmission: Friday 24 October 1975, BBC1, 8.30 p.m.

First repeat: Thursday 20 May 1976, BBC1, 8 p.m.

Cast: Norman Fletcher Ronnie Barker **Mr Barrowclough** Brian Wilde
Mr Mackay Fulton Mackay **Lennie Godber** Richard Beckinsale **Ives**
Ken Jones **Warren** Sam Kelly **McLaren** Tony Osoba **Lukewarm**
Christopher Biggins **Banyard** Eric Dodson **Mr Appleton** Graham Ashley
Mr Birchwood John Rudling **Gay Gordon** Felix Bowness

2. HEARTBREAK HOTEL

Original transmission: Friday 31 October 1975, BBC1, 8.30 p.m.

First repeat: Thursday 27 May 1976, BBC1, 8 p.m.

Cast: Norman Fletcher Ronnie Barker **Mr Barrowclough** Brian Wilde
Mr Mackay Fulton Mackay **Lennie Godber** Richard Beckinsale **Ingrid**
Patricia Brake **Mrs Godber** Maggie Flint **Jackdaw** Cyril Shaps

3. DISTURBING THE PEACE

Original transmission: Friday 7 November 1975, BBC1, 8.30 p.m.

First repeat: Thursday 3 June 1976, BBC1, 7.55 p.m.

Cast: Norman Fletcher Ronnie Barker **Mr Barrowclough** Brian Wilde
Mr Mackay Fulton Mackay **Lennie Godber** Richard Beckinsale
Mr Wainwright Peter Jeffrey **Williams** Philip Madoc **Warren** Sam Kelly
McLaren Tony Osoba **The Governor** Michael Barrington **Secretary
(Mrs Heskith)** Madge Hindle

4. NO PEACE FOR THE WICKED

Original transmission: Friday 14 November 1975, BBC1, 8.30 p.m.

First repeat: Thursday 17 June 1976, BBC1, 8 p.m.

Cast: Norman Fletcher Ronnie Barker **Mr Barrowclough** Brian Wilde
Mr Mackay Fulton Mackay **Blanco** David Jason **Warren** Sam Kelly
McLaren Tony Osoba **Banyard** Eric Dodson **The Governor** Michael
Barrington **Mr Collinson** Paul McDowell **Chaplain** Tony Aitken
Prison Visitors Ivor Roberts, Barbara New and Geoffrey Greenhill

5. HAPPY RELEASE

Original transmission: Friday 21 November 1975, BBC1, 8.30 p.m.
First repeat: Thursday 24 June 1976, BBC1, 8 p.m.
Cast: Norman Fletcher Ronnie Barker **Mr Barrowclough** Brian Wilde
Mr Mackay Fulton Mackay **Lennie Godber** Richard Beckinsale
Blanco David Jason **Norris** Colin Farrell **Mr Collinson** Paul McDowell
Medical Officer Terence Soall

6. THE HARDER THEY FALL

Original transmission: Friday 28 November 1975, BBC1, 8.30 p.m.
First repeat: Thursday 1 July 1976, BBC1, 7.55 p.m.
Cast: Norman Fletcher Ronnie Barker **Mr Barrowclough** Brian Wilde
Mr Mackay Fulton Mackay **Lennie Godber** Richard Beckinsale
Harry Grout Peter Vaughan **Jackdaw** Cyril Shaps **P.T.I.** Roy Sampson

SERIES THREE

1. A STORM IN A TEACUP

Original transmission: Friday 18 February 1977, BBC1, 8.30 p.m.
First repeat: Friday 27 January 1978, BBC1, 8.30 p.m.
Cast: Norman Fletcher Ronnie Barker **Mr Barrowclough** Brian Wilde
Mr Mackay Fulton Mackay **Lennie Godber** Richard Beckinsale **Harry
Grout** Peter Vaughan **Harris** Ronald Lacey **Warren** Sam Kelly **McLaren**
Tony Osoba **Lukewarm** Christopher Biggins **Spider** John Moore
Crusher John Dair

2. POETIC JUSTICE

Original transmission: Friday 25 February 1977, BBC1, 8.30 p.m.
First repeat: Friday 13 January 1978, BBC1, 8.30 p.m.
Cast: Norman Fletcher Ronnie Barker **Mr Barrowclough** Brian Wilde
Mr Mackay Fulton Mackay **Lennie Godber** Richard Beckinsale **Rawley**
Maurice Denham **Harris** Ronald Lacey **Warren** Sam Kelly **McLaren** Tony
Osoba **The Governor** Michael Barrington **Mr Collinson** Paul McDowell

3. ROUGH JUSTICE

Original transmission: Friday 4 March 1977, BBC1, 8.30 p.m.
First repeat: Friday 20 January 1978, BBC1, 8.30 p.m.
Cast: Norman Fletcher Ronnie Barker **Mr Barrowclough** Brian Wilde
Mr Mackay Fulton Mackay **Lennie Godber** Richard Beckinsale
Rawley Maurice Denham **Harris** Ronald Lacey **Warren** Sam Kelly
McLaren Tony Osoba

4. PARDON ME

Original transmission: Friday 11 March 1977, BBC1, 8.30 p.m.
First repeat: Friday 3 February 1978, BBC1, 8.30 p.m.
Cast: Norman Fletcher Ronnie Barker **Mr Barrowclough** Brian Wilde
Mr Mackay Fulton Mackay **Lennie Godber** Richard Beckinsale
Blanco David Jason **Warren** Sam Kelly **Lukewarm** Christopher Biggins
The Governor Michael Barrington

5. A TEST OF CHARACTER

Original transmission: Friday 18 March 1977, BBC1, 8.30 p.m.
First repeat: Friday 10 February 1978, BBC1, 8.30 p.m.
Cast: Norman Fletcher Ronnie Barker **Mr Barrowclough** Brian Wilde
Mr Mackay Fulton Mackay **Lennie Godber** Richard Beckinsale
Spraggon Alun Armstrong **Warren** Sam Kelly **McLaren** Tony Osoba

6. FINAL STRETCH

Original transmission: Friday 25 March 1977, BBC1, 8.30 p.m.
First repeat: Friday 17 February 1978, BBC1, 8.30 p.m.
Cast: Norman Fletcher Ronnie Barker **Mr Barrowclough** Brian Wilde
Mr Mackay Fulton Mackay **Lennie Godber** Richard Beckinsale
Jarvis David Daker **Warren** Sam Kelly **Ingrid** Patricia Brake
Crusher John Dair

CHRISTMAS SPECIALS

NO WAY OUT

Original transmission: Wednesday 24 December 1975,
BBC1, 8.25 p.m. (40-minute episode)
First repeat: Thursday 8 July 1976, BBC1, 7.50 p.m.
Cast: Norman Fletcher Ronnie Barker
Mr Barrowclough Brian Wilde **Mr Mackay** Fulton Mackay **Lennie Godber**
Richard Beckinsale **Harry Grout** Peter Vaughan **Prison Doctor** Graham
Crowden **Warren** Sam Kelly **Lukewarm** Christopher Biggins **Sandra**
Carol Hawkins **Nurse** Elisabeth Day

THE DESPERATE HOURS

Original transmission: Friday 24 December 1976, BBC1, 8 p.m.
First repeat: Friday 1 April 1977, BBC1, 8.15 p.m.
Cast: Norman Fletcher Ronnie Barker **Mr Barrowclough** Brian Wilde
Mr Mackay Fulton Mackay **Lennie Godber** Richard Beckinsale
Reg Urwin Dudley Sutton **Warren** Sam Kelly **McLaren** Tony Osoba
The Governor Michael Barrington **Keegan** Ken Wynne **Tulip** Michael
Redfern **Mrs Jamieson** Jane Wenham

PRODUCTION TEAM

All episodes written by Dick Clement and Ian La Frenais
Producer/Director: Sydney Lotterby
Executive Producer: James Gilbert (Pilot)

Music: Max Harris
Film Cameraman: Alan Featherstone (Pilot); Len Newson (S1, episodes 1, 2, 3 and 6); Keith Taylor (S1, episodes 4 and 5); Ken Willicombe (S2, episodes 2, 3, 4 and 6); Kenneth MacMillan (S2, episode 5); John Tiley ('No Way Out'); John McGlashan (S3)
Film Editor: Geoffrey Botterill (S1, episodes 1 and 2); Ray Millichope (Pilot; S1, episodes 3, 4, 5 and 6; S2, episodes 2, 3, 4, 5 and 6; 'No Way Out'); John Dunstan (S3)
Film Sound: Ron Blight (credited on 'No Way Out')
Make-up: Penny Delamar (Pilot); Sylvia James (S1); Ann Ailes-Stevenson (S2; 'No Way Out'); Suzanne Broad ('The Desperate Hours'; S3)
Costume: Penny Lowe (Pilot); Mary Husband (S1 and S3); Betty Aldiss (S2); Susan Wheal ('No Way Out'); Robin Stubbs ('The Desperate Hours')
Lighting: Peter Smee (Pilot; S1, episodes 1, 2, 3, 4 and 6; S2, episodes 1, 2, 3 and 4; 'No Way Out'); Peter Wesson (S1, episode 5; S3); Brian Clemett (S2, episode 5); Sam Barclay ('The Desperate Hours')
Sound: Mike McCarthy (Pilot); Anthony Philpot (S1; S2; 'The Desperate Hours'); Jeff Booth ('No Way Out'); John Holmes (S3)
Production Assistant: Ray Butt (S1); Dave Perrottet (S2); Alan Bell ('No Way Out'); Mike Crisp ('The Desperate Hours' and S3)
Technical Adviser: Jonathan Marshall (credited on S1, episodes 1–4)
Designer: Tim Gleeson (Pilot; S1, episodes 1, 2, 5 and 6; S2, episode 1; 'No Way Out'; 'The Desperate Hours'; S3); David Chandler (S1, episodes 3 and 6); Gerry Scott (S1, episodes 4 and 5); John Pusey (S2, episodes 2, 3, 4, 5 and 6)

PILOT

PRISONER AND ESCORT

1. OPENING TITLES

2. STREET

Fletcher, Mackay and a Police Constable walk towards a parked van. Barrowclough is sitting in the van reading a newspaper. He sees the men approaching and gets out. The others reach the back of the van.

POLICE CONSTABLE

Right, he's all yours then. Happy New Year, Jock.

MACKAY

Aye, escort duty on New Year's Eve.

POLICE CONSTABLE

Happy New Year, Fletcher.

Fletcher and Mackay get into the van.

FLETCHER

Oh yes, very witty, very droll.

Barrowclough gets in the van. The constable shuts the door, bangs on it and the van drives off. Zoom out as we see the van approach St Pancras station.

MAGISTRATE (*VOICEOVER*)

(*Offscreen*) Norman Stanley Fletcher, you have pleaded guilty to the charges brought by this court, and it is now my duty to pass sentence. You are an habitual criminal, who accepts arrest as an occupational hazard, and presumably accepts imprisonment in the same casual manner. We therefore feel constrained to commit you to the maximum term allowed for these offences – we sentence you to five years' imprisonment. Do you wish to address the court?

3. RAILWAY CARRIAGE

Mackay, Fletcher and Barrowclough are sitting in first-class compartment. The blinds into the corridor are drawn.

FLETCHER

Cobblers.

BARROWCLOUGH

What?

FLETCHER

What Brian Clough says about London clubs.

MACKAY
(*Grabbing the paper*) That's my paper.

FLETCHER
Can I have a look at your *Penthouse* then?

MACKAY
Get your own.

FLETCHER
How can I get my own? We're in motion, aren't we?

MACKAY
Shoulda thought of that at the station.

FLETCHER
At the station I wasn't even permitted a Jimmy Riddle.

MACKAY
Shut your mouth.
There is a pause.

BARROWCLOUGH
You can have a look at my *Angling Times* if you like.

MACKAY
No, he can't. God Almighty, mollycoddling him already! People seem to forget what prison's for. He's paying a debt to society. Not having an all-expenses-paid holiday with privileges and magazines. You're going to prison to be punished.
There is a pause. Then Fletcher leans across to Barrowclough.

FLETCHER
I spy with my little eye something beginning with (*indicating Mackay with his head*) C.

MACKAY
You watch it, sonny.

FLETCHER
Constable?

MACKAY
Don't come it with me.

FLETCHER
I wouldn't, Mr Mackay, I wouldn't – otherwise you'd wait until the train picked up a fair bit of speed outside Hemel Hempstead and chuck me out of the window. Put it down as attempted escape.

BARROWCLOUGH
He wouldn't do that.

FLETCHER
No, I suppose not . . . he couldn't spell Hemel Hempstead, he'd wait till Rugby.

MACKAY
I'm a reasonable man. But one more allegation of brutality and I'll knock your block off . . .

BARROWCLOUGH
Look, it's a long journey ahead so . . . so let's not conduct it in an atmosphere of hostility and aggression. Why don't we all have a nice cup of tea?
He starts to get to his feet.

BARROWCLOUGH
Both take milk and sugar?

MACKAY
You sit still, I'll get them.

BARROWCLOUGH
(*Looking for money*) Well, let me pay.
(*To Fletcher*) Anything you want?

FLETCHER

Thanks, mate. Tea with two sugars, and I'll have one of those individual fruit pies if they've got any . . .

Mackay slams the door shut before Fletcher finishes.

FLETCHER

He's a laugh, in' he?

BARROWCLOUGH

I suppose it's with bein' a Scotsman and being deprived of Hogmanay. I mean they do take it very seriously the Scots.

FLETCHER

Yeah, well they take any excuse for drinking seriously, don't they. Nothing social about their drinking, is there. With them it's not the case of a few friends mellowing over a glass of vino. No, no . . . they just drink to get drunk. (*Looking through a magazine*) Cor, look at 'er. Only one thing worse than a drunken Scot and that's a sober one.

BARROWCLOUGH

I'm Scots on my mother's side.

FLETCHER

Yeah, well second generation, in' it? Different fing.

BARROWCLOUGH

Anyhow, I'm a bit of all sorts. Scots, English, Irish . . . Polish –

FLETCHER

She got about a bit your mother.

BARROWCLOUGH

Oh no, I didn't mean . . .

FLETCHER

I'm pure London myself. In fact, pure North London. You go to the graveyard in Muswell Hill, it's full of Fletchers. Shall I tell you something? There's always been a Fletcher round my way, right back to . . . oh I should think Henry the Fourth Part One.

BARROWCLOUGH

Oh . . . I haven't got any heritage. I know me grandfather was an ironmonger in Accrington. But before that . . .

FLETCHER

My great-grandfather was William Wellington Fletcher. The last man in England to be hanged for horse-stealing. And Matthew Jarvis Fletcher – he was Newgate with Jack Sheppard, wun' he? That's well known.

BARROWCLOUGH

So it runs in the family, does it – crime, like?

FLETCHER

Possibly. I know there's a load of Fletchers in Australia.

BARROWCLOUGH

So you come from a rough neighbourhood?

FLETCHER

No, I told you – Muswell Hill. It's very suburban, Muswell Hill. Respectable.

BARROWCLOUGH

Broken home?

FLETCHER

Not at all. They've just celebrated their diamond wedding.

BARROWCLOUGH

Oh. I was just wondering why . . .

FLETCHER

Well, when I left school I went round the local Labour and appraised the professional opportunities open to me. Unfortunately my lack of scholastic achievement prevented me from doing the things I really fancied, such as stockbrokerin' or teaching tennis at a girls' school. And I didn't reckon working in a cardboard box factory. So I robbed this sub-post office off the North Circular.

BARROWCLOUGH

And you never looked back since, so to speak.

FLETCHER

No – nor have I ever been short of 3d. stamps.

BARROWCLOUGH

What have you gone down for this time?

FLETCHER

Aw, don't talk about it. Be a farce if it wasn't such a tragedy. Own fault, should have stuck to what I know best. Housebreaking. But I lifts this lorry. Impulse steal. You know what I mean, impulse steal. I think it's a doddle, don't I?

BARROWCLOUGH

I gather it wasn't.

FLETCHER

Yeah, you know why, though – flaming brakes failed. Criminal letting lorries on the road in that condition. And he

was overloaded. So there I was, wiv five ton on me back roarin' down bloody Archway.

BARROWCLOUGH

Wonder you weren't killed.

FLETCHER

I nearly was. Went through three back gardens, went clean through a brick wall and finished up in somebody's tool shed.

BARROWCLOUGH

Did they get you for wilful destruction of property? I mean, knocking that wall down.

FLETCHER

Yeah. And I asked for six other fences to be taken into consideration.

Barrowclough does not react to Fletcher's wit.

FLETCHER

Get it, get it?

BARROWCLOUGH

Pardon?

FLETCHER

Oh never mind.

There is a pause. He fumbles in his pocket and finds some chewing gum.

FLETCHER

Here – tell you what. Have a bit of this.

BARROWCLOUGH

You've only two bits left.

FLETCHER

Yeah . . . what made you take up this lark then?

BARROWCLOUGH

Prison service?

FLETCHER

Yeah, what made you fancy it like?

BARROWCLOUGH

I always wanted a vocation which would satisfy my desire to perform useful public service . . . and get a free house and uniform.

FLETCHER

What's it like, this nick?

BARROWCLOUGH

Oh very good. Modern you see. Experimental. With a cricket pitch and a psychiatrist.

FLETCHER

Oh yeah. Bird's bird though, in' it?

BARROWCLOUGH

Not with this one. If you took advantage of our courses, of our many occupational and/or recreational activities . . . well, you put your mind to it, you could come out an intermediate welder or an accomplished oboe player.

FLETCHER

Oh yeah.

BARROWCLOUGH

Pity you're not in longer, you could have taken up civil engineering.

FLETCHER

Oh pity. That is a pity. Pity I didn't get a ten stretch. Then I could have took my welding finals, and be a doctor of philosophy.

BARROWCLOUGH

(*Tentatively*) I'm a bit of an amateur botanist myself. So sometimes I take some of the prisoners out on the fells

to explore the natural phenomena of our countryside.

At this Fletcher's eyes register interest.

FLETCHER

Out on the fells, is it?

BARROWCLOUGH

Yes, lovely views.

FLETCHER

I might put down for that. That might interest me. Natural phenomena of our countryside – how far's the nearest railway station?

BARROWCLOUGH

Oh that's the beauty of it you see, we're miles from anywhere.

FLETCHER

(*Less enthusiastically*) Oh are we.

BARROWCLOUGH

We also have an arts and crafts section. Or you could learn woodwork.

FLETCHER

Listen, squire, I don't want no courses, no reconditioning, resettlement. All I want to do is mind me own business, do my porridge and count the days till I get out.

BARROWCLOUGH

You'll change you know.

FLETCHER

What?

BARROWCLOUGH

Even the most cynical and hardened criminals have changed at this place. They've responded you see to our approach which is based not on correction and punishment, but sympathy and understanding.

The door of the compartment slides open and an unsympathetic Mackay enters, carrying three cardboard cups.

MACKAY
I forget if you took sugar or not but it makes no difference 'cos I spilt most of yours on the way back, but what you gonna do about it?

FLETCHER
Where's this sympathy and understanding? How's he working at your nick? Blimey, he'd bring back the birch at the drop of an helmet.

MACKAY
What's he on about?

BARROWCLOUGH
Mr Mackay runs several of our group activities.

FLETCHER
Yeah. Like rock-breaking and compulsory pot-holing.

MACKAY
I'll soon have you in shape, Fletcher. I'll soon have you a shadow of your former self.

FLETCHER
I bet he's secretary to the Lord Chief Justice Goddard Appreciation Society.

MACKAY
Just keep your nose clean, lad. Just show me some respect and keep your nose clean, you'll be all right. I'm hard but fair.

FLETCHER
Like Leeds United?

MACKAY
If you like. You play ball with me, and I'll play ball with you, and you'll find me a reasonable man.

FLETCHER
Good, good . . . could I have a look at your *Penthouse* now?

MACKAY
Can you hell!

FLETCHER
You've got to admire consistency . . .

Barrowclough offers Fletcher his Angling Times.

FLETCHER
Try page twenty-four.

4. RAILWAY STATION

A train is leaving the station. As the last coach passes, Fletcher and Barrowclough are walking along the platform. They leave the station. Outside they walk to a waiting minibus.

FLETCHER
How far we got to go then?

MACKAY
About an hour and a half. Across the fells.

FLETCHER
Can I have a Johnny Riddle then?

MACKAY
You should have thought of that earlier.

FLETCHER
I did think of it earlier. There's been

nothing else on my mind for ages.
Why are you so reluctant to let me
go to the lavatory?

Mackay holds up handcuffs.

FLETCHER

Oh I see.

*Barrowclough starts undoing the
minibus doors.*

BARROWCLOUGH

You'd better let him go, we can't stop
in transit.

Mackay unlocks the handcuffs.

MACKAY

All right then, behind the bus.

FLETCHER

Thank you, Mackay.

*He goes round behind the minibus.
He looks at the petrol cap and his
expression changes. Fletcher checks
in the direction of Mackay and
Barrowclough to make sure they are
not watching and takes off the petrol
cap. Then he unzips his flies.
In the distance the minibus can
be seen driving along. Suddenly
it stalls. Mackay gets out. He
walks round to the front of the
minibus and lifts the bonnet.
Barrowclough and Fletcher
join him.*

BARROWCLOUGH

What do you reckon it is?

MACKAY

How do I know? I'm no mechanic.

FLETCHER

Plugs, is it? Or ignition?

MACKAY

Put the bracelets on him.

*Barrowclough starts to comply.
Mackay moves back to try
the starter.*

MACKAY

Don't you be thinking that fate's given
you a last chance of freedom.

FLETCHER

Don't believe in fate.

*The starter makes
unpromising noises.*

BARROWCLOUGH

Sounds like the carburettor.

FLETCHER

Have to get the bus then, won't we?

MACKAY

What bus?

FLETCHER

Hitch a lift then.

MACKAY

Who drives round here on New
Year's Eve?

BARROWCLOUGH

Who drives round here any time?

FLETCHER

Getting a bit parky, in' it?

BARROWCLOUGH

Be dark soon.

MACKAY

God Almighty!

FLETCHER

Don't you know how to fix it then?
Hasn't one of your many instructional
courses taught you how to cope with
mechanical failure?

BARROWCLOUGH

It's survival we'll need out here. Be dark soon. And they forecast snow.

MACKAY

Pull yourself together Mr Barrowclough.

FLETCHER

No need to take it out on him.

MACKAY

Look, there's one thing for it. I'm going on. Going on to the prison. Now listen to me. You do not move. You do not move from here and you do not take the bracelets off him. Right?

BARROWCLOUGH

Right, Mr Mackay.

MACKAY

(*To Fletcher*) And you behave yourself.

FLETCHER

Right, Mr Mackay.

Mackay walks off down the road. Fletcher and Barrowclough are shivering. To keep warm Fletcher flaps his arms across his chest, forgetting the handcuffs. He jerks Barrowclough.

FLETCHER

Sorry, mate.

5. MINIBUS

Outside the wind howls loudly. Barrowclough and Fletcher, still handcuffed, are sitting side by side in the minibus. Barrowclough blows on his hand, as Fletcher blows on his.

FLETCHER

By the time they find us we'll be dead with exposure. Like Robert Taylor at the end of that picture.

BARROWCLOUGH

What picture?

FLETCHER

Western about buffalo hunting. In the deep frozen North. And he had to spend the night out in the open. Up a tree he was.

BARROWCLOUGH

Why was he up a tree?

FLETCHER

What? Well I 'spect he was avoiding marauding buffalo, driven half-crazy by the extreme cold.

BARROWCLOUGH

Oh yes, marauding buffalo . . .

FLETCHER

Driven half-crazy by the extreme cold. Much as we'll be in an hour or two. Ain't there no houses or farms near here?

BARROWCLOUGH

There's a cottage not far.

FLETCHER

Well, let's go there then.

BARROWCLOUGH

Mr Mackay says we're not to leave the van.

FLETCHER

All right – we'll die in the van.

BARROWCLOUGH

Anyway it will be all locked up, they only use it in the summer.

FLETCHER

So what?

BARROWCLOUGH

How will we get in?

FLETCHER

Mr Barrowclough . . .

BARROWCLOUGH

Yes.

FLETCHER

I'm only a flaming housebreaker, in' I?

6. COTTAGE: LIVING ROOM

It is night time. Fletcher and Barrowclough come in from the kitchen. They walk to an old sofa and sit as near as possible to the glowing fire. They have mugs of black coffee in their outside hands, but their inside hands are still handcuffed together.

BARROWCLOUGH

I wish we had a drop of milk.

FLETCHER

It's the hot drink that counts.

BARROWCLOUGH

And you'd think they'd've had some sugar somewhere.

FLETCHER

Tell you what – try a drop of this in it.

He puts his hand in his pocket and produces a hip flask.

BARROWCLOUGH

What is it?

FLETCHER

I'm not sure –

With this he moves the two

handcuffed hands together to unscrew the cap. Then he sniffs it.

FLETCHER

Scotch.

BARROWCLOUGH

Oh no, anyway – I'm on duty.

FLETCHER

It's medicinal. Help to revive us. Take the chill out of our numbed bones.

BARROWCLOUGH

Where d'you get it?

FLETCHER

It must have accidentally fallen out the back of Mr Mackay's pocket, when he got off the van.

BARROWCLOUGH

You stole it!

FLETCHER

I didn't. I told you, it fell off the back of the van.

He drinks.

BARROWCLOUGH

Is whisky medicinal?

FLETCHER

Yeah. I always feel better after I've had a few.

BARROWCLOUGH

Oh all right then, if it's medicinal.

Fletcher pours some whisky into Barrowclough's mug.

BARROWCLOUGH

That's enough.

Fletcher takes a quick swig out of the flask before pouring some whisky into his coffee. Then he looks at his watch.

FLETCHER

Hey . . . it's New Year now, you know.

BARROWCLOUGH

Is it? Oh, all the best then.

FLETCHER

Yeah, and to you, mate.

They sip their drinks.

FLETCHER

Like *The Defiant Ones*.

BARROWCLOUGH

Beg your pardon?

FLETCHER

That was pictures an' all. *The Defiant Ones*. 'Bout these two convicts on the run, chained together like we are. Only one was black, one was white. Fact, if you had a bit of coloured blood in you, 'stead of all that Polish rubbish you've got, you could have been Sidney Poitier to my Tony Curtis.

BARROWCLOUGH

We have a Cinema Club at the prison. Only last Tuesday we showed *Irrigation in the Gobi Desert*. On the same bill with *Birds of the Farne Islands*.

FLETCHER

Standing room only, was it?

BARROWCLOUGH

No, we didn't have much of a turnout that night.

FLETCHER

I'm amazed.

BARROWCLOUGH

My wife likes the pictures. But we don't go much these days.

FLETCHER

No wonder – so bloomin' remote. Stuck in the middle of Cumberland where you going to find a cinema?

BARROWCLOUGH

That's the trouble. My wife, she feels very bad about being deprived of the excitement and amenities that a city can offer. She's always terribly unsettled every time we come back from our monthly day trip to Workington.

FLETCHER

Oh yes. I can see how the lights of Workington might turn a young girl's head.

BARROWCLOUGH

How d'you mean?

FLETCHER

Well, come on, mate. Amenities in Workington? Ain't got Christianity up here yet so you can't even go to a church social.

BARROWCLOUGH

Different for you – Londoners. My wife's always wanted to be cosmopolitan. Should have put in for a transfer to the Scrubs – or Brixton.

FLETCHER

No, if you was going to go to Brixton, mate, you'd have to be Sidney Poitier.

BARROWCLOUGH

(*Leaning back*) Too late now.

FLETCHER

So er, your old lady feels . . . deprived, does she?

BARROWCLOUGH

Well, she sees a future of frustrated ambitions stretching before her. She doesn't like what I do or where we live. So over the years she's grown bitter and unsettled, full of restless urges. Which have manifested themselves in various ways like bad temper, spots and sleeping with the postman. (*Drinks*) And there were liaisons with other men. We got to rowing all the time. Things went from bad to worse. Eventually we went to see this marriage guidance counsellor.

FLETCHER

That help, did it?

BARROWCLOUGH

It helped her! She ran off with him.

FLETCHER

Oh well, you're well out of it, aren't you, mate. You're well out of a slag like that.

BARROWCLOUGH

She's come back.

FLETCHER

Oh I see . . . well, people change.

Barrowclough moves along the sofa and lies back.

BARROWCLOUGH

I blame myself. I'm a failure. I'm only hanging on to this job by the skin of me teeth. I got so depressed I thought I'd take advantage of the prison psychiatric department. See them about my inferiority complex. Well, it's not a complex really – I am inferior.

FLETCHER

Aw come on, leave it off. Look, I don't know you very well. I can tell that you're a man of kindness, compassion and humanity. Now, you can't buy those, can you? Would you swap them for a colour telly and a penthouse in Workington? 'Course you wouldn't.

BARROWCLOUGH

I suppose not.

Fletcher empties flask into Barrowclough's mug.

FLETCHER

Here finish this. You can't go through life thinking that you should have been something else. You're doing the job you always wanted to do. You must think, this is what I am. I am what I am, and when it's all over I'll look God straight in the eye and say, I've done it my way.

BARROWCLOUGH

I've done it my way.

FLETCHER

Confidence in yourself.

BARROWCLOUGH

Confidence . . .

FLETCHER

Trust your own judgement and initiative.

BARROWCLOUGH

Initiative . . .

FLETCHER

Why don't you take these handcuffs off?

BARROWCLOUGH

(*Not hearing this*) D'you know, I've

never talked to anyone before – not really talked.

FLETCHER

Yeah – yeah . . . why don't you take these handcuffs off?

BARROWCLOUGH

Handcuffs?

FLETCHER

It's the circulation, in' it? Cuttin' off the supply to my head.

BARROWCLOUGH

We have rules . . .

FLETCHER

What about judgement – initiative. Are you going to do it their way, or are you going to do it your way? Confidence in yourself.

Barrowclough thinks very hard for a minute, then comes to a decision.

BARROWCLOUGH

I'm going to take them off. Yes. I am taking them off. I am taking them off because if I don't I'm betraying the principles of my prison and myself in approaching prisoners with sympathy and understanding.

Fletcher watches anxiously as Barrowclough fishes for the key.

BARROWCLOUGH

You are a criminal – habitual and hereditary. But until we show *you* trust, how are you going to *learn* trust?

FLETCHER

That is irrefutably true. What more can I say?

The handcuffs come off, and both men rub their wrists with relief. Barrowclough yawns, lying back against the sofa.

BARROWCLOUGH

Made me quite sleepy that whisky has. Quite drowsy.

FLETCHER

Another good reason for taking them off. We couldn't have kipped down there like Babes in the Wood, could we?

BARROWCLOUGH

I can hardly keep me eyes open.

FLETCHER

You get your feet up, my old son. Get a decent bit of shut-eye. I'll push these two chairs together.

He does so, settling in the chairs, but in a position to watch Barrowclough.

BARROWCLOUGH

You know, Fletcher, I hope you do decide to join my botany group.

FLETCHER

I'll give it serious consideration, squire.

BARROWCLOUGH

I feel a better man for tonight. More confident. I don't feel a failure. I feel that for once I've used my judgement, and I'm right.

FLETCHER

Right?

BARROWCLOUGH

Right about you, Fletcher.

Fletcher watches Barrowclough who has fallen asleep.

FLETCHER
Mr Barrowclough?
There is no reply. Fletcher gets up.
FLETCHER
Mr Barrowclough?
*Fletcher rushes out. Barrowclough
continues sleeping.*

7. COUNTRYSIDE

*It is night time. Fletcher escapes.
He is seen running and scrambling
up and down hillsides. Eventually
he reaches the edge of a farm but
the fierce barking of a dog forces
him to change direction. As dawn
breaks he is still running. As he runs
past a brick wall, he notices there is
a gap in it. Through it can be seen
a cottage. Fletcher comes back and
looks at the cottage. He decides
to check it out. He runs towards
the cottage.*

8. COTTAGE: SCULLERY

*Morning. Fletcher opens a window
and climbs into the scullery. He
moves one of the doors. Suddenly he
hears a cough (offscreen). He grasps
a heavy bucket and moves behind
the door. The door opens and
Barrowclough walks in.*
BARROWCLOUGH
Fletcher, are you out here?
Fletcher drops the bucket in surprise.
FLETCHER
Mr Barrowclough.
BARROWCLOUGH
What a shock you gave me. What are
you doing here?
FLETCHER
That's what I'd like to know.
BARROWCLOUGH
What are you doing with
that saucepan?
FLETCHER
Milk – milk . . . I've just been out to
get you some milk for your coffee –
thought I might find a stray
cow about.
BARROWCLOUGH
You look terrible, as if you've been up
all night.
FLETCHER
Couldn't sleep, could I?
BARROWCLOUGH
It was a very nice
thought but all the same
you shouldn't have done
it. You could have got lost. People are
always getting lost on these fells.
Wander around in circles they do.
FLETCHER
Do they?

9. FLETCHER'S CELL

Fletcher is lying on his bunk.
Mackay walks in.

MACKAY

So – whose good behaviour last night made him the Governor's blue-eyed boy?

FLETCHER

I must be the first man to have earned remission before I even got here.

MACKAY

Don't give me any of your officious lip, Fletcher. I know you were trying to work one last night.

FLETCHER

On what do you base that supposition, Mr Mackay?

MACKAY

On the evidence of our motor mechanic's report on the van.

FLETCHER

Oh.

MACKAY

It appears that the petrol tank had more in it after our journey than before. Only what was in it certainly was not 5-star. Now I'm going to be watching you like a hawk, 'cos nobody goes over the wall at this prison.

FLETCHER

No, Mr Mackay, no one takes the petrol out of you.

Mackay goes out, passing Barrowclough who walks into the cell.

BARROWCLOUGH

What did you say to the Governor?

FLETCHER

What?

BARROWCLOUGH

What did you say to the Governor?

FLETCHER

Why – give you a rollicking, did he?

BARROWCLOUGH

Far from it. He congratulated me on my handling of the situation. He said I was a credit to the service, praised my judgement and initiative and my capacity to remain calm under crisis.

FLETCHER

That's all right then.

BARROWCLOUGH

But you must have said something.

FLETCHER

All I said was that any naughty thoughts I'd harboured of escape were quickly dispelled by the cool authority of my escort, Mr Barrowclough. A man to whom I later owed my life, owing to the fact that he forced me from the vehicle against my will, to take shelter against the elements, supporting or half-carrying my exhausted body across several miles of rough terrain. Just what anyone would say, really.

BARROWCLOUGH

Did you mean all that, Fletcher?

FLETCHER

No – p'raps I coloured the incidents
of the night a little. But I see no reason
why you and I shouldn't start the
New Year on a good footing with
the authorities.

BARROWCLOUGH

I've never been praised before.

FLETCHER

How's it feel?

BARROWCLOUGH

Wonderful. You know, Fletcher, you've
done a lot for me the last twenty-
four hours. You've given me strength,
confidence and . . . friendship. Is
there nothing I can do for you
in return?

FLETCHER

Well, I expect a few things might occur
to me during the ensuing months . . .
in fact there is one little thing now.

BARROWCLOUGH

Yes?

FLETCHER

If you could see your way clear
to bringing me some reading matter,
nothing too heavy, the odd
glossy nude.

BARROWCLOUGH

Certainly.

FLETCHER

And when you've got turned round
p'raps you'd do something about this
cell – like, shifting me to one that faces
south-west 'cos I'm not going to get
much sun in here, am I? Oh, and this

botany club of yours, nature walks, is it?
Outside the prison?

BARROWCLOUGH

That's right.

FLETCHER

Put me down for it will you, as soon
as possible.

*He walks Barrowclough round the
cell, discussing what he can do.*

SERIES ONE

MEMORIES

Sydney Lotterby (Producer/Director)
Philip Jackson (Dylan in 'A Day Out')
Tony Osoba (McLaren in the series)

1 SERIES ONE

EPISODE ONE: NEW FACES, OLD HANDS

1. PRISON LANDING

A key is seen going into lock.
A door opens. Mackay, the chief
Prison Officer and Barrowclough
walk through. They lock the door
and walk along the gantry, stopping
outside a cell door.

MACKAY

The three new arrivals, Mr Leach.
Heslop, Cyril, forty-one. Three years,
robbery third stretch. Thick as two
short planks – no ulcers with that one.
Godber, Leonard Arthur, twenty-three.
First offender, two years breaking and
entering. Seems somewhat naïve.
Could be corrupted. Possibly by this
one – Fletcher, Norman Stanley, forty-
two. Five years. He's the one I brought
up from Brixton. Knows the score,
done a lot of bird, water off a duck's
back. (*Stepping back from spyhole*) I'll
be watching that one.

2. RECEPTION ROOM

Weak sun is filtering through a
barred window.

MACKAY

(*Voiceover*) What a beautiful day.
The camera reveals Mackay
standing at the window looking out.

MACKAY

For the time of year, quite astonishing.
Beautiful day.
The camera now shows Fletcher,
Godber and Heslop standing in a
line on the other side of the room.

FLETCHER

Oh lovely. P'raps later on we can all go
out for a cycle ride.

MACKAY

Know what they say about New
Year's Day? "What you do on the
First Day of the Year, you do all the
year round." In the case of you
three gentlemen that's perfectly true.
(*Addressing Lennie*) You, laddy –
you Mr Godber – first time, isn't it?
You must be wondering what an
average day in prison is like. Tell
him, Fletcher.

FLETCHER

It's exactly like the day before,
Mr Mackay.

MACKAY

The voice of experience. And tell him
how the average day begins, Fletcher.

FLETCHER

Begins at 7.00 a.m. You'll be woken
by a persistent and deafening bell.
Then the screws will come round –

MACKAY

I beg your pardon.

FLETCHER

The prison officers will come round.
Offering such encouragements as
'Wakey wakey, get your socks on,
move you 'orrible creatures.' We shall
respond to this badinage with such
remarks as 'Good morning, sir, Good
Lord is that the time,' or 'Who's been
having your old lady while you've been
on night duty?'

MACKAY

Very comical, Fletcher. Eight o'clock
slop out, eight ten breakfast. Eight
fifteen return to cell, nine o'clock –
yes, Fletcher?

FLETCHER

Slop out again, Mr Mackay, followed
by work till eleven fifteen when we –

MACKAY

Exercise. Walking in pairs, five to six
yards apart, no conversing to pairs in
front or behind. This is followed by the
highlight of the day, quiet Fletcher I'm
asking Heslop.

FLETCHER

Who?

MACKAY

You've been inside Heslop, what is,
the highlight of the day?

HESLOP

Er . . . er . . . visiting hours?

MACKAY

We're in Cumberland, man. A barren
windswept fell north of the Pennines.
We are two weeks from Euston! When
you see your loved ones it'll be the
highlight of the *year*.

*Fletcher turns to an increasingly
dismayed Lennie.*

FLETCHER

Glad you came?

MACKAY

Fletcher –

FLETCHER

Sir?

MACKAY

Highlight of the day.

FLETCHER

Highlight of the day – dinner, sir.

MACKAY

Which is –

FLETCHER

Nourishing.

MACKAY

Nourishing is it not.

FLETCHER

Can't wait, sir.

MACKAY

Midday, bang up.

Lennie looks hopeful.

MACKAY

Not what you think, laddy – back to your cells. Thirteen hundred, slop out, work, tea, evening association, which means in principle that you can follow a wide range of recreational activities; which in practice means television or ping pong.

HESLOP

Telly?

FLETCHER

Yeah, but only till seven. When there's only news and kids stuff. So if you're a fan of *Z Cars*, my son, forget it. You'll have to get your kicks from the Wombles of bleedin' Wimbledon.

MACKAY

Seven thirty, slop out, supper, seven forty-five, lights out, any questions?

FLETCHER

Any point?

MACKAY

None whatsoever. At ease.

He starts to prepare for documentation.

LENNIE

So this is Colditz.

FLETCHER

Colditz! You're joking. Compared to this place Colditz was a doddle. Load of public schoolboys playing leapfrog and making tunnels. This is nick this is. We spend our day slopping out and sewing mailbags. And by seven forty-five our lights are out. Colditz that time of night,

they'd be brewing cocoa and having pillow fights.

There is a knock on the door.
Lennie takes out a cigarette.

MACKAY

(*Crossing to Lennie*) Godber, who said you could smoke – did I say you could smoke?

FLETCHER

(*Taking the cigarette*) Don't think he wants you to smoke.

LENNIE

I was trying to give 'em up anyway.

FLETCHER

I'll help you.

Barrowclough comes in with documents.

MACKAY

I'm leaving you with Mr Barrowclough. Oh one more thing. Nice to have you with us.

He leaves.

HESLOP

My wife was coming next week.

FLETCHER

What? Who said that?

HESLOP

He says once a year. My wife was coming next week. Wrote to me. Staying overnight with her cousin in Barrow-in-Furness. Not fair. Not fair if she has to stay there indefinitely.

FLETCHER

Not fair on anyone to stay in Barrow-in-Furness.

BARROWCLOUGH

Heslop.

FLETCHER

Who?

BARROWCLOUGH

Will you step up here, please.
Christian name?

HESLOP

Cyril.

BARROWCLOUGH

Date of birth?

HESLOP

1st April 1933.

*He hands over his personal effects
to Barrowclough who puts them
in box.*

LENNIE

What's happening now?

FLETCHER

We're about to be dehumanised. First
they give us a number, take away our
personal possessions. Then they give
us a thorough medical check-up, and
we have a bath in six inches of
lukewarm water. Watch out for the
bath-house cleaners.

LENNIE

Why?

FLETCHER

Lot of trustee poofs work the
bath-house.

He crosses the room and sits down.

LENNIE

Know all the form, don't you?

He sits down.

Been here before?

FLETCHER

Not here – all the same though.
Porridge is porridge, in' it?

LENNIE

First time for me. Don't know how I'll
get through.

FLETCHER

Cheer up. Could be worse. State
this country's in. Could be free.
Out there with no work, and a
crumbling economy. Think how
'orrible that would be. Nothing to
do but go to bed early and increase
the population.

LENNIE

Won't be doing that for a while.

FLETCHER

Oh no, course not. Shouldn't have
said that, tasteless joke.

LENNIE

I'm going to feel ever so deprived.
'Cos I had this fiancée, Denise, who
was ever so active in that direction.

FLETCHER

You'll have to drink a lot of tea.

LENNIE

What good's a cup of tea going to do?

FLETCHER

It's what they put in it.

LENNIE

What?

FLETCHER

Something which will moderate your
memories of Denise.

LENNIE

I don't drink tea.

FLETCHER

You are in trouble.

He pauses.

FLETCHER

So's the bloke you share a cell with.

LENNIE

I'll have to throw myself into my mailbags – is that what you do here?

FLETCHER

Depends. Word of advice, son. What you tell 'em today can decide how tolerable your life here's going to be. I mean, if you want to work somewhere cushy and warm, like the kitchens or the library or the Governor's office, then you got to invent yourself a new career.

LENNIE

Oh.

Heslop, now in his underclothes, moves off to wait.

BARROWCLOUGH

All right. Let's have one of you.

Fletcher and Lennie get up. Fletcher gestures to Lennie to sit down.

FLETCHER

Me, Mr Barrowclough.

He winks at Lennie.

BARROWCLOUGH

It's Fletcher, of course, isn't it?

FLETCHER

Yes, Mr Barrowclough.

BARROWCLOUGH

Christian name?

FLETCHER

Norman Stanley.

BARROWCLOUGH

Date of birth?

FLETCHER

2–2–32.

BARROWCLOUGH

Next of kin?

FLETCHER

My beloved Isobel. The little woman. Well, she ain't so little. I said to her the other day, Isobel, I'll never get over you, I'll have to get up and go round.

He laughs and turns to the others for their reaction. Heslop does not react.

BARROWCLOUGH

Address?

FLETCHER

107 Alexandria Park Crescent, N.5.

BARROWCLOUGH

Occupation?

FLETCHER

Librarian during the day.

BARROWCLOUGH

During the day?

FLETCHER

Yeah. At night I was a chef. Library or the kitchen, I don't mind.

3. PRISON GOVERNOR'S OFFICE

Inside the office there is a tropical fish tank. Venables, the Governor, is sprinkling food on the surface of the water.

The office is furnished strictly to Home Office specifications in terms of furniture, filing cabinets and cream distemper. On one wall there is a professional diploma, and a photograph of a younger Venables as a policeman in Kuala Lumpur. On his desk is a photograph of his son, Guy, graduating at Keele University in Geography. Venables takes the Daily Telegraph which is on his desk. His books are about the law, reform, rehabilitation and the diseases of tropical fish. Venables looks into the tank rather anxiously when there is a knock at the door, and Mackay enters, coming to attention.

MACKAY

Good morning, Governor.

VENABLES

Not sure if it is, Mr Mackay, not sure if it is.

MACKAY

Oh, sir? What's wrong.

Venables beckons him across to the tank. Mackay registers impatience.

VENABLES

It's my four-eyed butterfly fish.

MACKAY

Would that be one with four eyes, sir?

VENABLES

No, no, it's just called that. *Chaetodon*

Capistratus. (*Pointing him out*) There's the little fellow, this one.

MACKAY

(*Bending down with Venables to look at the fish*) Poorly is he, sir?

VENABLES

You noticed?

MACKAY

I assumed, from your concern.

VENABLES

Yes. I'm rather afraid, Mr Mackay that he may have developed fin rot.

MACKAY

Oh dear, sir.

He stands up.

VENABLES

Either that or lymphocystis.

MACKAY

Oh dear, sir.

VENABLES

(*Stands up*) Contagious, you see. Have to isolate the little fellow.

MACKAY

Much as I've had to do with Evans, sir.

Venables turns away from his fish.

VENABLES

Evans?

MACKAY

Had to isolate him again, sir.

VENABLES

What has he done now?

He crosses to the desk.

MACKAY

Been eating light bulbs, sir.

VENABLES

Light bulbs? Did he say why he was eating light bulbs?

MACKAY

Yes, sir. Said it was because he couldn't get hold of any razor blades.

Venables sits down.

VENABLES

What have you done with him?

MACKAY

Locked him in his cell, sir. Taking the precautions first of all of removing the light bulb.

VENABLES

Is the MO free?

MACKAY

He's with the new arrivals at the moment, sir. But I can hurry them through.

VENABLES

As quick as possible. This is a very urgent situation.

MACKAY

I'll get him to Evans right away, sir.

VENABLES

I don't mean Evans. I mean here.

MACKAY

Here?

VENABLES

Fin rot can be fatal, Mr Mackay.

4. MEDICAL ROOM

Inside Fletcher, Lennie and Heslop are sitting on a bench waiting for the Medical Officer.

FLETCHER

Oh, I meant to tell you – when you see the doc tell him you've got bad feet.

LENNIE

Why?

FLETCHER

'Cos then you might get your brothel creepers back. Otherwise you'll have to wear those prison-issue shoes. Guarantee you bad feet for the rest of your life, they will.

LENNIE

Oh, I see.

Heslop starts to laugh. The others look at him.

FLETCHER

It's not funny. Perfectly true.

HESLOP

No, I don't mean that. I mean that's funny about your wife being a big woman and you havin' to get up and go round.

FLETCHER

Oh. I see. Thank you. Anyhow, remember that about the feet. What religion are you?

LENNIE

C of E, I suppose.

FLETCHER

That's no good. Get no perks with C of E. Whereas if you was a Sikh you could grow your hair long. Or if you was a Muslim they'd have to send you in special grub from outside.

LENNIE

Don't like Chinese food.

FLETCHER

Muslim ain't Chinese.

LENNIE

What is Muslim food then?

FLETCHER

What? . . . Well it's . . . it's well, it's more exotic grub than the filth you'll eat here, otherwise the Muslims wouldn't eat it, would they? Or you could say you were Jewish. Yeah, say you're Jewish. Oh no, you couldn't get away with that, could you? Doctor's just going to examine you. He'd spot the evidence.

LENNIE

Evidence?

FLETCHER

With Jews it's only circumstantial. (*Explaining*) They been circumstanted.

Medical Officer enters, coughing, and walks across to the table.

MEDICAL OFFICER

Tropical fish.

FLETCHER

Pardon?

MEDICAL OFFICER

Nothing . . . I'm the (*Coughing*) Medical Officer.

FLETCHER

That's reassuring, in' it?

MEDICAL OFFICER

Now I have to give you men a stringent medical. It's important that we ascertain your medical history and state of health. (*Coughing again*) Right, Fletcher.

Fletcher limps forward. During the questioning a cursory inspection takes place, with particular attention to the armpits.

MEDICAL OFFICER

Have you ever had crabs?

FLETCHER

No – I don't eat fish.

The Medical Officer winces.

MEDICAL OFFICER

Lice?

FLETCHER

No.

MEDICAL OFFICER

VD?

FLETCHER

No.

MEDICAL OFFICER

(*Looking in Fletcher's ear*) Suffer from any illness?

FLETCHER

Bad feet.

MEDICAL OFFICER

Suffer from any illness?

FLETCHER

Bad feet.

MEDICAL OFFICER

Paid a recent visit to a doctor or hospital?

FLETCHER

Only for my bad feet.

MEDICAL OFFICER
Are you now or have you been at any
time a practising homosexual?

FLETCHER
With these feet? Who'd want me?

MEDICAL OFFICER
Right – A1.

He stamps Fletcher's form.

FLETCHER
A1 – hang on, hang on. I can
hardly walk.

MEDICAL OFFICER
Fletcher – everyone in this prison's
trying to pull something, (*crossing to
the scales*) lying about their feet or
their teeth or their eyesight or their
appendix. And on top of that I've got
a Governor who's got fin rot.

FLETCHER
Got what rot?

MEDICAL OFFICER
Fish, tropical bloody fish.

*He puts Fletcher under the
height measure.*

FLETCHER
Oh? Interest of his, is it?

MEDICAL OFFICER
Obsession. That and pigs.

FLETCHER
Pigs?

MEDICAL OFFICER
(*Crossing to desk*) He's started a
prison farm to indulge his interest in
livestock. Only it's the rest of us
who have to look after it. His pigs and
his fish and his favourite Jersey cow.

I'm a man of medicine not a vet.
Half the pills in here are for animals.
Prisoner came in here yesterday with
earache and I gave him pills to dry up
his milk.

He takes a spoon of medicine.

FLETCHER
You must be rushed off your feet, doc.

MEDICAL OFFICER
I cannot cope, man.

FLETCHER
Good job they ain't bad feet like mine.

MEDICAL OFFICER
You're A1. I've told you. (*Pointing to
some flasks on the table*) You see
those flasks? I want you to fill one.

FLETCHER
From here?

MEDICAL OFFICER
Behind the screen. Now,
where's Heslop?

*Heslop walks toward the Medical
Officer as Fletcher takes the flask.*

LENNIE
Didn't pull that one did you, Fletch?

FLETCHER
What?

LENNIE
Prison shoes for you, eh.

FLETCHER
All right, sonny Jim. Lose a few, lose a

few. But my little chat was invaluable. Know something about the Governor, don't I? That's another priority for your first day.

LENNIE

Oh. I see, yes.

FLETCHER

Know your Governor.

LENNIE

Here, Fletcher.

FLETCHER

What?

LENNIE

What's he mean by practising homosexual?

FLETCHER

One who ain't quite got it right yet. Cheers.

Goes behind the screen.

5. PRISON MESS

Barrowclough and other Prison Officers sit at a table playing cards. Fletcher, Lennie and Heslop move to another table with trays of food.

LENNIE

Will we eat with everyone else tonight? *They all sit down.*

FLETCHER

Don't be in no hurry to get thrown in with the others. Bunch of criminals, they are. And don't eat too much of that stuff. Otherwise you might dull your palate for tonight's piss de resistance.

LENNIE

What's it likely to be?

FLETCHER

Likely to be lumpy, lukewarm, grey and gritty. I told you to say you was a Muslim.

HESLOP

Sheep's eyes.

FLETCHER

Yeah – what?

HESLOP

What Muslims eat. Figs. Desert. Wadis and things.

FLETCHER

Oh I see. Yeah well . . . thank you, Lawrence of Arabia.

LENNIE

Why didn't you put down Muslim?

FLETCHER

I don't need to, do I? Going to be working in the kitchens.

LENNIE

But they haven't allocated us jobs yet. *Fletcher indicates the card players.*

FLETCHER

Look, that screw. Barrowclough. Tall one. Looks like Arthur Askey on stilts. Well, I got him there, ain't I? Putty. He'll see me all right.

LENNIE

How come?

FLETCHER

He brought me up from Brixton. Handcuffed we was. Well, you establish a rapport with a man what you're handcuffed to on a long trip.

LENNIE
S'pose you must do. Specially when you go to the lavatory.

FLETCHER
(*Put out slightly*) Oh, you've got a sense of humour, I see. Come in handy during the grim nightmare of your next two years.

LENNIE
Will it be that bad?

FLETCHER
Listen – the important thing is to remember who you once was. And to keep a bit of that person intact up here.

He taps his temple.

FLETCHER
Don't get bitter, or militant, or try to screw the system, 'cos it'll only screw you. Just keep your nose clean, bide your time and do your porridge.

LENNIE
I'm only here due to tragic circumstances.

FLETCHER
Which were?

LENNIE
I got caught.

FLETCHER
Oh yes, I've had a few tragedies of that nature.

LENNIE
It was my fiancée, Denise. She has this nice flat in a tower block in Smethwick. Well, it's her mam's, like. Very nice. Overlooks the M6. So

I thought I'd get her some nice things for it. So I didn't want to have far to cart 'em, like, so I did the flat next door, 'cos I knew he'd be away, like, 'cos he drives a juggernaut from West Bromwich to Brussels. Only he had a puncture outside Coventry and came home and found me and kicked me head in.

HESLOP
Ramsgate.

FLETCHER
Pardon?

HESLOP
Took the wife.

FLETCHER
Took the wife where Mr Heslop?

HESLOP
To see *Lawrence of Arabia*. It was raining see. Couldn't go on the beach at Ramsgate. Took her to the pictures.

FLETCHER
Rains a lot in Ramsgate.

HESLOP
Rained the next day.

FLETCHER
Told you it would.

HESLOP
But she'd seen the film on at the other cinema so we come home. Although we did stop for a cup of tea at her sister's in Sidcup.

FLETCHER
Why don't you put that on a postcard and send it to Tony Blackburn's magic moments.

HESLOP

What?

FLETCHER

One thing I shall miss about not sharing
a cell with you two will be the cut and
thrust of your intellectual conversation.

LENNIE

Won't we all be in together?

FLETCHER

No, I'm having a single cell. I like my
privacy. I prefers to be alone see. Don't
like sharing. Don't like dominoes or
cribbage or other people's sweaty feet.

LENNIE

I'd prefer a single cell. 'Cos I want
to study.

FLETCHER

Study?

LENNIE

Well, I've had an education. I've got an
'O' Level in geography.

FLETCHER

Oh, that'll come in handy that will. If
there's an escape party from here
you're bound to be included 'cos
you'll know the way to Carlisle station.

LENNIE

Very interesting, geography. It's all part
of education.

FLETCHER

Yeah, but it's not the sort of
subject you can make a career
out of. Only reason people
learn geography is so they
can teach other people geography.
Ain't no use to anybody. No use

knowing the capital of Siam or what
an isthmus is.

LENNIE

Well, I don't have to use geography,
I can learn a trade they said.

FLETCHER

In principle; you can come out with
a diploma in some glamour occupation
like house-decorating or shoe repairing.
Or you can become a welder. There's a
riveting profession – get it, get it.

He looks at Heslop.

HESLOP

What?

FLETCHER

Oh never mind.

LENNIE

Here, won't I be able to learn a
trade then?

FLETCHER

Oh yes, there are certain things you can
learn inside that you can become expert
at. Like how to open a safe, steal a car,
forge a banknote. Bloke I was in
Maidstone with – Charlie Mossop, first
offender he was, by the time he come
out he was a brilliant forger. But brilliant.
And he only went in for reckless driving.

LENNIE

I'm fed up with crime, I want to
go straight.

FLETCHER

(*Looking appalled*) How old are
you, son?

LENNIE

Twenty-three.

FLETCHER

Twenty-three and you want to go
straight, what sort of attitude is that?
Got your whole life before you.

HESLOP

What's an isthmus?

FLETCHER

What, what? What is it now,
Dr Bronowski?

HESLOP

What you said – isthmus. What's
an isthmus?

FLETCHER

Oh. Well it's a thing in' it . . . a
thing in geography. A geographical
expression –

LENNIE

It's a strip of land joining together two
larger pieces of land.

FLETCHER

Yeah, strip of land, right.

LENNIE

See, education.

FLETCHER

I'm not saying don't put down for the
educational classes. Current affairs,
pottery, archaeology. I'll be putting
down for that. What. Hour every
night in a nice warm classroom. Bit
of luck you get a woman teacher.
See a bit of thigh when she drops
her chalk. Oh yes, I've nothing
against education.

*Lennie gets out a packet of
cigarettes, which he offers to
the others.*

LENNIE

Fag?

FLETCHER

Oh ta.

*Fletcher and Heslop both take
one and put them straight into
their pockets.*

LENNIE

Oh.

FLETCHER

We're not bein' impolite, Lennie, my
son. It's just that him and me we've
been inside before, and you see
inside, snout is like gold. You was mad
to give us those.

LENNIE

But you took them.

FLETCHER

Ah yes well, learn the hard way, isn't
it? Learn not to be so lavish, you're
not Paul Getty. Should have just lit one
and shared it.

*Heslop takes Lennie's cigarette
and has a puff at it, then passes it
to Fletcher.*

*Barrowclough gets up from the
card game and comes to them.*

BARROWCLOUGH

Right, drink up lads, shall we?

FLETCHER

What's next on the agenda,
Mr Barrowclough?

BARROWCLOUGH

Got to see the Governor, haven't we?
Right. Clear the stuff up. Put that
fag out.

Fletcher pinches out the cigarette and pockets it.

FLETCHER

Waste not, want not.

LENNIE

Here –

FLETCHER

Learn the hard way, son. Now come on, clear up.

Lennie and Heslop take their trays away. Fletcher takes Barrowclough aside.

FLETCHER

Did you er – get what I asked you for, Mr Barrowclough?

BARROWCLOUGH

Well, there wasn't much in the library, just this booklet. (*Gets it from his pocket*) *Know your Tropical Fish.*

FLETCHER

Oh good – it's my hobby, you see.

BARROWCLOUGH

D'you know, by an extraordinary coincidence that's the Governor's hobby.

FLETCHER

Really? Would you believe it.

BARROWCLOUGH

Likes all animals. On the local committee of the RSPCA. Between ourselves I often think he'd have been better off in charge of a zoo than a prison.

FLETCHER

Caged animals – well, we're all the same, ain't we? Talking of cages, you will get me one facing south,

won't you – on me own. I'm not a sharer you see. I mean the boy, he's all right, but he sniffs a lot. And Heslop, he's not on my intellectual level. Don't think he's on anybody's level really. If the Governor *did* open a zoo, Heslop'd be a big attraction.

BARROWCLOUGH

Fletcher, you must understand that I'm a Prison Officer and you are a prisoner. You must recognise that relationship. I am not here to be cajoled or coerced into doing what you want, when you want it.

FLETCHER

Mr Barrowclough, please, of course not. Would I ever?

He turns and leaves. Barrowclough is left holding Fletcher's tray.

BARROWCLOUGH

Well, as long as that's understood. *Barrowclough realises he has got the tray and bangs it down on the table.*

6. EXERCISE YARD

Camera shows the prisoners marching in the exercise yard. Fletcher is marching; Heslop is marching; Lennie is marching. Mackay watches Fletcher and Barrowclough march across the yard.

7. GOVERNOR'S OFFICE

Venables, Mackay and Barrowclough are in the Governor's office.

MACKAY

Fetch them in, Mr Barrowclough.
Barrowclough brings in Fletcher, Lennie and Heslop.

MACKAY

Stand straight in front of the Governor. (*Pointing them out*) Heslop, Godber, Fletcher, sir.

VENABLES

Thank you, Mr Mackay. Now you men have been sent here for varying offences and varying terms of imprisonment. This is not a top-grade security prison, you are C class prisoners. However, if any of you abuses the less stringent security measures which we impose here, you will quickly find that we are on you like a ton of . . .
He breaks off noticing that Fletcher is staring in another direction.

VENABLES

Are you listening, Fletcher?

MACKAY

Face the front.

FLETCHER

I am sorry, Mr Venables, sir. I just couldn't help noticing your aquarium. Interest of mine, you see, indoor fish, tropical fish.

VENABLES

Oh really?

MACKAY

All right, Fletcher.

FLETCHER

Sorry, Mr Mackay. Sorry, sir. But something is bothering me.

VENABLES

What is bothering you, Fletcher?

FLETCHER

Well, sir, this is only a first impression but . . . I think your four-eyed butterfly fish has got a touch of fin rot.

8. FLETCHER'S CELL

There are two bunks and a chair inside the cell. Heslop is lying on the top bunk rolling a cigarette. Lennie sits on the chair, while Fletcher lies on the bottom bunk reading a copy of Farmers Weekly.

LENNIE

Crafty old nurk, aren't you, Fletcher?

FLETCHER

Hang about, I'm just finishing this on Artificial Insemination what the Governor gave me.

LENNIE

Fell for it, didn't he? He really believed your interest in fish and livestock.

FLETCHER

Ain't been a bad day. I told you this is the day what conditions how tolerable your life'll become here.

LENNIE

I think he was impressed by my 'O' Level in geography.

The cell door is unlocked and Mackay enters, carrying a pair of shoes.

MACKAY

All right, lads, on your feet. Exam results. Been a full and exciting day. Firstly Godber – your shoes, courtesy of the M.O.

He hands Lennie his shoes.

FLETCHER

How d'you work that?

LENNIE

Told him about my flat feet, didn't I?

MACKAY

Which he believes, Fletcher. Young Godber's still got some credibility. Unlike yourself. I'm afraid we're having to split this lovely threesome up. One of you're going to a sing.

FLETCHER

Oh yes – only right.

He starts to gather his things.

MACKAY

Not so fast, Fletcher.

FLETCHER

You what?

MACKAY

Get your things together, Godber.

FLETCHER

Godber – him. A cell on his own.

MACKAY

Governor thought it would be more conducive to study.

LENNIE

Oh, that's lovely. I didn't fancy sharing – no offence.

FLETCHER

You didn't fancy sharing. What about me – you leaving me here with the Brain of Britain here?

MACKAY

There'll be three of you. We're moving Evans in here.

FLETCHER

Evans! That Welsh lunatic who eats light bulbs!

MACKAY

Only when he can't get razor blades.

FLETCHER

Oh marvellous. Can I have permission to grow a beard?

MACKAY

Jobs. Kitchen – Godber.

LENNIE

Oh that'll be nice – all warm and second helpings.

MACKAY

Library – Heslop.

FLETCHER

Library! Him! He's an illiterate.

HESLOP

I read a book once. It was green.

FLETCHER

And what's he got the kitchen for. First time in, God Almighty he should be breaking rocks or something – paying his dues. This is victimisation! I'm an old hand, I should have something befitting my seniority.

MACKAY

Special duties.

FLETCHER

What?

MACKAY

Special duties. Who's the Governor's blue-eyed boy?

FLETCHER

Well, we had a bit of a rapport yes. Cementated by our common interest in all things bright and beautiful, all creatures great and small.

MACKAY

Governor said you're just the man he's been waiting for.

FLETCHER

Oh. Oh I see. All right then. (*Turning to Lennie*) Kitchens – eat your heart out, Godber. Green it was.

9. PRISON FARM

The prison Governor and Fletcher are outside in the prison farm.

GOVERNOR

Good morning, Fletcher.

FLETCHER

Morning, sir.

GOVERNOR

It always gives me great pleasure to place a man in a job which gives him real fulfilment.

FLETCHER

Fulfilment, yes, thank you, sir.

Fletcher is cleaning out the pigsty. He is surrounded by pigs.

GOVERNOR

Oh, the article in *Farmers Weekly*, did you finish it?

FLETCHER

I'm afraid I didn't, sir. Oh, I would have done, only Evans ate it.

Fletcher continues digging.

1 SERIES ONE

EPISODE TWO: THE HUSTLER

1. HEN HOUSE

Chickens in a coop. Offstage the voices of Fletcher and Ives can be heard.

IVES

Come on, come on. You can do it, my love.

FLETCHER

Come on gel, come on gel. Force it out. Effort! Effort!

IVES

Come on, my son.

FLETCHER

Hang about. It's a girl, you nurk. 'My son'.

IVES

How d'you know it's a girl?

FLETCHER

Hens is all girls, Ives.

IVES

Are they?

FLETCHER

Course they are. All hens are females. Your male is your cock.

IVES

Oh yes . . . here, listen, there's a hell of a lot more females than males.

FLETCHER

'Course there are. That's why your cock always looks so smug. Always knows it's there. Hence the expression, cock sure.

They resume their encouragements.

FLETCHER

Come on gel, force it out.

IVES

Mine's looking inament.

Fletches takes a quick look at Ives's bird.

FLETCHER

Nodded off, she has.

IVES

Here, listen, want to double the bet?

FLETCHER

Certainly.

IVES

Right. Done.

FLETCHER

You certainly have been.

IVES

Why?

FLETCHER

Jackpot.

An egg rolls down its little channel.

Fletcher picks it up.

FLETCHER

Thanks, gel. And thank you, Ives.

Ives disgruntledly takes out two handed-rolled snouts from his breast pocket. He is about to hand them over when he has a thought.

IVES

Listen, double or quits.

He takes the egg from Fletcher and puts both hands behind his back.

IVES

Which hand's it in? Go on, fair's fair. Double or quits.

FLETCHER

All right.

Ives holds out his hands. Fletcher thinks, then taps one.

FLETCHER

That one.

Ives shouts with delight and opens an empty hand.

IVES

Ha! We're even.

FLETCHER

Oh in that one, was it?

He squeezes Ives's other hand breaking the egg within.

IVES

(*Shaking off the sticky egg from his hand*) Oh Fletcher, not funny, not funny.

FLETCHER

Can't take a yolk some people.

VOICE OFF

(*Shouting*) Ives!

Ives picks his bucket up and leaves.

Fletcher checks that he has gone and then moves to Ives's hen.

FLETCHER

Poor old Ives, what a loser. If Elizabeth Taylor had triplets and he was one of them, he'd be the one in the middle on the bottle . . . You're not a loser are you, gel? You'd 'a won by rights, if I hadn't cut off your access.

He removes a crumpled handkerchief from the channel beneath the chicken and an egg rolls down. He goes to the door and checks then puts some eggs in a bag of grain.

FLETCHER

This, girls, is what you might call one of the perks of this job. Now with those eggs I can get myself a quarter ounce of shag, or two tubes of toothpaste, or three bars of fruit and nut, or I could take them along to E Wing and see Smutty Garland, King of the Porn. Trade 'em in for one of his dirty books. Filled with full frontal naked nubiles . . . No, I'd rather have the fruit and nut.

2. PRISON FARM

Close up of a trough. Swill is being poured into it. Pigs come over to eat. Fletcher looks at them.

FLETCHER

Gawd, you're messy. And you eat like pigs. Here, can you lot run? There's a thought, pig-racing. That would make a nice little flutter, wouldn't it? The Slade Prison Selling Plate for Pigs . . . the Royal Cheltenham Pork Cup . . . I could have a book. Become an owner, and have my own stable – sty . . . Yeah, thought appeals, thought appeals. The Bacon Handicap.

He laughs and moves away.

FLETCHER

The Bacon Handicap.

A pig looks up at Fletcher.

3. HEN HOUSE

Fletcher walks into the hen house and looks at the chickens.

FLETCHER

Hello, darlings, still trying, are you?

BARROWCLOUGH

(*Appearing*) 'Morning, Fletcher.

FLETCHER

Oh morning, Mr Barrowclough. How's things?

BARROWCLOUGH

That man Ives, what was he doing round here?

FLETCHER

What – oh he was just dropping in on his way to the silos.

BARROWCLOUGH

Wasn't taking bets, was he?

FLETCHER

Bets?

BARROWCLOUGH

It has been suspected that he's Harry Grout's runner.

FLETCHER

(*Innocently*) Runner? Mr Barrowclough. Runner?

BARROWCLOUGH

Taking bets.

FLETCHER

Oh yeah.

BARROWCLOUGH

Harry Grout's a long-term prisoner and he's not the pleasantest of men, and he seems to exert an unhealthy influence. We're fairly sure that he runs both gambling and tobacco in this prison. I – I'm telling you this Fletcher because . . . well you're a good chap and I wouldn't want you to get sucked into that circle.

FLETCHER

Don't worry. Oh Mr Barrowclough, have no fear on that score. Gambling appals me. Seen the consequences too often.

BARROWCLOUGH

It's like a plague in this prison.

FLETCHER

Not one of my vices – got too many other things to do – 'ere do you think pigs can run?

BARROWCLOUGH

Run?

FLETCHER

Could they be trained to run?

BARROWCLOUGH

Why?

FLETCHER

What! Oh I just thought it would make a change for them. The exercise.

BARROWCLOUGH

Well, it's good to see you're taking an interest in your fellow creatures.

He goes to sit down but is stopped by Fletcher.

FLETCHER

Don't sit there, Mr Barrowclough. You'll dirty your uniform. I'll get you a chair.

He moves to get a chair and then back again.

BARROWCLOUGH

I gather you're settling in, down on the farm.

FLETCHER

(*Goes to sit, realises*) Oh . . . it ain't too bad, tell the truth. When I was assigned to it, well I took offence at first, 'cos I've never been a rural man. Always had a deep mistrust of animals.

BARROWCLOUGH

I thought you told the Governor you had a keen interest in farming and livestock.

FLETCHER

(*Guiltily*) Oh, yes, that. Farming and livestock, yes. Just that I ain't so keen on the animal end of it.

BARROWCLOUGH

(*Obviously not seeing*) Oh, I see. You're very lucky to be here, you

know. Normally a trusty gets a job like this. Privileged position.

FLETCHER

Don't think I don't appreciate it, Mr Barrowclough. I'm sure you had something to do with it, knowing your kind and generous nature.

BARROWCLOUGH

No, nothing to do with –

FLETCHER

(*Knowingly*) Say no more, say no more. When you going to get me a single cell then?

BARROWCLOUGH

It's not in my power, Fletcher.

FLETCHER

See, I'm not a sharer. And those two I'm in with, Heslop and Evans, well I mean there's no rapport . . . no intellectual stimulus. You know what I mean.

BARROWCLOUGH

Evans, yes, he's a strange fellow. Is he still eating light bulbs?

FLETCHER

No, he's got a taste for other things now. Ate my shaving mirror yesterday.

BARROWCLOUGH

I'm afraid there's little I can do. And it's wrong of you to ask me.

FLETCHER

What? Oh no. Wait. Please. You mustn't think – you must NOT think that I'm trying to influence you, to coerce you to . . . I can hardly bring myself to say the word . . . BRIBE you.

Barrowclough reacts.

FLETCHER

What – a prison officer what's been specially chosen by the Home Office for his integrity and honesty.

He has a quick look round.

FLETCHER

'Ere would a dozen eggs make a difference?

Barrowclough looks shocked.

FLETCHER

No, of course not.

4. PRISON FARM/PRISON

Barrowclough is seen locking up. Fletcher is waiting for him. Barrowclough moves to Fletcher and they walk off together to the prison gates. There they knock. The door is opened by a Prison Officer and they go in.

FLETCHER

Lovely day for it.

PRISON OFFICER

You won't be getting it for a long time.

FLETCHER

You obviously ain't had it for a long time.

Prison Officer reacting.

5. PRISON KITCHEN

Lennie is washing down one of the big hotplates. Also in the kitchen is

a trusty cook; he is called Lukewarm, after his cooking. Fletcher enters, putting down his boxes of eggs on the working surface. He has with him his plastic bag of grain with the concealed eggs. He's followed in by Prison Officer Appleton.

FLETCHER

There y'are, Lukewarm. Three dozen and two.

LUKEWARM

What? What's wrong with those hens since you took over? Shell shock?

APPLETON

Thievin' are you, Fletcher?

FLETCHER

No need for that is there, Mr Appleton, no need for that sort of defamatory.

APPLETON

Always pilfering, the whole lot of you.

FLETCHER

(*Outraged*) Now listen, Mr Appleton, I resent that. I may have done some bad things in my life, wouldn't be here if I hadn't, but I ain't a petty sneak thief, that's not my style at all.

APPLETON

All right, all right.

He turns away and Fletcher nimbly picks up a packet of margarine from the working surface and slips

it into his pocket, as he crosses to
the table, gingerly putting down his
bag of grain.

FLETCHER
Er . . . Lennie . . . anyone er . . . left a
message here for me?

LENNIE
Yeah. Bloke come in and said Harry
Grout said permission granted.

FLETCHER
Did he? Oh, good.

LENNIE
Permission for what?

FLETCHER
Permission to hold a game.

LENNIE
What game?

FLETCHER
Keep your voice down.

LENNIE
(*Quieter*) What game?

FLETCHER
A game of chance, my son.

LENNIE
How d'you mean?

FLETCHER
Oh for gawd's sake, Godber.
A gamble. A flutter.

LENNIE
But gambling ain't allowed.

FLETCHER
'Course it ain't allowed. That's
precisely why we're doin' it.

LENNIE
Why d'you have to get permission off
this Grout?

FLETCHER
(*Pained*) Godber, son, you've been
here a week, ain't you learned
nothing? Officially this hotel is run
by a governor appointed by the
Home Office, Mr Venables. But in
practice of course we knows
different. In practice General Harry
Grout can bring this nick to a
standstill if he so wishes.

LENNIE
What d'you play for – big stakes, is it?

FLETCHER
We will do if Lukewarm can nick some
from the meat safe. We play for
anything negotiable. Snout mostly. But
it won't be for chicken feed . . . pity
really 'cos I got plenty of that.

LENNIE
I've noticed people are always
betting on something. I suppose it's
their way of generating excitement
to counter the misery of their
monotonous existence.

FLETCHER
What? Oh yes – right. It ain't just the
excitement of the game, what you win
or what you lost. It's the pleasure what
you get for doing it under their noses,
surruptitious, like.

LENNIE
There's two blokes next door to me
who've had a bet on how many bricks
there are In their cell.

FLETCHER
Oh yes. Commonplace that.

LENNIE

I can't think or study. It's driving me mad, listening to 'em. Recount after recount. Three hundred and forty-one, three hundred and forty-two . . .

FLETCHER

Blokes doing stir'll bet on anything. Two flies going up a wall, hymn numbers in the chapel. Two flies going down a wall . . . I even laid an egg on a bet today – made a bet on egg laying. There was a big game last night in D Wing. Weren't you aware of the atmosphere in the air? It was electric – the tension.

LENNIE

Tension, I noticed that. But I thought that was because Tuesday's the day that female social worker comes round.

FLETCHER

What, gruesome Glenda? Her with the brogues and the bicycle. You'd be hard pushed to have an erotic fantasy about that one.

LENNIE

I dunno. Nifty Small's in love with her. He stole her bicycle saddle.

FLETCHER

Really? Gawd the ride back must have been painful for her. He won't have that long. They'll soon find it.

LENNIE

What, under his pillow! I bet they won't.

FLETCHER

(*Instantly*) All right, you're on. How much? Two fags?

LENNIE

'Ere, 'ere, I'm not gambling. My mother said gambling will get you into trouble.

FLETCHER

Son, it may have escaped your notice but you're in prison. Your mother was too late. You is in trouble.

LENNIE

Yeah, well nevertheless I'm not gambling. I'm not counting bricks or watching flies. Gambling's one thing I'm going to resist inside.

FLETCHER

Bet you can't.

LENNIE

Oh yes I can.

FLETCHER

Bet you a bar of soap you can't.

LENNIE

I bet I can.

FLETCHER

There you are. You bet me you wouldn't bet me. So you just lost your first bet. That's a bar of soap you owe me. Work that out.

Ives walks in carrying a sack of potatoes.

APPLETON

Where are you going, Ives?

IVES

Er just er . . . got the spuds, Mr Appleton . . .

APPLETON

Get on with it, Ives.

FLETCHER
(*Walking across*) Got the spuds, Ives?

IVES
'Ere listen, Fletcher. How much do they weigh then?

FLETCHER
You know already.

IVES
'Course I don't. No scales out there.

FLETCHER
What's the bet then?

IVES
All the eggs you've got in there.

FLETCHER
You crafty nurk.
Against what?

IVES
Ounce of snout.

FLETCHER
Fair enough.

IVES
Are you in, son?

LENNIE
No, I'm not.

Fletcher appraises the bag expertly then picks it up, testingly.

FLETCHER
Nearest one, eh!

IVES
Nearest one.

FLETCHER
Twenty-three pounds.

IVES
I'll say twenty-seven.

FLETCHER
Gave that a lot of thought, didn't you?

IVES
Just over twenty-seven.

Ives lifts the potatoes on to the scales. They weigh just over twenty-seven pounds.

IVES
Well I never, would you believe it?

BOTH
Just over twenty-seven.

IVES
Thank you . . . Sh-ting.

FLETCHER
You knew, didn't you?

IVES
Here listen. I ain't no cheat.

FLETCHER
What? You're in here for fraudulent conversion. It's your career that is, cheating.

IVES
Lose gracefully, come on, here listen.

FLETCHER
You're a crafty conniving gink, Ives.

IVES
Bad loser.

FLETCHER
Here you are then.

He hands over the eggs.

IVES
(*Putting them in his pockets*) Come in handy these. Owes Grout, don't I. Don't do to owe Grouty.

FLETCHER
Now naff off.

Mackay enters.

MACKAY

Morning, Mr Appleton.

Everyone redoubles their illusion of activity, including Appleton.

APPLETON

Morning, Mr Mackay.

MACKAY

Fletcher! What are you doing, Ives?

IVES

Oh – I just brought the spuds, Mr Mackay.

Fletcher tries to leave with his bag of grain.

MACKAY

Where are you going, Fletcher?

FLETCHER

Pig swill.

MACKAY

Pardon!!

FLETCHER

See about the pig swill, Mr Mackay. Little fellows need their swill this time of day.

Fletcher starts to go.

MACKAY

(*Gesturing*) Just a minute.

FLETCHER

I've swept all that Mr Ma . . .

MACKAY

Fletcher – come here.

Fletcher goes across.

MACKAY

I'm told your chickens are on short time. I'm told that since you arrived at the farm egg production has fallen drastically.

FLETCHER

Don't blame me, Mr Mackay. Perhaps they're in a foul mood . . .

MACKAY

Don't you come it with me, Fletcher. Now, what have we here?

FLETCHER

Crown jewels. Chicken meal, Mr Mackay.

MACKAY

Empty it. (*To Ives*) Ives, stands still.

FLETCHER

Empty it?

MACKAY

Empty it.

FLETCHER

Make ever such a mess.

Godber walks over.

MACKAY

Godber . . . Empty it.

Fletcher tips bag of grain on to table. Mackay pokes about in it with his truncheon.

MACKAY

All right, Fletcher. But if I catch you thieving . . .

FLETCHER

I won't.

MACKAY

Won't what?

FLETCHER

Let you catch me, Mr Mackay.

Mackay sees Ives.

MACKAY

Ives – where are you going, horrible Ives?

FLETCHER

Don't we knock, don't we knock?

IVES

No, no, 'ere listen. Word is you've got a game going.

FLETCHER

Oh say it a bit louder. Few people in E Wing didn't catch that. Why don't you bellow it from the bleedin' rooftops.

IVES

It's all right, the screws are brewing up.

FLETCHER

(*Sitting*) Subtle as an air-raid you are, Ives.

IVES

No, listen, is that gen? You got a game put together?

FLETCHER

Yup.

IVES

Grouty give the OK, did he?

FLETCHER

At a price, yeah.

IVES

When is it?

FLETCHER

Saturday afternoon. When the world is watching *Grandstand*, and the screws are playing E Wing at football.

IVES

Can I be in?

FLETCHER

Sorry, old son. Full house.

IVES

Who's in then?

FLETCHER

Myself. Mr Heslop, here. Lukewarm from the kitchen. And Mr Evans – providing he don't eat the dice.

IVES

Oh it's dice, is it?

FLETCHER

(*Rising*) What? Oh well, possibly, possibly. Said enough, said enough.

IVES

You can make room for one more.

FLETCHER

Not your sort, Ives.

IVES

'Ere listen –

FLETCHER

It's all been arranged, it's all set up, right? So naff off.

IVES

You telling me you going to set a game up? In this place. What? You ain't got a snowball's. Gambling here?

FLETCHER

Same in any nick. Question of integrity. Where there's a will there's a way.

IVES

(*Sitting*) You're so lairy, aren't you, Fletcher? Well it might have been a doddle in your last nick. But they cut off privileges here for the toss of a coin.

EVANS

I've had my privileges cut off.

FLETCHER

Oh yes, did it hurt much?

IVES

Oh yes, geraniums. Nice little fellas.
My cousin used to breed them.

FLETCHER

Grow them.

IVES

Grow them.

BARROWCLOUGH

Really? Now you know something,
I'm a bit of a horticulturalist myself.

FLETCHER

Oh really . . . oh gawd.

BARROWCLOUGH

Anyhow no time to go into that now.

FLETCHER

Oh. More's the pity.

BARROWCLOUGH

Come along Evans – time for your visit
to the psychiatrist.

IVES

'Ere listen – you still trying to work one
by eating things?

FLETCHER

Yes, he is. Playing havoc with my
personal possessions.

EVANS

Playing havoc with my digestion.

*He leaves the cell, rubbing
his stomach.*

IVES

Listen, Fletcher. Where d'you get the
dice then?

FLETCHER

Lukewarm made them in the kitchen.
Out of pastry. He baked them.

IVES

Won't they break?

FLETCHER

Not his pastry.

HESLOP

I'm very fond of geraniums.

Fletcher lies down. Ives sits down.

HESLOP

Flowers, things like that. Not that we
had a garden. My house just had a
yard. A yard with a wringer and a
bicycle in it. But the wife's sister's
house in Sidcup, that has a riot of
colour. What with his vegetables, she
never had to want for anything.

FLETCHER

Is that it?

Ives looks and nods.

FLETCHER

Comes in bursts like that. Another of
those poignant anecdotes from the
rich pageant of Mr Heslop's past, the
Patience Strong of Cell Block 11. You
can see how lucky I am to be in here
with him.

IVES

I can see why you dealt him in.

FLETCHER

First come, first served.

IVES

'Ere listen. You'll never pull it off.

FLETCHER

What you talking about?

IVES

Organise this game and get away
with it.

FLETCHER

(*Rising*) It's already organised.

IVES

But I bet you can't get away with it.

FLETCHER

Put your money where your –

IVES

Mouth is, I will do.

FLETCHER

Go on then.

IVES

How much?

FLETCHER

Try me.

IVES

A biggy.

FLETCHER

Big as you like.

IVES

How big?

FLETCHER

Try me.

IVES

Snout.

FLETCHER

Obviously.

IVES

All right then. Half a pound.

He says this as if expecting the reaction "Don't be ridiculous", but instead Fletcher agrees.

FLETCHER

Fair enough.

Fletcher's nonchalance unnerves Ives.

IVES

Did you hear me, Fletcher? I said half a pound.

FLETCHER

I heard you.

IVES

That's eight ounces.

FLETCHER

Nice one, Einstein.

IVES

Now let's get this perfectly clear – and you're a witness.

He indicates Heslop, then checks the door again.

IVES

I'm betting you half a pound of snout that you won't see your game through. You'll get found out, or busted, or whatever.

FLETCHER

You're on.

Ives looks visibly shaken at the size of the bet.

IVES

All right then. That's done then. I'll be off then.

FLETCHER

I'd lay a little of that off if I was you, my son.

Ives leaves.

HESLOP

Got a lot of bottle, Fletcher, a lot of bottle.

FLETCHER

Where there's a will there's a way. Here's my shoe polish.

HESLOP

When I was doing bird in Shepton Mallet we used to bet on the number of bricks in a cell.

FLETCHER

Oh original yes. How did you get on?

Fletcher walks to the table, then to the bed.

HESLOP

All I know is there was over thirty-seven.

FLETCHER

Oh roomy, wasn't it? When I was in Maidstone, d'you know what we had going? We only had a roulette game going that's all. With a dartboard, see. People bet on it. You could be on red or black, evens or odds, sequences or individual numbers. And your croupier was a bloke what was blindfolded and threw the dart. We used to play in association and we bribed this screw to turn a blind eye. Big game it was, mammoth.

HESLOP

Oh crafty that, roulette.

FLETCHER

Yeah . . . pity it came to such a tragic end.

HESLOP

What happened?

FLETCHER

One night the croupier got a bit careless. Now the screw turns a blind eye to everything.

9. COKE STORE

Inside the coke store Evans, Heslop, Lukewarm and Fletcher are sitting on boxes round a tea chest.

HESLOP

You sure they won't find us in here?

FLETCHER

Lukewarm here assures me they won't – he being a trusty, happens to have access to the coke store key. Cosy, ain't it?

LUKEWARM

They'll never look down here today.

FLETCHER

No – officially, as you know, we're all watching E Wing play the screws at football, a game that will occupy a lot of attention.

LUKEWARM

And the attention of the hospital as well later on, the way they go at each other.

FLETCHER

Yeah – should be quite a bloodbath, with any luck.

There are murmurs of approval and agreement.

FLETCHER

I did try to persuade Tommy Macready to put forward his escape attempt to today. 'Cos knowing Tommy he'll cock it up and the diversion would have come in very handy. However, he couldn't be swayed as he pointed out, quite rightly, state this country's in you can't rely on trains at the weekend.

HESLOP

I didn't know Tommy was going over the wall.

LUKEWARM

Oh yes, common knowledge.

EVANS

Domestic problems.

FLETCHER

Wife's got nerves or something.

LUKEWARM

Things are getting on top of her, are they?

FLETCHER

Quite the reverse. She's sleeping with a limbo dancer.

LUKEWARM

A limbo dancer? Is he black?

FLETCHER

Black and blue, I should think, knowing her. What a raver! Now then . . .

LUKEWARM

Oh, before I forget – something to nibble at for later.

He hands out packets of sandwiches.

EVANS

Ooh, lovely – I haven't had a square meal for ages.

FLETCHER

Not since my shaving mirror. Thanks, Lukewarm – you spoil us. I wish I'd had a mother like you. I might have gone straight.

LUKEWARM

Or bent.

HESLOP

Can I eat mine now?

FLETCHER

No you can't – he's like a big kid, ain't he? Soon as you get outside the front door, you want to start the picnic. Wait! Now the rules, gentlemen. One: Stakes – minimum bet, one fag. You cannot raise more than half the kitty. Two: Losers – and some of us have to lose, don't we? Divvy up within twenty-four hours – if not Mr Heslop here will come round with a reminder – just like the Post Office.

EVANS

The Post Office?

FLETCHER

Yeah, he'll stick one on you. Now we're all set. Right?

OTHERS

Right.

FLETCHER

Right.

LUKEWARM

And the game.

FLETCHER

And the game gentlemen.

He stands up and gets his shirt out from his trousers. There are snakes and ladders drawn on it.

FLETCHER

The game is snakes and ladders.

10. FILM

Mackay enters closely followed by Barrowclough.

MACKAY

I knew something was up,

Mr Barrowclough. My antennae told me. I know when there's a Big Deal at Dodge City in this place.

Mr Barrowclough shuts and locks the door.

BARROWCLOUGH

I sometimes think it's a waste of our manpower – trying to crack down on gambling – I mean, men will gamble.

Barrowclough and Mackay walk along the alley.

MACKAY

Gambling leads to debts, Mr Barrowclough. And debts lead to ill-feeling, antagonism. Lack of discipline.

BARROWCLOUGH

Did your antennae tell you where this game is taking place?

MACKAY

No, that was Ives, horrible Ives.

BARROWCLOUGH

No honour among thieves.

MACKAY

Not where there's gambling at stake, that's why it has to be stamped out.

BARROWCLOUGH

Where are they?

MACKEY

We're getting warmer.

They stop walking.

MACKAY

They're down there.

BARROWCLOUGH

What – in the boiler house?

MACKAY

In the coke store.

BARROWCLOUGH

Well, should we –

MACKAY

No, wait a moment. I've arranged for a special delivery.

He moves round the corner and gives the signal. Coal is seen going down the chute. Mackay and Barrowclough move to the doorway and wait. A door opens and Evans, Heslop, Fletcher and Lukewarm rush out covered in soot.

MACKAY

Welcome to the Black and White Minstrel Show.

They move up the alley.

11. CELL

Fletcher is collecting his things together inside the cell, when Ives puts his head round the door.

IVES

Evening, Fletcher.

Fletcher gives him no acknowledgement.

IVES

I – I heard this time the coke was on you.

FLETCHER

What? Oh yes, you're a very witty man. Full of that irrepressible Liverpudlian wit we've all heard about.

IVES

What the Governor say then?

FLETCHER

Said I'd abused his trust. Said I'd lost my privileged position on the farm. Said I'd lose my privileges for the next four weeks. Also said I was an evil influence and not the sort of man who should be sharing a cell and corrupting the likes of Heslop and Evans. So he's shifting me to a single cell.

IVES

Oh dear, how tragic. I am sorry.

FLETCHER

All right, don't give me all that. I know you grassed, Ives. As does the entire prison. As you will find out when you take your first turn round the recreation yard. I'm not saying there'll be any unpleasantness, but if I were you I'd try and borrow some shin pads from the PTI.

IVES

'Ere listen, Fletcher.

FLETCHER

Not that I bears you any ill-feeling, you 'orrible contemptuous despicable git you. No, no, you was just a pawn in my grand strategy.

IVES

Never mind about that, there's still the bet, there's still the bet – you owes me, Fletcher.

FLETCHER

That is true, that is true. And that half pound of snout may provide some consolation to you in the nightmare days that lie ahead.

Barrowclough comes in.

BARROWCLOUGH

Ready, Fletcher?

FLETCHER

Just coming, Mr Barrowclough.

IVES

'Ere listen, you take the heat off me and we'll forget about the bet. We're even. I mean you're never going to raise half a pound of snout, are you?

FLETCHER

No, there's no problem. I'll take it out me winnings.

IVES

Winnings? What winnings?

FLETCHER

Lose a few, gain a few. I was betting the whole landing half a pound of snout I'd be in a single cell by Sunday. I'm going to be rolling in it.

12. PRISON LANDING

Barrowclough and Fletcher come out of the cell and walk along the gantry. A prisoner passes Fletcher some tobacco.

They go down the stairs. Prisoners hand over tobacco to Fletcher. They go down more stairs. More prisoners give him tobacco.

1 SERIES ONE

EPISODE THREE: A NIGHT IN

1. PRISON

It is association hour. Lennie goes down stairs.
He walks past other prisoners on his way to Fletcher's cell.

2. FLETCHER'S CELL

Lennie walks in. Fletcher is sitting on the lower bunk writing a letter. Lennie is a bit diffident.

LENNIE
Oh er . . . hello, Fletch.

He is met with silence.

LENNIE
You er . . . you was expecting me? I mean they informed you?

FLETCHER
They informed me, yes.

LENNIE
Only temporary they said.

FLETCHER
You bet your life it's only temporary. Single cell this is, by rights.

LENNIE
Not my fault.

FLETCHER
I'm just saying

LENNIE
Only temporary.

FLETCHER
Look, park your stuff, get out the light.

Lennie pauses awkwardly, indicating the lower bunk.

LENNIE
Er . . . is this where you want me to sleep?

FLETCHER
What?

LENNIE
Well, I presume I'm in the bottom bunk. I mean, top bunk's status in the nick.

FLETCHER
'Course it is. You're in the bottom bunk, yes.

LENNIE
Well, if you wouldn't mind shifting your stuff, I could –

FLETCHER
What? Oh, all right. God Almighty.

He moves his stuff to the top bunk.

*Lennie begins to unpack his stuff
and make up his bunk.*

LENNIE

Not my fault.

FLETCHER

No no, so you keep telling me.

LENNIE

Not my fault if they have a riot on my
landing. My cell mate, Banksy, he was
one of the ringleaders, like. He set fire
to his mattress. And mine.

FLETCHER

Head case, that Banks.

LENNIE

He's being transferred.

FLETCHER

Head case.

LENNIE

He wasn't a bad bloke to share a cell
with. He was always very nice to me.
He showed me the ropes and taught
me cribbage. And he never displayed
no violence. He was the gentlest
of men.

FLETCHER

Oih . . .

*He nods to Lennie indicating that he
should go to the other washstand.*

LENNIE

(*Crossing over*) Oh . . . He found
this kitten and smuggled it into
the cell and from the way he handled
it you could see the gentle side of
his nature.

FLETCHER

You what? Before he lit his mattress

I heard he threw a screw off the
top landing.

LENNIE

Well, he weren't hurt. He hit the
safety net.

FLETCHER

That, Godber, is somewhat academic.
The point is that a fifteen-stone prison
officer was hurled from a top landing
by your cell mate, mighty Joe Banks.

LENNIE

Only because he said he couldn't
keep the kitten.

FLETCHER

Hardly an excuse, sonny Jim. Hardly
an excuse. Can't see that cutting
much ice with his parole board.

LENNIE

Where's the harm in keeping a kitten?

FLETCHER

It's not allowed, that's the point. It's
against prison procedure. Caged birds,
well yes, sometimes they'll let you keep
caged birds. Insects in a matchbox.
But you can't keep cats. And Banks
knows that, the porridge he's done.

LENNIE

It was only a little kitten.

FLETCHER

A kitten differs from a cat only in scale.
They share the same lavatorial
tendencies, they pee on your blankets.

LENNIE

Just don't see the harm.

FLETCHER

There are rules. For example, I have

certain rules in this cell here. Well, not so much rules as standards. This is my cell, in which you're a temporary resident, and as such you will honour those standards.

LENNIE

Which are?

FLETCHER

You don't rabbit, you don't snore, and you don't pick your nose.

LENNIE

I don't think I do any of them.

FLETCHER

Good, good. Then we should get on passably well.

LENNIE

Banksy never complained anyhow.

FLETCHER

Well, he wouldn't, not an animal like Banksy.

LENNIE

But I don't.

He sits down.

FLETCHER

Good good, fine fine – you're sitting on my paper.

LENNIE

Oh, sorry.

He gets up off a crumpled copy of the Sun and passes it over.

FLETCHER

Oh another thing. Newspapers. You can read the paper, but when, and only when I've finished with it.

LENNIE

All right.

FLETCHER

Right – get out of the way.

There is a pause while Fletcher climbs up into the top bunk and settles down with his paper. His shoes are off, and there is a big hole in one of his socks.

Lennie starts to set out a few personal possessions, including a photograph of his fiancée, only inscribed "Lennie – for always, Denise". He has also got some needle and thread, a tin of shag tobacco and some papers, a tin of throat lozenges, a box of liquorice all-sorts and shaving kit.

LENNIE

I've got some grey darning thread.

FLETCHER

(*Irritably*) What?

LENNIE

I've got some grey darning thread if you want that hole darned up.

FLETCHER

(*Politer*) What? Oh yes, thanks – yes.

He takes off his sock and hands it down to Lennie, who by his reaction registers that he had not expected to do the darning himself. He decides not to make a stand.

LENNIE

Your standards don't include sweaty feet, I notice.

FLETCHER

Man who don't sweat ain't healthy. Like a dog with a dry nose.

LENNIE

(*Getting the darning kit*) Settling in OK, are you?

FLETCHER

I'm all right, keep me pecker up. Can't grind me down. Bide your time, that's what it's all down to, bide your time.

Bells start to ring and doors start to slam, signalling lockup time. Voices are heard in the distance.

LENNIE

Unnatural in't it, men in cages.

FLETCHER

Bide your time.

LENNIE

I don't mind work. And as I'm in the kitchens I always get plenty of grub. And the screws ain't too bad, by and large . . .

A prison officer appears, gives a cursory check, then slams the door and locks it.

FLETCHER

Goodnight, sunshine . . . Charmless nurk. Oh dear, I forgot to put me shoes out to be cleaned.

Lennie walks across to the window.

LENNIE

This is the bit I can't stand though.

FLETCHER

What?

LENNIE

Lockup. It's only quarter-to-eight. Barely dark. If I was at home now I'd just be going out for the evening.

FLETCHER

That's the point you see, son. We're here to be punished, ain't we? Deprived of all our creature comforts. And the little things you've been taking for granted all these years. Like a comfy shirt, decent smoke, a night out.

LENNIE

A night out . . .

There is a pause.

FLETCHER

Look, if you're so keen we'll go out. We could find a couple of girls – two of them darlings what dance on *Top of the Pops*. Yes, Pan's People. Beautiful Babs – don't know what her name is. Arrange to meet them in some dimly lit Italiano restaurant. Then we could go on somewhere if you like. Some night club . . . dance till dawn. Then back to their luxury penthouse, and wallop. But you see I done all that last night so I'm a bit knackered. Also we'd have to get all ponced up and you'd have to darn me socks. So why don't we just have a quiet night in? All right?

LENNIE

If you say so, Fletch.

FLETCHER

That's what you've got to tell yourself. You're just having a quiet night in.

He goes back to the Sun. There is a pause.

LENNIE

(*Gloomily*) Trouble is I've got six

hundred and ninety-eight quiet nights in to go.

FLETCHER
Less than some.

Lennie looks at the picture of Denise.

LENNIE
D'you think she'll wait?

FLETCHER
(*Abstractedly*) What?

LENNIE
D'you think she'll wait?

FLETCHER
Who?

LENNIE
Denise. My fiancée.

FLETCHER
Oh yes, Denise, fiancée.

LENNIE
Well, do you?

FLETCHER
I dunno. I shouldn't think she'll wait *in* for six hundred and ninety-eight nights.

LENNIE
She is my fiancée.

FLETCHER
Yes, I know, but when she said she'd love you for ever she didn't know you were going to get put away for two years, did she?

LENNIE
I miss her so much. I can't sleep for thinking about her.

FLETCHER
Doesn't do no good that. Don't do no good lying awake at night brooding and twitching about what you ain't going to get no more. Carnal thoughts – well, best to give them the Big E, the elbow. Less you think about women the better – cor, look at that. 'Beauty Queen shocks Council. Lovely Sharon Spenser, twenty-two, shocked members of her town Council when they learned that she played the title role in the new sex-sational film *The Virgin and the Vicar*.'

LENNIE
I wonder which she played?

FLETCHER
'"Had we known," said a Council spokesman, "We would never have crowned her floral Queen." "I don't know what all the fuss is about," said Sharon, a former convent girl, whose hobbies include water ski-ing and carpentry. "I am proud of my body and what I do with it in my spare time is none of the Council's business".' She'd never get planning permission for that.

Both stare at the photograph for several seconds, their eyes glazing with obvious relish.

FLETCHER
Yes . . . yes . . . got every right to be proud of a body like that. Oh yes. Ravishing little thing, isn't she? Mischievous little mouth. Look at that mouth. Full of mischief. I bet that's been up to some mischief. Yes . . . what was I saying?

LENNIE

You were saying the less you think about women the better.

FLETCHER

Oh yes, yes, carnal thoughts, yes, fatal.

LENNIE

She reminds me of Denise a bit.

FLETCHER

Which bit?

LENNIE

No – Denise. My fiancée.

FLETCHER

Oh yes, the lovely Denise, yes right.

LENNIE

Not that they're similar in appearance, but they're both . . . physical. Know what I mean?

FLETCHER

You're not telling me your Denise is a star of the silver screen, are you? Albeit a grubby one in a backroom.

LENNIE

Oh no, nothing like that.

FLETCHER

Not a model, then?

LENNIE

Oh no, though I once took some provocative Polaroids of her when we were caravanning in the Gower Peninsula. I don't mean mucky, like. But she was sort of expressing herself . . . Posing, like.

He gives his impression of Denise posing provocatively on the Gower Peninsula. Fletcher looks disapproving.

FLETCHER

Come on, son! Leave it off! What will the neighbours think?

He is aware of the spyhole in the cell door.

LENNIE

Oh sorry, Fletch.

FLETCHER

Ain't thinking of me, son. They know which side my bread's buttered . . . It's you. Harm can come to a growing lad. You're the one could drive the fairies round here into a frenzy.

LENNIE

But I'm engaged to Denise.

FLETCHER

Means naff all to them, my son. They're all engaged to each other. Denise is a thing of your past. A letter in your top pocket. A photograph under your pillow. A warm tingle in your loins.

LENNIE

In me what?

FLETCHER

Your loins.

LENNIE

What are loins?

FLETCHER

(*Exasperatedly*) Loins is . . . look, when you think of her, when you thinks of Denise in the still of the night, think of the times you once had, don't you ever get a warm tingle?

LENNIE

Oh – yes.

FLETCHER

Well, where you gets it, that's your loins.

There is a pause.

LENNIE

I thought they were my –

He lies down on the bottom bunk.

FLETCHER

Well there's lots of words for them.

LENNIE

She is a very physical girl, Denise. She was a Beauty Queen. Finalist at the Office Machinery Exhibition. Miss Duplicating, she was. And her picture was in the paper and she became a pin-up of two thousand sailors in an aircraft carrier in Gibraltar. They wrote to her and said she was the girl they'd most like to ink their rolls.

FLETCHER

That must have made you very proud, Lennie, knowing that your fiancée was the sexual fantasy of an entire aircraft carrier.

LENNIE

Oh, I didn't know her then. That was before she moved to Smethwick, before that never-to-be-forgotten day when I met her at a supermarket in the Bull Ring – oh that's in Birmingham. She was stamping 'Special Offer' on giant-sized jars of pickled onions. I came round the corner from condiments and sauces and my wire trolley went

over her foot. It was a magic moment. We both knew. I said to her straight off 'Will you meet me outside?' I said. And she said, 'All right.'

FLETCHER

God preserve us, Godber. Romance.

He gets down from his bunk.

LENNIE

How d'you mean? I told you it was beautiful.

FLETCHER

I know, son, I know. But all I'm saying is if you had your time again, you might pick a more romantic setting to meet the love of your life. 'She was stamping "Special Offer" on giant-sized pickled onions,' I mean bloody hell, it's not Romeo and Juliet, is it.

He sits down. There is a pause.

LENNIE

Was your courtship any more romantic?

FLETCHER

Well no . . . in truth it wasn't really. I'm a city boy like you. And it was after the war. I had a bit more space than you, but that was mostly bomb sites. There was the pictures – the Muswell Hill Odeon. Or the back seat of a car – if I could open one. But somehow we had more chance to improvise. Today these great cold hostile concrete blocks. No hiding place. Can't make love in a launderette.

There is a pause.

LENNIE

We did.

FLETCHER

What? Oh . . .

LENNIE

It was very quiet at the time.

FLETCHER

That's a relief to us all.

LENNIE

We had three bagfuls to do . . . and it was bitter out.

FLETCHER

Hardly entitles you, I'd have thought. However I don't know Birmingham. Now, my eldest, Ingrid –

LENNIE

Ingrid?

FLETCHER

Yes, my old lady called her that after Ingrid Bergman what was a famous film star who was sweeping the country at the time, but I don't suppose you remember her, *For Whom the Bell Tolls, Casablanca, Spellbound*.

LENNIE

Oh I think I've seen that on the telly. Is that the one about the scientists in the secret laboratory in Arizona and this man drinks this substance by mistake and turns into a werewolf and carries off the mad doctor's niece and does things to her in the catacombs?

FLETCHER

No.

LENNIE

Oh.

FLETCHER

No, that weren't one of Ingrid's. No,

I can say without fear of contradiction that Ingrid was never in no catacomb with no werewolf. My daughter Ingrid might have been, but certainly not the lovely Miss Bergman.

He rises and crosses to stick up the photograph.

LENNIE

What were you going to say about your daughter Ingrid?

FLETCHER

(*Sitting down*) What? Was I? Oh yes, my point was that my eldest, was – this is between ourselves, Godber – she was conceived in Highgate Cemetery. You see we weren't married at the time. Of course we got married when we realised young Ingrid was on the way. But at the time we wasn't. And we needed somewhere to consummate the passion we felt for each other.

LENNIE

But a cemetery!

FLETCHER

Oh yes, but a very famous and historic cemetery.

LENNIE

Still seems a bit indecent to me.

FLETCHER

(*Indignantly*) No more indecent than doing it in your local launderette three bags full. Anyhow it wasn't premeditated 'cos we'd gone there to see Karl Marx's tomb. I was politically minded at the time, and very randy. Mind you, my political career never got beyond painting slogans on viaduct walls.

LENNIE

I've done that. Last thing I painted was Lennie Godber loves Denise Shorter on a warehouse wall.

FLETCHER

Denise Shorter?

LENNIE

My fiancée?

FLETCHER

Oh that Denise Shorter.

He gets up and gets a chair.

LENNIE

(*Hanging up photo*) I wrote to her in association hour. Helped to pass the time. I didn't have a class, you see.

FLETCHER

What class are you on?

LENNIE

Shoe repairing.

FLETCHER

Oh that's useful, yes. Very elevating, yes. You're not in the shoe repairing class are you? . . . Load of cobblers that.

LENNIE

Just helps kill the time. Anything to take me mind off the monotony of this place.

FLETCHER

Listen, this ain't so bad, this nick. Compared to Leicester, Parkhurst, high security places like that. Got closed circuit cameras there. Can't even go to the lavatory without it being on television.

Not that that would worry an exhibitionist like yourself, of course. Someone who makes love in launderettes.

The lights go out.

LENNIE

Oh, I ain't got me things off yet.

FLETCHER

Move over, will you, son?

He moves, then gives a yell of pain.

FLETCHER

Owww!

LENNIE

What's the matter?

FLETCHER

Something stuck in me foot.

LENNIE

That must be me darning needle.

FLETCHER

Well, what's it doing there?

LENNIE

I was darning your sock.

FLETCHER

Well, do it in the morning.

Lennie, trying to help, inadvertently steps on Fletcher's foot.

FLETCHER

Now you're standing on me other foot.

LENNIE

Oh, I'm sorry.

He moves.

FLETCHER

You've just injured both my feet, Godber.

LENNIE

I didn't mean –

FLETCHER

Just go to bed, son.

LENNIE

I'm not undressed yet.

FLETCHER

Just go to bed till I get into bed, then you can get out again.

Lennie complies. Fletcher climbs up on to the top bunk, muttering as he does.

FLETCHER

Not enough room to share . . . no privacy . . . bet he snores . . . he certainly rabbits.

LENNIE

D'you want a liquorice all-sort?

FLETCHER

No, I don't want a . . . liquorice all-sort.

There is a pause.

FLETCHER

How d'you get liquorice all-sorts?

LENNIE

(*Taking his shoes off*) I swopped them for a pound of marge I whipped from the kitchen.

FLETCHER

Learning, aren't you?

LENNIE

(*Taking his trousers off*) Little victories, you told me that.

FLETCHER

Shall we get some kip?

Lennie has been undressing and now gets into the lower bunk. There is a long pause.

LENNIE

Fletcher . . .

FLETCHER

(*Wearily*) Wha-at?

LENNIE

D'you know what I've found useful since I've been inside?

FLETCHER

What have you found useful, Godber?

LENNIE

I've started to do something which I haven't done since I was a kiddy.

Fletcher wonders whatever is coming next.

LENNIE

I find it helps. D'you know what I do?

FLETCHER

I shudder to think, son.

There is a pause.

LENNIE

I pray.

FLETCHER

Pray?

LENNIE

Yes, I've started saying me prayers.

FLETCHER

God preserve us.

LENNIE

That's what I keep asking him. So if you don't mind –

FLETCHER

If you must.

Lennie closes his eyes and starts praying.

LENNIE

Dear God, thank you for getting me through another day. Thank you for the letter from Denise and the liquorice all-sorts. Please look after Denise in your infinite wisdom. And the same applies to me Mum, Dad – wherever he is – and me Aunty Vi and Uncle Donald, Uncle Les and Aunty Con, me Aunty Rita in Newport Pagnall, and Cousin Rita in Walsall. And Cissie, and Stu, and Vic, and all the lads in the darts team at the Bell and Dragon.

He pauses.

LENNIE

And Norma and her husband who emigrated to Melbourne.

FLETCHER

Is this a prayer? Or a dedication on the Jimmy Young show?

There is a slight pause. We think Lennie has shut up but we are wrong.

LENNIE

And please God, look after Fletcher and forgive him for being such a bad-tempered, evil-minded, cantankerous old git.

Fletcher's face reflects his indignation.

3. PRISON

It is night. In the prison there is almost complete silence, save for a lone prison officer making his rounds on the landing and a few assorted snores.

4. CELL

Night time. A match flares as Fletcher lights up a smoke. Lennie speaks from below.

LENNIE

You awake, Fletch?

FLETCHER

No.

LENNIE

Oh.

There is a pause.

FLETCHER

Why?

LENNIE

Nor me neither.

FLETCHER

Your God in his infinite wisdom isn't giving you a peaceful night then.

LENNIE

Wasn't one of the things I asked for.

FLETCHER

That's true. He won't be getting much kip either, the list you gave him.

LENNIE

Don't be irreverent.

FLETCHER

You've changed your spots, ain't you? Day we come in, when we went through reception you didn't even know if you was C of E, Pressed Beef or a flaming Buddhist.

LENNIE

Don't think it matters much. I just believe in God – doesn't matter which lot you support. I admit my belief's only been revived since I come in here. 'Cos I prayed when I was a kid, like. When I was up in Juvenile Court and when Villa looked like doing well in the Cup. But I became disillusioned with religion. I got probation and Villa got knocked out by Rotherham one-nothing.

FLETCHER

That's typical, in' it? Most people never give a second thought, do they? When things are going well, ticking along with scant regard for the ten commandments. Stealing, committing adultery, coveting each other's oxes. Then, wallop. In the face of adversity – (*In a cringing falsetto*) 'Please God, please help your loyal and trusted servant.' Huh!

LENNIE

You're right. But I am in the face of adversity. I hate prison, Fletch. It makes me depressed and it makes me afraid. I hate the air of defeat and the smell of disinfectant. I hate the shouting and the keys. And I hate not having a handle on the inside of that door. *He nods towards the cell door. Fletcher is not unsympathetic.*

FLETCHER

(*Getting down from his bunk*) Kids like you shouldn't be in prison, son. It's the system, see. You ain't here to be reformed or rehabilitated. You're here because of public revenge. Now it's different for me. Occupational hazard being as my occupation's breaking the law. But my family ain't gone short, most years. Three kids and my old lady. Show you their picture when it's light. Now my youngest, he just got into Grammar School.

LENNIE

Has he?

FLETCHER

Yes, lovely school. Costs a bit, you know. Books, equipment. But when my son showed up first day he was short of nothing. Rugby boots, blazer, scarf, the lot. Now he wouldn't have had all that if his dad had been a struggling clerk or a – or a shoe repairer. No. The reason he had all that was that his dad robbed a school outfitters.

LENNIE

What would your son think if he knew the truth?

FLETCHER

He'd think 'Oh so that's why the blazer's a bit big.' But he'll grow into it.

LENNIE

So you only do it for your family then?

FLETCHER

And my old lady, yes. *He gets up and goes across for some water.*

FLETCHER

Twenty-four years we been together.
Married at nineteen see – too young,
'course it is, but that's Highgate
Cemetery for you.

LENNIE

You must love her very much.

FLETCHER

Yeah, well . . .

LENNIE

'Cos when you were asleep like, you
wore saying things.

FLETCHER

Who me – what? Saying what?

LENNIE

Just saying her name over and over
again. 'Gloria, my love – oh Glor, Glor,
my love.'

FLETCHER

Was I?

LENNIE

Yes. I found that very moving – even
though it woke me up.

There is a long pause.

FLETCHER

Thing is . . . my old lady's called
Isobel.

LENNIE

Then who's Gloria?

FLETCHER

(*Puzzled*) You may well ask. You sure it
was Gloria?

LENNIE

Positive.

FLETCHER

Gloria. Gloria? . . . (*Remembering*) Yes,
there was a Gloria once – well, more
than once in fact – many, many times.

LENNIE

Was that before you met your Isobel?

FLETCHER

(*Confidentially*) In truth er – it wasn't,
Lennie. This was a little indiscretion
round about 1955. I remember that
'cos at the time I was King of the Teds
in Muswell Hill. And Gloria she was a
machinist – clothing factory. So I used
to go round to her place, get me evil
way and get me trousers narrowed at
the same time.

LENNIE

I could never be unfaithful to Denise.

FLETCHER

Ah now, listen, listen. Don't get no
wrong impression. This was an
indiscretion. You must imagine my
position. You can't be King of the
Teds and say at ten o'clock I've got
to go home to the wife. Not after
you've just smashed up an
Amusement Arcade.

LENNIE

So you don't make a habit of
indiscretions?

FLETCHER

'Course not. Look, Isobel's my old
lady and she knows it.

There is a pause.

LENNIE

Then who's Sharon?

FLETCHER

Sharon!!

LENNIE
After Gloria you was moaning about
a Sharon.

FLETCHER
I couldn't have been, I don't know no
Sharons – here hang about! She was
the girl in the *Sun*, weren't she?
Beauty Queen shocks Council. Yes,
yes, I was having this dream and she
was in it, comes back to me now . . .

LENNIE
(*In censure*) Carnal thoughts.

FLETCHER
Listen, Godber. No one asked you to
eavesdrop on my dreams. It's about
the only place you have any privacy
inside – your head. You want to
remember that, son. Dreams is your
escape. No locked doors in dreams.
No boundaries, no frontiers. Dreams
is freedom.

This impresses Lennie.

LENNIE
Freedom.

FLETCHER
No locked doors.

LENNIE
That's true, Fletch, that's really true.

FLETCHER
Well, I'm getting back to mine and I
suggest you do the same.

LENNIE
I will do, I will. And thank you, Fletch.

FLETCHER
(*Quite grumpily*) All right. Goodnight.
He turns over.

FLETCHER
Now, where was I . . .

LENNIE
Beauty Queen shocks Council.

FLETCHER
Oh yes . . . the way she was
performing in my dream, I can see why.

5. PRISON
*The prison is bathed in the light
of dawn. Early morning sounds can
be heard. On the prison landing
officers walking along the building,
banging their keys against
the doors and shouting their
wake-up calls.*

6. CELL
Fletcher is waking up.

FLETCHER
There's my alarm call.

*He swings himself into a
sitting position and his feet hit
Lennie's head.*

FLETCHER
Oops. Sorry, son.

LENNIE
No, no, Fletch. It's your cell. Sorry if
my head hit your foot.

He gets up.

FLETCHER
How d'you sleep then?

LENNIE
Very well since our midnight chat.

FLETCHER
Did you dream? Did you find that

freedom I promised you, that land of exotic fantasy?

LENNIE

Oh yes. It was Denise and I. We were in the launderette and we got through five bagfuls without stopping. Trouble is this bloke came in and spoilt it.

FLETCHER

Oh what a pity.

LENNIE

It was you.

FLETCHER

Couldn't have been. I was with Sharon Spencer all night up at the Hylton.

LENNIE

Fletch . . .

FLETCHER

What?

LENNIE

In the rush, moving here I well, er – I like, mislaid something.

FLETCHER

What?

LENNIE

My toothpaste.

FLETCHER

Oh yes.

LENNIE

Well, er – could I possibly have a loan of yours?

FLETCHER

Have a loan of my toothpaste?

LENNIE

Just a squeeze, like.

FLETCHER

Have a loan of my toothpaste?

LENNIE

I'll give you a liquorice all-sort.

FLETCHER

Oh!

LENNIE

(*Getting them from under his pillow*) I've got some left.

FLETCHER

Got the round one with the pink coconut? There's only one, you know.

LENNIE

Yes.

FLETCHER

All right then.

There's a slight pause.

LENNIE

Fletch.

FLETCHER

Now what? Suppose you ain't got no shaving cream.

LENNIE

No. I just wanted to thank you.

FLETCHER

Oh?

LENNIE

For helping me out. With advice, like. You know, it's like that song – 'Help me make it through the night.'

FLETCHER

What song's that?

LENNIE

Don't suppose you'd know it. More contemporary than your era. Suppose as King of the Teds your tastes were more Eddie Cochran and Conway Twitty.

FLETCHER

No. No my tastes were a bit more mellow. What was it I used to like? Kay Starr. Rosemary Clooney. And what was that song . . . (*Sings*) 'See the Pyramids along the Nile' . . . Jo Stafford.

LENNIE

Don't know him.

FLETCHER

He was a girl you nurk. Jo's a girl's name. They don't write songs like that now. Had a bit of melody in them days.

LENNIE

You're a sentimentalist at heart.

FLETCHER

(*Suspiciously*) What?

LENNIE

I know that under that gruff unpleasant exterior there's a kind man with feelings.

FLETCHER

(*Gruffly*) Yes, well –

He sits down to put his shoes on, then leaps up in pain, hitting his head on the top bunk.

FLETCHER

Bloody hell, bloody hell.

LENNIE

Oh, was it the darning needle again?

There is the sound of a door being unlocked.

FLETCHER

I'll swing for you, Godber, I swear it.

The cell door is opened by a dour Prison Officer.

PRISON OFFICER

What's going on here then? Did you assault this man, Godber?

LENNIE

He sat on my darning needle.

PRISON OFFICER

Is that true, Fletcher?

FLETCHER

Oh naff off. Can't you see I'm in agony?

PRISON OFFICER

Why don't you get a move on?

FLETCHER

Why don't you go home and find out who's been sleeping with your old lady while you've been on night duty?

PRISON OFFICER

(*Re-entering*) Oh that's original, Fletcher. I've been having that for the last seven years.

He leaves. Lennie and Fletcher sit down.

FLETCHER

Yeah, and so has she.

A Prison Officer can be heard unlocking another door.

PRISON OFFICER (VOICEOVER)

(*Offscreen*) Come on, move it.

VOICE (VOICEOVER)

(*Offscreen*) Who's been sleeping with your old lady then?

Fletcher gets his boots and sits down to put them on.

LENNIE

Here you are, you can have these.

FLETCHER

What?

LENNIE

Go on – all of them. Present like.

FLETCHER

Oh, all right then. Not say no, son.

LENNIE

It's meant as a thank you. 'Cos when that door's locked I am depressed and I am afraid, and you – you know – just make it a bit more tolerable.

FLETCHER

You'll get used to it, Len. And the night's not so long, is it? It's your human spirit, see. They can't break that, those nurks. We'll be all right, you and me, son. Here, we'll go out tonight if you like.

LENNIE

With those dancers?

FLETCHER

If you like. Or I could ring Miss Sharon Spencer, eh? She'll have a big friend. Bound to. Soft lights, music, night club . . .

LENNIE

It's discos now.

He stands up.

FLETCHER

What? Oh well – as you say. Anyhow, think about it.

LENNIE

I will, I will. See how I feel. On the other hand, Fletch –

FLETCHER

Yeah.

LENNIE

If we don't feel like it, we might just have a quiet night in.

FLETCHER

Right. Right.

Fletcher picks up the pot. Lennie picks up the bucket and they move to the cell door.

Prisoners are walking along the landing with buckets etc. for slop-up. Fletcher comes out of his cell, followed by Lennie and they join the line.

SERIES ONE

EPISODE FOUR: A DAY OUT

1. PRISON

Prison Officers are seen knocking up prisoners.

2. FLETCHER'S CELL

Fletcher wakes up and sees that Lennie has almost finished dressing.

FLETCHER

Oh yes, what's your rush? Getting released, are you?

LENNIE

Been looking forward to today.

FLETCHER

What's so special about today? Only one good thing about a new day in here, it replaces the old one. Crossed one off, haven't we?

LENNIE

But we're going out today. Aren't we? Breath of fresh air. Trees. Walking on grass. The sounds of birds in the branches.

FLETCHER

Don't get so flaming lyrical,

Wordsworth. All we're going to do is dig drains for the council. Stooped six hours over a shovel. Doing a job they'd only give to prisoners, seeing as any civilised geezer would tell 'em to stuff it.

LENNIE

I don't care what they make us do. We're going outside that's all I care. A whole day out of here.

FLETCHER

You're like a kid on a school trip, aren't you?

LENNIE

You don't fool me, Fletch. You just mask your enthusiasm, you do. But if you were that indifferent, why would you have gone to the trouble of bribing yourself on to the party?

FLETCHER

Yuh, well . . .

LENNIE

Yeah, well.

FLETCHER

Well I can't deny the thought of fresh air appeals. Get the smell of disinfectant out me nostrils. Not to mention your festering feet.

LENNIE

I change my socks every day.

FLETCHER

Pity you can't change your feet.

LENNIE

If it ain't one thing it's another . . .
I don't complain about your
personal habits.

FLETCHER

What personal habits? I don't have
any personal habits.

LENNIE

Yes, you do.

FLETCHER

I do not!

LENNIE

You do.

FLETCHER

Like what?

LENNIE

You talk with your mouth full,
you whistle out of tune, you snore,
you spit . . .

FLETCHER

How dare you? I do not whistle out of
tune. You've got a cheek you have,
you've got a flaming nerve. This is
supposed to be a single cell, this is –
by rights, mine. You've got a nerve
talking about my personal habits.
You was dragged up in some
Birmingham backstreet.

LENNIE

I had a good upbringing, I did. We
may not have had much money but
my mother kept us spotless.

FLETCHER

Well you ain't spotless now, are you?
Your clothes are covered in gravy
stains. So don't give me no stick
about personal table manners.

LENNIE

Look, everybody at our table is
covered in gravy stains – it's your
gravy! I told you, you talk with your
mouth full.

Fletcher starts cleaning his teeth.

FLETCHER

You'd better watch it, Godber. I'm
warning you. I do not talk with my
mouth full.

LENNIE

Look, you're doing it now, I'm covered
in toothpaste.

FLETCHER

Cheeky young nurk.

LENNIE

Don't let's fall out, Fletch. We don't
want to spoil things this early. Today's
the big day.

FLETCHER

It ain't that big a day, son. Ain't a
coach trip to Southend. Not a day at
the seaside, with a trip up the pier and
a big nosh up and reduced rates at
the local knocking shop. We're only
going across a remote Cumberland
moor, to a remote Cumberland village
to dig drains. Sustained by the remote
possibility that the district nurse might
pass by on her bicycle and give us all
an exciting glimpse of stocking top.

LENNIE

A woman . . . a woman on her bicycle.

FLETCHER

Maybe, maybe.

LENNIE

No, Fletch, I can see her. Clear as day.
In her uniform, on her bicycle.

FLETCHER

District nurse, huh. Some old spinster
with brogues and bike rider's buttocks.

LENNIE

No, she's young, Fletch, honest,
young and nice looking. Well, more
than that, beautiful really. And the prim
uniform which she so proudly wears
can barely conceal the voluptuous
figure within.

FLETCHER

Oh. Voluptuous figure within, is it?

LENNIE

Yeah. Which her prim uniform
cannot conceal.

FLETCHER

Barely.

LENNIE

Her face is at once innocent
and knowing.

FLETCHER

I know them innocent faces.

LENNIE

Obviously primitive passions are
stirring deep within her breast.

FLETCHER

Oh deep one, is it?

LENNIE

Oh definitely.

FLETCHER

Here hang on, what's this gorgeous
deep-chested thigh-flashing bit
of nooky doing up this neck of
the woods?

LENNIE

(*Hesitates for only a second*) Well, you
see, she comes home to nurse her
dad what's been sick with a fatal,
tropical disease.

FLETCHER

Fatal is it, that could kill you.

LENNIE

She turned her back on the bright
lights like out of duty.

FLETCHER

Of course she did, didn't she? Could've
been a model, girl like that, cover girl,
chased by playboys and Arab princes.

LENNIE

Instead of which –

FLETCHER

Instead of which she returns to nurse
her ailing dad, trying hard to subdue
her primitive stirrings, until the day
when fate decrees she has a puncture
right next to the drain I'm digging.

LENNIE

Here, hang on, I saw her first.

FLETCHER

Naff off, Godber, age before beauty.
I'm at her side, picking her up, dusting
her down, and not failing to notice as I
do her proud, firm body. She's
sprained her perfectly formed ankle,
and I carries her over several miles of

ploughed sludge, staggering at last, exhausted, into her lonely cottage miles from anywhere, leaving the two of us thrown together as night falls.

LENNIE

What about Dad, then?

FLETCHER

Oh he's dead. There's just us. Me and her. Together. Alone. And she pours me a drink, after slipping out of her wet uniform. Slip, slip. Then she gets me some grub. And I eat, and we talk.

LENNIE

There you go again, Fletch.

FLETCHER

What?

LENNIE

Talking with your mouth full.

Fletcher throws a shoe at Lennie.

3. ASSEMBLY ROOM

Navyrum, Ives and Scrounger are waiting.

NAVYRUM

Hey Ives, how did you work your way on this doddle? Bribed a lot of people in high places.

IVES

'Ere listen –

NAVYRUM

You're not a working man. Not a bird bones skiving little git like you.

IVES

'Ere listen –

NAVYRUM

I'm a working man. Always have been.

Stoker. Paid my dues. Tankers. Persian Gulf. Big sweat I'll tell ye.

IVES

'Ere listen, Navyrum, I'll do my share, don't you worry.

SCROUNGER

I had a job once, worked on a road gang. Motorway. Naffing job that was. Had to live on a caravan site with the old woman and two nippers. Always mud. Work in mud, come home to mud.

IVES

Should feel at home today then.

The door is unlocked and Barrowclough brings Fletcher and Lennie in then locks the door again.

OTHERS

Hello, Fletch, Lennie.

LENNIE

Hello lads.

FLETCHER

Gentlemen . . . all right, Scrounger. Here, how did this little runt fiddle his way on this?

IVES

'Ere listen –

FLETCHER

Can't even shovel his peas he can't without getting tennis elbow.

IVES

Don't you worry, I'll do my share.

NAVYRUM

'E's a skivin' git.

FLETCHER

That's exactly what he is Navyrum,

you're not wrong there. And how are
you? D'you know young Lennie
Godber, my temporary cell mate?

LENNIE

(*Nods*) Hello.

NAVYRUM

Hello, son.

Fletcher and Lennie sit down.

FLETCHER

Me and Navyrum were in Maidstone
together. When he gets to know you a
bit better he might let you come round
one night and read his tattoos.

SCROUNGER

Who are we waiting for?

NAVYRUM

Dylan.

FLETCHER

Dylan! That long-haired anarchist nurk.
We've got a right lot here, ain't we, for
a hard day's work. A twelve-stone
weakling and the King of the
Huddersfield Hippies.

*The door is unlocked and
Barrowclough comes in with Dylan.
Dylan acknowledges the others with
a nod.*

FLETCHER

Well now, Dylan, speak of the devil.

DYLAN

Listen man, my name's Melvyn, what's
all this Dylan scene?

FLETCHER

Not out of malice, son, we calls you
that out of affection. We calls you that
'cos you reminds us of Dylan.

DYLAN

Bob Dylan?

FLETCHER

No, that hippy rabbit on *The
Magic Roundabout*.

DYLAN

I'm not a hippy.

FLETCHER

You're the nearest thing we've got to
one. You wear an earring and you got
chucked out of art school for writing
on the walls, and you're the only one
here what's tidied their prison uniform.

DYLAN

Oh man . . .

BARROWCLOUGH

I didn't know you watched *The Magic
Roundabout*, Fletcher.

FLETCHER

Yes, good ain't it?

DYLAN

Magic Roundabout.

FLETCHER

All right, all right. Gives a lot of
innocent people a lot of pleasure. Even
gives us guilty people a lot of pleasure.
Simple pleasures are very precious to
us, ain't they, Scrounger?

SCROUNGER

Like this day out.

LENNIE

Oh yeah, be great to see a bit of
grass, smell the flowers.

BARROWCLOUGH

Oh you'll have to join our Botany
Club, you'll enjoy that. I run it in the

summer. We get out on the fells exploring the natural phenomena of our countryside.

FLETCHER

Oh do you? All young Lennie and I want to explore is that young nurse, eh, son?

NAVYRUM

Nurse? What's this then? Which nurse?

LENNIE

She's mine. He commandeered my fantasy.

NAVYRUM

What we waiting for then?

BARROWCLOUGH

We're waiting for Mr Mackay.

FLETCHER

Oh dear, Scotland the brave – is he coming?

BARROWCLOUGH

Mr Mackay's in charge, yes.

NAVYRUM

Git.

DYLAN

Pig.

FLETCHER

Charmless nurk.

The door has been unlocked and Mackay enters.

MACKAY

What's going on then?

FLETCHER

Oh morning, Mr Mackay. Just voted you man of the year.

MACKAY

On your feet all of you.

They all stand.

MACKAY

None of your facetious lip, Fletcher.

FLETCHER

You'll get none of it today, Mr Mackay.

MACKAY

Now as this work party is composed of such a spineless, delinquent obstreperous rabble, let's make a few things crystal clear. There will be no skiving, no fraternising with members of the public, no kipping in the long grass, and another thing there will not be is visits to the nearest pub masquerading as Irish labourers working on a mythical motorway extension. Any questions?

FLETCHER

Yeah, I've got a question.

MACKAY

What?

FLETCHER

Is the ball and chain worn outside the wellington boot or inside?

4. PRISON

A bus approaches the prison gates. The warder opens the gate and the bus drives through and away.

5. ROAD AND DITCH

Camera shows a churchyard. Not far away a nurse is cycling up a hill. The prisoners' work party are at the roadside.

The nurse cycles past them. They come out of the ditch and react to her. She wobbles on her bicycle.

MACKAY
Quiet the lot of you.

He crosses to the ditch.

MACKAY
Just get on with it. Ives, put some effort into it.

IVES
'Ere listen, everyone picks on me. I do my share.

FLETCHER
I think you'd have us in chains, wouldn't you, Mr Mackay – if you had your way.

MACKAY
With the greatest of pleasure.

He turns to leave.

DYLAN
Pig.

Mackay turns back.

MACKAY
Did you speak, Bottomley?

DYLAN
Dig. I was just telling Fletcher to dig.

FLETCHER
Who're you calling a pig?

LENNIE
Can we sing?

MACKAY
Sing?

FLETCHER
What we got to sing about?

LENNIE
No, but it would help like. Keep our spirits up. Like the Negro slaves on

the plantations in the deep South. Work songs, things like that, kept their spirits up, didn't it? We're working in a gang, just like them.

FLETCHER
If you chuck much more mud about we'll all look like 'em an' all.

NAVYRUM
Used to sing in the Gulf. Stoking. Sing opera.

He starts singing. The others join in.

FLETCHER
Oh dear.

MACKAY
Thank God for that.

FLETCHER
Thank gawd for that.

MACKAY
I'm just popping down to the village to er . . . get some part for my lawnmower.

He moves to the door of the van and addresses Barrowclough.

MACKAY
So er . . . you take charge, all right?

BARROWCLOUGH
You'll not be long, will you?

MACKAY
(*Getting into van*) You're perfectly capable, man.

BARROWCLOUGH
Ah, but you see there's a lot of them and only one of me.

MACKAY
Pull yourself together, Mr Barrowclough.

The van starts up.
In the ditch Fletcher notices the
van's departure. The group cheers.
SCROUNGER
Where's he going then?
FLETCHER
He's going after that district nurse, he
ain't so fussy as us, is he?
BARROWCLOUGH
(*Moving to the ditch*) Now listen, you
men. Let's knuckle down. My
approach may not be as rigid as Mr
Mackay's but there's work to be done
and I'm here to see it gets done, so
there'll be no shirking, no slacking and
no taking advantage of my good
nature. Right.
ALL
Right, Mr Barrowclough.
They start chatting.

6. CHURCH
Inside the church the work party
are having a smoke and taking
it easy.
LENNIE
Nice this, isn't it Fletch? Being out
I mean.
FLETCHER
Oh yes, well, makes a change. Get a
bit more exercise. Mind you I'd like
today to be a bit more to write home
about. Pub just down the road.
Wouldn't half like to be in it. Pop in the
village shop. Get some sweets, and
a *Reveille*.

LENNIE
Ain't possible, is it?
FLETCHER
It's been done.
Barrowclough comes in.
BARROWCLOUGH
Oh no – now come along men,
you've had a good long smoke
break, it's high time we got back
to it. We shouldn't be smoking in
here at all.
FLETCHER
We had to have somewhere to sit,
couldn't sit on the damp grass, could
we? 'Cos it's bad for you, very bad
for you.
BARROWCLOUGH
It's usual to sit on the earth you dig
out – form little piles.
FLETCHER
Exactly, that's what I'm worried about,
forming little piles.
BARROWCLOUGH
That's enough, Fletcher. Now we really
must knuckle down. (*Counting*) One,
two, three . . . Now, where's Ives?
FLETCHER
He's outside desecrating holy ground,
isn't he?
BARROWCLOUGH
How do you mean?
FLETCHER
Gone for a slash in the churchyard.
At that moment there is a terrible
scream and Ives comes in clutching
his trousers.

IVES

'Ere listen, help, I've been stung.

FLETCHER

Obviously the Lord's retribution, you vulgar nurk. Bee, was it?

IVES

I don't know what it was, I ain't a flaming zoologist.

LENNIE

Maybe it was a wasp. Or a hornet.

IVES

What difference does it make?

FLETCHER

Makes a lot of difference. Different degree of pain and poison.

IVES

It was a great big thing.

FLETCHER

Oh hornet, fatal.

IVES

What you mean, fatal?

FLETCHER

Listen lads, if one of us don't suck the poison out of Ives's system he's going to die.

There is a silence.

FLETCHER

You're going to die, old son.

IVES

'Ere, listen, that's not funny.

BARROWCLOUGH

Don't joke, Fletcher, the man is in some distress – it's all right, Ives, it's almost certainly just a wasp sting.

IVES

I'm dying.

FLETCHER

(*Knocks Ives*) Yes, come on again.

(*Moving to Barrowclough*)

Permission to make a suggestion, Mr Barrowclough.

BARROWCLOUGH

What?

FLETCHER

Why don't someone go down the village get some ointment or TCP. Then the only problem's getting a volunteer to rub it on. I'd be willing to go and get some.

The others cough.

BARROWCLOUGH

Go to the village?

FLETCHER

I'd be willing to take that long walk on this mission of mercy.

BARROWCLOUGH

Well, I suppose . . . if you went straight there and back.

FLETCHER

What else, Mr Barrowclough? Man's life at stake. Need money, of course. Expensive those antibiotics.

BARROWCLOUGH

All right, well here, I've only got a pound.

FLETCHER

That should cover it.

BARROWCLOUGH

Now look, Fletcher –

FLETCHER

Mr Barrowclough please, every second counts.

He goes.

7. PUB

In the pub Fletcher hands over a pound note to the landlord and takes a pint of beer.

LANDLORD

Thank you, sir. You look as if you need that one.

FLETCHER

Thanks. I do, don't I? First one I've had for ages. Well, I'm not allowed, am I? Doctor says I'm not to drink – ulcer, you see. Can't take it any more. But just occasionally I have a little sip.

He sinks back the pint in about three seconds flat and bangs the glass on the counter.

FLETCHER

Fill it up, then.

The landlord takes the glass.

FLETCHER

Oh and six packets of crisps.

LANDLORD

With an ulcer?

FLETCHER

No – cheese and onion. Not for me, for the lads.

LANDLORD

Lads?

FLETCHER

What lads? Oh yes, what lads – oh well, we're working on the motorway, aren't we?

LANDLORD

What motorway?

FLETCHER

The . . . the *new* by-pass.

LANDLORD

But we've never heard of the new by-pass.

FLETCHER

No, it's that new, that's why you ain't heard of it. I've only just heard of it myself.

LANDLORD

But this is outrageous. This whole area's National Trust. What's the use in having a by-pass through here?

FLETCHER

Now look, mate, it's none of my doing, is it? I see your point of view, despoiling England's green and pleasant land, it worried me – that's how I got the ulcer, isn't it?

The vicar and his verger walk into the pub.

VICAR

Good morning all.

VERGER

Did you hear the thunder? It's going to p-pelt down in a minute.

LANDLORD

Vicar, have you heard?

VICAR

Heard what?

LANDLORD

They're building a new by-pass.

VICAR

Where?

FLETCHER

Where? Ah well. Over there, isn't it?

He points vaguely in the direction of the Gents.

VICAR

But what's the point of a by-pass? There's nothing to bypass, except for the prison, of course.

FLETCHER

What prison, eh?

LANDLORD

Six hundred bloody criminals on our doorstep.

VICAR

Now now, Frank, you mustn't pre-judge these men. They're serving their penance.

FLETCHER

Quite right, Rev. Public revenge, isn't it? Eye for an eye. Tooth for a nail.

VICAR

No, we must treat them with tolerance and compassion. I don't mean to sound pious but people must keep an open mind. My mind, like the doors of my church, is always open.

FLETCHER

Well spoken, Rev. Greater joy in heaven over a sinner what repenteth.

VICAR

Repenteth, yes indeed. I was wondering – would you like to –

FLETCHER

I would, yes. Pint, please.

VICAR

Oh fine, yes . . . would you do the honours Frank . . . in fact I was going to ask if you'd like to bring your chums over to evensong on Sunday.

FLETCHER

Oh? What? Well . . . much as we'd like to we may not be able to get out, er across. Tell you what, we'll come if we're free – all right? Cheers.

OTHERS

Cheers.

Mackay walks in.

VICAR

Ah here's a man with a different point of view. Morning, Mr Mackay.

MACKAY

Morning Padre, sir.

LANDLORD/VERGER

Morning, Mr Mackay.

MACKAY

Morning, gentlemen. Different point of view to what?

VICAR

To our friend here.

They turn to Fletcher but he has gone.

LANDLORD

Oh, where's he vanished to?

VICAR

Oh.

MACKAY

I'll have a whisky with a pint chaser.

LANDLORD

On duty?

MACKAY

I'm only half on duty. Got a works party down the road.

VICAR

Works party?

MACKAY

They're digging ditches down Felton Bank.

VICAR

Prisoners?

MACKAY

Oh yes.

VICAR

Verger, why don't you pop down to the church?

VERGER

But it's going to pour again any minute.

VICAR

You've got your bike, pop down and lock the church door.

VERGER

But why?

VICAR

You heard what he said – there's a bunch of criminals loose in the area.

8. PUB

Verger walks out of the pub. He puts on his bicycle clips, then turns to bike but there's an empty space where his bicycle should have been.

9. ROAD

Fletcher is cycling along the road. He puts his hand in his jacket and gets out a beer mug. He drinks from it, then chucks the mug over a fence. Sheep bleat in the background. Fletcher cycles on down the road.

10. CHURCH

Inside Navyrum is showing Lennie his tattoos. The other members of the work party and Barrowclough are also present.

NAVYRUM

This one was done in Valparaiso. That's in South America. Chile. Very Catholic country, Chile. Hence the religious overtones.

LENNIE

What's her name – Doris? Doesn't sound very Chilean.

NAVYRUM

No, she weren't. She were from Bootle. Stranded there with a juggling act. What with me being from the Pool that's how we got on so well, hence the affectionate overtones.

LENNIE

'I'll always . . .'

NAVYRUM

Don't read it out loud, son – not in here.

Fletcher walks in.

FLETCHER

What you all doing in here? You was just going out when I left.

BARROWCLOUGH

We heard the thunder and Navyrum assured me we were due for a heavy storm, him having been in the Navy he knows the signs. Well, have you got the ointment?

FLETCHER

Ointment?

IVES

I'm dying – 'ere listen.

FLETCHER

Oh, about the ointment, oh yes, thing is see the village shop it was closed, wasn't it? Closed for lunch hour.

BARROWCLOUGH

But it's only half-past eleven.

FLETCHER

Yeah well, it's not my fault, is it? They close for lunch earlier in the country, don't they, 'cos they get up earlier and they get hungry.

IVES

Oh come on, I'm in agony. I'm ablaze.

FLETCHER

Stick it in the font, then.

IVES

I might die.

FLETCHER

Anyone know the burial service?

NAVYRUM

I buried a bloke at sea once.

FLETCHER

Oh you're all right, Ives, then, there's a reservoir up the road.

BARROWCLOUGH

Oh dear, this day's turning into a disaster. Come on, there's not going to be any storm. It's passed over. We should be getting that ditch dug.

He goes to the door.

LENNIE

You crafty nurk, Fletch, you've been down the pub, ain't you?

SCROUNGER

You have, haven't you?

FLETCHER

Don't think I'd forget the lads, do you?

He hands out packets of crisps.

FLETCHER

Here you are, then. That'll put hair on your legs.

BARROWCLOUGH

Is all this out of my pound, Fletcher?

FLETCHER

It was, and me and the lads are more than grateful, aren't we?

LENNIE

Yes, Mr Barrowclough.

SCROUNGER

Thank you, Mr Barrowclough.

NAVYRUM

You're a toff, Mr Barrowclough.

FLETCHER

Eat up, lads. Now we've got all that protein inside us we can get on with the digging.

BARROWCLOUGH

Digging, yes, there's been precious little done so far. Come on, lads.

SCROUNGER

Come on, Ives, you're not dead yet.

LENNIE

That's funny, this door's stuck.

FLETCHER

Let's have a look. It's not stuck, it's locked.

11. ROAD AND DITCH

The verger is walking along the

*road. A van drives up to him and
stops. Mackay gets out.*

VERGER

Someone's stolen my bike, I bet it's
one of your lot.

MACKAY

Nonsense, my lot are hard at it. Without
my say-so they wouldn't dare move.

He moves to the ditch.

MACKAY

All right, you lot.

*He looks down and sees an empty
ditch.*

MACKAY

Oh my God, they've scarpered.

12. CHURCH

*The prisoners are locked in
the church. Barrowclough has
failed to find a way out and
joins the others.*

BARROWCLOUGH

The vestry's locked as well – there's no
other way out.

IVES

'Ere listen, we could break a window.

FLETCHER

That window's four hundred years old.
This is a church, you nurk. Have
you got no sense of reverence?
You're a Palestine, that's what you
are, a Palestine.

BARROWCLOUGH

Philistine, I think you mean.

FLETCHER

Yeah well, depends on your religion,
don't it?

DYLAN

Let's ring the bell, some cat might
hear that.

BARROWCLOUGH

They never use this bell. It's ancient,
you see, like the tower. Last time it was
heard in these parts was to warn the
villagers of marauding Scots.

FLETCHER

Marauding Scots, was it?

BARROWCLOUGH

In the sixteenth century, yes. They
came over the border, pillaging crops
and, well, ravishing the womenfolk and
all that.

FLETCHER

Oh well, that bell'll put the wind up a
few vests, won't it? Probably all flee
south with their possessions strapped
to the back of their Vauxhall Vivas.
Mind you, I reckon a few of the
womenfolk might stay. Eh? I mean, it's
been four hundred years since they
had a good ravishin'.

BARROWCLOUGH

Can't you do something? You've been
convicted for breaking and entering.

FLETCHER

Breaking and entering, yes. Entering, is
the operative word. I ain't never been
convicted for breaking out of nowhere.

LENNIE

Flippin' hell. We get one day out from nick and what happens. We get locked in.

13. FILM

Camera shows a telephone dial. A finger is dialling.

MACKAY

Chief Officer Barrett, Mackay here, sir . . . Mackay. Something has occurred, sir, to which I feel I ought to draw your attention.

Camera shows a van. Mackay and Barrett are inside it talking.

BARRETT

Just down this road, are they?

MACKAY

Not any more, sir. I still say you should put out a full scale alarm, Mr Barrett.

BARRETT

And I still say your judgement is impaired, Mr Mackay. And I am not making a fool out of Slade Prison or burdening the taxpayer with a full scale alert until I have personally verified the facts.

The van pulls up at the ditch and both men get out.

MACKAY

What did I tell you, there, what did I tell you?

The ditch is empty. The work party comes up and greets the officers.

BARROWCLOUGH

(*Standing up*) Afternoon, Mr Barrett,

sir. Mr Mackay. All present and correct, sir.

BARRETT

Pull yourself together, Mr Mackay. *Fletcher winks at Barrowclough who is looking at him.*

14. CELL

Fletcher, Lennie and Mackay are in Fletcher's cell.

MACKAY

I have been dropped in it, have I not, Fletcher? I have been put upon from a great height.

FLETCHER

Oh dear, Mr Mackay. I'm sorry to hear that, Mr Mackay. Anything we can do to alleviate it, as it were?

MACKAY

When I am in it, Fletcher, I absorb it with a stiff upper lip.

FLETCHER

No choice have you, if you're up to (*Gesturing*) here in it.

MACKAY

Stand still. I absorb it with cool Celtic calm, like a man. And then I relieve my frustrations by making sure that everyone down the line below me suffers.

FLETCHER

What?

MACKAY

Suffers.

LENNIE

Hey, that's not fair.

MACKAY

Fair?

LENNIE

Why take it out on us? Nobody's fault we got locked in the church.

FLETCHER

Yeah, we might still be there now if it hadn't been for that funeral.

MACKAY

Why were you in the church to begin with if you weren't skiving? Abusing our trust. Taking advantage of Barrowclough's laxity.

FLETCHER

I didn't know Mr Barrowclough had laxity, did you, Lennie?

LENNIE

No, poor fellow. 'Cos we were miles from anywhere.

MACKAY

Godber.

LENNIE

Sir.

MACKAY

Do not imagine that you will be excluded from my spiteful resentment. Over the next few weeks you'll both suffer some terrible indignities. Your feet Fletcher, your dinky little size sevens, will not touch the floor. I harbour grudges.

He goes out.

LENNIE

He means it.

FLETCHER

Yeah well.

LENNIE

It was worth it though, weren't it, Fletch?

FLETCHER

'Course it was, my son. A day out. Pint of beer, bag of crisps. Ives in agony. All that and him being dropped in, wallop! We did all right, son.

LENNIE

You did better than most, Fletch.

FLETCHER

Yeah well, naturally.

LENNIE

I got something out the day meself.

FLETCHER

Oh yes. What?

LENNIE

Something I nicked from the church.

He produces a crumpled surplice.

LENNIE

A surplice.

FLETCHER

You stole? From the church?

LENNIE

It's the only place you can get 'em.

FLETCHER

What do you want it for anyway?

LENNIE

It'll satisfy a need I've had for some time, this will.

FLETCHER

What you talking about?

LENNIE

It's to cover me from the gravy when you talk with your mouth full.

SERIES ONE

EPISODE FIVE: WAYS AND MEANS

1. PRISON WORKROOM

Fletcher, Ives, McLaren and other prisoners are making fishing nets. Barrowclough is supervising them.

FLETCHER

Oh shame on it.

BARROWCLOUGH

What's the matter?

FLETCHER

I've just dropped a stitch. (*Sewing*) Oh f . . .

BARROWCLOUGH

Is something wrong, Fletcher?

FLETCHER

'Course something's wrong. It's the job that's wrong, in' it? Grown men spending eight hours a day sewing fishing nets. Can you think of anything more demeaning or indignified?

BARROWCLOUGH

Mailbags. It's a step up from mailbags.

MCLAREN

This isn't a job, it's a punishment.

Everyone in this room's being punished, 'cos we haven't been good little boys.

IVES

Pity you lost that cushy job on the farm, eh? Fresh air – free eggs every day.

FLETCHER

Free – more like half a dozen.

BARROWCLOUGH

I knew you were pilfering eggs.

He walks across to Fletcher.

FLETCHER

Yeah, well it's like young McLaren says. I'm being punished, in' I? What chance has a man got? When all the establishment forces are aligned against him.

BARROWCLOUGH

Now, Fletcher, you've been in prison long enough to know the score. You've broken the rules. You've upset Mr Mackay and you must accept the consequences.

FLETCHER

I thought you was going to appeal to the Governor on my behalf, Mr Barrowclough.

BARROWCLOUGH

The Governor has no time for you, Fletcher. He's very disappointed in you, just as I am.

FLETCHER

All right, Mr Barrowclough, all right. We knows society's extracting its revenge on those what never had a chance to begin with. Look at McLaren here. Never had a chance, have you, son?

McLAREN

Cowing used to it, ain't I?

BARROWCLOUGH

Yes, he's being punished just like you.

FLETCHER

Why? What did he do?

McLAREN

I spoilt the stinking soup.

FLETCHER

He spoilt the soup! And for that he has to pay the penance – well, what chance has any of us got?

BARROWCLOUGH

McLaren, that's not the whole truth as you well know. You spoilt the soup because you held a prison officer's head under it for two minutes.

McLAREN

Yeah, well . . .

BARROWCLOUGH

You tried to drown that prison officer, McLaren. It was a vicious and unprovoked attack.

FLETCHER

(*Amused*) Tried to drown him!

McLAREN

He cowing asked for it.

BARROWCLOUGH

You could have severely scalded him.

FLETCHER

Not in this nick you couldn't. Not with the lukewarm soup we get. Poisoned him possibly, yeah, could have poisoned him.

IVES

What sort of soup, was it?

McLAREN

Mixed vegetable.

FLETCHER

Mixed vegetable. Stone me. I bet he was furious. All those bits of barley and carrot up his nose.

BARROWCLOUGH

It's not funny, Fletcher. It was a vicious attack, and that's why McLaren's here. And your attitude makes it quite clear why you're here.

FLETCHER

Oh I see, yes, well. Yes, well, I see, yes, well.

McLAREN

I was provoked.

FLETCHER

I bet you were, my son.

McLAREN

He called me a black bastard.

BARROWCLOUGH

Now if that were true if he really did say that, you could have gone straight to the Governor, McLaren.

FLETCHER

Oh yeah, fat chance. I mean technically he ain't got a leg to stand on. Technically the facts as stated by the prison officer are not wholly inaccurate. Being as how he is 'a' negroid, and 'b' illegitimate.

MCLAREN

It was the way he said it.

FLETCHER

I know that. You know that. He'll probably tell the Governor that in the course of conversation he simply observed that you were non-caucasian and born out of wedlock.

BARROWCLOUGH

Now that's enough talking, all of you. Work to be done.

FLETCHER

Work! Knitting string vests for hippopotamuses. This probably won't fit me anyway. They're cunning, ain't they? 'Cos giving you a job like this, they knows that we won't cock it up. They knows we wouldn't do nothing slipshod, 'cos we'd be screwing up those brave fishermen of England, wouldn't we? Leave a few holes in here and they'd be

coming back half a ton of cod short. And the price of fish fingers would rocker. Not to mention cod pieces. Whereas of course mailbags, well – don't care if we do a sloppy job there, do we? It makes it easier for our mates that rob mail trains.

BARROWCLOUGH

Fletcher, one just has to listen to you for a matter of minutes to know your type. When you first came here I had high hopes for you, I won't pretend I didn't. It has to be said, you're surly and hostile.

FLETCHER

Yeah, well, years of prison hardens you, doesn't it? Well-known fact.

BARROWCLOUGH

But you've only been here six weeks.

FLETCHER

I'm not really hostile, I'm just resentful. Well, when I first come in here I thought between the two of us there was some sort of rapport there, you know?

BARROWCLOUGH

(*Sitting down next to Fletcher*) You mean you thought I was 'in your pocket' – is that the term for it?

FLETCHER

Terrible thing to say. What a terrible thing to say. Just 'cos I asked you one or two little favours. What a terrible thing to say! In themselves they was meaningless but they would just have made life that little bit more tolerable.

BARROWCLOUGH

Your little favours were supposed to include getting you a new cell, with a window facing south-west, not to mention the extra blankets and the bit of carpet, the special soap, extra tobacco, carpet slippers, a set of darts, a roll of soft toilet paper and some Kendal mint cake.

FLETCHER

All right, don't exaggerate. I said you needn't bother with the darts if you were pushed.

BARROWCLOUGH

Now, I haven't forgotten that you've given me very helpful advice on . . . domestic matters. Don't think Mrs Barrowclough and I don't appreciate that 'cos we do. But I'll be damned if I'll let you treat me like some glorified batman.

FLETCHER

I ain't just referring to your . . . marital problems. Though one can't help reflect that there's been some change in your old lady's attitude . . .

BARROWCLOUGH

How can you tell that?

FLETCHER

Oh just little things. In the morning your general demeanour. A spring in your step. That certain smile that plays around your lips when you comes round in the morning ordering us to slop out.

BARROWCLOUGH

What certain smile?

FLETCHER

The smile of a man who's getting his oats.

BARROWCLOUGH

(*Embarrassed*) Fletcher!

FLETCHER

Are you denying it?

BARROWCLOUGH

Look, I've said I'm grateful.

FLETCHER

Oh yes. Well, yes. I don't want your gratitude, Mr Barrowclough. I've learnt my lesson. It's them and us.

BARROWCLOUGH

Look, Fletcher –

FLETCHER

Now, if you'll excuse me, I must get back to my knitting. Talking to you I'm getting all behind like a cow's tail. I might not get my full sixty pee this week. Sixty pee a week . . . Still it's just enough money to cover the cost of a jar of Wintergreen Ointment. 'Cos all my money goes on medicaments. 'Cos I've never been a well man. Always been suspect to lumbago and rheumatics . . . all those illnesses what are caused by not having enough blankets, having a cold draughty cell facing north-east, and walking around on concrete floors without carpet slippers.

BARROWCLOUGH

I'll see about the extra blanket.

FLETCHER

No. No, no, no, no. I want nothing from you or no one. Nothing, nothing, nothing . . .

Barrowclough moves.

FLETCHER

Well, there is one thing, since you insist. One very minor thing.

BARROWCLOUGH

What thing?

FLETCHER

I want a job in the library.

2A. FLETCHER'S CELL

He is washing his blistered hands. Fletcher's cell door is open as it is association hour.

FLETCHER

Gawd Almighty. I hope the fishermen of England flaming appreciate me. I won't never play the harpsichord again. I doubt if I'll even be able to wipe me own nose.

Fletcher picks up a towel and bar of soap and leaves his cell.

2B. PRISON LANDING

As he goes out he collides with McLaren, causing him to drop a newspaper, a couple of oranges and his metal comb.

McLAREN

Cowing hell.

FLETCHER

Sorry, son, sorry.

McLAREN

(*Threateningly*) Can't you watch where you're cowing going, Fletcher?

FLETCHER

(*Backing off*) I've said I'm sorry, son. My fault, my fault. Won't happen again. Promise you.

McLAREN

Watch it.

FLETCHER

I will, son. I promise. No borra, eh? I'm not a well man.

McLaren gives him another evil glance, then bends down to pick up his oranges.

As he does so his head is facing inside Fletcher's cell.

FLETCHER

I don't want no trouble with you, McLaren.

He kicks him up the backside causing him to fall on his face inside Fletcher's cell.

2C. CELL

Before McLaren can recover, Fletcher has grabbed the kid by the collar and hauled him to his feet, pushed him over the table, their faces a couple of inches apart. Fletcher speaks to him, disguising his genuine threat with a gentle, reasonable voice.

FLETCHER

Now I know you're an 'ard case, son.

We all do. We know you're full of nasty militant feelings. But if you ever speaks to me like that again, I shall twist your head round like a cork in a bottle of Beaujolais. Pull it off and give it to that poof Roland in B Block to keep his wigs on.

MCLAREN

(*Choking*) Yes, Fletch.

FLETCHER

And are we sorry?

MCLAREN

Yes we are, Fletch.

FLETCHER

Right. Don't lie about there. Got any snout?

MCLAREN

No.

FLETCHER

There's some under that pillow. Help yourself.

MCLAREN

Oh ta.

As he does so Fletcher picks up the oranges, the paper and the comb.

FLETCHER

Here you are – here's your things. Your own worst enemy, ain't you, son?
He sits down.

MCLAREN

Oh yes?

FLETCHER

Sit down, sit down. I know things ain't easy for you. Being black with a Scottish father. I mean, it's an unfortunate mixture. It's the Scottish side what brings out all that aggression in you.

MCLAREN

Is it?

FLETCHER

Yeah, course it is. I mean, it subdues your basic West Indian personality. Which is one of exuberant high spirits. All them steel bands, and carnivals, like. Lordy Lordy bit. Someone just has to score a boundary in a test match and they have a firework display.

MCLAREN

I've never set foot in the West Indies. I was born in Greenock. Or at least found. Some copper found me up an alley wrapped in a *Glasgow Herald*.

FLETCHER

Yeah, well, I did admit, didn't I, you ain't had it easy.

MCLAREN

I never knew my father. Mam who didn't want me. Flaming orphanage, and I'm black with a Scottish accent. What you want me to be, Fletcher, happy-go-bloody-lucky?

FLETCHER

It could be worse, son, couldn't it?

MCLAREN

Could it?

FLETCHER

(*Thinks hard*) . . . No, I don't suppose it could, in all honesty. But you don't want to let that illegitimate tag worry you. Lots of famous people was illegitimate. Royalty like. And William the Conqueror . . . Lawrence of Arabia . . . Leonardo da Vinci . . . Napper Wainwright.

MCLAREN

Who's Napper Wainwright?

FLETCHER

He was a screw in Brixton . . . mind you, he was a right bastard.

MCLAREN

Never let you forget.

FLETCHER

It ain't a stigma no more. Not these days, in these liberated times. Out of fashion, marriage is. All these glamour people, these trendsetters, your pop stars and television personalities, well all their offspring's outta wedlock, isn't it? Frankly, in a few years time, illegitimates is going to be fashionable figures. Like homosexuals are at the moment. In fact, being an illegitimate black poof's about as chic as you could get.

MCLAREN

(*Rising*) I'm not a –

FLETCHER

Oh come on, I know that –

MCLAREN

If anyone suggests –

FLETCHER

'Course no one won't. See the way you fly off the handle? Own worst enemy. Come the hard man, where's it get you?

MCLAREN

Got me pride.

Sits back on the bunk.

FLETCHER

Oh yes, pride is it? Listen, we ain't even got privacy in here, and where's a man's pride when he ain't got no privacy! You have to learn to turn the other cheek. Yes sir, no sir, three bags full, sir.

MCLAREN

Makes me sick to my guts.

FLETCHER

(*Rising and sitting at the bottom of the bunk*) Look sonny Jim, sonny Jock. You're nipping along the by-pass in a restricted area, right? And the police stop you. Then you think – what have I done, what's their game? So you leaps out the car and really has a go at them. 'Cos you're not going to take no stick from some jumped-up copper who's been watching too many *Z Cars*. In other words, you come on strong. So what happens? A night in the cooler – fifty-pound fine, lose your licence for six months. And they'd only stopped you to point out your rear light was wonky.

MCLAREN

Don't see the point.

FLETCHER

The point is if you'd leapt out, all smarmy and subservient, 'What, constable, my off-side rear? My word, constable – what a blessing you boys in blue are so diligent.' And it's cost you nothing has it? Except your pride and two tickets to the Police Ball.

MCLAREN

You obviously had no reason to hate the law like me. I hate 'em all. They even open letters from my girlfriend.

FLETCHER

Oh yeah. Passionate, are they?

MCLAREN

I can't enjoy them if I feel that lot's read 'em already. It's not right.

FLETCHER

'Course it ain't right, son, but they still do it, don't they? We've all had that. I was on remand once in Brixton. I done this job – a jeweller's in Southwark. Only they got me, but they didn't get the stuff, see. I hadn't . . . you know what I mean. (*Indicating stashing it*) I'd . . . So I'm in Brixton. And I writes to my old lady, Isobel, and says how sorry I was that I got done. Then I says, 'As you may well be a bit short this winter without me providing why don't you plant your own vegetables? I suggest you dig over the back garden as soon as possible.' 'Course next morning

there's twelve police round there with shovels, the devious nurks.

MCLAREN

Typical. Did they find the stuff?

FLETCHER

'Course they didn't, it was in the bottom drawer of the wardrobe. Just my way of getting the garden turned over, see. Why let Isobel do it when you've got twelve great big nosey coppers with spades – if you'll pardon the expression.

MCLAREN

You crafty nurk.

FLETCHER

We had some beautiful broccoli with Christmas dinner. I wrote to her next and suggested she swept the chimney, but they wouldn't buy that one.

MCLAREN

I get your point. You beat them at their own game.

FLETCHER

Subtle. Certainly more subtle than immersing a screw in the soup of the day.

MCLAREN

Wait till it's pea soup next time. Drown quicker in pea soup, it's thicker. Or maybe semolina pudding.

FLETCHER
How long you in for, son?

MCLAREN
Three years.

FLETCHER
You ain't going to be out for ten, the way you're going. Remission's all that counts. Gettin' out of here. I used to be like you once. Not 'ard but lairy, you know. Knew it all. But I wants out. And your time would come that bit sooner if you learned to turn the other cheek.

MCLAREN
I'm not as bad as people make out, you know. I ain't hit a screw for three months.

FLETCHER
No, you ain't actually hit one. But apart from the soup incident, you've tripped one down a flight of stairs, locked one in the deep freeze, caught one in the goolies with a football and put an overdose of cascara in the Padre's cocoa.

MCLAREN
Got a lot of pleasure out of that.

FLETCHER
Yeah, and a lot of solitary. Not as much as the Padre got. He was shut in the bog all week.

MCLAREN
Welfare Officer wants me to see a psychiatrist. Observation like. Thinks I need psychiatric help,

FLETCHER
Would you mind that?

MCLAREN
'Course not. I'd be crazy to turn it down. Cushy, hospital. Better grub, soft bed.

FLETCHER
So when you going to see him then?

MCLAREN
I'm not. Governor wouldn't wear it, would he? Said he knew my sort, I was trying it on.

FLETCHER
Yeah, he's shrewder than we credit him for, that Venables. It's my problem, see. Trying to ingratiate myself back in his good books. I've lost a lot of ground in the credibility stakes.

MCLAREN
Well thanks, Fletch, like. It's been more use than talking to the Welfare Officer.

FLETCHER
Turn the other cheek, son.

MCLAREN
I'll try. I know you're right in principle, like.

FLETCHER
For your own good.

MCLAREN
You're straight you are, Fletcher. Bloke can trust you.

FLETCHER
Don't forget your things.

MCLAREN
Oh, thanks. Where's me orange?

FLETCHER
Dunno son – in't it outside on the floor?

MCLAREN
(*Looking*) No, it's not there.

FLETCHER
Someone's had it – bunch of criminals in here, aren't they?

MCLAREN
Oh cowing heck. All right, tata Fletch.

FLETCHER
Mind how you go.

McLaren leaves. Fletcher gets the orange out of his pocket and starts to peel it.

3. FOOTBALL PITCH

Mackay blows his whistle and leaves the shot. A fight ensues among the players.
Mackay moves to the players to separate them.
Barrowclough and Fletcher are watching.
Mackay and the players argue. He sends McLaren off.

BARROWCLOUGH
He's got a natural talent that lad, but that's the third sending off in four games – it'll mean suspension.

FLETCHER
Own worst enemy.

BARROWCLOUGH
You know that lad needs help.

FLETCHER
Yeah . . . maybe I'm the one who could help him.

Camera shows the players and Mackay again. He blows his whistle and drops the ball.
An alarm bell sounds.

4. CELL

It is association hour and the cell door is open. Fletcher is sitting on the bottom bunk reading. The alarm bell is still ringing.
Barrowclough enters and walks across to the window.

FLETCHER
If that's for me tell them I'll ring back.

BARROWCLOUGH
It's McLaren.

FLETCHER
Oh he's gone over the wall, has he?

BARROWCLOUGH
He's on the roof and he won't come down. Threatening to chuck himself over, unless we answer his demands.

FLETCHER
Oh yes.

He gets up and walks to the table.

BARROWCLOUGH

Get the prison a bad name this sort of thing. If we don't get him down it'll be on *News at Ten*.

FLETCHER

(*Sitting on the chair*) Oh yes. Then *Panorama. World in Action.* Then the six-part serial in the *Sunday Times*, taking the lid off the penal system.

BARROWCLOUGH

It upsets the men this sort of thing.

FLETCHER

They'll be banging their mugs playing the *Anvil Chorus* on the radiators. You could have a full-scale riot on your hands by tea-time – hang about. What day is it?

BARROWCLOUGH

Thursday.

FLETCHER

Oh no, they won't riot this afternoon. Good tea on a Thursday, in' it? Cauliflower cheese.

BARROWCLOUGH

Fletcher, you take nothing seriously. There's a man's life in danger, to say nothing of the reputation of Slade Prison.

FLETCHER

Oh dear, we don't want to lose our goodwill do we? Or we won't get any bookings for next season.

BARROWCLOUGH

Your flippancy is in very bad taste at a time like this.

FLETCHER

How are they trying to get him down?

BARROWCLOUGH

At the moment the Padre's trying to talk him down through a megaphone.

FLETCHER

The Padre? Is he sober? I mean, the village pub's just closed, isn't it?

BARROWCLOUGH

He's not alone. He's with the Welfare Officer, Mr Gillespie.

FLETCHER

What's he know – the lad's just out of university. Got no experience of the practical. He's probably thumbing through his textbooks now. Trying to find the chapter on Negro nutters and how to deal with them.

BARROWCLOUGH

I think you're being a bit hard on Mr Gillespie.

FLETCHER

Mr Barrowclough! Permission to see the Governor.

He is putting on his jacket.

BARROWCLOUGH

What! Not now, Fletcher. Perhaps when it's all over.

FLETCHER

It's about now that I want to talk.

About the lad. I think I might be able to help.

BARROWCLOUGH

Help the lad?

FLETCHER

Come on then, are you going to take me or not?

BARROWCLOUGH

Well, I will if you think it might help – but Mr Mackay's in charge.

FLETCHER

There you are then. Anything's better than leaving it to Mr Mackay. He'd probably just let the lad jump . . .

Barrowclough goes.

FLETCHER

. . . and then jump on him.

5. PRISON GOVERNOR'S OFFICE

Fletcher and Barrowclough are standing in front of the Governor's desk. Mackay walks across and to the left of Fletcher.

VENABLES

In the circumstances I'm willing to listen to anybody. But what makes you think you can achieve what we can't, Fletcher? Do you know something we don't?

FLETCHER

I know something about what makes

the lad tick. I'm not saying you're not an experienced man in these matters, Mr Venables. As is Mr Mackay here and Mr Gillespie and the Padre. But in his mind you all represent the establishment which only inflames his feelings of hostility and persecution. I mean the Padre's been out there rabbiting for two hours, and all he's had for his trouble's a brick up his megaphone.

VENABLES

(*To Mackay*) How is the Padre?

MACKAY

He's very upset, sir. Very upset that he couldn't get through to the man. Very upset also about losing two of his front teeth.

BARROWCLOUGH

There'll be no sermon on Sunday.

VENABLES

Thank heaven for small mercies.

FLETCHER

You see, it's a question of attitude, isn't it, sir? Last thing the lad wanted was all that preaching and sermonising. Same with our well-meaning intrepid Mr Gillespie. Asked for trouble, didn't he, going up that ladder.

VENABLES

How is Mr Gillespie?

MACKAY

As comfortable as could be expected, sir.

BARROWCLOUGH

We must do something. We can't leave McLaren where he is, sir.

MACKAY

Why not? Let him sweat it out. Then tonight when that cold wind comes whistling over the Pennines, let him freeze it out. If we give way to him by just one inch, we'll establish a regrettable precedent. We'll have prisoners crawling on every inch of rooftop, clamouring for extra blankets, cleaner sheets, bigger helpings.

FLETCHER

On the other hand –

VENABLES

Yes?

FLETCHER

On the other hand, I could go up and talk to the lad. He don't trust you lot, right? And you can't send for friends or family 'cos the lad ain't got none. But maybe – and I say maybe – he may respond to the overtures of one of his fellow inmates.

MACKAY

Poppycock!

VENABLES

Quiet, Mr Mackay. There is a point here, a very good point. It could be quite dangerous, Fletcher.

FLETCHER

Yes, yes. I know. I'm aware that I'm putting life and limb in some jeopardy. But you try not to think about things like that. Try to ignore the tight knot of fear in the stomach, which I ain't had since Kuala Lumpur.

VENABLES

Kuala Lumpur?

FLETCHER

Yes, I was there National Service. Fighting those Malayan bandits for Queen and Country. Jungle warfare. Wading through swamps up to here, rifle above your head to keep the barrel dry. (*To Mackay*) You know what I mean. You'd had some of that, sir. Suddenly you're in a clearing, there'd be nothing but the sound of the night creatures in the undergrowth, and Taffy Williams's stomach rumbling. Anyway –

VENABLES

Has this any relevance to McLaren's predicament?

FLETCHER

Oh. Only to show that I'm no stranger to danger.

BARROWCLOUGH

Do you know I was in Singapore for my National Service. RAF Equipment.

FLETCHER

Oh, Singapore. Doddle, Singapore. We'd have given our eyeteeth for Singapore. All them historical temples and hysterical brothels.

VENABLES

Gentlemen, there's a man on the roof.

MACKAY

Sir, we cannot let a prisoner go up. We have to deal with our own problems, we can't leave them in the hands of a prisoner.

FLETCHER

Oh, in that case, sir, then we might as well accept the alternative.

VENABLES

What alternative?

FLETCHER

You'll have to go up.

6. PRISON BUILDINGS

McLaren is on the rooftop waving.
Camera shows emergency vehicles
and people watching, among them a
fireman, a medical orderly, a warder.
Fletcher walks into shot, looks up at
the roof and then at the fire engine.
Camera zooms to the ladder.
Fletcher looks at it.

MACKAY

Cold feet, eh?

FLETCHER

What me? No never. Let's get on with it.

He leaves the shot.

MACKAY

Kuala Lumpur!

Fletcher starts climbing up
the ladder.
Mackay is watching him.
The fireman is working the levers on
the engine as Fletcher goes up the
ladder. It extends.
Fletcher looks down at the scene

below and looks horrified.
The fireman is watching him.
Fletcher reaches the roof gutter and
starts to get off.

MCLAREN

Hi, Fletch. Lovely view up here.

Fletcher is panting on the edge of
the roof.

MCLAREN

Hey watch out for them slates, they're a bit dodgy.

FLETCHER

Yeah, yeah.

He scrambles up on the roof.

FLETCHER

High enough, in' it?

MCLAREN

It was your idea. You said climb a roof.

FLETCHER

Did you have to pick such a high one? I'm not a bleedin' steeplejack if you are.

MCLAREN

Makes you look more of a hero. Got more dramatic impact.

FLETCHER

Don't use words like impact, will you? Not at this height.

MCLAREN

Want a bit of chewing gum?

FLETCHER

'Course I don't. Let's get down off of here.

MCLAREN

We can't go yet. You're supposed to talk me out of it. I'm a nutter, remember. We'll be up here at least an hour before I succumb to your eloquent persuasion.

FLETCHER

An hour? I've got vertigo. I'm sick. I'm dizzy.

MCLAREN

We'll go down in time for tea. It's cauliflower cheese today, isn't it?

Fletcher falls out of shot. Slates rushing past. Barrowclough reacts to Fletcher's falling.

Mackay reacts. The camera reveals Fletcher is astride the chimney pot.

MCLAREN

Hey, Fletch, where you going – it's not teatime yet.

Fletcher is perched on the edge of the roof.

7. PRISON HOSPITAL

It is a small ward with seven beds in it. Only one is occupied, by Ives. A breezy-looking Fletcher enters, pushing a trolley with books on it.

FLETCHER

Ding-dong, Fletcher calling. Your friendly mobile library!

IVES

'Ere listen –

FLETCHER

Oh, it's you Ives – how'd you work this number?

IVES

What d'you mean, I'm ill – gastro-enteritis.

FLETCHER

Oh, they're not difficult symptoms to fake. Keep running to the bog every five minutes clutching your stomach and screaming in agony.

IVES

I didn't fake nothing. I really got it.

FLETCHER

(*Looking at chart*) Oh, that's unusual. Must be some sort of record, a genuine illness in this hospital.

IVES

What about you? I heard you was in here last week.

FLETCHER

I had a few bruises, but they say I can still have children.

IVES

I heard it was shock. They told me you couldn't stop shaking for two days.

FLETCHER

All right, Ives – wouldn't you be shaking after an heroic ascent like that?

IVES

Your descent weren't so heroic. The kid had to bring you down on his back.

FLETCHER

Look, don't needle me, Ives. Otherwise you won't be getting anything worth reading off here at all. I shall be palming you off with *Lamb's Tales from Shakespeare* without benefit of mint sauce.

IVES

'Ere listen –

FLETCHER

No, you listen to me, Ives. That little rooftop caper was all set up, it was all arranged between McLaren and me. He went up there so I could rescue him.

IVES

Oh yeah.

FLETCHER

All right, I didn't expect to get a dizzy turn like I did. But at least I goes up a hero and he comes down one. As a result of which I have leapfrogged my way back into the Governor's good books. My slate is clean and all my misdemeanours is writ off. And here I am – assistant librarian. And the kid McLaren, who they've decided to treat with sympathy and understanding . . .

IVES

Yeah, I've seen him – hospital orderly – cushy number. 'Ere listen, what about a decent book – know what I mean.

FLETCHER

You mean something a bit risqué.

IVES

Won't be risky, I won't tell anyone.

FLETCHER

Risqué means dirty, you nurk.

IVES

Oh dirty, yes. That's what I mean, yes.

FLETCHER

Well, I could offer you this one – it's all about the sex-starved lady pygmies of the Malaysian jungle.

IVES

What's it called?

FLETCHER

Little Women.

IVES

Little Women.

FLETCHER

It's an erotic classic. Don't you remember that trial at the Old Bailey?

IVES

Er, vaguely like. 'Ere, what's it doing in the prison library?

FLETCHER

Library? What? I nicked that from the Governor's private bookshelf. It was concealed next to the tropical fish year book for 1973. Here listen to this . . .

He opens the book and starts reading.

FLETCHER

'She come out of the clearing her flimsy shift soaked by the sudden monsoon. Through it Gilbert could discern the firm contours of her proud young Malaysian body. She stood there unashamed staring him straight in the kneecap. She was everything that he had imagined on that long train ride from Kuala

Lumpur. He gazed in awe at her half-naked uptilted perfectly formed –'
He shuts the book.

IVES

'Ere listen, perfectly formed what, perfectly formed what?

FLETCHER

I'll give you a clue. There was two of them, and they went up and down when she ran, and I don't mean her eyebrows. Now if you was to borrow this torrid saga of Malaysian love rites, well it could be yours for only two snouts, couldn't it?

IVES

Done.

FLETCHER

In advance.

IVES

Done.

FLETCHER

You certainly have been.
He wheels the trolley off.
As he does so, McLaren comes up with another trolley and they bump into each other.

MCLAREN

Just watch it, you clumsy nurk.

FLETCHER

Hey, hey, hey. Have we learnt nothing? Where did that ever get us?

MCLAREN

Oh . . . sorry, Mr Fletcher.

FLETCHER

That's all right, Mr McLaren. And how's things in the medical world?

MCLAREN

Cushy, Mr Fletcher. And the library?

FLETCHER

A doddle, Mr McLaren.

MCLAREN

Did you get me *The Godfather*?

FLETCHER

Did you get me the Wintergreen Ointment?
McLaren hands Fletcher the ointment and Fletcher hands McLaren the book.

1 SERIES ONE

EPISODE SIX: MEN WITHOUT WOMEN

1. PRISON

Camera shows the prison warder. Then zooms to Warren who is sweeping. He looks and sees Fletcher planting flowers. Warren glances at the warder, then moves towards Fletcher.

WARREN
'Ere, Fletch . . .

FLETCHER
Naff off. I'm thinking.

WARREN
Thinking?

FLETCHER
Yes – thinking. I realise, Warren, that to you and the rest of that lot, thinking is an alien pastime. But some of us – more endowed with a bit of grey matter where it matters, namely up here, preserve our identity and sanity in this place by thinking.

WARREN
But what are you thinking?

FLETCHER
At the moment I'm thinking 'Why won't this bloke Warren naff off and leave me alone?'

WARREN
Look, Fletch, I realise you're a man of . . .

FLETCHER
Intellect.

WARREN
Intellect, yes –

FLETCHER
And erudition.

WARREN
That an' all, Fletch, if you say so. But that was why I wanted to have a word, see. I got this letter . . .

He produces a letter.

FLETCHER
(*Taking letter*) Oh yes. Yes. From a woman, I would assess.

WARREN
That's right. How can you tell?

FLETCHER
It's in the handwriting, isn't it?

The warder is approaching. Fletcher drops the letter and starts to dig.

The warder walks past.
Warren reacts to letter being buried.
Fletcher stops digging after warder
has passed and bends down to pick
up the letter. He sniffs at it.
FLETCHER
Female handwriting, in' it? And judging
by the stationery and the perfume, a
woman of little sophistication or class.
He hands the letter back to Warren.
WARREN
That's right, it's from the wife.
FLETCHER
Oh, I don't mean to infer –
WARREN
No, you're a clever bloke, Fletch.
That's why I wanted your help, really.
FLETCHER
Oh, I see another one. My counsel is
it? Advice to the lovelorn. Now you
want me to assess the situation and
compose an appropriate response.
WARREN
No, it's simpler than that . . . Just want
you to read it to me . . .

2. ASSOCIATION ROOM
Fletcher is sitting at a table with
Warren, Heslop, Lukewarm and Tolly.
He has Warren's letter in front
of him.

FLETCHER
Now, this letter of Warren's – it's very,
very typical. It's your classic wives' letter
after you've done eight months to a
year – that sort of period. I mean wives
make all those marital vows, but you
have to be around to make sure they
do love, honour and obey, don't you?
TOLLY
Yuh.
WARREN
Right.
HESLOP
Yes.
LUKEWARM
How true.
FLETCHER
You see, after a while a wife gets restless
urges. So having got restless, chances
are they weaken and gets naughty.
Warren thumps his fist against
the table.
WARREN
I'll kill her. I'll throttle her.
FLETCHER
Yes . . . that is one solution, but what
we're looking for here is something a
little more constructive. Besides, you're
in here and she's in Bolton.
WARREN
It's visiting day next week.
FLETCHER
Yes, yes, we know. But if you was to
strangle your wife on visiting day
there's a good chance you'd lose half
your remission.

WARREN

I'm just saying.

LUKEWARM

Ooh, he's so impulsive.

WARREN

I'm just saying.

TOLLY

Leave it off, Warren. Leave it to Fletch, he knows, doesn't he?

FLETCHER

Thank you, Tolly, for the vote of confidence. Now, where was I?

LUKEWARM

Just getting to the naughty bit.

FLETCHER

Oh yes. Now having got naughty she gets guilty. So in my reply that I've written out here I have sought to achieve subtlety with strength. An obvious display of affection but carrying beneath it a hint of menace.

The others murmur. Fletcher starts reading.

FLETCHER

'My darling – I realise these are difficult times for you. Here we are, men without women – and you are women without men with all your attendant frustrations' – nice phrase that, isn't it?

They murmur assent.

LUKEWARM

Well chosen.

FLETCHER

Got it out of the *Reader's Digest*. 'I realise my love, that it is a lot to ask, to ask you to wait for me. But I will be upset, dearest one, if I hear about you having a nibble of something you shouldn't. In other words, dear heart, I have friends on the outside, who have friends who have friends. And any word of hanky panky will be followed by swift and merciless retribution. I hope the weather is nice and you are feeling well in yourself. Yours etc.' – blah, blah, blah.

LUKEWARM

Subtlety with strength, oh yes.

TOLLY

Very good, Fletch. I told you, Warren, Fletch knows.

HESLOP

My wife's sister lives in Sidcup. And sometimes we stay there, or drop in for a cuppa when we bin to the coast.

The others exchange looks.

HESLOP

(*Leaning forward*) Anyhow, once we was there, and while my wife was upstairs powdering her nose prior to going to see *Paint Your Wagon* by the Sidcup Operatic, her sister touched me.

There is an expectant pause, but Heslop fails to go on.

FLETCHER

Where, where?

HESLOP

In the kitchen. She got very . . . heated. Had me pressed up against the Aga.

FLETCHER

'Spect you got fairly heated then didn't you, up against the Aga?

HESLOP

She was saying how she'd always fancied me, she knew it was wrong, being as she was the wife's sister, but she couldn't control her true feelings no longer. I had to say 'Now listen Gwendolyn' – that was her name, see – I said, 'Listen, Gwendolyn, this is no way to behave. It's not right, it isn't decent and what happened must never happen again.'

WARREN

But nothing did happen.

FLETCHER

All you did was give her a lecture.

HESLOP

That was an hour later when we were getting out of bed.

FLETCHER

Look, look, what point is it you're making, Einstein? You're on a different time scale to all the rest of us. His head's about twenty minutes slow. Now then, I'd done copies of this letter . . . (*Starts distributing them*) . . . there's one for each of you. You just have to write 'em out in your own handwriting. I'll do yours Warren for a small fee, as you can't write. And of course you must fill in the names of your loved ones. (*To Heslop*) My beloved Iris . . . (*To Tolly*) My darling Norma . . . (*To Lukewarm*) My dearest Trevor. Now post these sharp 'cos we want them to read these before they comes up visiting day. So that they can be duly humble and apprehensive.

HESLOP

There's no evidence that my Iris has strayed from the straight and narrow.

FLETCHER

What? Oh well, post it in any case. A stitch in time saves a hole in the trousers.

HESLOP

Oh right, I'll post it then.

FLETCHER

No sense leaving these things to the last minute.

A bell sounds.

FLETCHER

Now gentlemen, haven't we forgotten something?

WARREN

Oh yes, fair's fair. Cough up, lads.

They all produce little tins of tobacco and hand over a hand-rolled cigarette.

TOLLY

You got no problem on this score then, Fletch? Marriage, like?

FLETCHER

No, no. I been married a bit longer than you lad, ain't I? And she knows her place.

LUKEWARM

Doesn't she get upset that you keep going inside all the time?

FLETCHER

I don't keep going inside all the time.

LUKEWARM

You are fairly consistent. And she's got a home and three kids to run – I don't know how she does it, I don't know how she does it.

FLETCHER

Oh, I'm not saying it ain't hard, obviously. A few weeks ago she had to build a new coal bunker. That's a terrible job for a woman, isn't it?

LUKEWARM

You mean she had to mix all the cement and all that?

FLETCHER

Oh no, no, no, that was all right. Her mother came over and did that.

BARROWCLOUGH

Come on now, lads . . . Well, Fletcher, have you employed yourself usefully this evening?

FLETCHER

Just giving the lads the benefit of my experience, Mr Barrowclough.

BARROWCLOUGH

I've heard that your opinion is sought in this prison. Mr Gillespie, the Welfare Officer, he was saying he's running out of customers.

FLETCHER

Yeah, well, Welfare Officers – like the Padre, they're not to be trusted.

BARROWCLOUGH

I think you're being a bit harsh on a very well-meaning body of men and women.

FLETCHER

I ain't saying they ain't well-intentioned. But the lads, you know, they bring me their problems, they know I speak their language.

He sits down.

FLETCHER

By the way, how's things with your old lady?

BARROWCLOUGH

What? Oh well . . . difficult, you know, Fletcher, she's been a bit better since you and I had that chat, but well, things could be easier. She's not an easy woman to live with, my wife.

FLETCHER

No, no . . . not still the postman, is it?

BARROWCLOUGH

Oh no – heaven forbid. He's in the sorting office in Carlisle now.

FLETCHER

Sorted him out, did they?

BARROWCLOUGH

Pardon?

FLETCHER

Nothing, nothing. Shouldn't joke at your expense.

BARROWCLOUGH

No, no. Well, I'm afraid I'll have to ask you to . . .

Fletcher picks up chair.

FLETCHER

Yeah, I know. Time I turned in.

BARROWCLOUGH

I hate this part of the job you know, Fletcher. Shutting men up, caging them in.

FLETCHER

Yes – it is a shame. Just when the good telly's starting an' all. All we ever see's the flaming news. And *Town and Around*. Fat lot of interest to us that is. Locked in here.

BARROWCLOUGH

No. I've never got used to bolting those doors. I think of you in that little cell . . . and I think of me going out of here, and going home, to my house. To my wife, who's waiting for me.

He stops as if something's occurred to him.

FLETCHER

(*Rising*) What's wrong, Mr Barrowclough?

BARROWCLOUGH

I sometimes wish I was in here with you lot . . .

3. PRISON LANDING

The cell doors are open, leaving the prisoners free to fraternise within their own landing. Prisoners with towels and slop buckets are moving among themselves. Camera follows Warren as he walks along the corridor and enters a cell.

4. FLETCHER'S CELL

Fletcher is on his bunk reading when Warren enters with a slop bucket.

WARREN

Fletch . . . Would you do the honours?

He produces another letter and hands it over.

FLETCHER

What read this you mean? All right . . . (*Sniffing the letter*) . . . the wife?

WARREN

(*Sitting*) Yeah, knows her perfume anywhere.

FLETCHER

Not surprised, Warren. It's very distinctive. Should think it kills ninety-nine per cent of all known germs.

WARREN

Don't you like it – should I tell her to change it?

FLETCHER

No, no, my son. You're safe from other men as long as she wears this.

He starts to read.

FLETCHER

'My dear Bunny'. Bunny?

WARREN

Yes, Bunny Warren.

FLETCHER

Oh – Bunny Warren. 'I got your letter, for which many thanks. It's wonderful that already prison has taught you to write and spell proper. Who knows what you may come out . . .' – what's this word? Oh . . . 'qualified as'. It was the k-w that fooled me . . . 'Now

Bunny, about this other thing. I don't know where you've got these doubts from. I spend my nights watching the box on which is placed your picture which I cut out the *Manchester Evening News*. It is the one of you resisting arrest, but I have cut off the two policemen. I've left the Alsatian on as I know how fond you are of animals. I did go out Sunday I admit, but only to see your mother who has had to go into Salford again with her feet.' How she usually go in then – on her hands and knees?

WARREN

No, no, what she means is er – she's had to go back to chiropodist like. She's always had these feet, you see.

FLETCHER

Has she? The same ones? Oh. Anyhow . . . 'Never mind the expense, I am coming up visiting day, to put your mind at rest.'

Warren gives a thumbs up sign.

FLETCHER

'I will get Saturday morning off at the laundry. I miss you and I think of us when you were at home and you used to take my . . .'

He breaks off.

WARREN

What – used to what?

FLETCHER

Oh well, this last bit's a bit intimate, Warren, I don't think I should read it aloud in front of me. Personal, isn't it?

WARREN

What is it? What's she say?

FLETCHER

Er . . . well, how can I say it? Well, the gist of it is . . . she missed your er – no. Put it another way . . . which you obviously did. No, it's just that . . . well, she regrets that you're not home providing for her.

WARREN

Oh. Oh good. Anything else?

FLETCHER

Anything else would be a bit of an anti-climax. It just says 'I wish you were here. Oh well, I must stop and get on my lover . . . Oh, must stop and get on, my lover . . . See you Sat. Elaine.'

WARREN

Oh. Yes, she's a good girl Elaine. No problems there – what you think, Fletch?

FLETCHER

It's a nice letter, Warren. Heartfelt. You can tell. And coming up Saturday, isn't she?

WARREN

Aye. And so is Heslop's missus. All the way from Kent. And Tolly's wife. You're a clever lad, Fletch.

FLETCHER

Yeah, well.

WARREN

Your ole lady coming, is she?

FLETCHER

She'll be here.

WARREN

You had a letter like?

FLETCHER

No, I ain't actually but . . . she'll be here.

WARREN

I think Lukewarm's fella's coming
up as well.

FLETCHER

Is he now? 'Course Lukewarm's got a
different sort of problem from the rest
of you. His Trevor's the insecure one
there, isn't he? I mean there's six
hundred men in here. So whereas
you're all worried what your wives are
up to on the outside, Trevor's worried
what Lukewarm's up to on the inside.

Mackay walks in.

WARREN

Morning, Mr Mackay. See you, Fletch.
And thanks again, mate.

He leaves.

MACKAY

Thanks? What was all that about?

FLETCHER

Bit of advice . . . Matter of the heart,
Mr Mackay. Between him and me.

MACKAY

Tell me, Fletcher, is it true that this
is the office of Slade Prison's
Miss Lonelyhearts?

He laughs.

FLETCHER

That why you're here then, is it?
Problems of that nature.

MACKAY

I do not have problems of that nature.

FLETCHER

Oh come on, Mr Mackay, all screws,
beg your pardon, all prison officers
have problems in that area. I mean
matrimonially you and me are very
similar. 'Cos while we're in here we
can't be too sure what our old ladies
are getting up to, can we? No difference.

MACKAY

There is a major difference, Fletcher.
Your wives are criminals' wives.
They belong to the criminal classes
with all their inherent traits of
slovenliness and promiscuity. Our
wives are the wives of uniformed men,
used to a life of service and duty,
decency and moral fibre. My house
reflects my wife.

FLETCHER

Big, is it?

MACKAY

It's spotless. And when I get home of
an evening my uniform for the next
day has been cleaned and pressed,
the jacket with its buttons gleaming,
the trousers with razor sharp creases
and the shirt crisply laundered.

FLETCHER

Oh yes? So what's that prove? Your
old lady's having it away with the bloke
from the dry cleaners.

MACKAY

I refuse to rise to your bait. It's obvious that your cynicism derives from some bitter personal experience of your own.

FLETCHER

No, no, no, no. Nothing wrong with my marriage. No doubts about my Isobel. My wife and I have always got on very well.

MACKAY

You've spent half your married life in prison, man.

FLETCHER

Absence makes the heart grow fonder in our case. Bet your old lady wouldn't mind a break from all that ironing and cleaning.

He sits on the bed.

MACKAY

My wife has never had any desire other than to be by my side. Before Prison Service you know, Fletcher, I was in the Army. I was a drill sergeant in the Argyll and Sutherland Highlanders.

FLETCHER

I'd never have guessed that!

MACKAY

And even though I was posted to some far-flung places, Marie would always be with me.

FLETCHER

I bet she was. Brassing up, polishing, blancoing. Female batman. I can just see you coming in of an evening off the parade ground – 'Marie, Stand by your ironing board!!!'

MACKAY

Seventeen years of domestic contentment.

He starts to go.

FLETCHER

Er – Mr Mackay – drill sergeant, was it?

MACKAY

That's right, Fletcher, drill sergeant.

FLETCHER

Do everything by numbers, did you?

Mackay returns.

MACKAY

I am not rising to your bait, Fletcher, and it's naïve of you to assume that I would.

Finally he leaves.

FLETCHER

Even with your old lady. Numbers is it. 'Marie, I am about to make passionate love to you – stand by your bed. Wait for it! Wait for it! Knickers down – two three!'

An enraged Mackay re-enters, pointing his truncheon at Fletcher threateningly.

MACKAY

I'll have you, Fletcher!

FLETCHER

Don't you hit me!

5. COUNTRY ROAD/COACH

A coach is seen travelling along a country road. Inside are Elaine, Iris, Norma and Ingrid talking.

NORMA

Couldn't be much farther this place, could it?

INGRID

I've had to come from London. Had to be at Euston by eight. And there was no buffet on the train.

NORMA

Never is, is there? Or if there is, it's only yesterday's sausage rolls.

ELAINE

I've only come from Bolton. But it's taken me all morning to get here. Change at Manchester. Change at Carlisle. Least when he was in Strangeways I only had a bus ride.

NORMA

It's us that suffers chuck. Us that has to cope with no money and a family to run, and no man around the house.

IRIS

They thinks you've got a man about the house. I've come all the way from Kent because of his suspicious mind. I had this letter.

ELAINE

Me an' all.

NORMA

Me too.

IRIS

Yeah but what a nerve – listen to this.

She gets her letter out and starts reading.

IRIS

'I realise my luv that it is a lot to ask, to ask you to wait for me. But I will be upset dearest one, if I hear about you having a nibble of something you shouldn't.'

The other wives get their letters out. Trevor also produces his letter. The bus arrives at the prison gates, they open and the bus drives in.

6. VISITING ROOM

Heslop, Warren, Lukewarm and Tolly are jostling at a window to catch a glimpse of the arriving visitors.

HESLOP

There's my girl, there she is.

WARREN

Can see my Elaine.

HESLOP

Look at the little darlings. Don't you want to have a look, Fletch?

FLETCHER

See her soon enough, won't I? I know what she looks like.

BARROWCLOUGH

Come on now, sit down, let's have some order.

The prisoners move away from the window and take up their seats.

TOLLY

Did the trick then, Fletch?

FLETCHER

Yeah, well.

HESLOP

Kent's a long way, you know.

LUKEWARM

Trevor's come all the way from Southport. He'll have had to close the shop. He's a watch repairer.

WARREN

I did a watch repairer's once.

FLETCHER

Yeah and now you're doing time for it.
Did you get that, Mr Barrowclough?

BARROWCLOUGH

Oh yes, very funny, Fletcher, very funny.
Nice to see you all in such good spirits.

WARREN

I'm sure I can smell Elaine's perfume.

FLETCHER

No, that's the sheep dip from the
prison farm, that is.

There is a knock on the door.
Barrowclough unlocks it. The wives
walk in and join their husbands.
Ingrid moves to Fletcher.

FLETCHER

Ingrid!

INGRID

Hello, Dad.

FLETCHER

Where's your mother?

Others are immediately captivated
by this.

FLETCHER

I said, where's your mother?

INGRID

She couldn't come, Dad.

FLETCHER

Not ill, is she?

INGRID

No, she –

FLETCHER

She, what?

INGRID

She's found another man, Dad.

7. GOVERNOR'S OFFICE

VENABLES

(*Crossing to his desk and sitting down*)
Morose you say, Mr Barrowclough.

BARROWCLOUGH

I have the Welfare Officer's report here,
sir. Mr Gillespie feels that psychologically
Fletcher is overcompensating for the
traumatic shock of –

VENABLES

Oh, don't spout that university clap trap
at me. Young Gillespie – what does he
know? These lads come in here with no
experience of life. How can they have?
Not two minutes ago they were in rag
parades, blowing clarinets and throwing
flour bags at old ladies.

BARROWCLOUGH

I think you're being a bit harsh on a
very well-meaning body of men, sir. Mr
Gillespie has done work in the field, sir.

VENABLES

In Welwyn Garden City! Hardly a walk
on the wild side. What is it?
Compassionate parole?

BARROWCLOUGH

Just forty-eight hours to help him sort
out his problems. They have been
married twenty-four years.

VENABLES

Alright – wheel him in then.

Barrowclough walks across to the door and opens it to admit a melancholy Fletcher who stands in front of the Governor's desk.

VENABLES

Now, Fletcher, as we all know . . . you've had this domestic . . . well, I suppose, crisis isn't too strong a word, is it?

FLETCHER

My wife's scarpered. Yes, I think crisis is a very good word.

BARROWCLOUGH

She hasn't actually left you yet, Fletcher.

FLETCHER

She's about to.

VENABLES

What do we know about the other man?

FLETCHER

Well apparently, from what I 'licited from my eldest, he's a heating engineer – see we was getting new central heating installed. So obviously he was round there quite a while . . . younger man, bit of patter, from what I heard, new Capri in mustard yellow with wing mirrors.

VENABLES

Younger man, was it?

FLETCHER

Yeah, with wing mirrors, bound to turn a woman's head.

VENABLES

It couldn't just be an infatuation?

FLETCHER

Not according to my eldest, Ingrid. She knows the score, my girl. She says they're planning a new life together in Hemel Hempstead.

BARROWCLOUGH

Oh I know Hemel Hempstead. Pass through it on the train – it looks nice there.

Venables and Fletcher look at him.

VENABLES

Yes, yes . . . well now the Welfare Officer seems to think it would help if we gave compassionate parole.

FLETCHER

Parole – what get out, like?

VENABLES

Not so much get out as go out. For forty-eight hours only. You could go on Friday. Report to the local police on arrival, but otherwise the weekend would be your own.

FLETCHER

I see . . . well, no harm in trying, get a decent Sunday dinner I suppose.

VENABLES

Now, Fletcher, if that's your attitude –

FLETCHER

No, no, Governor, I'm sorry. My flippancy was only masking my deep wounds. If you see fit, sir. I shall go. For the sake of my marriage and your trust in me I'll go. I wonder if Spurs are playing at home?

8. POLICE STATION

Camera shows sign outside the police station. Then Fletcher and Sergeant Norris come out. They

*walk round a corner and carry on
up the street.*

FLETCHER

Look I've checked in – you know where
I live, you don't have to walk me home.

SGT NORRIS

I don't mind, Fletch. Breath of fresh air.

FLETCHER

I'm going home to see my old lady. It's
personal, matters of a personal nature.
That's the reason for my parole.

SGT NORRIS

It's the personal nature that concerns
me Fletch. Want you to greet your wife
with sympathy and understanding.
Don't want you to force her head
through the mangle.

9. FLETCHER'S HOUSE: HALLWAY AND STUDIO

*Ingrid opens the front door to see
Fletcher and the Sergeant.*

INGRID

Hello, Dad.

FLETCHER

Hello, love. Your mother in, is she?

INGRID

In there.

FLETCHER

You know Sergeant Norris, don't you?

INGRID

Met him in court.

SGT NORRIS

Only stopping a minute, love.

*They file through into the living room.
Isobel is waiting, standing in front of*

*the fireplace, composed and
assured. She is an attractive woman
in her forties, dressed neatly.*

FLETCHER

Isobel . . .

ISOBEL

Norman . . .

FLETCHER

I got this compassionate parole.

ISOBEL

So they told us.

FLETCHER

Yeah well . . .

ISOBEL

There's no need for you to stay
Sergeant Norris. Thank you.

SGT NORRIS

I just thought that –

ISOBEL

Yes, well, there's no need for worries
on that score is there, so if you'll
excuse us?

*Fletcher and Isobel greet each
other with warmth and affection.
They hug each other.*

ISOBEL

Hello, Norman!

FLETCHER

Hello, my love.

ISOBEL

It worked then?

FLETCHER

Like a flaming charm.

ISOBEL

I knew it would. It worked in
Maidstone. Knew it would again.

FLETCHER

Like a flaming charm. 'She's found another man . . .'

ISOBEL

Ingrid, go and get your dad's slippers and put the kettle on.

FLETCHER

And don't be in too much of an hurry to come back, neither. Your mother and I have got a lot to make up.

INGRID

It's just like when I was a kid – if you give me some money I'll go to the pictures.

FLETCHER

It's worth it. (*Goes to get money then stops*) Hang on – that's how her brother was born. Puddle off.

10. STREET

On the street is parked a car. A man is washing his car.

11. LIVING ROOM

Fletcher, shoes off, feet up, is reading a Sunday paper. Isobel comes in with grip and carrier bag.

ISOBEL

You'll have to move I'm afraid, love.

FLETCHER

Won't take long to get to Euston on a Sunday.

ISOBEL

Did Sergeant Norris say he'd drive you there? I've given you some apples. And a banana. And some tangerines – what a price they are. But you need the fruit, it's good for your complexion. You should get shaved, love. Norris'll be here soon.

Fletcher gets to his feet and turns off the TV set.

FLETCHER

Yeah, I suppose so.

ISOBEL

It's been lovely having you, Norman.

FLETCHER

Done me a power of good, Isobel. See you and the kids. Colour telly, home cooking . . . Spurs winning at home, and soft lavatory paper.

ISOBEL

It's all here when you come out. Just bide your time, love.

FLETCHER

Tell you one thing, gel. I ain't going back in again after this stretch.

ISOBEL

You've said that before.

FLETCHER

I mean it. I've had me fill of porridge. It's full of kids these days. Talk about a generation gap. Father figure, I am. No, it's been a mug's game my life. And seein' and seein' the kids, and realising I'm missing them growing up . . . and all the things this weekend gave me. I tell you . . . . the best things in life ain't free . . . but the best thing in life is bein' free.

ISOBEL

Oh Norman, you say lovely things, what made you think of that?

FLETCHER

I didn't . . . Randolph Scott said it just before you came in.

12. OUTSIDE PRISON

The minibus carrying Fletcher approaches the prison gates and drives through.

13. ASSOCIATION ROOM

Prisoners are carrying on with their activities. Fletcher and Barrowclough enter the area. Lukewarm sees Fletcher and nudges Heslop. They all see Fletcher.

WARREN

Er . . . you all right, Fletch?

FLETCHER

What?

WARREN

No, Fletch, listen – me and the lads just wanted to say – we're sorry. I mean I know we laughed about it last week but, you know – well, look, the fact that you're not so clever after all, just makes you more human like the rest of us.

FLETCHER

Oh yeah. Let me ask you something Warren – what you done – this weekend?

WARREN

What? Well –

FLETCHER

I'll tell you. Same as you did last weekend. Had a freezing shower, cleaned your shoes, washed your vest, had your dinner, had another freezing shower, spent the evening lying on your bunk picking your nose. Some of us was in the pub, some of us was eating roast beef, or watching Spurs play at home, or having a sing-song with their friends and relatives. (*Crossing to behind Heslop*) Or lying in a big crisp bed with their crisp old lady. (*To Heslop*) Have a banana.

He crosses to his cell.
Mackay and Barrowclough are walking along.

MACKAY

All right, let's have you – come on.

BARROWCLOUGH

You can see the difference in Fletcher. I think Mr Venables sending him home has made him realise what he's missing. It's suddenly dawned on him that he's been on a mug's game all these years.

MACKAY

Oh yes. He's had the cockiness knocked out of him. We've seen the last of his lairy insolence. You can't beat the system, Mr Barrowclough.

They reach Fletcher's cell door and Mackay flicks open the eyepiece. Fletcher is sitting on the lower bunk, looking depressed. He looks up: gives an evil grin and thrusts up two fingers in a vulgar gesture.

MEMORIES

Sydney Lotterby (Producer/Director)

'As soon as I saw the pilot script, "Prisoner and Escort", I knew I wanted to direct it. It was such a good script and just pleading to be done. It revealed the essence of Dick and Ian's writing: they don't write jokes, they write situations and explore the personalities of the characters, which is why they're such good writers. The humour in their scripts comes from the situations they put their characters into. With *Porridge*, their work was very accurate and seemed to reveal how a prisoner felt – it was almost as if they'd experienced prison life themselves!

'Despite the quality of the pilot script, however, I doubted whether the idea for a prison-based sitcom gave enough scope for an entire series, it was too confined – that is until I received the scripts for the first series.

'A director's job is easy when you have quality scripts; there are no problems with the dialogue or the situations, all you have to do is make sure that both you and the actors interpret the script accurately and without ostentation, and the end result will be perfect.'

Philip Jackson (Dylan in 'A Day Out')

'*Porridge* was one of my first TV jobs. Syd Lotterby had seen me in a *Play for Today* called *Blooming Youth*, an improvised film about students. He obviously thought I was the man to play Dylan, the Huddersfield hippie; mainly, I suspect, because of my extraordinary hairstyle! It was the first time I was ever offered a job with no interview or audition.

'Rehearsals in London were hilarious, then much bonding was made in the hotel bar when we filmed the outside scenes in South Wales. During frequent stoppages for the bad weather, Ronnie played poker with the crew, taking care not to win! The studio was my first experience of recording in front of a live audience, and I found it incredibly nerve-wracking. Just before we began, I saw Ronnie in the wings and even he looked petrified, but as soon as he went on, the panic disappeared from his face and you never for a second could have believed he was nervous.

'The initial scene with Richard and Ronnie was a bit edgy at first, and Ronnie did a deliberate cock-up halfway through, which relaxed the audience and actors alike. He was brilliant at gauging the atmosphere at any one time and constantly came up with ideas to relieve any tension. If an actor (me, for example) had a good line that didn't get a laugh, he was always able in some way to do something funny and make it look as if it wasn't you who'd messed it up. This was a total comedic instinct on display and I learned a great deal from watching him. Several of his lines came from larking about, ad-libbing in rehearsal, and the best ones stayed in. I remember the line about cheese and onion crisps in the pub came from such a moment.

'Looking back after nearly thirty years, I think there was a great sense that we were involved in something special. The show has lived on and my amazing hairstyle is still on regular display!'

Tony Osoba (McLaren in the series)

'Although transmitted fifth out of the six episodes of series one, "Ways and Means" was actually the last to be recorded and I recall joining a team which had been together for several weeks and who had all got to know each other well. However, I was made very welcome and soon felt at ease, thus dispelling the natural nervousness that I had been experiencing in the lead up to rehearsals.

'A week or two before, I had been invited to attend a casting to meet Ronnie Barker and Sydney Lotterby at the BBC rehearsal block in west London. I later discovered that a television director I'd recently worked with had recommended me and I shall be eternally grateful to Mike Vardy for that. When I learned that I had been offered the part, I was consumed with excitement and nerves in equal measure and couldn't wait to start work.

'As I say, I was quickly made to feel at home by the cast and crew and filming at the various locations passed all too quickly as I revelled in playing the rather hotheaded prisoner, McLaren, wonderfully written by Dick Clement and Ian La Frenais. Among the many kindnesses, I recall the reassurance and humour shown to me by Ray Butt, the PA, who later received great acclaim as a comedy producer/director in his own right.

'The scene on the roof which ends with Fletcher sliding down the tiles and straddling a drainpipe is one that always brings tears to people's eyes: tears of sympathy as well as laughter. Two roofs were used during the shooting of the scene: a school roof in Ealing for the close-ups and the roof of a psychiatric hospital near Watford for the longer shots. As we filmed in the hospital there would be many people milling around the grounds – crew and technicians, cast, patients and hospital staff; it was difficult telling who was who at times! I remember standing talking to a female member of the crew and a hospital doctor. We chatted for several minutes and then the doctor suddenly pulled the woman's skirt up before running off. It turned out, of course, that the "doctor" was actually a patient.

'In the studio, I was new to the tricky technique of playing television comedy in front of a live audience, but adapted fairly well under the sure but gentle guidance of Ronnie and Syd. However, I was mortified at one point when, during a break in recording, a voice from the audience called out: "Where's my orange?" It was a tag line from a part of the show that we hadn't arrived at yet. Ronnie looked startled and whispered under his breath: "How do they know that?" I didn't have the nerve to tell him that I had recognised the voice as that of my sister Trish. She and my mother were in the audience that evening and a few days earlier I had proudly been showing them the script and discussing my role, including that tag line. Fortunately, as ever in the studio, time was pressing and we could no longer dwell on the possible identity of the mystery caller!

'The evening was a success and I was delighted when the character of McLaren was incorporated into the subsequent series. I owe a great deal to *Porridge* and this episode in particular.'

Patricia Brake (Ingrid in the series)

'In September 1972 I starred in a *Play for Today* purely because I happened to be in the right late stage of pregnancy with my daughter Hannah. My part in *The Bouncing Boy* was arduous and when I had a really early call the make-up artist Ann Ailes, as she was then, came to my home. We became good friends and it was a great piece of luck that she then went on to work on *Porridge* and recommended me to Syd Lotterby. Luckily, I had already appeared in a sit-com called *Second Time Around*, playing the young wife, so I had a little experience of recording with an audience.

'In my first episode, *Men Without Women*, I had to say, "Hullo, Dad" several times which seemed to make Ian and Dick laugh, and thankfully they wrote me into more episodes where I had a great deal more to do. Ronnie was a delight to work with and I learnt a great deal from him. Always generous, he often made sure that the camera was on me for a particular moment during a scene together, very unusual in this business, and the way he could develop and add to an already very funny script was simply pure genius. In *Heartbreak Hotel* I appeared not wearing a bra, very risqué in 1975, and hanging on my bathroom wall now is a certificate made by the props department commemorating this momentous occasion. Later on I was cast several times in *The Two Ronnies*. Ronnie B said it was simply because my surname began with a B, and when he'd been through *Spotlight*, the actors directory, several times and got back to me he said, "She'll do." Now, many years later, I'm so proud to have been a part of *Porridge* and watch the repeats with delight, and I'm still rather secretly pleased that Clive James fancied me.'

2 SERIES TWO

MEMORIES

Sam Kelly (Warren in the series)
Tony Osoba (McLaren in the series)
Philip Madoc (Williams in 'Disturbing the Peace')

SERIES TWO

EPISODE ONE: JUST DESSERTS

1. FLETCHER'S CELL

Fletcher is searching anxiously among his meagre possessions. He is obviously angry at losing whatever it is he cannot find. He goes to Lennie's bed and looks under the pillow.
He looks at the picture of Denise and replaces it.
An air of resolution comes over his face. And he goes out of the cell. Fletcher walks along the catwalk and down the stairs into the association area.
He goes up to the table where Lukewarm, Banyard and Warren are sitting.
Ives is next to them at a table alone reading the paper.
They all greet him with 'Good mornings, etc.'

FLETCHER

Never mind the good mornings.

WARREN

What's up, Fletch?

FLETCHER

What's up, I'll tell you what's up. Are you listening, Ives?

Ives looks up from his reading.

IVES

(*Putting the paper down*) Oh sorry – yes.

FLETCHER

I don't know how to tell you this, gentlemen, but . . . there is a thief among us.

The others look at each other.

WARREN

There's nigh on six hundred people in this prison and I should think two-thirds of them are in for stealing something.

FLETCHER

That was stealing on the outside, Warren. Against civilians. That's work, that is. Making a living. Skullduggery. But the theft to which I'm referring has been perpetrated within these walls. Which is despicable. A crime which offends the dignity of any normal law-abiding criminal.

BANYARD

What is the nature of this alleged offence?

FLETCHER

There's nothing alleged about it,

Mr Banyard. Someone has crept into my cell and lifted a two-pound tin of pineapple chunks.

IVES

(*Impressed*) Pineapple chunks?

FLETCHER

Keep your voice down. We are discussing contraband after all.

IVES

(*Quieter*) Pineapple chunks?

FLETCHER

Correct. One tin of chunks, pineapple. Thickly cut chunks of delicious pineapple, soaked in a heavy syrup, from the sunkissed shores of Honolulu.

LUKEWARM

Mmmm, lovely.

FLETCHER

(*Sharply*) I trust the look on your face doesn't convey a pleasant memory, Lukewarm?

LUKEWARM

'Course not, Fletch. I haven't had your chunks.

BANYARD

Have you any idea who took them?

FLETCHER

I was hoping that our little chat might throw some light on the matter. 'Cos I can tell you, I'm extremely dischuffed about this. Luxuries are few and far between in this neck of the woods. I'd been looking forward to that, I had. Particularly partial to tinned pineapple. Very fond of all tinned fruits but particularly tinned pineapple. In the absence of tinned pears, that is. Bad enough if I'd had some snout nicked, or a new razor blade. Or even money, God forbid. But never my tin of pineapple chunks.

WARREN

When did you discover they was missing, Fletch?

FLETCHER

Just now, you nurk! I was going to have some of them after my Sunday lunch. For dessert. To supplement your wretched cuisine, Lukewarm.

LUKEWARM

I do the best I can with the materials provided.

IVES

'Ere listen, I had something whipped last week.

The others laugh.

IVES

No, honest, listen. You remember visiting day when Ronnie Arkwright's old lady said she weren't coming back no more, 'cos she was going to live with a Maltese ponce in Morecambe. And Ronnie went berserk and attempted to strangle her until restrained by that Scottish screw with the harelip.

FLETCHER

You paint a pretty picture, Ives, go on. They could use you on *Jackanory*.

IVES

Well, during the commotion my missis slipped me a jar of her mother's homemade gooseberry preserve. Now, 'ere listen . . . on the Tuesday, I'd had most of it, and d'you know I was only out the cell for half an hour, but in that time some scroat whipped the rest. While I was in the Hobby Shop making me Bugs Bunny Money Bank.

FLETCHER

(*Sarcastically*) Oh yes. Well, now we're getting somewhere, aren't we? We've narrowed the trail down. The net is closing in. We know the thief has a sweet tooth.

Banyard seems bored with the proceedings and gets up as if to go.

BANYARD

Look, any speculation you have about who took your pineapple chunks, I hardly think applies to me.

FLETCHER

Oh yes, Mr Banyard. Would you mind reseating yourself and elaborating on that if you would.

BANYARD

Well, unlike the rest of you, I'm not a common criminal.

FLETCHER

Has it escaped your attention that you're doing porridge and have been for eighteen months now?

BANYARD

You know what I mean. I'm a professional man, a dentist, and consequently –

FLETCHER

Just let's get the record straight. You

was a dentist. It's been some time now since they struck you off their list. Following those regrettable incidents with the laughing gas. You may not consider yourself a criminal but to the ladies in question it certainly weren't no laughing matter.

LUKEWARM

He is a good dentist though. He did a lovely job on my bridge when the old one fell in the soup.

FLETCHER

I'm not questioning his dental ability. Just making the point that he can't set himself above the rest of us.

The others react with indignation.

IVES

'Ere listen.

FLETCHER

No, you 'ere listen. Pass the word round, right? I'm going for me shower now to stretch me legs, an' wash 'em an' all. Then I'm going to chapel to contemplate the errors of my ways and make peace with my bookmaker. If, when I come back my tin of pineapple has not been returned, we'll have to open a full scale enquiry. A thing like this can spread. If we can't live 'ere together and trust one another then where are we?

There is a murmur of reluctant agreement and Fletcher leaves.

WARREN

Quite right.

He goes to get some Polos.

WARREN

Here – who's pinched my Polos?

Fletcher enters his cell, and gestures for the others to follow.

The prisoners troop in. They include Banyard, Ives, Lukewarm and Warren, and about five others. The cumulative effect is a bit like the cabin scene in Night at the Opera. As they walk in Fletcher is saying:

FLETCHER

Come on in, make yourselves as comfortable as possible . . .

WARREN

(*Enjoying himself*) Pass right down the cell, please.

FLETCHER

This is not a laughing matter, Bunny.

WARREN

Sorry, Fletch.

FLETCHER

Who's keeping an eye open?

IVES

Gay Gordon. He's at the end of the landing.

FLETCHER

Bit conspicuous, isn't she? She's got her hair in curlers.

LUKEWARM

Nifty's at the other end.

BANYARD

I take it that the pineapple chunks have not been returned?

FLETCHER

No, they haven't. Now I've established when the crime was committed, and each of you lot had the MMO. Means, motives and opportunity.

BANYARD

(*Very Agatha Christie*) Are you saying that the thief is one of us . . . here in this very room?

FLETCHER

That's exactly what I am saying, Monsieur Poirot, yes.

They all look at each other uneasily.

FLETCHER

You lot were all on this landing before bang-up last night.

WARREN

Weren't you?

FLETCHER

Not all the time. At one stage I went over to see genial Harry Grout, didn't I, to negotiate the tobacco concession.

McLaren enters with difficulty.

MCLAREN

Kangaroo court aye, heard about it.

FLETCHER

Ah, McLaren, can we make room for McLaren, budge up.

It is difficult, but they manage it.

MCLAREN

No reason to exclude me you know, Fletch. All in this together. Finger of suspicion points at everyone. Just like to mention, of course, that if anyone points it at me, I'll clobber 'em.

FLETCHER

Good of you to be so reasonable, McLaren. Now just to recap, I've established that the crime was perpetrated during the fifteen minutes before bang-up last night.

MCLAREN

I was in the gym, working on me weights.

LUKEWARM

I was playing ping pong. With these two and Gay Gordon. Mixed doubles.

BANYARD

I was teaching Atlas chess.

WARREN

I was watching telly – (*To another*) Well you were as well, weren't you? And Crabs.

FLETCHER

Oh hello, Crabs, I didn't see you there. We don't need sworn statements from everybody.

BANYARD

Nevertheless, we should adhere to the fundamental principles on which our legal system was founded.

FLETCHER

You mean that every man is innocent until proven guilty.

BANYARD

Quite.

FLETCHER

True, true. On the other hand it's nearly lunch and there is amongst us one who is notorious for this kind of petty two-faced gittery, so I suggests we grab hold of Ives now and extract a swift confession.

All eyes turn to Ives.

IVES

'Ere listen . . .

MCLAREN

I'll extract the confession.

He gets Ives in a headlock.

IVES

'Ere listen, it wasn't me, straight up. I was in the Hobby Room. Making me toys, honest.

MCLAREN

Oh wait. That's true, that is. Saw him meself. On the way back from the gym. Making a big fluffy panda he was. He's good. Have you seen his Bugs Bunny Money Bank?

FLETCHER

No, is he doing it now?

MCLAREN

I think you're barking up the wrong tree, Fletch.

IVES

(*Hoarsely*) Could you let me go?

MCLAREN

Fletch?

FLETCHER

Yeah. Let him go, let him go.

McLaren does so.

FLETCHER

So we still live with the knowledge that there's a thief among us.

BANYARD

Where d'you get the pineapple in the first place?

FLETCHER

Stole it from the kitchen, didn't I?

A head peeps round the door. It is Gay Gordon.

GORDON

Mackay . . .

He disappears.

FLETCHER

(*Quietly*) All right, lads – we all know what we're here for. The initial gathering of the newly formed Slade Prison Cowboy Club. All together now . . .

He conducts them and they sing.

ALL

Home, home on the range . . . Where the deer and the antelope play, Where seldom is heard –

MACKAY

Quiet the lot of you, you horrible rabble!

Mackay arrives.

FLETCHER

(*Speaking*) A discouraging word?

MACKAY

What is going on here?

FLETCHER

Oh Mr Mackay. It's Mr Mackay, pardners.

ALL

Howdy, Mr Mackay.

MCLAREN

How.

MACKAY

I said, what is going on here?

FLETCHER

Cowboy Club, sir.

MACKAY

The what?

FLETCHER

Friends of the West. Kindred spirits, brought together by a mutual love and interest in those far-off days of the new frontier. We plan to meet, sing the songs –

MACKAY

Poppycock! This is an unlawful assembly, Fletcher. Prison regulations clearly state that no more than three prisoners will at any time congregate in a cell.

FLETCHER

Ah there, Mr Mackay, you have the advantage over me. Try as I might I have been unable to obtain a copy of the current Home Office Regulations.

MACKAY

Get on your feet the lot of you. There are only two rules in this prison. One: you do not write on the walls. Two: you will obey all rules. Back to your cells, the lot of you.

FLETCHER

All right lads, you'd better mosey along.

They start to troop out.

WARREN

See you later, Fletch. I'll bring round me Gene Autry songbook.

LUKEWARM

Adios, amigos . . .

Fletcher and Mackay are left alone.

FLETCHER

Well . . . highlight of the week coming up, Sunday lunch – can I offer you a sherry?

MACKAY

There is a growing current of insubordination and laxity in this prison. A definite rise in insolence. And pilfering.

FLETCHER

Pilfering, yes. Me and some of the lads have noticed that.

MACKAY

I'm not referring to petty sneak thieving amongst yourselves. That's to be expected amongst incorrigible criminals. I'm referring to thefts of prison property. Mark my words, Fletcher – it will not be tolerated.

Lennie enters in his kitchen whites and small chef's hat and spots Mackay.

LENNIE

Oh.

MACKAY

Ah yes, Godber. What are you up to?

LENNIE

Off work, sir. Been up since six this morning.

FLETCHER

Yes the lad's tired, sir. So if you'll excuse us –

MACKAY

This is a very unfortunate combination.

FLETCHER

Oh yes, how's that?

MACKAY

Godber with his opportunities to steal from the kitchen. And you with your distribution network.

LENNIE

Here, I don't steal, I resent that!

MACKAY

Oh you resent that, do you, Godber? Butter wouldn't melt in your mouth.

FLETCHER

That's a good idea, how much could you get in your mouth?

LENNIE

Don't make waves, Fletch.

Mackay starts to search Lennie.

LENNIE

No, I want to say. This is not on, Mr Mackay. (*As Mackay searches him*) All right, I'm inside, I have done wrong, and I've got that stigma to bear. But I'm paying my penance, I'm paying my dues.

MACKAY

What makes you think you're any different from anyone else?

LENNIE

Certain circumstances brought me here. Environment. Lack of parental guidance. Times were tough, I did go off the rails but I did have a few decent qualities underneath and I've learnt my lesson. Now I won't grass and I won't cheat and I will not steal.

MACKAY

Hmmm. All right, sonny Jim, we'll say no more . . . for the present.

Mackay goes.

FLETCHER

Well said, son. You even impressed

Mackay with your eloquence and
obvious sincerity.

LENNIE
Should think so. Suspicious old scroat.

FLETCHER
Good thing you were clean though.

LENNIE
Good job he didn't look under me hat.
He takes it off, revealing half a
pound of marge perched on the
top of his head.

3. PRISON
Camera shows the prison in the
early evening, after lock-up but
before lights out.

3A. CELL
It is night time. Fletcher is cleaning
his teeth in his underclothes,
Lennie is looking for something
under his bed.

LENNIE
Fletch?

FLETCHER
Whah?

LENNIE
Can I have a loan of your black
boot polish?

FLETCHER
(*Spitting*) Why?

LENNIE
Why? Why do you think? Me mascara's
run out.

FLETCHER
Don't be cheeky, young Godber.

LENNIE
I just want to clean me shoes.

FLETCHER
Borrow someone else's.

LENNIE
It's after lock-up.

FLETCHER
Then you should have thought of
that earlier.

LENNIE
Aren't you going to give me a measly
bit of shoe polish?

FLETCHER
No. I think that in the light of certain
events, it would be better if in the
future what one has one keeps.

LENNIE
I notice you didn't say this till after I
shared my margarine with you.

FLETCHER
I've done enough for you, Godber.
Boot polish, snout, toothpaste – the
first night you moved in here I give you
my toothpaste.

LENNIE
You give me one squeeze.

FLETCHER
On three successive nights! That adds
up to a lot of toothpaste.

LENNIE
Your squeezes don't.

FLETCHER
That weren't no ordinary toothpaste,
neither. That had hexochloroform in

the stripes. I got that special to match
my pyjamas.

Lennie starts to darn his socks.

LENNIE

I gave you liquorice all-sorts for that
toothpaste. Fair exchange is no robbery.

FLETCHER

When you were at death's door last
month with your inflamed bronchs,
who gave you a TCP throat lozenge?

LENNIE

Yeah. Lozenge. Singular.

FLETCHER

Who saved you all those matchsticks
when you wanted to make a model of
the *Cutty Sark*?

LENNIE

And who sat on it?

FLETCHER

Well, it was a pointless exercise. You
need a ten stretch to finish the *Cutty
Sark* in matchsticks. You should have
used chair legs like I told you.

LENNIE

Who stole nails for you from carpentry
classes so you could stick your pin-ups
on the wall? And who gave you half his
mother's home-made shortbread?

FLETCHER

Home-made shortbread, yeah. I used
that to hammer the nails in with.

LENNIE

You ungrateful nurk.

FLETCHER

Who loaned you their darning
wool then?

LENNIE

You did. And who's darning whose
socks then?

FLETCHER

Oh. Oh are they my socks?

LENNIE

'Course they are. I don't go through
my socks.

FLETCHER

Oh I didn't realise . . .

LENNIE

Apparently.

FLETCHER

Yeah well. Ta very much then.

LENNIE

(*Sulkily*) My pleasure.

FLETCHER

Go on then, here's me shoe polish.
Don't take too much.

*Lennie takes a small smear on
his brush.*

LENNIE

You told me when I moved in here that
our best protection against those
nurks out there was mutual interest.
Team spirit.

FLETCHER

Yes, but my trust has been
misplaced, hasn't it, as that missing
tin of pineapple has proved. I was
careless enough to forget that this
is a jungle in here. You can't trust
no one.

LENNIE

Here! Are you including me in
that remark?

FLETCHER

What remark was that?

LENNIE

About not trusting anybody.

FLETCHER

Look after number one, that's what it's
all about.

LENNIE

That's not answering my question.

FLETCHER

What question's that then?

LENNIE

Do you think I nicked your chunks?

*Fletcher is deliberately vague
and evasive.*

FLETCHER

Who knows who took them?

LENNIE

Fletcher, don't evade me. This is a
very critical point in our relationship.

FLETCHER

Never mind that. You just darn your
socks . . . my socks.

LENNIE

No. No. I want an answer. I respect
you, Fletch. I owe you a lot, and I'm
not talking about stripey toothpaste.
I've never pretend to be cool or off-
hand about doing stir. It bleeding
petrified me. But you made it tolerable.
You taught me the right approach. In
me head. I get by now. Just, but I get
by. I'm grateful, very grateful. And do
you think I'd repay that by stealing
your tin of naffing pineapple chunks
. . . not even me favourite fruit.

FLETCHER

(*Pacifying him*) Here, here, here . . .
it never entered my head, Lennie.
If there's one person I know didn't
take them it's you.

LENNIE

Yeah well.

FLETCHER

Of course. You and me. Oppoes,
ain't we?

LENNIE

I dunno.

FLETCHER

You know we are. Living like this, like
caged animals we're bound to get
the needle sometimes. But I trust you.
Implicit. I know you didn't take
my pineapple.

LENNIE

How can you be sure?

FLETCHER

'Cos I know you. I know the type of
person you are.

*There is a pause while Lennie
digests this.*

FLETCHER

'Sides, when you were in the shower
I went through all your gear!

4A. CORRIDOR

*Camera shows Barrowclough
walking along a corridor towards
library door.*

4B. LIBRARY

To describe this as a library is an overstatement. It is a small dusty room, full of old books with broken spines and grubby paperbacks. There is a locked door with a meshed grille at the back of the room. A chipped table has an old filing cabinet on it. There is also a very ancient typewriter behind which sits Fletcher, tapping out index cards as he catalogues new books. Barrowclough unlocks the door and walks in. Fletcher looks up.

FLETCHER
Ah, morning, Mr Barrowclough.

BARROWCLOUGH
Fletcher . . .

FLETCHER
Have a nice weekend then, did you?

BARROWCLOUGH
Not especially.

FLETCHER
Least the weather kept nice.

BARROWCLOUGH
Did it? The sun rarely shines in my household.

FLETCHER
You should put another window in.

BARROWCLOUGH
I wasn't referring to the architecture.

FLETCHER
Oh dear.

BARROWCLOUGH
But I haven't come to discuss my domestic situation . . .

FLETCHER
Your problems are my problems.

BARROWCLOUGH
I'm aware of that. I'm aware that's true at times. And that's why I've been lenient with you, Fletcher.

FLETCHER
Lenient?

BARROWCLOUGH
I haven't had a chance to talk to you since I went off duty for the weekend, but on Saturday afternoon when you were all out watching the football match, Mr Malone and I were detailed by Mr Mackay to do an RSC.

FLETCHER
A what?

BARROWCLOUGH
A random security check.

FLETCHER
Oh yes. The vocabulary varies from nick to nick. In practice it's the same thing though, isn't it? Burgling, a despicable infringement of civil liberties.

BARROWCLOUGH
The practice is justified though, Fletcher, when one finds stolen tins of pineapple chunks.

There is a long pause. Then Fletcher makes a game try.

FLETCHER
Where?

BARROWCLOUGH
Don't play games with me, Fletcher.

It was in your cell as you well know, and by rights I should have reported it.

FLETCHER

(*With a glimmer of hope*) You didn't then?

BARROWCLOUGH

No. As it happened, Mr Malone's attention was distracted. He was in the showers at the time, taking up the tiles looking for a missing hatchet. Fletcher, if I had reported that find you would have lost this job, had loss of privileges and probably solitary confinement.

FLETCHER

(*Contritely*) Well, what can I say, Mr Barrowclough?

BARROWCLOUGH

You can promise me to keep your nose clean. I reckoned I possibly owed you a favour, and the consequences would have been a bit severe. But that's wiped the slate clean. Now we're all square, right?

FLETCHER

Right, sir.

BARROWCLOUGH

You know this is a very cushy number here. This is a better job than most *trusties* have got.

FLETCHER

It's not all that easy. I've got a very complicated index to complete.

BARROWCLOUGH

Yes and you've been doing it for five weeks.

FLETCHER

I want to avoid mistakes, don't I?

BARROWCLOUGH

You want to avoid finishing it. 'Cos then you've got to decorate the room, which is why you were put in here in the first place.

FLETCHER

Waiting for the paint, sir.

BARROWCLOUGH

Where is it?

FLETCHER

Stolen, sir.

BARROWCLOUGH

What is happening to this prison?

FLETCHER

Strong criminal element in here, sir.

BARROWCLOUGH

There's just too much petty pilfering going on. Mr Mackay is on my back to stamp it out. I've let you off the hook, Fletcher. And in return I expect to see a sharp decrease on your block.

FLETCHER

Rest assured, sir.

Barrowclough seems satisfied with this.

FLETCHER

By the way . . . the tin of pineapple, did you manage to return it to the food store?

Barrowclough now looks slightly uncomfortable.

BARROWCLOUGH

Not exactly. I took it home and the wife did gammon steak Hawaii.

FLETCHER

Oh very nice, very nice. Gammon steak Hawaii. So the pineapple has been consumed!

BARROWCLOUGH

I hadn't intended to. But the wife found it and . . . insisted that we ate it. I could do very little about it.

FLETCHER

Only eat it.

BARROWCLOUGH

Under protest.

FLETCHER

On top of gammon. Well now we have quite a different situation here, don't we? I mean, if I did commit the alleged offence – which in the absence of evidence is somewhat difficult to prove – you are unquestionably an accessory before, after and during the facts. You're a felon same as me.

BARROWCLOUGH

I am aware of the situation. I would suggest that we purchase another tin of pineapple, and replace it in the food store.

FLETCHER

What do you mean we? I can't just troll down the village store at will.

BARROWCLOUGH

Oh no. I realise that, Fletcher. I shall get it. You shall pay for it.

5. KITCHEN

It is mid-morning, before lunch. There is a bustle of activity. Huge cauldrons of soup are bubbling. Several prisoners are going about their various tasks under the watchful eye of a Prison Officer.
Lennie brings over a tray of Cornish pasties to a hotplate by which Lukewarm is standing. He talks to him quietly.

LENNIE

Hey, Lukewarm. Make a bit of a commotion in a minute, will you?

LUKEWARM

What for? You're not going to escape, are you? It's a good lunch today. We've got jelly.

Lennie looks around to make sure no one's in earshot.

LENNIE

I'm going to whip Fletch a tin of pineapple.

LUKEWARM

What for?

LENNIE

Surprise, like.

LUKEWARM

Bit dodgy. There's only one tin left.

LENNIE

Well . . .

He moves across the kitchen towards the store cupboard. Then turns and nods at Lukewarm. Lukewarm looks sadly at the tray of pastries.

LUKEWARM

(*To self*) They came out lovely an' all.
He drops them on the floor.
The Prison Officer comes over
to Lukewarm.

PO

What's all this, Lewis? Get all this
mess cleared up at once!

While the hubbub is going on Lennie
goes into the store cupboard.
Warren goes past the cupboard with
a laundry basket. A hand drops a tin
into it. Lennie comes out and reacts
with pleasure, but then reacts again
in alarm. Mr Birchwood, the civilian
catering administrator, walks across
to the cupboard and goes in.

BIRCHWOOD

Good morning, Mr Appleton.

APPLETON

Morning, Mr Birchwood.

Warren and Lennie exchange
anxious glances as he goes into
the cupboard. Birchwood comes
out of the cupboard and
confronts Appleton.

BIRCHWOOD

Mr Appleton – there's a tin of
pineapple chunks missing.

APPLETON

All right . . . (*Turns to a prisoner*) You –
fetch Mr Mackay from the Mess Hall.
The prisoner goes.

APPLETON

Everyone stay just where they are.
(*To Lennie*) You, where you are off to?

LENNIE

I've forgotten where I was.
He moves back. Appleton starts
to search them.

APPLETON

Come on, arms up.

LUKEWARM

Come on, Mr Appleton, we haven't
got time for all this – I've got a whole
trayful of pasties to get ready.

APPLETON

They'll have to wait, won't they?

LUKEWARM

They can't wait, they have to do
twenty-five minutes on Regulo 6.
They continue talking as
Barrowclough enters and crosses
over to the store cupboard. He looks
very shifty and nervous. He opens
the door and puts the tin back on the
shelf. He comes out of the cupboard
and moves away. Mackay comes
into the kitchen.

MACKAY

All right, what's going on here?

APPLETON

Pilfering we think, sir.

BIRCHWOOD

Tin of pineapple chunks, sir. There was
a tin in that cupboard half an hour ago.
I'm sure of that.

MACKAY

Who was last seen in that vicinity?

APPLETON

(*Indicating Lennie*) Godber was there
a minute ago.

MACKAY

Oh, was he? Well, that makes sense. Your come-uppance is well overdue, Godber.

As Mackay speaks, he approaches Lennie.

MACKAY

Why is your hat standing to attention, Godber?

He prods it with his stick.

LENNIE

Ow, Mr Mackay.

Mackay removes the hat. Naturally there is nothing underneath it. Mackay is disappointed.

MACKAY

All right. Now just stand there. All of you. Very well, Mr Birchwood. Where was the crime perpetrated?

BIRCHWOOD

From this cupboard, Mr Mackay.

He leads Mackay to it.

BIRCHWOOD

I saw straight off, 'cos there was only the one tin there.

He opens the cupboard door. Mackay goes in and comes out with a tin of pineapple. He hands it to Birchwood.

MACKAY

Is this the one that's missing?

BIRCHWOOD

(*Looking at it*) That's the one, yes, sir.

MACKAY

Pull yourself together, Mr Birchwood.

Lennie reacts with relief. Warren is on his knees praying.

6. CELL

Lennie is alone in the cell finishing a shave.

WARREN

Here . . .

Warren produces the tin of pineapple chunks from under his jacket, and hands it to Lennie who quickly hides it under his pillow.

WARREN

(*Wanting reassuring*) Now, listen. Tell me. There were two tins there, weren't there?

LENNIE

Just the one.

WARREN

Then I was right. It were a miracle.

LENNIE

Apparently. No other explanation.

WARREN

Scares you a bit though, doesn't it?

LENNIE

I don't pretend to understand.

WARREN

'The Miracle of Slade Prison'. I tell you something, Len, I was brought up a Catholic – not a very good one. But after this – well. Makes you think, doesn't it?

LENNIE

God moves in a mysterious way. His wonders to perform.

WARREN

See you in church.

He goes. Lennie takes the tin from under his pillow. He gets a label with 'surprise, surprise!' written on it in large letters and ties it round the tin. He looks at Fletcher's bunk. There is a towel on it. With a grin he places it under Fletcher's towel.

He moves away quickly on hearing Fletcher enter. Fletcher is not in the best of moods.

LENNIE

'Lo, Fletch.

FLETCHER

Oh yes . . .

LENNIE

What's the matter?

FLETCHER

What's the matter, some new paint's arrived.

LENNIE

So?

FLETCHER

So, it means I've got to decorate that library, doesn't it?

LENNIE

Can't you get rid of it, like all the other consignments?

FLETCHER

No – not a chance. There's not a screw left who hasn't got a gleaming front fence.

LENNIE

(*Happily*) Well never mind, life could be worse.

FLETCHER

Oh yes?

Fletcher picks up his towel, but still looking at Lennie, not noticing the tin.

Lennie starts to snigger. In pleasurable anticipation of Fletcher's discovery.

FLETCHER

What's got into you, Godber?

He throws his towel on the tin again.

LENNIE

You'll find out soon enough.

Mackay enters.

FLETCHER

Oh that's all we need, isn't it?

MACKAY

Haven't come to see you, Fletcher.

FLETCHER

What a shame, sir.

MACKAY

Came to see Godber. Now laddie, don't want you developing a chip. Don't want you to think I'm picking on you. I have a job to do. And whatever else I am, I'm firm but fair. I want you to know that I treat you all with equal contempt.

LENNIE

I appreciate that, Mr Mackay.

FLETCHER

What's all this about?

LENNIE

He thought I'd been pilfering again.

FLETCHER

Oh, did he? Well that should come as no surprise to you, son. They think

we're all at it, don't they? Think we're
all thieves in here. We're under
continual harassment. Suspicion.
Sneaking around, poking through our
belongings, with any justification
whatsoever. Now if you'll excuse me
I'm going for a shower.

LENNIE

No.

FLETCHER

You what?

LENNIE

You don't need to, Fletch. You're
so . . . clean.

FLETCHER

What's got into you, Godber?
(*To Mackay*) You lot are warping this
lad's mind.

*Fletcher picks up towel and moves
towards the door. The tin of
pineapple is left uncovered. Mackay
sees it.*

MACKAY

Fletcher . . .

*Lennie winces. Fletcher
comes back.*

FLETCHER

What?

MACKAY

What is that?

FLETCHER

What's what?

*He looks to where Mackay
is pointing.*

FLETCHER

Bloody hell!

MACKAY

Come along with me, Fletcher.

FLETCHER

Now, listen.

MACKAY

You won't need your towel.

FLETCHER

It's a plant.

MACKAY

Oh no, it's not, it's a tin of pineapple.
Come along with me.

FLETCHER

I've been framed.

*Mackay leaves. Fletcher follows,
picking up his shirt.*

*Lennie moves across to get the tin.
Takes off the label and makes for
the door. Camera shows Mackay,
followed by Fletcher, walking along
the catwalk.*

*Lennie comes out of the cell with
the tin.*

LENNIE

Anyone got a tin opener?

Fletcher reacts then moves on.

SERIES TWO

EPISODE TWO: HEARTBREAK HOTEL

1. FLETCHER'S CELL

A small transistor radio is on in the cell.
From it comes the voice of a DJ with romantic mood music playing in the background. Lennie is sitting on his bed, darning his socks and listening intently.

DJ
Here's a request from Brigit in Dundee for a boy, she only knows him as Ricky but he has blue eyes, dark curly hair and looks a bit like David Essex. Brigit is sixteen and works in product control in a cake factory and her job is to spot flawed almonds.

Fletcher comes into the cell as the DJ gives the last fascinating piece of irrelevant detail.

DJ
Brigit was on a coach trip to the Ayrshire coast last summer and met Ricky briefly at a dance. All she knows is that he's from Glasgow.

Fletcher turns off the radio and takes over from the DJ.

FLETCHER
She knows he's from Glasgow and his hobbies include getting drunk and beating up lavatory attendants.

LENNIE
Here, I was listening to that.

FLETCHER
Yeah, well, I'm not. Teenage sentimental slush.

LENNIE
I have to sit through your *Gardeners' Question Time* and *Friday Night is Music Night*.

FLETCHER
All right, all right. And I sit through *Rosko's Round Table* but I draw the line at David 'Diddy' Hamilton. The wireless is never off in this nick.

LENNIE
Well, the screws think it makes us work harder. They're piping Tony Blackburn through to the kitchens now.

FLETCHER
They're doing that 'cos they believe we're in prison to be punished.

LENNIE
I wanted to hear that bit. 'Cos that was their special request slot. That was their 'Hello Young Lovers' corner.

FLETCHER
Oh yes?

LENNIE
And I'd written in, like. For a record.
For Denise.

FLETCHER
Denise?

LENNIE
My fiancée.

FLETCHER
Oh yes, that Denise, of
course, yes.

LENNIE
Just wanted to convey my undying
feelings of affection and devotion.
'Everlasting Love' that was the record
I asked for.

FLETCHER
You should have asked for 'My Ding-
a-Ling'.

LENNIE
I been listening all week, but it ain't
been on yet. Not fair. You'd think my
needs were greater than an almond
sorter's from Dundee.

FLETCHER
Hang about. Did you write this on
prison notepaper?

LENNIE
Yes. If you remember I gave you me
last sheet of Basildon Bond.

FLETCHER
That's it then.

LENNIE
Why? Are they biased
against prisoners?

FLETCHER
P'raps not officially. But I don't
recall ever having heard a prisoner's
request on the air. Forces yes.
Aircraft carriers or ack-ack batteries,
but never heard nothing from no
one from the *nick*.

LENNIE
It's a disgrace. We have a rotten
enough life in here without having our
requests refused. That's discrimination
that is. And five five and a halfpenny
stamps up the spout.

FLETCHER
You can see it from their point of view.
The public what pay their radio licence
faithful every year. Take offence,
wouldn't they? Sitting down to Sunday
lunch with their beloved *Family
Favourites*. Suddenly they read out a
card with a Parkhurst postmark. Says
could Tommy 'Mad Dog' Hollister
please have 'Clair de Lune'.

Mackay enters.

MACKAY
'Clair de Lune'?

FLETCHER
Oh. Yeah, it's French, Mr Mackay.
French for 'By the light of the
silvery moon'.

MACKAY
I thought for a moment, Fletcher, you
were having a cultural conversation.

LENNIE
P'raps you could tell us the ruling,
Mr Mackay.

MACKAY

The ruling, Godber?

FLETCHER

Miss Lonelyloins here, lovelorn Lennie, he wants to know whether the BBC plays prisoners' requests?

MACKAY

No. The answer to that is no, on the grounds that it caused embarrassment.

LENNIE

Embarrassment?

MACKAY

To the prisoners' families. The family might have excused his absence by telling the neighbours that the felon in question was abroad, or working on a North Sea oil rig.

LENNIE

Oh I see.

MACKAY

No doubt your wife, Fletcher, has told your friends that you're on a five-year safari.

He laughs.

FLETCHER

(*Reading paper*) No, no. She tells them I'm doing missionary work in Scotland.

MACKAY

No, Godber. The practice was also open to abuse. There was nothing to stop prisoners sending messages in code across our airways.

FLETCHER

Ah, that's a point – yeah, that's a point. Listen to some heartwarming

Christmas message from some poor lag. To his beloved wife and family and little Tiny Tim. Could he please hear Harry Secombe with 'The Impossible Dream'. Translated what he really meant was 'Nobby, have the ladder round the back of E Wing, Boxing Day – and bring me a mince pie.'

LENNIE

Oh it's a good idea, that.

MACKAY

It's an abuse of privilege, Godber. Which is why I'm here.

FLETCHER

Oh, I thought it was a social call.

MACKAY

Six rolls of soft toilet paper have disappeared from the Governor's closet – the Governor's own personal water closet.

FLETCHER

Oh dear. Would you Adam and Eve it? What next?

MACKAY

Knowing you, Fletcher, probably the seat.

Lennie laughs.

FLETCHER

Don't look at me.

LENNIE

Nor me. It's writing paper I'm short of.

MACKAY

It's not right. We've had to give the Governor standard prison issue tissue.

LENNIE

That's rough.

FLETCHER

Not half, it ain't. That'll wipe the smile off his face.

They both laugh.

MACKAY

Fortune has given you two privileged positions in this prison. You would be foolish to jeopardise them by any infraction of the rules . . . I'll say no more.

He leaves. They call after him.

FLETCHER

Thank you, Mr Mackay.

LENNIE

Yes, thanks for the advice.

FLETCHER

To which we'll pay great heed . . . now naff off.

LENNIE

Always picking on us, isn't he?

FLETCHER

Well, that's his devious suspicious mind, the nosy nurk. Care for a glass of toilet roll?

He tips up the jug, revealing a pink roll of soft toilet tissue.

LENNIE

Eh, you've got one!

FLETCHER

Yeah. I had six.

LENNIE

Where's the other five?

FLETCHER

I traded them, didn't I?

LENNIE

Who to?

FLETCHER

There are a few inmates with some refinement in this nick. Bottom landing, call at the end, there's some embezzlers in there. Mr Banyard, the unfrocked dentist. Well those middle-class white-collar felons . . . leapt at 'em, didn't they?

LENNIE

What d'you get?

FLETCHER

Well, they owe me, don't they? Lot of nice middle-class merchandise. I'm promised a cricket sweater, a pair of Hush Puppies and a box of after-dinner mints.

Fletcher sits down, retrieves his socks and bundles them up.

LENNIE

Hey.

FLETCHER

What?

LENNIE

Share and share alike.

FLETCHER

Yes. What!!

LENNIE

Rule of the house, isn't it?

FLETCHER

Share my toilet roll?

LENNIE

Only fair.

FLETCHER

Share my toilet roll!!! Godber.

LENNIE

Only fair.

He sits glowering.

LENNIE

Look at all them darned socks.

FLETCHER

All right then.

He picks up the toilet roll and tears off one piece, handing it to Lennie.

FLETCHER

Mind how you go.

2. VISITING

A door is unlocked and wives, sweethearts, mothers, a few dads and brothers are ushered in under the watching eye of Mackay. The camera picks out Ingrid, Fletcher's daughter, and an older woman soon to be revealed as Mrs Godber, Lennie's mother. They move to their respective prisoners, who greet them at their individual tables. Fletcher and Lennie are sitting at adjacent tables.

INGRID

Hello, Dad.

FLETCHER

Hello, Ingrid, love.

LENNIE

Hello, Mum.

MRS GODBER

Hello, son.

Fletcher registers Lennie's visitor and Lennie makes the introductions.

LENNIE

Oh er – this is me mum, Fletch.

MRS GODBER

Hello, Mr Fletcher.

FLETCHER

Oh, pleasure's mine, Mrs Godber. Got a fine lad there. This is my eldest, Ingrid.

INGRID

Hello.

MACKAY

(*Calling out*) Sit down, Fletcher! And you, Godber! This is not a royal garden party.

He laughs. They sit down, muttering at Mackay.

Ingrid and Fletcher lean in closely towards each other and speak intimately.

INGRID

Who's he then?

FLETCHER

That's Mr Mackay. Charmless Celtic nurk.

INGRID

And who's the boy?

FLETCHER

Oh that's Lennie. Lennie Godber, my temporary cell-mate. He's from Birmingham but he's got an 'O' Level in geography.

INGRID

Oh.

FLETCHER

Well, you have to find your way round Birmingham. Well, how's your mother then?

INGRID

Oh fine, Dad. Sends her love and everything.

FLETCHER
How's your sister?

INGRID
Oh, Marion's fine. Got a new job.

FLETCHER
Gawd, does she never keep a job for more than three weeks?

INGRID
It's the bosses she has trouble with. They molest her, she alleges.

FLETCHER
Well, that's her. Skirt right up to her expectations. Where is she now?

INGRID
Timothy White's.

FLETCHER
Oh. Oh, that's better. Shouldn't get molested there. All qualified pharmacists, aren't they?

INGRID
Her flat fell through.

FLETCHER
What flat's this?

INGRID
The one behind Olympia that she shared with six other people.

FLETCHER
Six? Fell through to the flat below I should think.

INGRID
No, the rent went up so she's home again, pro tem.

FLETCHER
And how's young Raymond?

INGRID
Oh, Raymond won the mile in the school sports.

FLETCHER
Oh, did he? Wish I had, I might not be in here now.

INGRID
And he came in second in the high jump. And he's swimming for the school. And he's stage manager in the play.

FLETCHER
Why isn't he in it? Last year he was Yum Yum in the *Mikado*.

INGRID
His voice has gone.

FLETCHER
Oh.

INGRID
Well, he's on thirty a day.

FLETCHER
Thirty a day, that's shocking. At fourteen! What a waste of money.

INGRID
He does save the coupons, Dad. He wants to buy himself an aqualung.

FLETCHER
He'll need one if he sticks to thirty a day.

INGRID
Wants to go skin diving in St Ives.

FLETCHER
I notice all his achievements are extra-curricular. Isn't there anything he fancies inside the classroom?

INGRID
Mostly the girls, Dad.

FLETCHER

(*Speaking as a parent*) Here, here!
Tell him to watch that, to curb his
appetites. Don't want him getting no
girl into trouble.

INGRID

If you hadn't I wouldn't be here.

FLETCHER

Ingrid, there's no need for coarse
remarks of that nature. I can't believe
my ears when I talk to kids today.

INGRID

There's nothing wrong, Dad. You and
Mum have proved that your love
wasn't just a passing infatuation.
Silver wedding.

FLETCHER

Nevertheless, I don't want my
adolescent love life held up as a
yardstick to young Raymond. He's
only fourteen. When what happened
happened to your mother and me we
was mature responsible sixteen-year-
olds. We had something behind us.
We was in Highgate Cemetery – it was
the tomb of Karl Marx. Your mother
had a steady job in Gamages
hardware department. And I had my
plastering diploma from Borstal.

INGRID

Yes, Dad.

FLETCHER

Speaking of Highgate Cemetery, how's
your love life? Not still that Eddie
Risley, is it?

Her look shows that it is.

FLETCHER

I warned you enough about him, gel.
He's a crook is Eddie Risley.

INGRID

Oh he's straight, Dad. Just he's a
tough businessman. It's not fair what
people keep saying about him. They
tell you he'd sell his own mother.

FLETCHER

I heard that on very good authority.

INGRID

Who from?

FLETCHER

The two blokes who bought his mother.

INGRID

It's no use talking to you about Eddie.
You got a blind spot about him.

FLETCHER

So have you, my gel. He's giving you a
bad time. Isn't he?

INGRID

I just don't know where I am with him.

FLETCHER

You do pick them, Ingrid. You're a
bonny girl with a lovely nature. You
could have anyone, you could. And
you're not getting any younger, you
know. You're twenty-four, girl. Has to
be said.

INGRID

That's not old.

FLETCHER

It is for a teenager, and a spinster.

INGRID

Oh Dad . . . things have changed
since your day. Girls want to be . . .

well, lots of girls don't want to be tied down so quick. They feel there's alternatives to marriage.

FLETCHER

Not in Muswell Hill, they don't. Nothing's changed there.

INGRID

They've twinned the Odeon.

FLETCHER

I'm talking about standards. Moral standards. All these social commentators – they don't know Britain. They all live within a stone's throw of each other in NW1. They ain't never been north of Hampstead or south of Sloane Square. But in the real world – Birmingham, Bristol, Muswell Hill – the fundamentals haven't changed – here, are you wearing a bra?

INGRID

I don't need to, Dad.

FLETCHER

You what?

INGRID

I haven't done for years. My breasts are firm and pliant.

FLETCHER

(*Whispering*) Ingrid, please. This ain't San Tropay you know, this is Slade bleedin' Prison. There's six hundred men in here would go berserk at a glimpse of shin, never mind unfettered knockers.

It's Ingrid's turn to be embarrassed.

INGRID

Dad!

FLETCHER

I'm sorry, gel, but it has to be said. You're very naïve in certain ways. Very naïve about the effect your body has on the shackled male.

INGRID

Dad, you're naïve in certain ways. I shouldn't think anyone's even noticed.

They look round. The camera reveals that all the male heads, Lennie's included, are focused firmly on Ingrid's unfettered womanhood.

3. LANDING

It is night time. There is the sound of snores and coughs.

3A. CELL

Lennie is asleep. Suddenly his bunk is shaken.

FLETCHER

Godber . . . Godber! . . . GODBER!!

Lennie opens his eyes, trying to emerge from a deep sleep.

LENNIE

What, what, what???!!!

FLETCHER

Are you awake?

LENNIE

I am now . . . what's the matter?

FLETCHER

Got any snout?

LENNIE

No. Would you believe it?

FLETCHER

(*Grumpily*) I'd believe it, you inconsiderate nurk.

LENNIE

I thought you'd given it up.

FLETCHER

I feel like starting again.

There is a pause. Fletcher gets out off the bunk and lowers himself to the floor. He looks uncharacteristically worried and preoccupied.

FLETCHER

Mind your head.

LENNIE

Me mum brought me some Maltesers.

FLETCHER

No, thanks.

LENNIE

And some of her Parkin cake.

FLETCHER

No, thanks. If you ain't got no snout, naff off back to sleep.

LENNIE

Oh thanks very much, you bad-tempered old scroat. What's wrong with you anyway?

FLETCHER

Things on my mind, ain't there?

LENNIE

Like what?

FLETCHER

My business.

LENNIE

Oh come on, Fletch. Might as well talk it out. I mean, you woke me up.

FLETCHER

Get depressed at times that's all. Stinking stir.

He kicks the table.

LENNIE

That's not like you, Fletch.

FLETCHER

A father's place is at home, with his kids – giving them affection, parental guidance. I got three of 'em, you know.

LENNIE

Yes, I know.

FLETCHER

Fourteen, nineteen and twenty-four.

LENNIE

Quite a gap between each.

FLETCHER

Circumstances dictated that.

LENNIE

How?

FLETCHER

Kept going in prison for five years, didn't I?

LENNIE

Oh.

FLETCHER

The two youngest – well, that's a terrible age the teens, in' it? You expect trouble. But Ingrid, my eldest, you'd think she'd have learnt some lessons by now.

LENNIE

She looked a nice girl to me. She had lovely –

FLETCHER

(*Quickly*) I know what she's got lovely,

Godber. It's her father you're talking to, be very careful!

LENNIE
(*Calming him*) Eyes, I was going to say. Eyes. Big and blue.

FLETCHER
(*Mollified*) Oh.

LENNIE
Nice smile too which seemed to indicate a nice disposition and a warm and generous nature.

FLETCHER
Yes, yes. True, true. That's all right then.

LENNIE
(*Carefully*) Fletch, I hope you don't mind but I couldn't help overhearing a bit of what you was saying – well, most of us did.

FLETCHER
Oh yes?

LENNIE
Doesn't sound good enough for her, that Eddie Risley, if you ask me.

FLETCHER
He ain't. He used to say he was in the motor trade – know what he did? Forged car log books. Not that she'd believe it.

LENNIE
How could you be sure?

FLETCHER
'Cos I bought two off him.
There is a pause.

FLETCHER
They weren't much cop. He'd spelt Citroën with an S . . .

LENNIE
Well, with a bit of luck he'll get rumbled sooner or later and sent away. Give her a chance to find someone new. I should think your Marion awakening to the possibilities of her sex, she'll settle down at Timothy White's. And I wouldn't worry too much about your Raymond either. I was on thirty a day when I was fourteen. Oh, and by the way, congratulations on your silver wedding.

FLETCHER
Godber, did you earwig all my conversation? Couldn't you have talked to your poor old mum? It's a long shlep from Birmingham.

LENNIE
She doesn't have much to say for herself does Mum. She's a canny old soul but she only gives me a catalogue of family ailments.

FLETCHER
What about news of the lovely Denise?

LENNIE
She don't talk about Denise 'cos she don't approve of her.

FLETCHER
Why?

LENNIE
'Cos she uses green nail varnish and doesn't wear a bra.

FLETCHER
Sounds as if she and my Ingrid have got a lot in common.
There is a pause.

LENNIE

Your Ingrid's got nicer knockers.

4. ASSOCIATION AREA

Fletcher is playing draughts. As he makes a move, Barrowclough shouts from the landing above.

BARROWCLOUGH

Fletcher . . . could I have a word.

Fletcher calls out from the table.

FLETCHER

I'm playing draughts, ain't I?

BARROWCLOUGH

It is rather important. Wouldn't ask otherwise.

FLETCHER

So's this important . . .

He makes a move. The other player makes a move and takes four of Fletcher's men.

FLETCHER

Still, if duty calls, better abandon this game, Cecil. Call it a draw. Half each.

He gets up and takes half the board with him. He walks to the stairs.

4A. CELL

Barrowclough walks in, followed by Fletcher.

BARROWCLOUGH

I'm sorry to interrupt you in association hour.

FLETCHER

'S all right. Only draughts.

BARROWCLOUGH

Not your game as a rule, is it?

FLETCHER

What else is left? Only news on the telly and someone's trod on the ping pong ball.

BARROWCLOUGH

Oh, I am sorry. Anyhow I wanted a quiet word.

FLETCHER

I'm all ears.

BARROWCLOUGH

Do you know where Godber is?

FLETCHER

He'll be at one of his poxy evening classes. What is it today, Tuesday? Tuesday – woodwork.

BARROWCLOUGH

He's up in front of the Governor.

FLETCHER

What? The kid? What's he done?

BARROWCLOUGH

He attacked another prisoner. At work, in the kitchens. He attacked Jackdaw with a soup ladle.

FLETCHER

I don't believe it.

BARROWCLOUGH

It's true. A severe and unprovoked attack the officer said.

FLETCHER

I don't believe it. I know Jackdaw gets on your wick, he gets on all our wicks but young Lennie's a passive lad, he wouldn't hurt a fly.

BARROWCLOUGH

That's why I came to you. I thought

you might be able to shed some light
on the matter.

FLETCHER

I dunno. He was his usual self this
morning. And at lunch he was quite
cheerful. Mind you, one of your
colleagues, Mr Pringle, did slip on
some orange peel and fall down
some stairs hurting his back – so
we were all quite cheerful.

BARROWCLOUGH

Fletcher, you must be serious. Godber's
in trouble. It's so irrational. I mean I like
that lad, I think he's got a lot of promise.

FLETCHER

Well, that's prison, isn't it? The system.
Already turning a nice quiet lad into a
violent criminal. You're sitting on a
volcano which at any time might erupt
in an explosion of desperate violence
and mayhem.

BARROWCLOUGH

Fletcher – you've got your finger on
the pulse. What can we do to avert it?

FLETCHER

There's only one thing which might help
to postpone the inevitable holocaust.

BARROWCLOUGH

What? What?

FLETCHER

You'll have to indent for some new
ping pong balls.

4B. FILM

*A warder unlocks the gate. Lennie
enters and walks along the catwalk*

*and past Barrowclough into
Fletcher's cell.*

4C. CELL

*Lennie goes to the bed and takes
off his jacket. Fletcher watches him
for a moment.*

FLETCHER

Well then . . .?

LENNIE

Well then what?

FLETCHER

I heard.

LENNIE

Heard what?

FLETCHER

I heard you hit Jackdaw with a ladle.

LENNIE

Heard right then, didn't you?

FLETCHER

(*Fishing*) I'm sure you had your reasons.

LENNIE

Yes, I did.

*Fletcher waits but nothing else
is forthcoming.*

FLETCHER

Ain't you going to the cooler then?

LENNIE

No. I'm not.

FLETCHER

Well, you're a lucky lad then, aren't you?

LENNIE

Lucky, am I?

FLETCHER

Assault! Ladling a fellow prisoner.
Automatic cooler offence, ladling.

LENNIE

(*Staccato*) Governor gave me a severe reprimand and loss of privileges. Would have got cooler. But accepted my mitigating circumstances.

FLETCHER

Oh . . . mitigating circumstances. Well, you must have had . . .

There is a pause.

FLETCHER

Don't have to tell me.

He gets off his bunk.

FLETCHER

Don't have to tell me what drove a normal affable lad like yourself to the pitch where he suddenly launches himself on another prisoner with a deadly weapon, to wit a ladle.

LENNIE

I won't then. Rather not.

FLETCHER

I see.

There is a pause.

FLETCHER

Doesn't occur to you that your hitherto blameless record is due in no small part to yours truly. I'm just the bloke who showed you the ropes, helped you get by, kept you on the rails, loaned you his soft toilet paper.

LENNIE

I'm not ungrateful, Fletch, honest. Every time I go to the bog, I'm not ungrateful.

FLETCHER

Godber, having eavesdropped into

every aspect of my private life, don't you think I'm entitled to know a bit of yours!

Lennie sighs then says reluctantly.

LENNIE

I had some news. Which upset me. Jackdaw thought it was a joke. Kept taking the mick. Wouldn't leave it off. So I hit him. While the balance of my mind was disturbed.

FLETCHER

News?

LENNIE

Yeah.

There is a pause.

FLETCHER

(*Sitting by Lennie*) What news?

Lennie takes a letter out of his pocket and hands it to Fletcher, who opens it.

FLETCHER

Oh, I see, it's a 'Dear John' letter, ain't it?

LENNIE

Yeah – Dear Lennie, in my case.

FLETCHER

Naturally, yours, no longer for ever, Denise, eh?

LENNIE

'S right.

FLETCHER

Dear, dear. So it's the demise of Denise then?

LENNIE

Not funny, Fletch.

FLETCHER

Was I making a joke?

LENNIE

Not what I call a joke, no.

FLETCHER

Don't you think I haven't seen this happen many, many times? Only natural. You could say inevitable. Least your Denise has been honest enough to write a letter. 'Cos they're all at it like knives while we're in here.

LENNIE

Came out of the blue though this, Fletch. No hint of it a fortnight ago in her last letter. Her only concern then was whether we should have a canary or a budgerigar.

FLETCHER

In your future life together?

LENNIE

Yes.

FLETCHER

Well, that's one decision you don't have to make.

LENNIE

No.

There is a pause.

FLETCHER

I know it's now academic, but speaking personally, from personal experience, I would say I would always without doubt plump for the budgerigar.

LENNIE

Oh, why?

FLETCHER

Budgies is friendlier. And they're very prone to draughts, canaries – it's the angle of the tail.

LENNIE

Oh.

FLETCHER

I speak from experience as I say. We had a canary once . . . surly little bleeder he was.

LENNIE

Yes, well as you say, it's a bit academic now, Fletch.

FLETCHER

So your Denise . . . has . . . er . . . she er . . . I mean er, there's another man is there, presumably?

Lennie nods.

FLETCHER

D'you know him?

LENNIE

His name's Kenneth – he's in the Merchant Navy. Third engineer, qualified. No contest, is there?

He gets up, walks across the cell and sits down again.

FLETCHER

Oh well, Jack the lad, isn't he? The blue-eyed boy with his navy blue uniform and the gold braid. Oh well, the sun shines out of his pot-hole. It's all temporary, son, all temporary. When he goes back to sea – sailor beware then. You'll be out with Denise, he'll be in the Persian Gulf. That's when you resume your rightful position, in her affections that is. I tell you, this is only a temporary setback.

LENNIE

I don't think so, Fletch.

FLETCHER
No sweat.

LENNIE
She's married him.

FLETCHER
She done what!

LENNIE
Last Saturday, Smethwick Registry Office. She thought it was my right to know.

FLETCHER
Married!

LENNIE
Apparently it kept fine for them and the Cross Keys did them proud. Pâté and ham salad.

FLETCHER
(*Rising and walking across*) Pâté and ham salad. Well, I'm appalled. Words fail me. I'm speechless. Nothing will surprise me any more. *Jackdaw comes in with his arm in a sling and his head bandaged.*

FLETCHER
Jackdaw!

JACKDAW
Now look 'ere . . .

FLETCHER
God preserve us, Jackdaw, what do you look like?

JACKDAW
All right, all right.

FLETCHER
You been driving golf balls in your cell again.

JACKDAW
Ask him!

LENNIE
(*Walking over to Jackdaw*) I'm sorry, Jackdaw, straight up. There was no call for that.

JACKDAW
What d'you get?

LENNIE
Didn't get the cooler. Deserved it.

JACKDAW
'Ere listen, no hard feelings.

LENNIE
That's good of you, Jackdaw. 'Cos you're entitled.

FLETCHER
Yes, very commendable, Jackdaw. Why don't you shake on it?

JACKDAW
I'd sooner not.
He indicates his bandaged right arm.

JACKDAW
I just come in to say that I realise that you er . . . you er . . . that there were –

FLETCHER
The circumstances was mitigating.

JACKDAW
That's it. As you say, Fletch. That I bear no grudges, 'cos obviously you've suffered a great emotional upheaval. And it'll take some time to get over. Thing like this does, doesn't it, like? But as soon as you're back to normal and my wrist is better I'll er –
He points to his head.

JACKDAW
I'll get you for this!!

5. VISITING ROOM
Ingrid is sitting in the same seat as before, facing Fletcher.
INGRID
Mum's definitely coming up next month. She would have come today only the doctor expressly forbade it. Said she'd be a fool to herself.
FLETCHER
It's nothing serious though?
INGRID
Just something going round he says.
There is a pause. Then comes the news.
INGRID
Marion ain't with Timothy White's no longer.
FLETCHER
(*With heavy sarcasm*) Dispensed with her services, did they?
INGRID
It wasn't molestation this time. But she got a job selling shirts. She shows them round the offices.
FLETCHER
Well, make a change from showing her knickers round the office.
INGRID
And she's found a flat in Maida Vale, which she's sharing with some nurses. And what you'll be most glad to hear is that Eddie and me have split up.

FLETCHER
Not before time, gel. That's a relief to us all.
A voice can be heard from their right. The camera reveals Lennie, sitting opposite his mum again.
LENNIE
Yes, we was worried about that liaison.
FLETCHER
(*Indignantly*) Do you mind, Godber! I'm sorry Mrs Godber, no offence, but I've warned the lad about this before. Ain't you got any news from your home front?
MRS GODBER
I'm sorry, it's my fault. I can never think of what to say to him. It's like visiting people in hospital.
FLETCHER
Force yourself.
Mackay bears down on them.
MACKAY
Here, here, here, here! You all know the procedure. Conversations will be confined to the relative or friend opposite the prisoner in question. There will be no fractricide.
FLETCHER
That's what I was telling him, Mr Mackay. (*Then pointedly to Lennie*) So if you'll excuse us, Godber.
LENNIE
Sorry, Fletch. Sorry miss.
He smiles at Ingrid, who smiles back.
INGRID
That's all right.

FLETCHER

So anyhow, you give Eddie the elbow then? Good for you, girl. Just listen to your old dad in future.

INGRID

I do, Dad. Ain't you noticed how much more discreet I am today?

FLETCHER

How d'you mean?

INGRID

Well, last time I was here I obviously embarrassed you in front of your friends. Well, this time, I ain't given you no cause, have I?

FLETCHER

Ain't you? I don't get you, girl.

INGRID

Oh Dad . . . look – I'm wearing a bra. *She pulls up her sweater to reveal a black bra. The entire room is goggle-eyed and sick with lust.*

6. CELL

Lennie is folding a letter into an envelope and then licks and seals it. Fletcher enters, taking something furtively from his pocket.

FLETCHER

Look at that.

It is a ping pong ball.

LENNIE

What?

FLETCHER

New ping pong ball. Two star.

LENNIE

But you don't play.

FLETCHER

(*With an expression that says, will he never learn*) I don't play. But all you other nurks do, don't you? There's a severe scarcity of ping pong balls in this nick. I'll get a quarter-pound of snout for this.

LENNIE

Oh. (*Seriously*) Fletch – can I ask you something?

FLETCHER

(*Looking for a hiding place*) Feel free.

LENNIE

You know when I was very down the other day. After Denise's letter.

FLETCHER

Yes.

LENNIE

When I was worried about the stigma of being an ex-con . . .

FLETCHER

Yes . . .

LENNIE

Well, will it be a problem for me? I mean, will I be able to work me way back into society?

FLETCHER

That depends, son. Depends on the breaks.

LENNIE

Have there been any problems for you? When you get out?

FLETCHER

Not for me, no. I've never had to worry about no references, no testimonials. 'Cos I've always gone straight, straight back into crime. It's different with you,

Lennie – you're young, you're healthy, you've got an honest face.

LENNIE
Is that enough?

FLETCHER
Yes, yes. Character. That's what I can read. And you've got it, son. You're a good lad.

LENNIE
So you think, if someone really cared for me, a girl, like . . . she'd overlook my past misdemeanours?

FLETCHER
Certainly. If she's any sort of human being of course she would. Like anybody would. Lennie, my son, you have to learn to believe in yourself. I believe in you.

LENNIE
Do you, Fletch?

FLETCHER
'Course I do.

Lennie is cheered by this.

LENNIE
Oh good. I'm going to send this then.

He holds up the letter.

LENNIE
Would you give it to your mucker Barrowclough? To post in the village.

FLETCHER
(*Reading the address*) BBC . . .?

LENNIE
It's on plain notepaper, so they won't know it's from a prisoner.

FLETCHER
'Hello Young Lovers Corner.' Oh gawd.

Is all this soul-searching for the benefit of that slag Denise?

LENNIE
No, not her.

FLETCHER
Well who?

LENNIE
Ingrid.

FLETCHER
(*Quietly*) My Ingrid . . .

LENNIE
(*Quoting his letter*) Yeah . . . 'Our eyes met across a crowded room . . .'

FLETCHER
My daughter Ingrid!

LENNIE
'And though we didn't know each other, we both knew . . .'

FLETCHER
(*Exploding*) You think I'd let my beloved Ingrid take up with the likes of you! A bleeding juvenile delinquent from the backstreets of Birmingham!

He raises his fist, about to bring it down on Lennie.

LENNIE
(*Urgently*) Fletch, be careful, be careful.

FLETCHER
(*Checked*) What?

Lennie unclenches Fletcher's fist.

LENNIE
You've crushed your ping-pong ball!

SERIES TWO

EPISODE THREE: DISTURBING THE PEACE

1. LIBRARY

Fletcher is stacking the old books on to a trolley when the door is unlocked and Barrowclough enters.

BARROWCLOUGH

Right, Fletcher, you'd better get on your rounds, hospital and Governor.

FLETCHER

Just picking something out special for the Governor, Mr Barrowclough. Got a good one for his wife an' all. 'A Perilous Odyssey of Love and Anguish Set in Turbulent Tuscany'. Very torrid according to the write-up.

BARROWCLOUGH

Not too torrid, is it?

FLETCHER

Have no fear. It's done in very good taste. They always put the lights out.

BARROWCLOUGH

Come on then, let's get along.

He is trying to rush Fletcher. Fletcher produces a paper.

FLETCHER

Oh, just before we go, could you sign this, Mr Barrowclough? Requisition for new books. I know

how busy you are so don't trouble to read it, just sign at the bottom where I've indicated.

Fletcher has placed the paper in front of him, but Barrowclough hesitates.

BARROWCLOUGH

Just have a quick glance through . . .

FLETCHER

(*Disapprovingly*) Well, we are a bit behindhand, I mean, chop chop.

Barrowclough, however, insists on checking the list, then frowns.

BARROWCLOUGH

There's several here quite unsuitable, not suitable at all. Look at this . . .

FLETCHER

What?

BARROWCLOUGH

(*Shocked*) The Great Escape . . . Nudes of the Naughty Nineties . . . A History of Erotica.

FLETCHER

I couldn't find it on the map.

BARROWCLOUGH

I can't let these through, Fletcher. They're mostly sexual or subversive.

He scratches them out.

FLETCHER

Oh, leave *Voodoo Woman*. It's a classic, that.

BARROWCLOUGH

You've got a very privileged job in this library, Fletcher. Take care you don't lose it.

He gives the list back to Fletcher, who, disgruntled, looks at what has survived the censor's pen.

FLETCHER

I see you've allowed the Enid Blyton Omnibus. The lads'll be chuffed about that.

BARROWCLOUGH

There is a limit.

FLETCHER

Yes, yes, I can appreciate your point of view. There's always two sides, isn't there? Sort of thing I want to bring out in my forthcoming book.

BARROWCLOUGH

Book!

FLETCHER

Well, working in the library has rekindled my literary aspirations. So I'm working on this book, see. On prison life. From the man within, like.

BARROWCLOUGH

(*Not keen*) Prison life.

FLETCHER

Ah, but don't worry, I'm very objective. I haven't overlooked the difficult task which confronts you brave boys in blue and I've sought to shed light on your problems as much as the ones faced by my fellow felons.

BARROWCLOUGH

(*Reassured*) Oh good, good. What are you going to call your book, Fletcher?

FLETCHER

Don't Let the Bastards Grind You Down. *Fletcher exits, pushing his trolley.*

2. GOVERNOR'S OFFICE

Mr Venables is sitting at his desk going through the mail with his secretary, Mrs Heskith. She is in her latish thirties, a local lady wearing sensible shoes.

VENABLES

Is this all the mail then, Mrs Heskith?

MRS HESKITH

Yes, Mr Venables. The Home Office have confirmed the dates of Mr Mackay's promotion course.

Venables picks up the relevant letter, studying it doubtfully for a moment.

VENABLES

What? Yes, yes . . . it's difficult enough running a prison without losing someone of Mr Mackay's calibre.

MRS HESKITH

Don't forget Tuesday is the magistrates' inspection.

VENABLES

Oh is it? We'd better put on a bit of a

show for them. We'll have a roast, and get out the tinned pears . . . with cream.

MRS HESKITH
Cream?

VENABLES
Well, you know . . . Carnation milk or whatever it is.

MRS HESKITH
Right, I'll get along then.
She goes to the door and bumps into Fletcher who enters, pushing his little trolleyload of books.

FLETCHER
Oh good morning, Mrs Heskith, what a rare treat.
She gives him a coy smile and tries to edge round his trolley, a little flustered.

MRS HESKITH
Oh yes, good morning, Fletcher.

FLETCHER
What a lovely cardigan. Goes with your eyes, two of your best features if I may say so, tho' I expect you've been told many times before –

VENABLES
Fletcher, what is it?

FLETCHER
Oh. Morning, sir.

VENABLES
Thank you, Mrs Heskith. You'd better go and get me that release form to sign.
She leaves. Fletcher gives her a quick appraisal as she goes.

FLETCHER
(*Sotto voce*) Well I would, if you wouldn't.

VENABLES
What is it, Fletcher?

FLETCHER
Books, sir. New consignment, sir. You always like to have first pick of a new consignment.

VENABLES
It's not a question of first pick. I like to look them over to ensure there's nothing unsuitable for the men.

FLETCHER
I found one book you wanted, sir.
He gives him a book.

VENABLES
(*Puzzled*) Tom Brown's Schooldays.

FLETCHER
The title's irrelevant, sir. Point is it's exactly three-quarters of an inch thick, which is just what you said you wanted to prop up your wobbly bookcase.

VENABLES
Oh splendid, Fletcher. Thank you.
Venables bends down to prop up the desk with the book, withdrawing a telephone directory. Fletcher automatically takes the opportunity to pocket what he can: a rubber, a pencil sharpener, a felt pen, two cigarettes from an open packet and a paper clip. He also cranes his head to read the letter about Mackay, showing more than a passing interest in it. Then he straightens himself up, just as Venables is also doing so.

VENABLES

Yes, that's much better. Much better. Well, Fletcher, cut along.

Mrs Heskith re-enters with a release form for signature. Fletcher again watches her, as he makes to go.

MRS HESKITH

The release form, sir.

VENABLES

Oh good . . . where's my pen?

Not surprisingly, he cannot find it on the desk.

FLETCHER

Oh . . . borrow mine, sir.

He produces Venables's pen.

VENABLES

Oh, thank you, Fletcher.

He takes it and signs the form, handing it back to Mrs Heskith and pocketing the pen.

Meanwhile Fletcher is looking at her, causing her some slight embarrassment.

VENABLES

Go on then, Fletcher.

FLETCHER

Yes sir, it's just –

VENABLES

What, what?

FLETCHER

My pen, sir.

VENABLES

Oh I'm terribly sorry.

He hands it back.

FLETCHER

They all look alike, don't they, sir?

3. ASSOCIATION AREA

It is evening, association time.
Mackay walks around the men.

3A. CELL

Fletcher is emptying his pockets and putting the items on the table.

LENNIE

Is that it, then?

FLETCHER

Yes – apart from a very interesting bit of information. I always learn something when I go in the Governor's office.

LENNIE

Like what?

FLETCHER

Well . . . apart from the fact that there's something simmering between him and Mrs Heskith – which we'll bear in mind for future reference, won't we – I also saw a memo on Venables's desk. Upside down of course, but years of being in the nick have taught me to read memos upside down.

LENNIE

What did it say?

FLETCHER

'Eciffo emoh, laitnedifnoc'.

LENNIE

What the hell's that mean?

FLETCHER
'Home Office, Confidential', backwards.

LENNIE
What was it about then?

FLETCHER
Something to do with Mackay's going
on a course.

LENNIE
When, where, what course?

FLETCHER
Naff off, you nurk, I only had four
seconds. But I reckon it must be
something to do with promotion
or transfer.

LENNIE
He ain't let on, like.

FLETCHER
He don't know yet, only me and the
Governor knows so far.

MACKAY
(Offscreen) Come on, you men!

LENNIE
Aren't those his dulcet tones now, on
the landing? Shall we ask him?

FLETCHER
No, no, no. We've got a situation here
which I can turn to my advantage.

MACKAY
(Offscreen) Get your hair cut.

FLETCHER
(Getting paper) No time like the
present – pretend you're listening.
*Fletcher reads the paper. Lennie
gets on his bunk.*

FLETCHER
I see here, Godber, that with Saturn

passing through your opposite sign
of Cancer, this may be an exhausting
and turbulent month for you. Must
be moving you out the kitchens on
to dustbins.

MACKAY
Seeking solace in the stars now,
are we?

FLETCHER
Oh evening, Mr Mackay. If you'll
excuse me – 'As Uranus is one of
the most powerful and unpredictable
planets – future events will be
likewise unpredictable.'

MACKAY
I should have thought all your futures
were somewhat predictable – hm, hm,
hm . . . Now if your stars were true
they would say, 'Little change for the
next four years. No opportunities for
travel, and absolutely no prospect of
romance on the horizon.'

FLETCHER
Only a question of scale. When
you're deprived of romance as what
we are, a chance brush with the
Governor's secretary is like a naughty
weekend in Boulogne with a teenage
nymphomaniac, see it's only a
question of scale.

LENNIE
When's your birthday, Mr Mackay?

MACKAY
April the twenty-fifth.

FLETCHER
(Looking in the paper) Oh yes, Taurus.

Not the subtlest of signs. The bull.
Here we are. 'Endeavours you have
been hoping for come to fruition.'
Oh look at this . . . 'A favourable
time for a move and seeking
opportunities elsewhere.'

MACKAY

Poppycock.

FLETCHER

No, they're rarely wrong. You must be
moving on, Mr Mackay.

LENNIE

Holiday?

MACKAY

Not till August.

LENNIE

Your retirement's not due just yet, is it?

MACKAY

Don't be insolent, Godber.

FLETCHER

Well, it's very clear in the stars, very
clear. A move is clearly indicated.

MACKAY

Out of the question.

FLETCHER

Want a bet?

MACKAY

You'd wager on this nonsense?

FLETCHER

When it's as clear as this I would.
Doesn't do to deride what you don't
know. The paranormal, the psychic.
Take my Uncle Godfrey. Walked
under a ladder one day. Laughed
about it he did. Walked under it.
Purposely, like. And d'you know,

over the next forty-three years he lost
all his teeth.

MACKAY

You'd lose your shirt betting on this
astronomical nonsense.

FLETCHER

It's not nonsense. I'll bet you
anything that within a few days
you'll be leaving your familiar
surroundings.

MACKAY

Step outside, Fletcher.

FLETCHER

What have I said now?

MACKAY

Step outside.

*Fletcher gets up, passes Mackay
and goes out. Mackay follows him
out of the cell.*

MACKAY

You have the nerve to offer to bet
with a prison officer? In front of
young Godber.

FLETCHER

Oh, I never thought, Mr Mackay.

MACKAY

What are you trying to do, disillusion
the boy?

FLETCHER

Sorry, Mr Mackay.

MACKAY

How much then?

FLETCHER

A quid?

MACKAY

You're on.

4. PRISON GATES

Camera shows a minibus. Mackay approaches it, shakes hands with Venables and gets in. Cheering is heard from prisoners on work detail.

5. ASSOCIATION AREA

It is night time. Fletcher is at a table with McLaren, Warren and Williams, who are playing draughts. Fletcher himself is reading the Sun. The mood is relaxed.

WARREN

Eh, did he pay up, Fletch?

FLETCHER

Certainly. With all the ill-grace you'd expect from that charmless Celtic nurk.

They grin in satisfaction.

McLAREN

Twos up with that paper, eh?

FLETCHER

When I've finished.

WARREN

You've had it long enough. Are there some nice birds in it?

FLETCHER

I ain't looking at birds, am I? I'm reading the editorial. I'm not like you lot. All you want out a paper is horses and nudes. Some of us is a bit curious about what's going on in the world. I like to keep abreast.

Lennie joins them at the table, wearing his kitchen whites.

LENNIE

Yes, he does. Got breasts pasted all over our cell.

Fletcher looks at him.

FLETCHER

What!

The others chuckle.

WILLIAMS

I'm not a breast man myself.

FLETCHER

I beg your pardon, Mr Williams?

WILLIAMS

My initial interest is always awakened by the leg.

FLETCHER

Just one of them?

McLAREN

I hear you're a bit of a ladies' man on the outside, Williams.

WILLIAMS

I've had my moments. I have a large sexual appetite, see. Probably compensating for those years of deprivation in the Bridge End Choral School. Consequentially I suffer more than most in prison.

Fletcher finishes reading the paper, which is grabbed by McLaren.

FLETCHER

Well listen, from what I just been reading I think we're better off in here. This country's on the verge of economic ruin. This once great nation is hovering on the brink of the abyss.

MCLAREN
That's the bosses' fault.

FLETCHER
It's not the bosses, Vanessa, it's the average man. The people who'd rather draw National Assistance than take a job. People who won't do a decent day's work for a decent day's wages . . . people much like ourselves.

WARREN
My Elaine says she doesn't know where it's going to stop.

FLETCHER
What?

WARREN
Prices, like. No one's got any money.

LENNIE
By the time you lot get out of here, there'll be no one worth robbing.

FLETCHER
By then Britain should be reaping the benefits of North Sea oil. Can tell the A-rabs to stuff it and can we please buy London back.

MCLAREN
Scottish oil. Don't forget that. Scottish oil.

FLETCHER
Oh, listen to the Scottish Nationalist, all of a sudden. Well, well, would you believe it. A dusky Rob Roy. What tartan do you wear, the Black Watch?

MCLAREN
Naff off, Fletcher.

FLETCHER
All right so it's Scottish oil. It's English expertise what'll get it out.

LENNIE
Texan.

FLETCHER
(*Exasperated*) I don't know why I get drawn into these pointless arguments with you nurks. The only point I was trying so painstakingly to make is that we're better off inside.

WARREN
He's not wrong, I've known worse stir.

WILLIAMS
Me an' all.

FLETCHER
Right. And with Mackay gone . . . happy days are here again. Chance to work a few things, in't there?

WILLIAMS
True. Old Barrowclough don't exactly rule with a rod of iron, does he?

FLETCHER
We can start having a flutter again. What about frog racing? We could revive that. Get them from the farm.

WILLIAMS
Should I tell you something about frogs? Which is a fact. Like me, the frog has an exceptional sexual appetite. When the frog and his mate, mate, he's at it for twenty-eight days non-stop.

LENNIE
Twenty-eight days.

WILLIAMS
Non-stop.

FLETCHER

No wonder his eyes bulge out.

Barrowclough enters through the gates with Wainwright.

FLETCHER

Oh gawd.

WARREN

What's up, Fletch?

FLETCHER

Happy days. Life of Riley. I think they're over.

LENNIE

What you talking about?

FLETCHER

You heard me mention a screw in Brixton, Napper Wainwright. Right bastard.

LENNIE

Yeah, why?

FLETCHER

He's just walked in the door, that's why.

They all turn to see Wainwright and Barrowclough walking behind one of the other tables to the guarded curiosity of the prisoners sitting at it.

WARREN

He looks a right one.

MCLAREN

You don't suppose he's Mackay's replacement?

FLETCHER

That's exactly what I am supposing.

LENNIE

Living legend, isn't he, in the Prison Service?

FLETCHER

Not only that, he's got promotion. Stripes, isn't it? Well, lads . . . let's hope success has mellowed him.

As if for an answer, we hear Wainwright bawl out an unfortunate prisoner, in a voice which reveals him as a Londoner.

WAINWRIGHT

(*Rapidly*) Something to say to me, have you? Have you? Well my name's Wainwright. You address me as 'Mr Wainwright' or 'Sir'. Now button your lip!

FLETCHER

It has!

WARREN

He's coming over.

Wainwright approaches them.

WAINWRIGHT

Norman Stanley Fletcher, on your feet. I knew our paths would cross again, my son. The day you left Brixton I said to you, 'This is not goodbye, Fletcher, this is merely au-revoir.'

FLETCHER

I have to admit you did, Mr Wainwright, and I said to you, 'Why don't you . . .' That is, I gave you certain advice regarding the Warders' Comfort Offertory Box.

WAINWRIGHT

I haven't forgotten what you said!

FLETCHER

And did you manage it?

Wainwright's narrowed eyes promise future retribution.

WAINWRIGHT

It doesn't pay to come it with me, Fletcher. You remember me.

He widens his audience to include the rest of the group at the table.

WAINWRIGHT

I have this mean streak, see. I know it's despicable but I'm prejudiced.

MCLAREN

That'll make a nice change.

WAINWRIGHT

Sonny Jim, I'm not just prejudiced against you lot . . . *I'm* prejudiced against – *(Rapid-fire)* liberals, longhairs, pill-heads, winos, queens, slags, squealers, pikeys and grease-balls. Are you in there, sonny?

He has suddenly switched his attention to Lennie.

FLETCHER

Isn't everybody?

WAINWRIGHT

Quiet, Fletcher, I was talking to the boy. I said, are you in there?

Lennie thinks seriously about it, then speaks with some relief.

LENNIE

I don't think so, I'm Church of England.

Wainwright's look once more promises further retribution. The others snigger.

WAINWRIGHT

We've only just met, and already he's given me a grudge to bear.

Barrowclough comes over to join Wainwright.

BARROWCLOUGH

Oh, I see you men have been getting acquainted with Mr Wainwright.

CHORUS

(Not thrilled) Yes, yes . . .

FLETCHER

Some of us have had that dubious privilege earlier in our careers.

BARROWCLOUGH

Oh really?

WAINWRIGHT

(Indicating Fletcher) This one passed through Brixton on a couple of brief but memorable occasions.

BARROWCLOUGH

Oh well, it's nice to bump into old faces, old . . .

FLETCHER

Adversaries.

BARROWCLOUGH

No no, that's not the word, Fletcher. I keep telling these men, Mr Wainwright, that our role is to help them . . . to encourage them in a programme of self-improvement and rehabilitation. To prepare them for going back into society.

WAINWRIGHT

Our role, Mr Barrowclough, is to keep them away from society. Our role is to keep these scheming bastards locked in.

He strides away.

BARROWCLOUGH

Yes, well I . . . I expect he's a bit tired after the long journey.

He goes after Wainwright.

MCLAREN

Spoke too soon, Fletch.

WILLIAMS

(*Singing*) Happy days are here again . . .

They all join in.

WAINWRIGHT

(*Offscreen*) Quiet!

The singing stops abruptly.

6. CANTEEN

Wainwright comes in, surveys the scene, then walks along behind the line of men being served. Lennie is dishing out potatoes. As Wainwright gets level with Lennie some potato drops on Wainwright's shoe. He indicates for Lennie to come to him.

Lennie does so. He wipes the potato off Wainwright's shoe, then goes back to serving again.

6A. ASSOCIATION

A group of prisoners is watching a boxing match on television. Camera shows a hand which switches the set off. It is Wainwright, who says:

WAINWRIGHT

Beddy byes . . .

6B. CORRIDOR

Fletcher and other prisoners are washing the floor. Camera shows feet as they walk over floor leaving marks.

FLETCHER

Oh Mr Wainwright, now look what you've done.

Wainwright walks back to Fletcher.

FLETCHER

Have to do it all again now.

He gets a cloth from the bucket and throws it on the floor. It splashes Wainwright's boot. Fletcher washes the floor. Wainwright moves and steps on his hand.

7. CELL

Fletcher is unbandaging his hand. Lennie is building a model.

LENNIE

What a swine, stepping on your hand like that.

FLETCHER

Be fair. Complete accident. His foot slipped. He was aiming for my head.

LENNIE

What are we going to do about it, Fletch?

FLETCHER

I'll have a word with Warren and McLaren, they're dab hands at sabotage.

LENNIE

Your stars didn't predict this, did they?

FLETCHER

Yes, well, that's all a load of cobblers isn't it? . . .

Barrowclough appears at the cell door.

BARROWCLOUGH

Mind if I come in?

FLETCHER

All right, wipe your feet.

Barrowclough enters.

LENNIE

You look a bit bushed, Mr Barrowclough.

BARROWCLOUGH

Well, I am. It's that Mr Wainwright. He's been through this prison like a dose of salts. He's reorganised the entire duty roster.

FLETCHER

Oh, tough titty. Any idea how many curtailments we've suffered? No fraternising in the exercise yard. Shorter telly hours. And he's only commandeered our ping-pong table for your bleeding mess.

BARROWCLOUGH

Only until our billiard table's been recovered.

FLETCHER

Oh yes, well . . .

BARROWCLOUGH

Well, it's your fault it needed recovering.

FLETCHER

Our fault?

BARROWCLOUGH

Some prisoner certainly tampered with it.

FLETCHER

Can you prove that?

BARROWCLOUGH

We can at least surmise it. When Nosher Garrett went over the wall he was picked up in Blackpool wearing a green baize suit.

FLETCHER

Look, I'm not being drawn into any more pointless arguments.

BARROWCLOUGH

No . . . well, I really came to say cheerio, 'cos you won't be seeing so much of me in the future. He's got me down for a transfer to the farm.

LENNIE

What?

BARROWCLOUGH

Says I should just be in charge of trusties. Says I'm not really suited to a cell block. Where I'm at the mercy of infractious and recalcitrant prisoners like yourself, Fletcher – no offence you understand, these are his words, not mine.

FLETCHER

Look, Mr Barrowclough, we've got to prevent this.

He gets up and goes across to Barrowclough.

FLETCHER

Trouble is you see, if truth be told,

your humanity is mistaken by them
nurks as mollycoddling.

BARROWCLOUGH

I've only tried to be fair and
encourage them –

FLETCHER

'Course you have. I knows that, and
you know that. But you'll have to
change your ways. If you don't want
to spend the rest of your life down
the farm, knee deep in cow dung in
charge of trusty udder-pullers.

BARROWCLOUGH

Change my ways?

FLETCHER

Yeah. Don't let people take advantage.
Come on strong. Wield the big stick.

LENNIE

Put on a bit of a show, like.
You know . . . Mean, moody
and magnificent.

There is a pause.

BARROWCLOUGH

Oh, I don't know.

8. CANTEEN

*Camera shows food, trays, men
being served. A Prison Officer is
walking up the line of prisoners.
Lennie, who is serving, looks at
McLaren. McLaren looks at
Fletcher. Fletcher gets up and goes.
He looks at the clock. Fletcher
nods. Warren receives nod and
nods the other way. McLaren
receives nod and turns to Lennie.*

MCLAREN

Hey you. I'm talking to you.

LENNIE

Me?

Heads turn.

MCLAREN

Yes you, Fanny Craddock . . . there's a
caterpillar on my plate.

LENNIE

Well a caterpillar don't eat much.

MCLAREN

You what?

*He leans across the counter and
grabs Lennie.*

LENNIE

Ease up, Mac, it's only a make-
believe riot.

MCLAREN

I know kid, but I have to make it
look authentic.

LENNIE

But you're strangling me.

MCLAREN

I know, but nothing personal, you
understand. This food's no fit for
swine. We've had enough, lads.

Warren gets up.

WARREN

We want a riot.

*Camera shows tables being turned
up, food being upset, plates
dropped, Lennie with peas over his
head thrown by McLaren. A Prison
Officer blows his whistle and is
showered with potatoes.
Alarm bells start ringing.*

Prison warders come running.
There is the noise of cell doors
being slammed. The warders run
along the catwalk.
Camera shows Wainwright's head
as he comes into view. The door
is unlocked and he goes into
the canteen.
The prisoners stop.
Wainwright starts to speak but food
is thrown at him and he finally
backs out.

9. GOVERNOR'S OFFICE

Camera shows a tray with a
glass of water and two pink pills.
Mrs Heskith gives it to Venables.

VENABLES

Thank you, Mrs Heskith.

He gulps the pills down.

MRS HESKITH

You're only supposed to take two
before retiring.

VENABLES

If we don't put a stop to this riot, that
may be tomorrow.

Mrs Heskith leans over the desk.
Fletcher comes in at that moment,
pulling his trolley load of books.

FLETCHER

Oops! Oopsadaisy! Sorry.

VENABLES

What on earth do you want, Fletcher?

FLETCHER

Another load of new books, sir.

VENABLES

At a time like this!

FLETCHER

Oh yes, well I wasn't to know, was I . . .

VENABLES

I'm referring to the riot!

FLETCHER

Oh, the riot, yes. Another nasty
situation, sir.

VENABLES

It is indeed. At the moment there's a
systematic and wilful destruction of
furniture and crockery. They're knee
deep in plates in there.

FLETCHER

Like a Greek restaurant on New
Year's Eve.

VENABLES

Don't be flippant, Fletcher. I'd've
thought Mr Wainwright would have
been the ideal man for this situation,
but he seemed to make matters worse.

FLETCHER

If truth were told, sir, it's Mr Wainwright
what aggravated the situation now in
the first place. Now that's just between
me, you, Mrs Heskith and the bedpost.

MRS HESKITH

I'll just get this typed up then.

VENABLES

I suppose I'll have to go down
there myself.

FLETCHER

No offence, sir, but there's only one man in this prison who could quell that riot. Only one man who could confront that ugly vicious mob and defuse the powder keg of emotion.

VENABLES

Who? Who?

10. FARM

Barrowclough is supervising the prisoners working on the pig farm. He turns.

BARROWCLOUGH

Me, what do you mean me?

11. CANTEEN

Riot is still going on.
McLaren is shouting 'Load, aim, fire!' Food is being thrown. The firing party throws potatoes. Barrowclough goes to the canteen door. A PO unlocks it and Barrowclough walks in. The door is shut behind him. Barrowclough walks into the canteen. The prisoners stop.

BARROWCLOUGH

Now we . . . why don't we all put those things down?

The prisoners do so.

BARROWCLOUGH

This mess will all have to be cleared up, you know.

They start to clear up.

BARROWCLOUGH

Not yet though . . . In the meantime, why don't we all file back to our cells in an orderly fashion.

The prisoners start to file out of the canteen. As Lennie passes Barrowclough he stops.

LENNIE

Mean, moody, magnificent!

11A. YARD/LANDING

Camera shows Warren and McLaren being marched across the yard. They enter through the gate on to the prison landing and walk along the catwalk. The prisoners congratulate them.

12. CELL

Fletcher and Lennie are in their cell.

FLETCHER

(*Speaking through the door*) Well done, lads.

LENNIE

Congratulations.

Warren and McLaren walk in.

MCLAREN

Worth it, wasn't it?

FLETCHER

Well worth it, my son.

MCLAREN

Barrowclough's back on the landing, then?

FLETCHER

Yes and Wainwright's back in Brixton, where he belongs. Loss of face, wasn't it? Had to leave, bloke like that.

MCLAREN

So happy days are here again, eh?

FLETCHER

Normal service has been resumed.

They all laugh.

Meanwhile Mackay has entered the association area and is looking around, when he hears laughter from Fletcher's cell. He walks to it and goes in. Fletcher catches his eye at last.

Mackay looks.

FLETCHER

Oh . . . Mr Mackay, what a nice surprise. Nice surprise, isn't it, lads?

McLaren and Warren leave.

MACKAY

I thought it might be, Fletcher. I think some of you wrongly assumed that I had left, gone for good, but as you see nothing could be further from the truth. Only I'm somewhat disturbed to hear what's been happening in my absence. So now, we're going to have a new regime here. Based not on leniency and laxity but discipline, hard work, and blind unquestioning

obedience. Feet will not touch the ground, and lives will be made a misery – I'm BACK and I'M IN CHARGE HERE.

Mackay leaves.

Fletcher and Lennie look at each other.

Mackay is walking along the catwalk when suddenly he hears Fletcher and Lennie singing 'For he's a jolly good fellow'. The camera shows Fletcher and Lennie singing in their cell. Gradually other prisoners are heard joining in the singing.

2 SERIES TWO

EPISODE FOUR: NO PEACE FOR THE WICKED

1. ASSOCIATION AREA
Fletcher walks along the catwalk with a mug of tea and a magazine towards his cell. McLaren is fixing his boots. Then he moves off upstairs towards Fletcher's cell.

1A. FLETCHER'S CELL
Fletcher comes into his cell with the mug of tea and magazine. He is singing to himself.

FLETCHER
Born free . . .
Till somebody shopped me
Now I'm doing solitree.
McLaren walks in.

MCLAREN
Got any chewing gum, Fletch?

FLETCHER
(*Chewing*) No, never use it.

MCLAREN
Aw come on, you mean old scroat.
Fletcher reluctantly scoops a piece of gum out of his pocket, tears it in half and hands it over.

FLETCHER
Here you are – don't eat it all at once.

MCLAREN
Ta. Going to watch the game?

FLETCHER
Naff off.

MCLAREN
Be a guid game.

FLETCHER
What, A and B Wing, that bloodbath.

MCLAREN
If we win we win the trophy.

FLETCHER
What trophy?

MCLAREN
It's a silver cup.

FLETCHER
Correction. It was a silver cup. It disappeared from the Governor's office on Tuesday night.

MCLAREN
Who'd have done that?

FLETCHER
I can't be sure but I've narrowed it down to six hundred suspects.

MCLAREN
Never see that again. Be melted down by now.

FLETCHER

Just have to play for the honour
of the wing, won't you?

MCLAREN

You should cheer us on, Fletch.
It's your wing.

FLETCHER

It's not my wing. I just happen to be
incarcerated in this wing. At Her
Majesty's pleasure. It's not your wing
neither, is it? I'm surprised at you
coming the Tom Brown's schooldays
bit. Tom Black's schooldays, yes.

MCLAREN

I'm not. When I'm out there I'm
playing for Morton. Against Celtic at
Hampden. And we stuff them.

FLETCHER

I've got better things to do than watch
people being stuffed at football.

MCLAREN

Got visitors?

FLETCHER

No.

MCLAREN

Got a card game going?

FLETCHER

No.

MCLAREN

Just watching the box, are you?

FLETCHER

No. Three times wrong in a row.

MCLAREN

What you doing then?

FLETCHER

I'm going fox-hunting, aren't I?

MCLAREN

No, seriously – you ought to do
something. You've got five years,
Fletch. If you don't do anything your
stretch will be endless.

FLETCHER

Here listen to me, sonny Jock.
Don't tell me how to survive in here.
I was doing time when you was
running around stealing mangoes on
the plantation.

MCLAREN

What do you mean, plantation? I
was brought up in a Greenock
housing estate!

FLETCHER

All right, when you were
stealing mangoes on a Greenock
housing estate.

He gets up on his bunk.

MCLAREN

It's a beautiful day out there as well.

FLETCHER

It's a beautiful day in here as well –
d'you know why? 'Cos all you lot are
out there. That's what I like about the
weekend. You're playing football,
others are gambling away their hard-
earned money, some of them are
indulging in their pathetic hobbies.
And I ends up with some peace and
quiet. Go on then – enjoy your game.
Take no prisoners.

*McLaren goes. Fletcher gets off his
bunk and walks across the cell,
humming to himself.*

FLETCHER

'I believe for every drop of rain
that falls . . .'

Warren walks in.

Fletcher notices him.

FLETCHER

Oh – what do you want?

WARREN

Me and Mini Cooper want to go and
play ping-pong.

FLETCHER

Don't let me stop yer.

WARREN

Er well . . . there aren't any balls, like.
And Lugless Douglas said you had one.

FLETCHER

Who told Lugless?

WARREN

He just heard.

FLETCHER

He just what?

WARREN

Is it true?

FLETCHER

I've got one hidden – yes.

WARREN

Would you lend us it then?

FLETCHER

Lease. Let us discuss the possibility of
leasing you the ball, Bunny. Then we
might have some basis for negotiation.

WARREN

How much is it then?

FLETCHER

One snout . . .

Warren starts to get one.

FLETCHER

Ah, ah, ah . . . per hour. Minimum
three hours.

WARREN

You're a hard man, Fletch.

FLETCHER

No. I'm not hard – I'm just taking
advantage of something which
happened to bounce my way. If you
was dealing with Harry Grout's
syndicate you'd have to leave your
wristwatch as a deposit against the
ball being trod on. And if you didn't
return the ball your wristwatch would
get trod on . . . ad infinitum.

WARREN

All right, Fletch, you're on.

He hands over the snout.

FLETCHER

What's this then?

WARREN

It's good shag, honest.

FLETCHER

All right . . .

He puts it away.

WARREN

Where's the ball then?

FLETCHER

Oh yes.

He gets the ball.

WARREN

It's a funny colour.

FLETCHER

I got it off McLaren.

WARREN

D'you want a game yourself later?

FLETCHER

Certainly not. Don't do you no good exercise.

WARREN

Helps to pass the time.

FLETCHER

I don't need any help to pass the time, thank you.

Warren leaves.

FLETCHER

Next?

Banyard puts his head round the door.

BANYARD

Erm, Fletcher . . .

FLETCHER

(*With a look saying what is it now!*) Yes?

BANYARD

Erm . . . a few of us have formed a drama group.

FLETCHER

(*Unenthusiastically*) Oh yes.

BANYARD

Well, I was wondering – do you have any theatrical inclinations?

FLETCHER

No.

BANYARD

You don't necessarily have to act. You could be prompter or work the lights or operate the wind machine.

FLETCHER

(*Getting on to bunk*) The wind machine, what you want one of those for, just enlist Ives, he's a walking wind machine he is.

BANYARD

We want to do some contemporary plays, we thought we'd start with a thriller, *Wait Until Dark*, d'you remember that one? They made a film of it with Audrey Hepburn.

FLETCHER

I don't think I could slim down in time.

BANYARD

Oh there's no shortage of Audrey Hepburns, it's prompters and lighting men we need.

FLETCHER

I don't really go for the theatre much. Now if you was getting up a concert party, well . . . could maybe help you out there. Singing. 'Cos in the old days I was always round the pubs in North London you know, like the Angel, Walthamstow, Friday nights. 'Ladzangenelmen . . . let's have a big hand for Frankie Fletcher.' 'Course it's Norman really, but Frankie sounded better, was more showbiz, know what I mean? What was the one we used to do? I say 'we' 'cos I was backed by Ted Prendergast and the Organaires. You remember Ted Prendergast?

BANYARD

I don't think so.

FLETCHER

You should do. He was on *Workers' Playtime* once. A cardboard factory in Letchworth.

BANYARD

No, I would have remembered.

FLETCHER

Yes – I suppose you would. We used
to do – (*Singing*) See the pyramids
along the Nile

Watch the sunrise on a tropic isle . . .

BANYARD

No, we're not doing a concert party.

FLETCHER

Oh well then, naff off Sir Lawrence,
leave me be, eh.

BANYARD

I just thought it might relieve
the boredom.

FLETCHER

The boredom will be relieved as soon
as you leave this room.

BANYARD

Oh charming . . .

He starts to go.

FLETCHER

Give my love to Miss Hepburn.

*Fletcher settles back on his bunk
and opens Penthouse.*

FLETCHER

(*Singing*) Time on my hands . . .

*He opens the centrefold and looks
at the girl.*

FLETCHER

You in my arms . . .

*He glances towards the door
where a large wooden mule
can be seen peering round.
Fletcher looks away, then looks
back again.*

FLETCHER

What are you looking at?

The mule is still there.

FLETCHER

All right then, I give up.

*Blanco comes in through
the doorway.*

FLETCHER

Hello, Blanco.

BLANCO

Hello, Fletch.

FLETCHER

Would you mind explaining?

BLANCO

(*Wheeling mule in*) It's my Muffin.
It's Muffin the Mule. You know him
what's on television.

FLETCHER

Muffin the Mule on television.
When was the last time you
watched television?

BLANCO

Some time back. I've been too busy
making him.

FLETCHER

Well, he's very lovely. Is there any
particular reason why you bring him
round here though?

BLANCO

Just finished him. I wanted you to
be the first one to see him. Taken
me nigh on fifteen year.

FLETCHER

Fifteen years – has it? Still worth it
though, isn't it?

BLANCO

D'you know now it's done . . . I'm at a bit of a loose end.

FLETCHER

Yes, well I expect you are, Blanco. You could always study – improve your mind.

BLANCO

I tried that once – I got a book out of the library, on memory training. Studied it for months. Then I had to pack it in.

FLETCHER

Why?

BLANCO

I forgot where I left the book.

FLETCHER

Oh dear. Here, try smoking yourself to death instead.

BLANCO

Bless you, Fletcher. I was making it for my three-year-old niece. She's grown up a bit, works as an air hostess. Never thought it would take this long.

FLETCHER

Time flies when you're having fun.

BLANCO

Oh. Aye. Can I borrow your magazine?

FLETCHER

No, you can't.

BLANCO

After you've finished with it.

FLETCHER

No, you can't.

BLANCO

See, now that I've finished Muffin I want to catch up on me reading.

FLETCHER

You should start with something a little less controversial, you know what your blood pressure's like. Try the *Radio Times*. Tell you what, will you settle for a Jaffa cake?

BLANCO

Have you got some?

FLETCHER

No. But let's see what providence will provide. Just get me boots on. (*To the mule*) Come on, Muffin, walkies . . .

2. ASSOCIATION AREA

Fletcher goes out of the cell followed by Blanco with the mule. They walk along the catwalk and arrive at a cubby-hole door. Fletcher knocks.

COLLINSON

(*Offscreen*) Come in.

Fletcher goes in.

3. CUBBY-HOLE (OFFICER'S ROOM)

Inside the cubby-hole is a desk with papers on it.

On the wall is a 'switchboard'
referring to each cell on the landing
with lights that illuminate when a bell
is rung from the cell. There are keys
on the wall, some faded regulations,
a single-bar electric fire. A youngish
Prison Officer, Collinson, sits at the
desk. He has a mug of tea, and on
the desk a packet of Jaffa cakes.
He is not the friendliest of men.

COLLINSON

What is it?

FLETCHER

(*Quietly*) Mr Collinson, sorry to
disturb you – I can see you're busy –
not take a minute . . . It's just old
Blanco. He's finished his wooden
mule, and er, he'd like you to
see it, know what I mean. Not
take a minute.

COLLINSON

Oh. Oh, all right . . .

He gets up, squeezes past
Fletcher, who eyes the Jaffa cakes
on the desk.

4. ASSOCIATION AREA

Collinson comes out of his cubby-
hole. Blanco is waiting there.

COLLINSON

Oh yes . . . this is the mule is it, Blanco?

BLANCO

Yes, sir, fifteen years.

COLLINSON

Oh well, it's worth it, you don't often
see craftsmanship of that quality.

BLANCO

Thank you, sir, nice of you to say so.

COLLINSON

All right then, off you go,
Blanco, then.

BLANCO

Yes, sir.

FLETCHER

Very kind of you, Mr Collinson.
I mean a word from someone like
yourself – you don't know how
we appreciate that.

COLLINSON

All right then.

He returns to the cubby-hole.
Outside Fletcher gives Blanco
a biscuit.

BLANCO

You're a lad, Fletch.

FLETCHER

Yeah, well, say no more.

BLANCO

Sorry if I disturbed you.

FLETCHER

Any time for you.

BLANCO

I think I'll nip down and
watch *Grandstand*.

He picks up the mule.

FLETCHER

Oh yeah, while you're down there put
the word round, I'm incommunicado.

BLANCO

You're in the where?

FLETCHER

I don't want to be disturbed.

BLANCO

We'll tell 'em.

He moves off down the stairs.

5. CELL

Fletcher enters his cell and walks to the bed. He climbs on to the top bunk and settles down with his magazine. He has an 'Alone at last' expression. After a moment we hear someone clearing his throat.

FLETCHER

Yes?

Barrowclough is in the doorway.

BARROWCLOUGH

Oh Fletcher . . .

FLETCHER

Mr Barrowclough – on your way out would you lock me in so's I can get some privacy?

BARROWCLOUGH

On a lovely afternoon like this? I thought you'd be out in the yard, or in the hobby shop. Seems such a waste to be stuck in here.

FLETCHER

It's not a waste to me. I like to spend my Saturday afternoons in my cell. With my feet up and a bit of reading matter. I don't want to play games, or do exercises. Nor do I want to carve

toys, take saxophone lessons, form an amateur dramatic group, or watch *The Blue Lamp* on BBC2, a film glamourising that despicable bunch what put me here in the first place.

BARROWCLOUGH

It's a damn sight better than lying on your bunk reading that lewd lascivious rubbish. If a man puts his mind to it a man can better himself in here. There's a lot more opportunities now than when I first joined the service. Spraggon, you know him in E Block, Spraggon has made a six-foot space rocket out of milk bottle tops.

FLETCHER

Really.

BARROWCLOUGH

It's a work of art. Belongs to a museum. He used three colours. The nose cone's in red, homogenised, the bulk of it's made out of ordinary silver top, and the Governor's gold tops provided a nice motif round the centre.

FLETCHER

Well, he'll never get it off the ground.

BARROWCLOUGH

There's Rafferty having his watercolours exhibited in a Carlisle art gallery. Not to mention all the professional qualifications that vocational training has given people in this prison. Brickies, plasterers. Even the Tooley brothers left here with a diploma in welding.

FLETCHER

Yes and what did they do with it, soon

as they got out? Welded their way into Barclays Bank in Blackburn High Street.

BARROWCLOUGH

Yes – well – the point I'm trying to make is that we at least gave them the opportunity to do something legitimate with their lives.

FLETCHER

And the point I'm trying to make is that they'll just abuse the opportunity. They're felons, Mr Barrowclough. You get a bloke in here. Teach him how to use a printing press. What's he do when he goes out? Does he join the *Northern Echo*, does he fairycakes. He stays at home and forges premium bonds – only sensible.

BARROWCLOUGH

I won't accept your cynicism. I just don't like seeing a fully grown man with a good brain – 'cos you're not stupid, Fletcher – wasting his time. You should do something whatever it is.

FLETCHER

Oh – is that the lecture over? Is that what you come in to say, Mr Barrowclough?

BARROWCLOUGH

I didn't come in to lecture you.

FLETCHER

No, well, we never did discover the purpose of your visit, you never said.

BARROWCLOUGH

Didn't I . . . I don't know – (*Thinks*) Oh well, I just dropped by 'cos I had nothing better to do.

FLETCHER

Would you believe it, would you Adam and Eve it? Your lives are emptier than ours.

BARROWCLOUGH

They are not! I have my allotment.

FLETCHER

Your allotment – listen, Mr Barrowclough, if the system wants to do something really constructive for us chaps, give us more freedom, better grub. Give us conjugal visits.

BARROWCLOUGH

Give you what?

FLETCHER

Conjugals. From the Latin, *conjugo*, meaning to have it off.

BARROWCLOUGH

We can't do that –

FLETCHER

With our old ladies! All above board, Bristol fashion. It's what some prisons do, have special quarters. Where wives come up, and we spend the whole weekend . . . manifesting our long-felt wants.

BARROWCLOUGH

I don't know of any prisons where they -

FLETCHER

Maybe not here. But certainly abroad. Certainly Holland, and America, where they have more enlightened penal systems.

BARROWCLOUGH

They just allow the wives to visit, and they spend the whole weekend . . .

FLETCHER

Conjugating, yeah.

BARROWCLOUGH

That's more than I'm allowed at home.

Barrowclough moves off, shaking his head.

FLETCHER

Mr Barrowclough.

Barrowclough stops in the doorway.

FLETCHER

Here you are, Mr Barrowclough, your needs are greater than mine.

He offers Barrowclough the magazine.

BARROWCLOUGH

Certainly not, Fletcher.

He leaves.

FLETCHER

(*Spreading out the centrefold*) Well, my little treasure. Alone at last.

6. ASSOCIATION AREA

Mackay unlocks the door and three visitors enter the association area. Mackay closes it again.

MACKAY

This is a typical cell block.

WOMAN

Why do you have the nets?

MACKAY

Suicide, ma'am. The prevention of.

WOMAN

Do you have many instances of that?

MACKAY

Certainly not, ma'am. It's against the rules.

OLDER MAN

I suppose it's also useful if any of these chaps get violent and take it into their heads to throw each other over the edge.

MACKAY

If they get violent, sir, they generally throw us over the edge.

YOUNGER MAN

Do you have a bad record of violence in this prison?

MACKAY

Oh no, sir. That's because we at Slade Prison encourage a wide range of activities. This helps the men express themselves in various ways, releasing much of the pent-up aggression endemic to the incarcerated male.

WOMAN

Is that what most of them are doing now?

MACKAY

Absolutely. You will notice how at the weekend every prisoner has seized the opportunity to enjoy the extensive facilities which we provide.

Mackay looks into Fletcher's cell and then looks back again.

MACKAY

There are always some exceptions, of course.

WOMAN

Could we have a look in a cell?

MACKAY

Certainly, ma'am . . .

He ushers them into Fletcher's cell.

7. CELL

The three visitors and Mackay enter Fletcher's cell. He is still lying on his bunk reading.

OLDER MAN

Is this man sick?

MACKAY

Are you sick, Fletcher?

FLETCHER

I'm sick of interruptions.

WOMAN

Oh please, this fellow's probably trying to relax.

FLETCHER

Oh be my guest.

OLDER MAN

Please don't get up.

MACKAY

This is a typical cell.

WOMAN

Single or double?

MACKAY

Double, ma'am, as indicated by the presence of the two bunks. Prisoners are, of course, allowed to personalise

their cells. You notice the radio, the matches. And, of course, they're allowed to decorate their lockers with mementoes of family and home.

He opens the cupboard door and is faced by several photographs of nudes.

FLETCHER

Those two are the wife, and that's the wife's sister.

MACKAY

Perhaps you would like to see the recreation room.

OLDER MAN

Yes, we are rather disturbing this man's privacy.

FLETCHER

Privacy! Precious little of that in here.

MACKAY

Fletcher!

YOUNGER MAN

No, no, please, let the man speak.

FLETCHER

Well, have you noticed any signs of privacy on your rounds? Seen a door without a peephole? Seen a shower curtain or a cubicle door in the latrines? Very hard, you know, to retain a vestige of human dignity when you're sitting on the bog and a whole football team clatters past on their way to the showers.

WOMAN

Yes – well –

FLETCHER

Yes well – notice the way Mr Mackay

barged in here. Never so much of a by my leave or kiss my foot. Paid no more regard to me than he did the washbasin – in fact less.

MACKAY

Privacy is one of the privileges you forfeit when you transgress the law. This is not a hotel. They do forget that they're in here to be punished.

FLETCHER

Oh yes. Eye for an eye. Tooth for a nail.

OLDER MAN

You sound as if you're a Londoner.

FLETCHER

I am, sir, yes. It's the accent.

OLDER MAN

Long way from home up here. What's a Londoner doing in this neck of the woods?

FLETCHER

This particular Londoner is doing five years. What are you doing?

MACKAY

Fletcher!

OLDER MAN

No, no, fair question. Well, Fletcher, we're all attached to the Home Office in one capacity or another. And it's through these visits that we learn more about our penal system. And only by seeing things for ourselves and talking to people like yourself are we able to make recommendation for change and reform.

FLETCHER

Change yes . . . well, if you can supply

a new coat of paint, give us an improved supply of ping-pong balls. But reform, save yourselves the bother.

MACKAY

I don't think this particular prisoner's opinion is particularly instructive.

FLETCHER

Oh, isn't it? Let me tell you I've been in more nicks than he has. So whose opinion is more instructive?

WOMAN

I would value it.

FLETCHER

I bet you would – oh, I see. Well, obviously we can't have total amnesty. Got to keep a few hard cases locked away so we can walk the streets at night. But you should do with the rest of us what they do in Scandinavia. Make us work off our debt to society. On farms, building sites, factories, hospitals.

WOMAN

That's one school of thought, of course.

OLDER MAN

You know despite what this man says about rehabilitation, I think his attitude proves the contrary.

MACKAY

You what?

OLDER MAN

Now this system of working off your sentence, I can see it working with men like you.

YOUNGER MAN

If you had a choice, what area would you choose to work in?

FLETCHER

Well, if I had the choice I'd probably choose the building site.

WOMAN

The fresh air?

FLETCHER

Yes . . . but mostly 'cos I could nick meself a fortune.

He goes back to reading the magazine.

FLETCHER

(*Reading*) Cor look at her!

OLDER MAN

The recreation room next is it, Mr Mackay?

Mackay ushers the visitors out.

MACKAY

Hopeless case, sir. Classic recidivist.

YOUNGER MAN

Bit of a surly character.

OLDER MAN

Yes, but articulate.

MACKAY

Like a lorry.

They leave.

FLETCHER

(*Getting off his bunk*) Is there anybody else?

8. ASSOCIATION AREA

Fletcher comes out of his cell and stands on the catwalk. He looks around for any more interruptions, then goes back inside the cell.

9. CELL

Fletcher enters his cell. He swings straight up on top of his bunk and settles himself down, bashing his pillows and lying on his side. There is a pause. Then Warren's voice can be heard.

WARREN

'Scuse me, Fletch –

FLETCHER

What!!

He leaps straight up in the air, falls off his bunk and lands face to face with Warren.

WARREN

Were you asleep?

FLETCHER

Sleep, what chance have I had to sleep?!! More chance of having a sleep at Waterloo in the rush hour! What's wrong with you nurks in here? Can't you see when a man wants to be left alone?

WARREN

I'm sorry, it's just . . . your ball's got a crack in it.

Fletcher has to think about this for a moment.

FLETCHER

Pardon?

Warren holds up the ball.

WARREN

Cracked.

FLETCHER

(*Menacingly*) Better than having no balls at all.

WARREN

Spoilt the game though –

FLETCHER

I'll have it back then.

WARREN

I'll have the fag back then.

FLETCHER

You will not. You should have examined the merchandise when the transaction was transacted.

WARREN

That's not fair, Fletch.

FLETCHER

Fair? Since when was life ever fair? Is it fair that I should suffer this continual bombardment of people who don't know how to occupy their own time and minds? Saturday afternoon provides a few sacred hours when one can enjoy one's own company. It's not much to ask. It don't last long. Only till teatime when we traipse across to have that hideous mixture masquerading as cottage pie. When will you blokes learn that surviving in stir is a state of mind? It's an attitude. It's learning to live with yourself.

WARREN

(*Sniffing*) Sorry, Fletch.

Fletcher turns away, then softens his attitude to another approach.

FLETCHER

I like you, Warren. Believe me there are many times when I crave your company. I love those action-packed anecdotes of yours of the days when you worked in your father-in-law's ironmonger's in Bury.

WARREN

Bolton.

FLETCHER

Bolton, yes, even better. I was only too eager to look at your snaps the other day. Of your wife's day trip to Lake Windermere.

Warren reaches towards his top pocket.

WARREN

Oh, I've got some more.

Fletcher turns away and grasps the edge of the top bunk to prevent himself from grasping Warren's neck.

FLETCHER

God, give me strength.

WARREN

They didn't come out too well, I expect it was the rain.

FLETCHER

(*Controlling himself*) Just . . . just put them on the table, Warren, and they'll help to while away my evening.

WARREN

Oh, fine, right.

He does so.

WARREN

I'll be off then, Fletch, I'll not disturb you no more.

FLETCHER

Promise?

WARREN

Yeah.

FLETCHER

Here – d'you promise?

WARREN

I promise.

Warren goes. Fletcher laughs. Puts the photos down but drops them. Goes down on his knees to pick them up.

FLETCHER

Dear God, you might think it's a bit of a liberty me asking you favours, but on the other hand there is more joy in heaven when a sinner repenteth. Isn't that right, sir? It's only a small thing I ask . . . keep these nurks off my back, can't you? 'Cos if anyone else walks through that door I might not be answerable for the consequences. Know what I mean, God?

The Chaplain appears at the doorway.

CHAPLAIN

Ah, Fletcher . . . I'd been meaning to have a bit of a chat for some time.

Fletcher rises and moves towards the Chaplain.

10. GOVERNOR'S OFFICE

The office is empty. Then camera shows the door opening and Mackay's voice can be heard.

MACKAY

Left, right, left, right, left, right . . .

Fletcher is marched in by Mackay.

MACKAY

Halt. Face the front. Stand still. For the chop, you know that. No exit. If ever I have any doubts about the system it's people like you that reassure me. Because in the final analysis, in the final analysis, your criminal character will always show through like ink on blotting paper.

VENABLES

(*Offscreen*) They're in there already, are they?

Venables enters. He is wearing a football scarf, which he removes.

VENABLES

Mr Mackay.

MACKAY

Yes sir, Fletcher, sir. Sorry to fetch you from the game.

VENABLES

Not at all. This is a serious matter, a desperately serious matter. These Home Office visitors, they weren't around when the incident took place?

MACKAY

No, sir. Fortunately I had them in the woodwork room at the time.

VENABLES

Thank heavens for that, 'cos we must hush up a thing like this.

MACKAY

Face the front.

VENABLES

Did anyone witness it?

MACKAY

Only old Blanco Webb, sir. And Mr Collinson heard the scream.

VENABLES

Fletcher, what got into you?

Fletcher shrugs.

MACKAY

Face the front.

VENABLES

I'm talking to you, Fletcher.

FLETCHER

Everyone's talking to me, sir. End of my tether, see. Think I'm losing my mind, sir. Possibly I should have psychiatric observation in the hospital, sir.

VENABLES

Psychiatric observation . . . well, I don't know . . .

MACKAY

No, you don't. Sir – an unprovoked attack. And even Slade Prison, which has had its share of violence, has never known a chaplain thrown off a balcony.

FLETCHER

I knew the safety net was there, sir.

VENABLES

That's hardly the point. The chaplain was shattered.

FLETCHER

He'll bounce back, sir. He did a bit.

VENABLES

Don't be insolent, Fletcher. I have no alternative but to give you the maximum period of solitary confinement. Then we'll have to discuss the matter further.

FLETCHER

Yes, sir.

VENABLES

You've only yourself to blame. You have a very regrettable attitude, Fletcher. Perhaps you'll dwell on that over the next three days in isolation.

FLETCHER

Three days is it, sir?

VENABLES

Yes, it certainly is. All right, wheel him out.

FLETCHER

Could I just ask one thing, sir?

VENABLES

What?

FLETCHER

Couldn't make it a fortnight, could you?

Mackay marches him off.

SERIES TWO

EPISODE FIVE: HAPPY RELEASE

1. MEDICAL OFFICER'S ROOM

The Medical Officer is examining a prisoner. Mackay enters.

MACKAY

Is it true about Fletcher, sir?

MO

What? Oh morning, Mr Mackay.

MACKAY

Is it true about Fletcher, Doctor?

MO

Oh yes, I'm afraid it is.

MACKAY

Oh – definite?

MO

Yes, we had him down at Carlisle General, they verified it.

MACKAY

Where is he now?

MO

He's back here. We've just got him to bed.

MACKAY

No possibility of a mistake?

MO

No, no. The X-rays are positive.

MACKAY

In other words there's nothing we can do about it?

MO

Nothing.

MACKAY

Fletcher of all people.

MO

That's the way it is.

MACKAY

How long would you say?

MO

Three weeks. Maybe a month.

MACKAY

I had him down for the drainage detail you know . . . and now he gets three cushy weeks on his back with a -broken ankle, there's no justice.

Mackay starts to go.

MO

I said it could even be a month.

2. HOSPITAL WARD

*Fletcher is in bed with his plastered
leg in traction. Screens surround
his bed.*
*Next to him is the old lag, Blanco,
who is asleep. Opposite is Norris,
another prisoner.*
*A prison orderly removes the
screens from around Fletcher.*

FLETCHER
Thank you, Charlie. I'll do the same for
you one day.

Mackay enters.

FLETCHER
Oh, Mr Mackay, how kind. I don't think
it's official visiting hours, you know.

MACKAY
You're a lucky man, Fletcher.

FLETCHER
No grapes then?

MACKAY
I just wanted to verify with my own
eyes that you weren't malingering.

FLETCHER
No, no. My foot is broken. You
can see the plaster. The evidence
is irrefootable.

Fletcher laughs at his own joke.

FLETCHER
Did you hear that Blanco, oh
you're asleep.

MACKAY
I won't pretend your indisposition isn't
very frustrating, Fletcher.

FLETCHER
Not to me, it isn't. Better grub in here.

Better beds an' all. Got me own
cushion here.

MACKAY
Since you lost your soft number in the
library I was all ready to make your life
a misery.

FLETCHER
I gathered that when you sent me up
that twenty-foot ladder to clean pigeon
droppings out the guttering.

MACKAY
Wouldn't surprise me if you
fell intentionally.

FLETCHER
No, no, it's just poetic justice. You was
out to victimise me, and all you've
done is give me a passport to comfort
and seclusion. Mind you, I do have to
put up with that scroat Norris for the
next few days.

NORRIS
Oh yeah, well it cuts two ways,
don't it?

FLETCHER
Shut your face, Norris, or I'll hit you
with me frying pan.

NORRIS
Violence now, eh?

MACKAY
Quiet, both of you.

BLANCO
(*Waking up*) What is it?

FLETCHER
Ssh, it's all right.

MACKAY
And you.

NORRIS

He started it. He's been at me all afternoon, Mr Mackay.

MACKAY

That's one thing I can't blame Fletcher for, Norris. You're not the pleasantest of men. In fact you're a horrible creature.

NORRIS

Here! I done my bird! I'm being released in two days.

MACKAY

Yes, and you're skiving to the last.

NORRIS

I've had surgery. Ingrown toenail.

MACKAY

I know the kind of surgery I would give you had I my way.

FLETCHER

Couldn't have waited till you got out, could you? Had to burden our overworked prison medical service.

MACKAY

Which is exactly what you're doing, Fletcher.

FLETCHER

Yeah, well we know whose fault that is, don't we?

MACKAY

Four weeks. Maximum. I can bide my time. I'll soon have you up on your foot.

FLETCHER

Not before it's mended.

MACKAY

You're in discomfort, are you?

FLETCHER

Well, nothing to speak of.

MACKAY

Oh come on, Fletcher, it's giving you hell, admit it.

He pulls the traction.

FLETCHER

No.

MACKAY

Not even the odd twinge?

FLETCHER

No, no. Not now the plaster is on.

MACKAY

There's no justice. (*Lets traction go*)

He lets traction go, shakes his head and leaves.

FLETCHER

And the next object is, a thwarted screw, a thwarted screw . . .

NORRIS

I'm in pain.

FLETCHER

Pardon?

NORRIS

I'm in pain.

FLETCHER

Good.

NORRIS

I've had surgery.

FLETCHER

I've had X-rays.

NORRIS

X-rays isn't surgery.

FLETCHER

Surgery. Ingrown toenail.

NORRIS

I haven't slept for days with the pain. Shadow of my former self I am.

FLETCHER

Well, your former self wasn't much to begin with, Norris.

NORRIS

Naff off.

FLETCHER

Soon as my broken foot's better I'm going to use it to stand on your ingrowing toenail.

NORRIS

Have to hurry, won't you? I'm out of here Thursday!

The door is unlocked by a Prison officer.

Lennie is admitted, wearing kitchen whites and pushing a food trolley.

LENNIE

Meals on wheels.

FLETCHER

Oh, look at this. Look at this, Blanco. What's on the menu then, Lennie? Apart from yesterday's gravy stains.

LENNIE

Braised steak and carrots, mashed potatoes, bananas and custard.

Starts to serve.

FLETCHER

Oh good – what's for afters?

LENNIE

Tomato soup.

FLETCHER

Hear that Blanco? Bananas and custard.

BLANCO

I've got no appetite.

FLETCHER

You've got to eat, Blanco. Keep your strength up. If you don't eat you will be ill – oh you are ill, aren't you?

NORRIS

If he won't have it, I'll have it.

FLETCHER

You will not! You leave it by his bedside, Lennie. Anything he don't fancy now he can have later . . . or I'll have it.

LENNIE

How are you then, Fletch?

FLETCHER

All right – surviving. How's yourself?

LENNIE

Not as comfy as you are. Look at those crisp, clean sheets.

FLETCHER

Yeah well – give us some more carrots.

NORRIS

Don't leave me short.

LENNIE

Shut up, Norris. Here you are, Blanco. I'll just put this here then. He don't look too chipper, does he?

FLETCHER

He's all right. Just a bit depressed that's all.

LENNIE

Looks at death's door to me.

FLETCHER

Shut up – gawd, you youngsters. Don't have much tact, do you? You don't make remarks about death's

door to people. Not in hospital.
Specially when they're at death's door.

BLANCO

(Laughing weakly) Ha ha . . . that's a
good one, Fletch.

FLETCHER

Well, you've got to laugh, ain't you?

LENNIE

(Serving Norris but addressing
Fletcher) You're cheery enough.

FLETCHER

Can't complain. Life of Riley, in' it? And I
had a nice day out, Lennie. Went down
to Carlisle General and got plastered.

Lennie laughs.

FLETCHER

And there was some lovely nurses
there – kept popping their heads
round the door. Giggling like. 'Cos
there I was, a convict. Mister Menace
– handcuffed to a wheelchair.

LENNIE

Sort of like Ironside – only bent.

FLETCHER

Well yeah . . . it was my air of villainy
what titillated them. 'Course some have
bigger titillations than others. (Lowering
voice) I was in this cubicle with this
ravishing West Indian sister . . .

**A Prison Officer appears at
the doorway.**

PRISON OFFICER

Come on lad, you've had long
enough fiddling around with that.

FLETCHER

That's what she said.

LENNIE

Oh can I just hear the end of this . . .

PRISON OFFICER

No you can't, come along.

LENNIE

Tell me tomorrow then, Fletch.

FLETCHER

It'll keep.

Lennie starts to wheel trolley away.

LENNIE

Sleep well.

FLETCHER

And you. Look after yourself.

LENNIE

I will. Nice change having a cell to
meself. It don't half smell fresh in there
without your feet.

NORRIS

How do you think we feel?

LENNIE

Shut up, Norris.

He leaves.

FLETCHER

I should think you'll be glad to get
out of here on Thursday, Norris, it'll
give you a better opportunity to be
more revolting to a larger number
of people.

BLANCO

I'll certainly be glad to see the back of
him. You know I never had much.
Possessions like. But in the last three
days before you came in here he's
had 'em all.

FLETCHER

How d'you mean?

BLANCO

He's had me wireless. And me silver snuff holder. Real silver, Fletch. Antique. I kept me snout in it. He had all the snout an' all.

FLETCHER

(*To Norris*) Is this true?

NORRIS

Fair and square.

BLANCO

And me musical box which plays 'Waltzing Matilda' when you open the lid.

FLETCHER

What'd he do, he just took 'em? Well, he's going to put 'em right back I tell you that, Blanco.

NORRIS

Fair and square. Cards, wasn't it?

FLETCHER

Oh dear, oh dear, Blanco. You don't play cards with him.

BLANCO

Brag, nine-card brag.

NORRIS

Fair and square.

FLETCHER

You'll give those back, Norris.

NORRIS

Will I . . . heck.

He goes.

FLETCHER

Don't worry, Blanco, me old son, I'll get them back for you.

BLANCO

It doesn't matter, Fletch. What do I need with a 'Waltzing Matilda' music box where I'm going?

FLETCHER

You ain't going nowhere, mate, you've got another two years to do.

BLANCO

I'm going out of here sooner than that.

FLETCHER

You're too old to escape, Blanco. You'll never get over the wall. You been watching too much of that *Colditz*, you have.

BLANCO

I'm going out of here in a wooden overcoat.

FLETCHER

Oh come on, Blanco – dear me, what kind of talk's that?

BLANCO

No, me time's about up, Fletch. I'm not going to last the distance. Tired heart the doctor says. Tired everything more like. I come in here to die.

FLETCHER

No, you didn't. You come in here yester-die. Get it, get it?

BLANCO

(*With a wan smile*) Oh Fletch, they were cracking that when even I was at school.

FLETCHER

Well, that raised a smile.

BLANCO

You don't have to gee me up, lad. I'm not afraid. It's time I went to that great cell block in the sky.

FLETCHER

Rubbish. Bloke like you ain't ready for celestial porridge yet awhile. You're not old. You look old but that's prison. Prison puts years on a man's physical appearance. Got to remember you're only twenty-nine.

BLANCO

(*Smiling*) Sixty-three.

FLETCHER

Sixty-three, you're not past it at sixty-three. Most of the government's older than that.

BLANCO

And look at the state this country's in. Mind you it weren't much better when I were a lad. Depression. Hard times. No work. Took to stealing. Such a waste. Spent nigh on half me life in one nick or another. Lost all me family. Mostly through neglect. Mine. That's why I'm resigned to passing on. Well, more than that, relieved.

FLETCHER

Come off it, there's years of wear left in you yet. Charlie Chaplin become a father nigh on eighty. Winston Churchill was at least your age when he had his finest hour. As was my Uncle Wilfred.

BLANCO

What did he do?

FLETCHER

When he was seventy he married this gorgeous young dental assistant. 'Course it killed him. But you should have seen the smirk on his face in the coffin.

BLANCO

Died with his boots off, did he?

FLETCHER

Yeah – and his teeth out. Couldn't get the coffin lid down for three days. State of mind, age. You're as young as you feel. For instance, this old boy goes to the doctor, see. The doctor says, 'What's wrong then?' And the old boy says, 'Well it's the wife and I – we ain't getting any pleasure out of sex any more.' The doc like, he's a bit taken aback. He says, 'How old are you?' 'Eighty.' 'And the wife?' 'Seventy-nine.' He says, 'Well, when d'you first notice this?' And the old boy says, 'Last night . . . then again this morning.'

They laugh.

BLANCO

I heard that at school an' all.

3. HOSPITAL WING

The camera shows the exterior of the hospital wing at night.

3A. HOSPITAL WARD

It is night time. The room is lit by a dim hospital night light and some moonlight through the barred window. Blanco is coughing, unable

to sleep. Norris is sound asleep,
snoring lightly.
Fletcher is asleep but moves
restlessly in his bed. Blanco
coughs again.

BLANCO
(*Quietly*) Fletch . . . Fletch!

FLETCHER
Mmmmh?

BLANCO
Want to talk to you.

FLETCHER
Whassamatter?

BLANCO
Wanted to tell you something –
important, like . . . while he's asleep.
He indicates Norris.

BLANCO
He is asleep, isn't he?
There is an answering snore
from Norris.

FLETCHER
Unless he snores when he's
awake, yes.

BLANCO
Well, you see, I've got something
of value.

FLETCHER
How do you mean?

BLANCO
Well, you see, I've got no family – I
told you that. And the few things I've
got – well, Norris has got them now,
since the nine-card brag. But I still got
one thing of value. And I'd like to
bequeath it.

FLETCHER
You're getting morbid again.

BLANCO
I'm not. I'm being practical. 'Cos if owt
happened to me, no one would know
about my legacy.

FLETCHER
Listen, if you want to make a will, it's
no good talking to me, Blanco. You
want a solicitor, we got one on our
landing. He'll see you right. Straight
as a die, he is.

BLANCO
What's his name?

FLETCHER
Corkscrew Carter. Nice bloke.

BLANCO
My legacy is not the sort I
can legalise.

FLETCHER
Why not?

BLANCO
It's ill-gotten gains. Buried somewhere
in Leeds.

FLETCHER
Oh, ill-gotten gains, is it? Oh, I see.

BLANCO
Shall I tell you about it?

FLETCHER
Not now.

BLANCO
Well it was like this. There were three
of us. And we done this wages van
on the way to a fridge factory near
Otley. Don't you remember reading
about it?

FLETCHER

I don't Blanco, no.

BLANCO

It were in *Yorkshire Post*.

FLETCHER

If it didn't make the *Muswell Hill Examiner* or *Titbits* I wouldn't have seen it.

BLANCO

I s'pose not. Anyway it were an untidy job. Lot of things went wrong.

FLETCHER

You wouldn't be here if they hadn't.

BLANCO

The other two lads were brothers, Jack Brackett and Harry erm . . .

FLETCHER

Brackett, was it?

BLANCO

That's right. Did you know him?

FLETCHER

No, no. Only through his brother.

BLANCO

Oh, 'cos their escape were in *Yorkshire Post*. They got away in a fishing boat from Bridlington –

FLETCHER

Will this take long, Blanco – only my foot's gone to sleep, and I'd like to catch it up.

BLANCO

Not that the Bracketts knew where I'd put loot in any case.

FLETCHER

Blanco – fascinating as it is to stroll down felony lane with you –

BLANCO

I'm the one who's got the map. I'm the one who knows where it's buried.

FLETCHER

Oh gawd, it's bleeding Treasure Island now, is it?

BLANCO

Eight thousand quid.

FLETCHER

(*Eyes widen*) How much? **Norris's eyes open but he remains still.**

BLANCO

Eight thousand quid.

FLETCHER

Eight big ones?

BLANCO

Maybe nine. Used notes. Didn't have time to count 'em. According to *Yorkshire Post* it were fifteen, but that were the thieving company, trying to diddle Lloyds.

FLETCHER

Now listen, me old son. I obviously never realised the magnitude of your legacy.

BLANCO

The map's yours, Fletch. **He gives him the map.**

FLETCHER

I don't know what to say. Words fail me. I shall use the money wisely, Blanco, rest assured. Let me ask you one question. If you don't snuff it – which we all hope and pray for, that you won't that is – then on your release you'll presumably want your map back.

BLANCO

Oh . . . oh well, if I did last the distance I suppose so, yes.

FLETCHER

And you'd trust me to give it to you?

BLANCO

Of course I would, Fletch.

FLETCHER

D'you know, Blanco, in all my life I don't think anyone's ever shown me trust like that . . . probation officers, Borstal principals, judges. And yet here you are – a man who ain't known me long, or in great intimacy, entrusting me with everything he's got in the world.

BLANCO

I am that, Fletch.

There's a pause.

FLETCHER

You must be bleeding barmy.

4. HOSPITAL WARD

Later that night, on his rounds, Barrowclough looks through the glass panel on the ward door, which adjoins the medical room. He moves off. Fletcher is fast asleep, as is Blanco in the next bed. Norris appears at Fletcher's bed. He is searching Fletcher's possessions.

He checks the pockets of Fletcher's hospital issue robe. Nothing.

Norris freezes as Fletcher rolls over, but he now has his back to Norris, who pushes a cautions hand under the pillows. Fletcher moves again restlessly, rolling on to his back, thus trapping Norris's hand. Norris hesitates a moment, looking down at the sleeping Fletcher. Then he carefully slips his hand into the breast pocket of his pyjamas. Again nothing.

More gingerly than ever, Norris now starts to search under the sheets. His hand moves lower in the bed. Fletcher opens an eye, at first unsure what is going on. Then:

FLETCHER

Help!!

Norris, as if stung, leaps back and scurries across the room.

FLETCHER

Help – what the hell's going on here? Who was that? Was that you, Norris?

Norris slides back in bed and starts snoring before his head has even hit the pillow.

FLETCHER

Norris, was that you?

BLANCO

(*Waking*) What's going on – what's happening?

FLETCHER

I'm not sure, Blanco. I think I've just been molested.

The door is unlocked and the lights go on. Barrowclough enters, wearing his most anxious expression.

BARROWCLOUGH

What is it? What was all that noise, what is it?

FLETCHER

Oh, Mr Barrowclough, thank God it's you!

BARROWCLOUGH

Why, Fletcher? Whatever's happening – what's going on?

NORRIS

(*Feigning waking*) What's happening? What going on?

FLETCHER

Don't give me that parrot fashion, Norris, you despicable nurk!

BARROWCLOUGH

Will you answer my question, Fletcher?

FLETCHER

I was awoken, Mr Barrowclough. Woken by a foreign hand.

BARROWCLOUGH

A foreign hand?

FLETCHER

Well, you know what I mean, Norris was over here, sir.

BARROWCLOUGH

What were you up to – stealing?

NORRIS

I haven't been up to anything.

FLETCHER

Don't give me that, you were over here rummaging in my pyjamas.

BARROWCLOUGH

Have you got any valuables here, Fletcher?

FLETCHER

Only what I always keep in my pyjamas.

BLANCO

He could have been after your lemon barley water.

FLETCHER

What – in my pyjamas? Funny shaped bottle.

BARROWCLOUGH

What have you got to say for yourself, Norris?

NORRIS

What's he got that I'd want to nick? One orange and a pair of smelly slippers.

FLETCHER

You've just put yourself right in it there. I got those slippers off Mr Barrowclough. Present they were. My first week in here.

BARROWCLOUGH

Yes well, we don't need to go into that now. They were second hand, and I happened to be finished with them.

FLETCHER

Nevertheless I appreciated and grew to love those, Mr Barrowclough. And I wouldn't like to see them falling into the wrong hands – or in this case, feet.

NORRIS

I don't want your tatty old slippers.

BARROWCLOUGH

They are not tatty. They cost thirty-two and six in the old currency.

He looks at Norris's table.

BARROWCLOUGH

You go out of this prison in two days' time, Norris. You must be ruddy mad to risk losing remission by going back to your nasty little habits.

NORRIS

Why d'you take his word for it?

BARROWCLOUGH

Fletcher's not the sort of person who's likely to scream out in the middle of the night over nothing. Though for the life of me I can't think what there is to steal. You're not hiding anything are you, Fletcher?

FLETCHER

Hiding?

He looks at Blanco.

BARROWCLOUGH

You're not hiding a bottle of surgical alcohol?

FLETCHER

Hide? No, sir.

Barrowclough tugs at Fletcher's blankets.

FLETCHER

Gerroff.

BARROWCLOUGH

Fletcher!

Fletcher reluctantly releases his grip on the blankets. Blanco reacts anxiously. Barrowclough pulls back the blankets. While he makes

a cursory inspection of the pillows and sheets, Fletcher is moaning bitterly.

FLETCHER

Isn't it marvellous? Eh, Blanco? Marvellous, isn't it? The suspicion, the mistrust. Even in our sick beds, racked with pain we're still subject to these indignities.

BARROWCLOUGH

This won't take a moment, Fletcher, I just want to get to the bottom of this.

FLETCHER

Yes, you're well on your way an' all!

He pulls the blankets back and examines underneath the bed, looking inside the slippers.

BARROWCLOUGH

I thought for once I'd have some peace and quiet on this shift. But there's never a moment when one of you isn't up to something.

He picks up the slippers.

BARROWCLOUGH

Oh, you've broken the pom-poms.

Sudden thought strikes him.

BARROWCLOUGH

My God.

FLETCHER

Where are you going now?

BARROWCLOUGH

It just occurred to me that this whole farce has all the classic elements of a diversionary tactic. When I get back I'll probably find that the rest of the wing has tunnelled their way to freedom.

He starts to go.

FLETCHER

'Ere.

BARROWCLOUGH

What?

FLETCHER

Lights out.

Barrowclough leaves.

FLETCHER

He's left that door unlocked. It's not good enough is it – a burglar could walk straight in here.

5. PRISON

Camera shows the prison in the morning.

5A. HOSPITAL WARD

Lennie is serving breakfast.

LENNIE

Here you are, Blanco. Nice bit of marmalade here.

FLETCHER

What's the news from the outside world?

LENNIE

Mackay's in an ever so rotten mood. Villa drew. At home. Weather forecast said winds moderate to light. (*Giving food to Fletcher*) The hot water's working again. If you're quick. And it's cauliflower cheese for your supper tonight.

FLETCHER

Dear, oh dear. That's the trouble with being cooped up in hospital. You miss it all – don't you?

LENNIE

I only give the highlights. I missed out the boring bits.

FLETCHER

Well, when you come back later, can you bring me a newspaper – the *Sun*. And something to read. I've finished these two books . . . Oh er . . .

He looks to see if Norris is watching but he is eating his breakfast.

FLETCHER

Would you make sure these books go back to my cell?

He gets the map from his plastered leg and puts it inside a book. He hands it to Lennie, winking at him.

FLETCHER

I don't want those thieving nurks on the landing getting at them.

PRISON OFFICER

Come on, Godber.

LENNIE

Oh naffing hell. See you then, Fletch.

FLETCHER

Yes, drive carefully.

Lennie wheels the trolley away.

FLETCHER

(*To Blanco*) How's your tomato then, Blanco?

BLANCO

Had worse. But not much.

NORRIS

I'll have his.

FLETCHER

You'll have it all down your front if you're not careful.

NORRIS

Listen you two, I'd like a word. I'll come straight to the point. I was awake last night. I heard.

FLETCHER

Heard – heard what?

NORRIS

About the map.

FLETCHER

Don't know what he's talking about, do you Blanco? What map's this then?

NORRIS

Come on, Fletch, don't pee around. Listen, you could cut me in.

FLETCHER

I don't know what you're talking about.

NORRIS

You know what I'm talking about. The map, the gelt – the buried gelt, in Leeds.

BLANCO

Why should we cut you in?

NORRIS

Ah see – there is a map, isn't there?

FLETCHER

All right, then, all right, there is a map. But why should we cut you in?

NORRIS

I'm going out tomorrow.

FLETCHER

So.

NORRIS

Well, Blanco ain't out for two years, and you're not for three. Anything could happen. They could find it . . . or, or build a multi-storey car park on top of it. So I could keep it safe, couldn't I? Put it in a building society. Invest it, like.

FLETCHER

I know what you'd invest it in, Norris. You'd invest it in a brighter future for your despicable self. By the time we come out there wouldn't be a penny left. You'd squander it in a vulgar orgy of wining and dining northern tarts in northern night clubs.

BLANCO

Yeah. That's what I'd planned to do with it.

FLETCHER

You're entitled, Blanco. It's your money.

NORRIS

It won't be if he snuffs it, will it? You're going to cop it.

FLETCHER

I happens to be his chosen benefactor. And you happen to be someone he can't bear the sight of. You're only the bloke what cheated him out of his most treasured possessions. His snuff box and his radio, and his little Matilda what goes round. Tell you what though, Norris, if you can find the map you're welcome to a share.

BLANCO

Here, Fletch.

FLETCHER

Go on then, straight up. I mean I ain't been able to leave this room, have I? Not with this plaster.

NORRIS

That's a deal, is it?

FLETCHER

Have to find it first.

NORRIS

I know where you hid it.

FLETCHER

You ain't that clever, Norris.

Norris lunges at Fletcher's plaster and tries to pull it off. Fletcher yells in agony.

6. LANDING

Norris, now fully dressed, makes his way up the steps towards the upper landing through the bustle of association hour.

6A. CELL

It is night time. Lennie is lying on the upper bunk, reading a paper, when Norris enters.

NORRIS

'Ere, Godber.

LENNIE

Oh hello, Norris. Come to say your goodbyes, have you?

NORRIS

No, it's just that er – Fletch said when he give you those books, did he leave a bit of paper in it? By mistake, like.

LENNIE

Why?

NORRIS

He just wanted it. I said I'd take it over to him.

LENNIE

(*Suspiciously*) Bit of paper, like?

NORRIS

Yeah, quite meaningless.

LENNIE

Why's he want it then?

NORRIS

I dunno, it's meaningless –

He sees the two books on a chair and grabs them. There is nothing in them.

LENNIE

Meaningless, is it?

NORRIS

Was there a bit of paper in here?

LENNIE

Could be.

Norris tries another tack.

NORRIS

Look, Godber – I mean, Lennie – how d'you like to make some money? I mean real money. On the outside.

LENNIE

Not much use to me as I'm on the inside, is it?

NORRIS

All right. I've got gear on the inside. And my back wages.

LENNIE

What for – a meaningless bit of paper?

NORRIS

Ask no questions, son.

*Lennie swings down from
his bunk.*

LENNIE

No questions about the fact that
this is behind my mate's back.
This, obviously, whatever it is,
belongs to Fletch.

NORRIS

Never mind about Fletch. He only
worries about number one. Look I'm
offering you all my back pay. And
my snout.

LENNIE

Fletch's my cellie. My mate.

NORRIS

(*Producing goods one by one*) I've got
a silver snuff holder. Antique. Worth a
lot of money.

LENNIE

He's been good to me, Fletch.

NORRIS

And a music box. Plays
'Waltzing Matilda'.

LENNIE

Contrary to popular belief in here, we're
not all without scruples. Fletcher's
shown me friendship. You can't buy
that. Without him I'd've gone under
in here.

NORRIS

There's a radio as well. Japanese.

LENNIE

All right, then, done.

Norris grins in satisfaction.

7. PRISON GATES

*Camera shows the prison gates.
Norris walks out with a carrier bag
and parcel and to a waiting minibus.
He gets in and the minibus drives off.*

8. HOSPITAL WARD

*Lennie wheels the lunch trolley into
the ward.*

FLETCHER

(*Indignantly*) Oh here he comes! The
Judas Iscariot of Slade Prison.

BLANCO

Don't know how he dares show
his face.

FLETCHER

Judas. You betrayed us, didn't you,
Godber – you betrayed us to that
evil Norris.

LENNIE

(*Unfazed*) Yes, I did.

FLETCHER

Thank God for that – how did it go?

LENNIE

Like a charm.

FLETCHER

(*To Blanco*) Like a charm – D'you hear
that – like a charm.

They all laugh.

*Lennie picks up the cover on one
of the trays.*

LENNIE

What have we here? One radio.

One snuff holder. And one Australian
music box.

*He puts them on Blanco's
bedside table.*

FLETCHER

There you are, Blanco, with all thy
worldly goods we thee endow.

BLANCO

(*Chuffed*) Oh lads, lads.

FLETCHER

(*To Lennie*) What did you do with
Norris's snout?

LENNIE

There was so much there wasn't
room for it! And I've stashed the
back pay.

FLETCHER

Split it three ways, fair enough?

LENNIE

When d'you cook this up, Fletch?

FLETCHER

That first afternoon when Norris was
having his bath.

LENNIE

Lovely idea. He really thought you *had*
some money buried.

FLETCHER

It's him. Lovely bit of acting. He had
me going, he did in the small hours.
'Course we knew Norris would
be earwigging. Person like that
always does.

BLANCO

D'you think he'll go straight there?

FLETCHER

Oh gawd yes, the best is yet to come.

LENNIE

Should think he'll be in Leeds
by midday.

FLETCHER

Yes. Then he'll go to an ironmonger's
and buy a shovel – 'course he'll lie
low this afternoon. Won't go there till
everyone's gone home. (*To Blanco*)
Here we'll listen to your wireless
tonight. Might hear something on the
nine o'clock news.

They all laugh.

9. FIELD

*A man is walking along. He stops,
looks at a map, turns and walks on.
Further along he stops walking, puts
the map away and starts to dig.
Lights start coming on. The sign
'Leeds United' can be seen. It is a
floodlit football ground. A guard with
a dog is walking towards Norris.*

10. HOSPITAL WARD

*Fletcher and Blanco are listening to
the radio.*

ANNOUNCER

(*Voiceover*) Later a man was detained
at Leeds Police headquarters,
charged with trespass and causing
wilful damage to the property of
Leeds United Football Club. He is
being remanded . . .

SERIES TWO

EPISODE SIX: THE HARDER THEY FALL

1. ASSOCIATION AREA 1.

Lennie is seen walking through the association area and going upstairs. A prisoner at a table speaks to him.

PRISONER

Hey, Len, heard you made the team.

LENNIE

Yeah, well . . .

He carries on up the stairs. At the top he meets Barrowclough.

BARROWCLOUGH

The champ, is it?

LENNIE

Not yet.

BARROWCLOUGH

Double rations then.

LENNIE

If I want 'em.

BARROWCLOUGH

I thought that was the whole point in boxing. Getting a double ration chit.

LENNIE

Well, you see, if I have double rations of Slade Prison's food I won't be a middle-weight, I'll be an overweight.

BARROWCLOUGH

I trust you're not complaining about the food, Godber?

LENNIE

No complaints, sir.

BARROWCLOUGH

It's a jolly sight better than a lot of people get in their own homes. And I speak from experience. Of prison food, that is.

LENNIE

Yes, sir. I mean it's not much to look at, but then neither is ready-mixed concrete, and that doesn't taste very nice either.

BARROWCLOUGH

Well, that's all right then . . . I'm glad to hear you're taking a sensible . . .

Lennie has gone.

BARROWCLOUGH

Pardon?

2. CELL

It is evening. Fletcher has just finished a game of draughts with another prisoner. They pack up.

FLETCHER

Cheerio – thanks for the game.

The prisoner goes, passing Lennie on his way in. Lennie is wearing a tracksuit.

LENNIE

'Lo, Fletch.

FLETCHER

Oh gawd, the athlete.

LENNIE

Nothing wrong with that. Keep in shape. Better than draughts. You could do with losing a few pounds, Fletch.

FLETCHER

Thanks to draughts, I just won two pounds, ain't I?

LENNIE

You cheat at draughts.

FLETCHER

Here, you watch your tongue, or I'll knock your block off.

LENNIE

Oh no, you won't, Fletch . . .

He starts to shadow box at Fletcher.

LENNIE

Made the boxing team, didn't I . . .

He starts slapping Fletcher's face in an irritating manner.

LENNIE

Didn't I, didn't I . . . Come on, Fletch, where's your guard?

FLETCHER

He's outside, want me to call him in? Naff off, sit down, will you? Boxing now, is it?

Lennie nods.

FLETCHER

Gawd, Godber, you've taken every miffing course in this prison. Arts and Crafts, 'O' Levels, Pottery, Spanish. What are you going to do with Spanish, become an interpreter, are you?

LENNIE

Si, si, Señor.

FLETCHER

That's it, is it? Six weeks of concentrated study and what have we got – 'Si, si, Señor!'

LENNIE

No, listen . . . No tiene vaca, pero tiene uno burro.

FLETCHER

Go on then, I'll buy it.

LENNIE

I haven't got a cow, but I have got a donkey.

FLETCHER

Oh that'll come in handy, that's extremely useful, that is. On your first Spanish holiday, pick up a shy little señorita, she starts whispering sweet nothings up your nose and what do you say? 'Well, I haven't got a cow, darling, but I have got a donkey.'

LENNIE

Vaya con Dios – that's Spanish.

FLETCHER

People like you from Birmingham
would be better off learning English.
I hope this boxing lark won't last long.
'Cos you do bring a terrible smell of
sweat and liniment into my room.

LENNIE

Takes away the smell of your aftershave.
Seriously though, Fletch, I'm dead
chuffed at making the boxing squad.
Big match next week.

FLETCHER

You're only boxing for our wing.

LENNIE

I know but . . .

FLETCHER

Against another wing.

LENNIE

Even so.

FLETCHER

Hardly Madison Square Garden, is it?

LENNIE

It's a start, Fletch. I'm going to
work at this. It's the great working-
class escape, sport. That and rock
and roll.

FLETCHER

No doubt you'll get round to that
sooner or later.

LENNIE

I've got all the credentials to be a
fighter. Deprived childhood, terrible
background. Mr Hopkins, the PTI,
says I've got natural ability.

FLETCHER

If you show all the flair in the ring that

you show for Spanish, my son, you
ain't half due a clobbering.

LENNIE

Que sera, sera . . .

FLETCHER

Kiss her what?

Jackdaw comes in.

JACKDAW

Hey, Fletch, Grouty wants to see you.

FLETCHER

Pardon?

JACKDAW

Grouty. Wants a word.

FLETCHER

Are you running for Harry Grout, now,
Jackdaw?

JACKDAW

I'm one of his firm.

FLETCHER

He must be scraping the barrel.

JACKDAW

Watch it.

FLETCHER

Oh hark at him. Now that he's under
the protective wing of genial Harry
Grout he's full of bravado, isn't he?

JACKDAW

Well are you coming then?

FLETCHER

I might stroll across in due
course, yeah.

JACKDAW

I'm supposed to take you with me.

FLETCHER

I'm a bit heavy to lift, Jackdaw.
Tell you what, you scurry back,

I know the way. Tell Harry I want
to change me socks and cut me
toenails, all right?

JACKDAW

On your head be it.

He leaves.

LENNIE

Was that wise?

FLETCHER

Yeah – he's all right Harry. I know he has
a long past of mayhem and violence,
but this is the last year of a long, long
stretch. He ain't going to come the
heavy and cock up his release at this
stage, is he?

LENNIE

S'pose not.

FLETCHER

He's happy being the tobacco baron,
and running all the rackets.

LENNIE

Wonder what he wants to see
you for?

FLETCHER

Maybe he wants a slice of my
draughts action.

They laugh.

FLETCHER

Now where's me clippers?

LENNIE

Oh Fletch, you're not going to cut
your toenails in here.

FLETCHER

Well I ain't going to grow them
indefinitely, and I'm not tall enough to
get me feet out the window.

LENNIE

All right, but you always cut 'em on
my bunk.

*He walks over to the table and
sits down.*

FLETCHER

Oh I'm sorry if it offends your sense of
Birmingham propriety. I hope you're
going to take a shower to wash that
liniment off. Smells like a Turkish
wrestler's jock strap in here.

LENNIE

Yes well, you've travelled Fletch, you
know these things.

*Mackay comes in and walks across
to Lennie.*

MACKAY

Hello, Godber. No, sit down. I'm told
congratulations are in order.

LENNIE

Oh, the boxing. Thank you, Mr
Mackay, yes.

MACKAY

Fine outlet, boxing. The noble art.
Teaches you discipline, dedication and
team spirit. Oh yes. I was no slouch
myself at your age. I once boxed for
Midlothian Boys.

FLETCHER

Who against, Lanarkshire Girls?

MACKAY

In the Army I boxed for the battalion.

LENNIE

Did you, Mr Mackay?

MACKAY

First Battalion. Argyle and Sutherland

Highlanders. Great regiment, great
tradition. A regiment I was proud
to serve.

FLETCHER

A regiment which is now defunct.
Despite all those nurks who put
stickers in their car windows.

MACKAY

I expect you were in the Ordnance
Corps, Fletcher. Something which kept
you well out of the line of fire. Probably
served your time embezzling stores in
some cushy posting like Shoeburyness.
He laughs.

FLETCHER

Well, you're wrong there. I did active
service. Malaya. Kuala Lumpur. That's
where I did my embezzling. And I
wasn't in no Ordnance Corps. I was
in the RASC.

LENNIE

What's that stand for?

FLETCHER

Run Away Someone's Coming.
He laughs.

MACKAY

National Service would have done you
good, Godber. The Army's good to
its boxers.

FLETCHER

I don't reckon boxing's such a noble
art at all.

MACKAY

No?

FLETCHER

I had a friend once – haven't told you

this before, have I? He was a light-
heavy. Good strong, boy. Won a few
fights. Suddenly thought he was the
bee's knees. Fast cars, easy women.
Classic story of too much, too soon.
He just blew up. He got into debt and
ended up in one of those travelling
booths. Four fights a night, seven
night a week. Well the body can't take
that punishment. His brain went soft,
his reflexes went. You know – punchy.
Just became like a vegetable – an
incoherent non-thinking zombie.

MACKAY

What became of him?

FLETCHER

He joined the prison service as a
Warder. Doing very well.
Mackay knows he's been had.
He goes.

3. LANDING

*It is evening. Fletcher moves up on
to the landing. He passes a Prison
Officer on the stairs and gives a
polite nod.*

3A. GROUT'S CELL

*It is evening. Grout's cell is extremely
well furnished. It is a single cell with
a quilted counterpane on the bed;
an expensive radio and record
player; a lamp made from an old*

*Chianti bottle; and several framed
pictures of friends and well-known
sporting personalities. He also has
chintzy curtains, a rug, a magazine
rack and a budgie in a cage. Harry
Grout himself is a heavy-set man;
an affable East London villain
though one should be aware of a
sense of power when he chooses to
switch off the charm. He is listening
to the radio on stereo headphones
when Fletcher enters. Harry looks
up and sees him, indicating that he
should wait a moment till he has
finished listening.*

*Fletcher enters the cell, looks around,
touches the birdcage and waits.*

GROUTY

Archers. Never miss.

FLETCHER

They still on, are they?

GROUT

Doris is in a bit of a state. She's got
Dutch Elm disease.

FLETCHER

Oh dear, poor Doris.

GROUT

Don't you follow *The Archers*?

FLETCHER

I don't, Grouty. Not for some years.
Not since Grace copped it when I was
in Shepton Mallet. That's nice.

Grout is putting on a dressing gown.

FLETCHER

I like the radio, mind. *Gardeners'
Question Time* and *Desert Island Discs*.

GROUT

I like a good play meself. And a *Book
at Bedtime*, never miss that.

FLETCHER

I like that. But of course they don't
allow us the wireless that late.

GROUT

Don't they? No one's ever told me.

FLETCHER

Don't suppose anyone's ever dared.
Nice place you got here.

GROUT

Do you like it?

FLETCHER

All the creature comforts. Like the lamp.

GROUT

Memento. Of Alassio. That's in Italy
that is.

FLETCHER

Wasn't it Alassio that they extradited
you from?

GROUT

That's right. I came back handcuffed to
Scotcher of the Yard on Alitalia. I paid
the extra and moved us both up into
first class. Bit of a perk for him, he's
never been south of Worthing before.
Bought the Chianti for me, duty free,
and got him a bottle of Sambuca.

FLETCHER

In the light of your subsequent
sentence, it might have been better if
you'd given the judge the Sambuca.

GROUT

I offered him five hundred quid, what
more could I do?

FLETCHER

Oh I suppose not . . .

Jackdaw enters with a tray of cocoa.

GROUT

Yes, come in, Jackdaw. Cocoa, Fletch?

FLETCHER

Oh, don't mind if I do.

GROUT

Sugar?

Hands Fletcher a two-pound bag.

FLETCHER

Thank you.

JACKDAW

(*Holding up a packet of bird seed*)

Should I feed Seymour, Harry?

GROUT

Yeah, go on.

Fletcher looks round.

FLETCHER

Seymour? Oh your feathered friend.

Very nice.

GROUT

He's company of an evening. When

I was in Parkhurst I had a pigeon.

FLETCHER

Oh like the Birdman of Alcatraz.

GROUT

Not really, no.

FLETCHER

No, not really I suppose. Took a

bit more room though, didn't he?

A pigeon.

GROUT

Just a bit, yeah. On the other hand

how else could I keep in touch with

the bookmakers?

FLETCHER

Oh I see – yeah.

He pauses.

GROUT

Brought me in a few bob.

FLETCHER

Yeah, must have done. What

did you do with it when you had

to leave?

GROUT

I ate it.

FLETCHER

Oh very nice. I should watch your step

if I were you, Jackdaw.

JACKDAW

Will we – that be all then, Harry?

GROUT

Probably, but hang about . . . oh

and Jackdaw?

JACKDAW

Yes, Harry?

GROUT

We're in conference so do the

minding, right?

JACKDAW

Yes, Harry.

He withdraws.

GROUT

Do you want a Bath Oliver?

FLETCHER

You got a bath in here an' all?

Grout offers him a biscuit.

FLETCHER

Oh, biscuit.

GROUT

With your cocoa?

FLETCHER
No thanks, Grouty. Got to watch the weight, you know what I mean.

He spoons four heaped spoonfuls of sugar into his cocoa.

GROUT
Well then; Fletch . . .

FLETCHER
Well then, Grouty . . .

GROUT
They're going to have this boxing match, aren't they?

FLETCHER
So I hear. Inter prison championships or something.

GROUT
Well then – money to be made.

FLETCHER
You mean a flutter?

GROUT
Sport means competition, don't it? Which means there's a winner and a loser. Which is all right providing you're on the winner.

FLETCHER
Forgive me for saying this, Grouty, but do you need the funds? I mean if you want money all you have to do is go to people and they give it to you.

GROUT
Where's the fun in that? We're talking about sport, my son. The speculation, the excitement, the tension, the thrill of the outcome.

FLETCHER
Oh the thrill of the outcome, yes.

GROUT
That's what I enjoy.

FLETCHER
Yeah, yeah.

GROUT
That's why I want you to fix the fight.

FLETCHER
You what?

GROUT
Well that's putting it a bit strong. What I mean is what I want you to do is to feed me certain information so that I get all my thrill of speculation and excitement from knowing that I'm on a certainty.

FLETCHER
Feed you what information, Harry? There's seven fights. Wing against wing.

GROUT
I know that, but as they all have to train in the same gymnasium, it just needs someone with an experienced eye to run over the form. Someone like yourself. As you know, in this nick I have a bit of a rival. Namely the presumptuous upstart, Billy Moffatt.

FLETCHER
That nurk, Moffatt. No contest, Harry.

GROUT
Nevertheless he's running a book. Without my seal of approval. So I'd like to take him to the cleaners.

FLETCHER
Yes, I sees your point, Harry, but you know me, I'm a loner. I sees myself as

the Randolph Scott of Slade Prison.
I don't like being responsible to nobody,
not even someone as distinguished
as yourself. So I think really the best
thing is for me to say straight off, very
adamantly, that I decline this flattering
invitation. Thanks for the cocoa.

He starts towards the doorway.
There is a very large prisoner
standing there.

GROUT

You disappoint me, Fletch.

Fletcher changes his mind and
returns to Grout.

FLETCHER

When do I start?

4. GYM

Lennie is sparring with Larry in the
ring. The PTI is watching them.
Fletcher walks into the gym.

REFEREE

What are you on, Fletcher? Charity
walk, is it?

FLETCHER

You know me, Mr Bayliss. I'm not a
man what gets involved in the
recreational pastime of this prison.
When all around me's a frenzy of
activity, I'm happy to be on my bunk
whittling. But I was lying there, you
know, and I was thinking about the
honour of the wing, and I realised that
it would be a crime if I didn't offer you
the benefit of my experience.

Mackay approaches.

MACKAY

What experience is this, Fletcher?

FLETCHER

Oh hello, Mr Mackay. My experience
of ringcraft, the noble art. Just telling
Mr Bayliss how my know-how is at
his disposal.

MACKAY

Well, we don't know what to say,
do we, lads? We're overwhelmed.
All right then, Fletcher. In the ring.

FLETCHER

In the ring? What d'you mean, in
the ring?

MACKAY

Show the lads a thing or two.

FLETCHER

I'm offering you my advice.
My expertise.

MACKAY

Have to show the lads a thing or two.
Show 'em the old magic's still there.
How else will they believe in you?

He starts putting gloves on Fletcher.

FLETCHER

The England Squad believe in Don
Revie, but he don't get on the park
and kick a ball around. Angelo Lundee
– he don't spar with Ali. Stays in the
corner, muttering words of advice and
minding the gumshield.

MACKAY

He wants to work for the squad, lads,
he has to show willing, doesn't he?

The prisoners agree. Fletcher
is trapped.

REFEREE

Go on then, Fletch, out you come, Larry.

Larry gets out of the ring. Fletcher climbs in. Fletcher walks up to Lennie who pushes his gloves forward in the prematch gesture.

FLETCHER

Now just go easy, sonny. Don't make me lose my rag. Hey, watch it.

LENNIE

Keep your guard up, Fletcher.

REFEREE

Seconds out.

He rings the bell.

FLETCHER

Fire drill, oh – back to the cells everyone.

He walks to the ropes.

MACKAY

Fletcher.

FLETCHER

Oh sir, sorry, sir. Yes, sir.

He returns to Lennie and starts ducking round him. Lennie just stands there in amazement. Finally he takes one punch at Fletcher. Fletcher falls to the ground.

5. UTILITY ROOM

It is evening. Jackdaw, followed by Fletcher, comes down the corridor and up to the door. He unlocks it. Grout is sitting on an old deckchair, smoking a cigar, when Jackdaw ushers Fletcher into the utility room.

GROUT

Come in, Fletch. How are you?

FLETCHER

I'll live, I suppose.

JACKDAW

Should I er – ?

GROUT

Yeah, keep an eye.

Jackdaw withdraws. Fletcher looks around him with some distaste.

FLETCHER

Preferred your other place.

GROUT

The less you and I are seen together the better. So what's the form then?

FLETCHER

Well there's not much to choose between any of the matchings, Grouty. Anybody's guess who'll win the flyweight, since they're both equally stupid and cowardly. Question of which one bursts into tears first. I think Big Mac's a certainty in the heavyweight.

GROUT

Well we all know that.

FLETCHER

The other certainty, I must say, is young Godber. 'Course being his second, I've been able to give a bit extra, y'know – phuh phuh.

GROUT

Yes, I heard from other quarters, he's well favoured. Good strong boy.

FLETCHER

And his opponent, young Nesbitt – he just hasn't got it. No contact.

GROUT

Well that's the one then.

FLETCHER

You won't get very good odds
on Godber.

GROUT

No, but I will on Nesbitt.

Fletcher realises instantly the
implications of this.

FLETCHER

Oh now, Harry . . .

GROUT

Tell the lad to make it look good. And
then go down in the second.

FLETCHER

Oh Grouty, please! Not the lad. It
means a lot to him.

GROUT

Means a lot to me, Fletch. Billy Moffatt
will be on your boy.

FLETCHER

But why him? Why not nobble
Big Mac? Get even better odds on
his opponent.

GROUT

Don't be daft. Where's the credibility
in Big Mac going down? He put
four screws in the hospital last
year when someone knocked his
jigsaw over. Can you see Hermigton
beating him?

FLETCHER

David beat Goliath.

GROUT

With a sling full of shot, not a
left hook.

FLETCHER

Put some shot in his glove?

GROUT

No, no, it's got to be Godber.

FLETCHER

But, Grouty, I'm not sure the lad will
do it. He's young, he's idealistic.
He's still got his scruples.

GROUT

If he don't do what I ask, he may not
have them much longer.

6. FLETCHER'S CELL

Lennie is doing press-ups on the cell
floor when Fletcher enters, diffidently
and watches him for a moment.

FLETCHER

Oh, anyone we know?

LENNIE

Just a minute, Fletch . . . twenty-four
. . . twenty-five . . .

He collapses, then staggers on to
his bunk.

LENNIE

Twenty-five, Fletch.

FLETCHER

That's very commendable.

He gives Lennie a mug of tea.

LENNIE

Thank you. And I did twenty pull-ups
on the wall bars before I left the gym.

FLETCHER

Twenty? Really?

LENNIE

Pull-ups. Yes.

Fletcher looks at Lennie panting on the bed for a minute and then shakes his head.

FLETCHER

Is it worth it?

LENNIE

How d'you mean?

FLETCHER

All these press-ups, and pull-ups. All these deep breathing exercises. And this weight-lifting. It's a bit daft in' it? I mean it's just punishment.

LENNIE

It's for the boxing, Fletch.

FLETCHER

I know, Len, I know. That's my worry, you see.

LENNIE

Why?

FLETCHER

My concern, my very genuine concern is that you're neglecting your pottery classes. And all those other arts and crafts activities in which you indulged so diligently. And what's happened to your elementary plumbing – that's gone down the drain an' all. You see there's no future in boxing. It's a mug's game. Snout?

He offers him some.

LENNIE

No, I'd better not.

He pats his chest.

FLETCHER

Suit yourself. Oh here, that reminds me. I got you some chocolate – your favourite, fruit and nut.

He gives it to him.

LENNIE

Oh that's ever so kind, Fletch. I'll save it till after the fight.

FLETCHER

Suit yourself.

LENNIE

You all right, Fletch?

FLETCHER

What do you mean, am I all right?

LENNIE

Well, the snout, the tea and the chocolate. It's not you, normally you're so mean.

FLETCHER

What do you mean – mean?

LENNIE

(*Standing up*) I was wondering if my right cross had done some permanent brain damage. I think you ought to go to the MO and have your bumps felt.

He laughs.

FLETCHER

(*Walking over to Lennie*) Now you listen to me, Godber, you listen to me. Just shut your mouth and hear me out, you cocky young scroat.

LENNIE

(*Sitting down*) That's better. That's the old Fletch.

FLETCHER

(*Crossing to Lennie*) No, it isn't. It isn't

your old Fletch you see before you but a very troubled man.

LENNIE

Oh?

Fletcher paces the floor for a few moments, then says.

FLETCHER

I'm a cynical old so-and-so . . . well, I don't have to tell you. It's 'cos I've seen it all. You on the other hand haven't seen anything. That's what gives you your naïve charm I suppose. You ain't had all the idealism ground out of you. Yet! But I have to ask you – well *tell* you – what someone has asked me – well *told* me – they were wondering – well they was insisting – if you could see your way clear – not that you have very much choice . . . I don't know how to say this, kid . . .

LENNIE

What is it you're trying to say, Fletch?

Fletcher looks him in the eye.

FLETCHER

Tomorrow night's not going to be your night, Lennie.

LENNIE

How?

FLETCHER

(*Taking a deep breath*) Harry Grout wants you to take a dive in the second.

Lennie stares at him blankly.

FLETCHER

Don't look at me in that way, son. You're shocked, of course you are . . . and me . . . I'm ashamed.

There is a pause before Lennie says, quietly.

LENNIE

I can't do that, Fletch.

FLETCHER

I knew you'd say that, Len . . . and I respect you for it. But you have to see the position I'm in.

LENNIE

I appreciate that, Fletch. But I just can't do it.

FLETCHER

But it means nothing! What does it mean after all! It's a wing against a wing. It's meaningless!

LENNIE

I know that.

FLETCHER

Then why can't you do this? For me!

LENNIE

I've already promised Billy Moffatt to take a dive in the first.

Fletcher is outraged.

FLETCHER

You've what! You're going to take a dive –

LENNIE

Keep your voice down, Fletch.

FLETCHER

(*Voice down*) You're taking a dive for Moffatt?

LENNIE

Yes.

FLETCHER

I don't pretend to understand the younger generation. I really don't.

Would you mind telling me why?

LENNIE

They asked me first.

FLETCHER

Oh, they asked you first. So you're in the market for corruption, are you? Case of the biggest bidder, is it?

LENNIE

Oh come on, Fletch! You know the score. I may be innocent and naïve but I'm not bloody daft. I'm au fait with the realities inside. I'd rather be clobbered in the ring than out of it. It's the easy way out – no skin off my nose.

FLETCHER

It's me that's going to get skinned! And not just off the nose neither.

LENNIE

'Spose you want your fruit and nut back.

FLETCHER

I most certainly do.

He takes it and starts eating it.

FLETCHER

You've disappointed me you have. You could have been a contender, you could.

LENNIE

But you just said . . .

FLETCHER

Never mind what I just said, you forget what I just said, it's none of your business what I just said! Things have changed between you and me. I'm disappointed, bitterly disappointed in you. I've never been so let down since

my son Raymond broke into his school one night and had a prior peep at the exam papers.

LENNIE

Did he?

FLETCHER

Yes he did, and he still didn't pass.

7. UTILITY ROOM

It is night time. Grout is still sitting in the same chair. He is talking to Fletcher.

GROUT

Well, I don't know what to make of youngsters today. No moral fibre.

FLETCHER

They won't be told.

GROUT

Poses a problem though, don't it?

FLETCHER

Now wait a minute, Grouty. Godber's still going to lose. We're all on Nesbitt to win, so there's no conflict of interests, is there?

GROUT

There's no odds neither. All the big money in this nick's on Nesbitt – wouldn't even get evens.

FLETCHER

Why don't we just withdraw gracefully from this one, Harry? It's getting ever so complicated. Why don't you just go back to demanding money with menaces?

GROUT

That doesn't satisfy my sporting

instincts, I told you before, I like the excitement, the old adrenalin. Only one thing for it. If they've nobbled Godber we've to make sure that he wins.

FLETCHER
How?

GROUT
You nobble Nesbitt.
Fletcher looks in pain.

8. GYM
Prisoners are coming in to take their seats. Grout and Jackdaw are among them. Grout looks at Moffatt.

9. CHANGING ROOM
The boxers are getting ready for the fight. Fletcher and Lennie come in.

LENNIE
What's up, Fletch?

FLETCH
I want a word.

LENNIE
What?

FLETCHER
The fix is on.

LENNIE
Well I know that, don't I? I'm going down in the first.

FLETCHER
Yeah, well don't hang about, 'cos so is Nesbitt.

LENNIE
Is he?

FLETCHER
Which is serious for all three of us. If you win, you're in trouble with Moffatt. If Nesbitt wins he's in trouble with Grouty. And whoever wins I'm in trouble with both of them. One of us is going to suffer, and it's going to be me twice. It ain't the customs of the fight I'm worried about, it's the outcome of the outcome.

LENNIE
Whatever it is it's going to be serious.

FLETCHER
That much is certain, my son. In fact the only element of speculation in this fight is which one of you hits the flaming canvas first.

LENNIE
What are we going to do?

10. GYM
The boxers enter with their seconds and climb into the ring. The Referee calls the boxers over to him.

REFEREE
All right, lads, let's have a good fight. If you go down take a mandatory count of eight, you break when I say break and you fight fair, right?

THE BOXERS
The boxers touch gloves and return to their respective corners.

FLETCHER

(*Putting gumshield in Lennie's mouth*)
Go in and may the best man lose.
*Nesbitt in his corner is also getting
his gumshield.*
The bell rings.

VOICE

(*Offscreen*) Seconds out, round one.
*Grout and Moffat are watching the
fight when both boxers go down.
Lennie is on the floor apparently
knocked out. The referee starts to
count. Fletcher, relieved, counts
with him.
Grout leaves, as do Moffat and the
other prisoners.*

11. FLETCHER'S CELL

*It is night time. Lennie is on his
bunk. Fletcher is brought into the
cell by a Warder.*

FLETCHER

Thanks very much, James. I'm
sorry I don't seem to have any
small change.
*The Warder goes and slams the
door shut.*

FLETCHER

(*To Lennie*) Are you all right?

LENNIE

'Course I am. Hardly touched me.
What did Grouty say?

FLETCHER

Couldn't say anything, could he?

LENNIE

He didn't suspect?

FLETCHER

He's all right. Bets were void, weren't
they? So he didn't gain anything – on
the other hand he didn't lose anything.
Nor did he lose any prestige to that
Billy Moffat.

LENNIE

A great idea. Nobody won, and none
of us lost.

FLETCHER

Er yeah . . . well, that's not exactly true.

LENNIE

How d'you mean?

FLETCHER

There was somebody who came out
of this ahead.

LENNIE

You?

FLETCHER

Confidentially, I made quite a bit of
money off of that bent warder who
works in the bakery.

LENNIE

How?

FLETCHER

I was the only bloke in this nick what
bet on a draw. Chocolate?

MEMORIES

Sam Kelly (Warren in the series)

'Can you imagine the joy in speaking the lines and working with those actors for someone who had hardly set foot in a television studio in 1975? That was me playing the illiterate Bunny Warren, a man who was inside because he couldn't read the sign that said "burglar alarm". And who better to be inside with than the brilliant Mr Barker. Don't mistake Ronnie for a comedian, he's a great actor with the skill and generosity that made newcomers like me gain in confidence with each episode, and the knowledge that with good actors around him the show would work and that he would shine. And shine he did! Norman Fletcher is without doubt one of the greatest creations in the history of television.

'Syd Lotterby had used me previously in an episode of *The Liver Birds* and in a one-off sitcom playing, of all things, Cilla Black's boyfriend. To have crossed his mind when casting *Porridge* has helped my career to take off in all directions, both in television and the theatre. Innumerable sitcoms later I give thanks to Syd.

'What do I remember of a fantastic couple of years? The hilarious weekly read-throughs (I deliberately didn't read the scripts beforehand); the rehearsals with Ronnie putting in his little looks, double takes and the odd extra line; Fulton Mackay fussing around on his way towards that marvellous performance. I watched relentlessly, instinctively knowing that I was learning all the time. I watched everyone: Beckinsale, Osoba, Biggins, Ken Jones. I learned things from actors far less experienced than I, and now that Ronnie has retired I can safely say that I stole some of his expressions and "takes" and shamelessly use them to this day.

'Favourite moments are many: Philip Madoc on the mating habits of spiders; Lukewarm knitting while waiting for a visit from his boyfriend; Fletcher wangling a weekend at home in his big bed with his big wife; the food riot (which nearly brought Ealing Studios out on strike); the two episodes with the legendary Maurice Denham as a bent judge; great visiting actors such as Ronald Lacey, Dudley Sutton, Madge Hindle, Patricia Brake and Peter Jeffrey. And a great comic coup was the fey governor who couldn't cope with anything, least of all Norman Stanley Fletcher.

'*Porridge* worked because it was truthful. Despite the laugh, jokes and hilarious characters there was no doubt that these men were in prison. Acting is about being truthful, nothing else, and we were blessed with two writers who knew that and who could write in no other way.'

Tony Osoba (McLaren in the series)
' "Disturbing the Peace" is one of my favourite episodes and I vividly recall filming the riot scene on the set at Ealing film studios. The *Porridge* sets were always quite superb – testimony to the brilliance of the designers Tim Gleeson, John Pusey, David Chandler and Gerry Scott. Many people were convinced that we shot the series in a real prison.

'I think the writing beautifully sets up the character of Napper Wainwright and his relationship with Fletcher. The late Peter Jeffrey captured the essence of Wainwright magnificently and later I was privileged to enjoy hooking and slicing my way round the golf course in the company of this delightful man.

'Meanwhile, back at the riot, can you imagine turning a group of thirty people loose in a canteen scene and encouraging them to chuck the food around? What we'd all have given for that to have happened at school dinners! And nobody telling you off. To make sure everything was suitably messy we were supplied with appropriate victuals: vats of mashed potatoes, tureens of mushy peas, etc.

'The downside to all of this delinquent fun was that we ran out of time whilst filming the scene and had to return the following day to complete it. Continuity meant that the costumes couldn't be washed and the set had to remain exactly as it had been left. Even now I recall with nauseous clarity climbing into my costume, still wet in patches with the congealing mushy peas, cracking in other places with hardened mashed potato and squelching around the set, slipping and sliding on unspeakable concoctions formed from our previous day's efforts. And as to the smell, well I won't even begin to describe that. Ah, all in the name of art! Fond memories.'

Philip Madoc (Williams in 'Disturbing the Peace')
'The first sight of Machu Picchu, the approach through the Sik and entry into Petra, the advent of sliced bread – could these moments in my life compare with the phone call from Ronnie Barker inviting me to be in *Porridge*? Comparisons are odorous [sic] and the jury is still out – but I can certainly say – without fear of contradiction, that the week spent with Ronnie and that splendid cast made upon me the most indelible of impressions. Ronnie, Richard, Fulton and Brian were perfect and we worked with an impeccable script. In Mr Williams I had the most interesting of parts.

'*Porridge* has always seemed to me to be underpinned with truth, subtlety and delicacy, and Sydney Lotterby was most clearly in tune with it all. I would love to have developed my character in other episodes, but Sydney later told me – unsolicited – that he had himself found the character fascinating, had tried to get hold of the writers (Dick Clement and Ian La Frenais) to suggest that they might like to extend Mr Williams's lease, but they were in America at the time and he failed to contact them. Nevertheless it was an experience just to be in this one episode, "Disturbing the Peace", and I know that whenever it still appears, it continues to provoke much laughter and is sheer enjoyment.'

SERIES THREE

MEMORIES

Colin Farrell (Norris in 'Happy Release')
Christopher Biggins (Lukewarm in the series)
Cyril Shaps (Jackdaw in 'The Harder They Fall')

SERIES THREE

EPISODE ONE: A STORM IN A TEACUP

1. FLETCHER'S CELL

Fletcher sits at the table reading a tatty paperback. He has a mug of tea. Warren walks in, eating an apple.

WARREN

What are you reading, Fletch?

FLETCHER

A book.

WARREN

No, I meant what sort of book?

FLETCHER

A paperback sort of book, lots of bits of paper all stuck together down the left-hand side.

WARREN

Is it a good book?

FLETCHER

I won't know that till I've finished it, will I? Which will be some time if I get these continual interruptions.

WARREN

I'd read books, if I could read.

Fletcher, for the first time, looks up, then looks back to his book.

WARREN

Is it a dirty book?

FLETCHER

Yes, filthy. Coming back from lunch, I dropped it in a puddle.

McLaren approaches.

MCLAREN

Reading a book, Fletch?

FLETCHER

No, I'm ironing.

McLaren peers over his shoulder, reading.

FLETCHER

Don't do that. Read over my shoulder. Can't stand that. Height of bad manners, that.

McLaren lowers his head to read cover.

MCLAREN

Mandingo . . . what's that about then?

FLETCHER

Curiously enough, it's about your lot. Slaves in the Deep South.

MCLAREN

Scots, are they?

FLETCHER

Blacks, sonny Jock, blacks. Your – ancestors. Toiling in the cotton fields.

MCLAREN

My ancestors are from the West Indies. Or at least half of them.

FLETCHER

All the same. Slaves an' that. This lot picked cotton. Your lot picked bananas. Comes down to the same difference. A load of blacks toiling in the fields under a boiling sun picking something.

WARREN

I thought slaves were in Roman times. In galleys, rowing like.

FLETCHER

Well yes, them, Warren, them was your galley slaves.

WARREN

But they was white. I know they was 'cause I've seen all them films. Set in Roman times. And they always had slaves in them. And Rosanna Podesta. Oh and Steve Reeves. Did you see Jason and the Golden Fleas?

FLETCHER

Jason and the Golden Fleece – fleece would be the word you had in mind, Warren – if you had a mind to have it in, that is.

WARREN

Oh what was that other one – I loved it at the time. Oh yes! Jason and the Astronauts.

MCLAREN

You dim nurk, Warren. You're thinking of Jason and the Juggernauts. I know that because . . .

FLETCHER

(*Interrupting*) Gawd! Listen Philip Jenkinson, if you'll excuse me I think this is where I came in. I remember it was that bit in the picture where Rod Steiger hit Sidney Poitier over the head with a cup of tea 'cos he wouldn't let him read (*Standing up*) his book in peace.

MCLAREN

(*Standing up*) Sorry, Fletch – we're just going.

FLETCHER

No, carry on – you might as well stay and see the shoot out at the end. With any luck, Jason there might get his argonauts blown off.

Fletcher leaves with his mug of tea and his book.

WARREN

That's funny. I didn't think they had guns then.

MCLAREN

When?

WARREN

In the days of Kirk Douglas.

2. ASSOCIATION AREA

Fletcher walks down the stairs with his book and his mug of tea. He goes to the table where Lukewarm is sitting. He looks at Lukewarm and then sits opposite him and starts to read.

LUKEWARM

Reading a book, Fletch?

FLETCHER

Oh gawd, don't you start. Just carry on with your balaclava, there might be another war. In fact, there will be if I don't finish this book.

He takes a sip of tea and puts the mug down.

MACKAY

(*Offscreen*) Harris!

Mackay walks up.

MACKAY

Stand where you are – stand still!

HARRIS

Me, Mr Mackay?

MACKAY

Yes, you. Don't move.

Lukewarm and Fletcher look up at Mackay.

MACKAY

You've been to the medical room.

HARRIS

Yes, sir. Just had me dressing changed like.

MACKAY

The orderly thinks you may have palmed some pills.

HARRIS

Not me, sir.

Mackay starts to search Harris. Fletcher looks up.

FLETCHER

Never a dull moment.

He takes a sip of tea, puts the mug down and goes back to reading. Mackay is still searching Harris who looks down.

Pills drop out of Harris's trouser leg and he kicks them over the edge. Pills drop down splashing Fletcher.

FLETCHER

Who did that?

LUKEWARM

Did what?

FLETCHER

Bleeding sparrows in our roof again? Anything on my face?

Mackay finishes searching Harris.

MACKAY

Come with me, Harris.

HARRIS

'Ere listen, I'm clean. You got no right. This is harassment.

MACKAY

(*Walking away*) I'll harass you, Harris – I'm going to strip you down.

LUKEWARM

Ooh, some girls have all the luck.

He turns away. Mackay looks for the voice. Then he indicates to Harris to come and marches him off.

LUKEWARM

He'd whip anything, him. Don't know what he wants with pills.

FLETCHER

(*Getting up as he speaks*) Oh come on. You know the racket in here. Always someone who wants to be picked up or zonked out. Inside same as outside, in' it? Can't see it meself. Not my cup of tea, drugs. *He walks off with his mug of tea and his book.*

3. CELL

Lennie is still in his chef's outfit, washing, when Fletcher enters, carrying his mug of tea and his book.

LENNIE

'Lo, Fletch.

FLETCHER

Oh, they've gone, have they?

LENNIE

Who?

FLETCHER

Warren and McLaren – the black and white minstrels.

LENNIE

Oh yeah. Hey, I did the lunches on my own today – did you like it?

FLETCHER

Tell me something – what was the name of that pudding?

LENNIE

Tapioca.

FLETCHER

Oh, tapioca was it? *He sits down.*

FLETCHER

D'you think you could sneak a dollop back here?

LENNIE

P'raps. Liked it that much, did you?

FLETCHER

No, but I need something to stick down the sole of my shoe with.

LENNIE

I'll ignore that. Can't bait me. Tapioca off a duck's back. *Fletcher takes a sip of tea.*

FLETCHER

Tea's cold now.

LENNIE

(*Crossing to his bunk*) Tapioca off za duck's back. *He laughs.*

LENNIE

What was the kerfuffle? I heard Mackay nabbed Harris.

FLETCHER

Oh that. Thought he'd been pinching pills from the MO's.

LENNIE

(*Removing trousers*) Had he?

FLETCHER

Probably. Didn't find nothing. Must have stashed 'em.

LENNIE

Wonder where?

FLETCHER

Why?

LENNIE

Wouldn't mind them dropping into my hands. Windfall that.

FLETCHER

You don't even knows what they was.

LENNIE

Wouldn't matter to the blokes in here. Currency.

FLETCHER

Oh I see, you'd sell them, would you? You'd take on the might of genial Harry Grout.

Lennie thinks.

LENNIE

No, p'raps not. I'd have 'em myself.

FLETCHER

Drug addict!

LENNIE

Oh come on, Fletch. Your generation has a lot of prejudice about drugs. It's fear through ignorance.

FLETCHER

My generation's sensible enough to know that drugs don't do no one no good no how. They're anathema to me, they are.

LENNIE

There's even drugs for that.

FLETCHER

What?

LENNIE

Anathema.

FLETCHER

Anathema is an expression, not an ailment.

LENNIE

I know, I was only making a joke.

FLETCHER

Godber, you have used up your joke ration for the month with that tapioca pudding.

4. LANDING

Harris comes out of Mackay's office, thinking.
He climbs up stairs and walks along the landing.
Arm comes out from a cell and pulls him inside.

5. GROUT'S CELL

Crusher has pulled Harris into the cell and he swings him round to face Grouty, who is sitting in his chair with a tray on which are the remains of his lunch.

HARRIS

Oh, hello, Mr Grout, sir.

GROUT

Thank you, Crusher. Would you take the tray away.

CRUSHER

Yes, sir.

He picks up the tray and hands it to Spider.

SPIDER

Didn't you like your tapioca?

GROUT

Oh that's what it was.

SPIDER

Want me to open a box of those crystallised fruits?

GROUT

No, I mustn't.

Patting stomach.

SPIDER

Tins of mandarins then? They ain't fattening.

GROUT

I didn't know we had any.

SPIDER

We hadn't but young Tomkiss had a food parcel, didn't he, Crusher?

CRUSHER

(*Laughing*) Yeah . . .

GROUT

And he gave us some?

SPIDER

In a manner of speaking. I know you likes a mandarin.

GROUT

I'll have 'em for me tea. On your way.

Spider leaves, followed by Crusher. Grout crosses to the right of Harris, picks up a napkin ring and puts his napkin into it.

HARRIS

Mandarins eh – rare treat.

GROUT

Harris.

HARRIS

Yes, sir.

GROUT

What did Mackay just do to you?

HARRIS

Frisked me over.

GROUT

Why?

HARRIS

Dunno.

GROUT

Must have had a reason.

HARRIS

Oh well, he alleged I took some pills from the MO's.

GROUT

Had you?

HARRIS

'Course not.

GROUT

Dangerous things to do. Dangerous things, drugs. If they get taken injudiciously, they can be harmful. Leads to addiction. Seen it happen too often.

HARRIS

Oh I see. Well, that's a good reason for me not to whip pills, isn't it?

GROUT

Oh I agree.

HARRIS

I didn't honest.

GROUT

Harris, you're a born tea leaf. It's force of habit. Whip now – think later. That's your motto.

HARRIS

Honest – I only went in there to get me bandage changed.

GROUT

(*Moving closer*) I see. By the way, how is the arm?

HARRIS

Oh well. It's coming on quite nicely –

He screams as Grout pulls at the arm.

6. FLETCHER'S CELL

Fletcher is on the top bunk reading.
Lennie is standing.
They are both startled by the scream.

LENNIE

What was that?

FLETCHER

I dunno. Someone's gone on hunger strike and they're force-feeding him your tapioca.

LENNIE

(*Going to the door*) No, but it was a terrible scream. Bloodcurdling.

FLETCHER

Probably one of your drug addict friends taking the cold chicken cure.

LENNIE

Cold turkey.

FLETCHER

Yeah, well they use chicken in here, don't they?

LENNIE

(*Returning to the bunk*)
You just don't understand, Fletch.
Fear through ignorance.

FLETCHER

(*Sitting up*) Listen, I'm not ignorant. I'm just more aware of the abuse than you seem to be. I've seen it happen. Saw some of my comrades in arms got addicted to morphine.

LENNIE

When was this?

FLETCHER

Comrades in arms. Wasn't in the launderette – when I was in the Army.

LENNIE

Why did they have morphine?

FLETCHER

To ease the pain of the gunshot wounds.

LENNIE

Where was you stationed, a rifle range?

FLETCHER

You're an impudent nurk, you are, Godber. While you were safely sleeping in your Smethwick crib, some of us was doing our bit for Queen and country. In the steaming Malayan jungle at the height of the terror.

LENNIE

You told me you was in the stores.

FLETCHER

In Kuala Lumpur.

LENNIE

There wasn't any fighting in Kuala Lumpur.

FLETCHER

There was in the stores. Anyway, I'm not talking about that. I'm talking about when I lay wounded in hospital.

LENNIE

You told me that an' all – four days with a septic toenail, wasn't it?

FLETCHER

(*Getting off his bunk*) Oh, it's easy for you, isn't it? Not being there in the heat of it. You heard that scream just now. When I was in hospital that would go on all night.

LENNIE

It's your own fault – you should have left the nurses alone, shouldn't you?

FLETCHER

Oh shut up. (*Looking at his mug*) I must wash this out.

He crosses to the washbasin. Grout walks in. Crusher stands in the doorway.

FLETCHER

Oh hello, Crusher – hello, Grouty.

GROUT

Hello, Fletch.

LENNIE

Hello, Grouty.

GROUT

Goodbye, Godber.

Lennie leaves. Crusher also leaves and shuts the door.

FLETCHER

What's up then, Grouty?

He puts the mug down on the table.

GROUT

Oh – I just er had a word with Harris.

FLETCHER

Oh, I heard you, yes.

GROUT

He whipped some pills.

FLETCHER

Comes as no surprise.

GROUT

Said that when Mackay frisked him, he dropped them over the landing.

FLETCHER

Really?

GROUT

Immediately under which there were only two people at the time.

FLETCHER

Yeah, that's right, me and Lukewarm.

GROUT

Well, Lukewarm wouldn't, would he – I mean anything for a quiet life, him. As long as he's got his knitting.

FLETCHER

Just a minute – wouldn't what?

GROUT

Take advantage.

He sits down.

FLETCHER

Take advantage?

GROUT

Of a windfall. Have a chair, Fletcher.

FLETCHER

Oh – thank you very much.

GROUT

See, this is the problem, Fletch. I want those pills back where they belong.

FLETCHER
In your pocket?

GROUT
Dear me no. In the MO's office.

FLETCHER
Oh I see. I didn't know you shared my views on the evils of drugs, Grouty.

GROUT
It's not that exactly. It's just that despicable pilfering of this nature could mess up my own pill-peddling operation.

FLETCHER
Oh I didn't know about that.

GROUT
(Gets out a cigar) Very few people do. That's one of its virtues. Now unless those pills are returned, Mackay is going to ask the MO to take an inventory to establish what's missing. And if that happens they're going to find that there's more pills missing than they ever imagined.

FLETCHER
Oh dear me, yes. Couldn't you replace them from stock?

GROUT
I haven't got any stock. I don't keep 'em. I peddle them.

FLETCHER
Yes, I see your point.

GROUT
Well then, we've got an hour.

FLETCHER
Oh, we've got an hour have we? Oh I see, yes.

GROUT
Yes. Fortunately the MO's over in the married quarters for an hour or so lancing Mrs Barrowclough's boil.

FLETCHER
Now Grouty, you and me know each other. I give you my solemn word – you know it's sacrosanct – that I ain't got the pills.

GROUT
The point is you're one of the few people in this nick in a position to acquire some *more* pills.

FLETCHER
How?

GROUT
Come on! You work the admin block. The Governor, secretaries, typists. Doesn't matter what sort of pills they are. As long as they're back in the MO's office – then I'll get the word to Mackay it's taken care of.

FLETCHER
Yeah, well that will solve it. Even supposing I can do what you suggest – what am I looking for?

GROUT
Pills is pills, Fletch. Aspirin, allergy pills, slimming pills.

FLETCHER

Here – those typists are all on the pill. They're all ravers over there.

GROUT

Now steady on Fletch, there are limits. If you whip those and the MO issues them to some poor bloke with toothache, what then?

FLETCHER

Stop his teeth getting pregnant, won't it.

He laughs. Grouty does not react.

FLETCHER

It's a serious matter, isn't it? (*Looking away*) Well, I can't guarantee anything, Grouty. But of course I'll do the best I can.

GROUT

(*Rising*) I'm sure you will, Fletch.

He walks to the door, then turns back.

GROUT

Oh, if there's any codeine while you're there, get a couple for Harris. Apparently his arm's playing him up.

He leaves. Fletcher is furious. He gets up and goes to the window.

LENNIE

(*Entering*) What were that about?

FLETCHER

Grouty wants me to whip some pills for him.

LENNIE

Why?

FLETCHER

To replace the pills Harris whipped.

LENNIE

Well, where are the pills Harris whipped?

FLETCHER

Precisely. Where are the peppers that Peter Piper picked? If we knew that, sonny Jim, there'd be no problem, would there?

LENNIE

(*Sitting by the table*) Barrowclough has pills.

FLETCHER

Does he?

LENNIE

All sorts. Nerve pills, indigestion pills. And he's a vitamin freak. He takes so many of 'em, I should think when he makes love he rattles.

FLETCHER

Don't think he'll be having a rattle for some time – apparently his old lady has a boil.

He sits down.

LENNIE

Depends where the boil is.

FLETCHER

The boil is in a very nasty place.

LENNIE

Where?

FLETCHER

Married quarters.

LENNIE

Ooh, nasty.

FLETCHER

And what is more, it is being attended to by the MO.which is why we've still got fifty minutes.

LENNIE

We?

FLETCHER

Oh come on, Godber, you're
supposed to be my mate, aren't you?

LENNIE

I'm your mate,
Fletch. Always have
been, always will be
I hope.

FLETCHER

(*Rising*) Then help
me get some pills!

LENNIE

I would do but for one thing.

FLETCHER

What?

LENNIE

You told me not to have anything to do
with drugs.

*Fletcher raises his arm as if
to backhand Lennie, when
Barrowclough comes in.*

BARROWCLOUGH

Fletcher?

Fletcher freezes, arm still raised.

FLETCHER

What?

BARROWCLOUGH

Raised arms.

Fletcher looks round for one.

FLETCHER

Raised arm, sir – where?

BARROWCLOUGH

(*Pointing*) There.

Fletcher sees it.

FLETCHER

Oh that. That is not a raised arm, sir.
That is a flexed arm. It's me muscles –
can't clench, you see.

He demonstrates.

FLETCHER

Muscular stress. It's due to me nervous
condition. I wish I had something for
nerves. A pill or something.

BARROWCLOUGH

I have pills for my nerves.

FLETCHER

Really – what an unbelievable
coincidence! Are you telling me you
have something which can alleviate
the suffering?

BARROWCLOUGH

Well, I don't carry them around with me.

Fletcher lowers his arm immediately.

FLETCHER

Oh don't you. No, I noticed you
weren't rattling.

He sits down.

BARROWCLOUGH

They're prescribed, you see.
They're only mild tranquillisers,
but they help me cope with the
horrors of life.

FLETCHER

Yes. How is Mrs Barrowclough?

BARROWCLOUGH

Not too good, I'm afraid. As you know,
she's not the easiest of women to live
with at the best of times, but now that
she can't sit down . . .

FLETCHER

Oh, we thought that's where it was.

BARROWCLOUGH

What?

FLETCHER

The boil.

BARROWCLOUGH

How did you know about my wife's boil?

FLETCHER

Oh – it just leaked out.

BARROWCLOUGH

We're hoping a hot poultice will help.

FLETCHER

You want to slap a dollop of Godber's tapioca pudding on it. That would make her sit up and take notice.

BARROWCLOUGH

Oh, that's what it was.

LENNIE

I'd like to see you lot do any better.

FLETCHER

Well, of course, a lot of these blemishes is caused by lack of vitamins.

LENNIE

Oh, I don't think so. I think a boil's more to do with the bloodstream.

FLETCHER

Shut your face, Godber. When I want a second opinion I'll go to Harley Street.

BARROWCLOUGH

I've always been a great believer in vitamins. I think that's why I have such a good complexion.

FLETCHER

(*Standing up*) Yes, that's what I need you know. 'Cos my nerves is caused by vitamin deficiency. You haven't got any to spare, have you, Mr Barrowclough?

BARROWCLOUGH

I'll bring you some in the morning.

FLETCHER

Oh – too late then, don't bother.

BARROWCLOUGH

Well, it's never too late to improve your health.

FLETCHER

By tomorrow morning my health might be a lot worse. Got anything for broken kneecaps?

BARROWCLOUGH

I don't think I follow.

FLETCHER

I shan't be able to either with broken kneecaps.

LENNIE

(*Mumbling to himself*) I do me best with the ingredients provided. Chef said my raspberry blancmange was the finest he'd ever tasted.

They look at him.

FLETCHER

No seriously, Mr Barrowclough, the main problem with my nerves and my lack of vitamins is the terrible indigestion it brings on.

BARROWCLOUGH

Oh, really?

FLETCHER

Yes, terrible.

BARROWCLOUGH

Oh I can help you there.

He produces a packet of Alka-Seltzer from his pocket.

BARROWCLOUGH

Have you got a mug, or something?

He picks up Fletcher's mug and goes to the washbasin to rinse it when Fletcher interrupts him.

FLETCHER

(*Holding two tablets*) No, don't bother. They're too big.

BARROWCLOUGH

What on earth do you mean, too big?

FLETCHER

Oh well . . . I mean my condition's too chronic for anything as big as that. I even get indigestion if I eat Rennies too quickly.

BARROWCLOUGH

I must say you seem to be in pretty poor physical shape, Fletcher.

FLETCHER

Oh, I can put up with it. The thing that really gets me is the blinding headaches.

BARROWCLOUGH

(*Taking the tablets back*) Then I suggest you go on sick parade tomorrow. Get a couple of codeine from the MO.

He leaves. Fletcher follows him to the door.

FLETCHER

That was no flaming help, was it? (*To Lennie*) And nor was you!

LENNIE

Not talking to you.

FLETCHER

Pardon?

LENNIE

Not talking to you.

FLETCHER

Just proved yourself wrong. Why do you think you aren't talking to me?

LENNIE

Had enough of your derogatory remarks about my culinary prowess.

FLETCHER

Has your culinary prowess got any relevance to the urgent matter at hand? No, it has not. When Grouty asks you a favour it is with the clear understanding that the favour will be done. If it isn't, he takes it as a personal affront and sends round his big henchmen to mete out retribution – from Crusher with love.

LENNIE

That'll solve your problem then – you'll end up in the hospital. No shortage of pills there.

Harris walks in.

HARRIS

'Lo, Fletch.

FLETCHER

You've got a bleeding nerve, Harris.

HARRIS

What?

FLETCHER

Showing your face round here.

HARRIS

Why?

FLETCHER

Cause of all the trouble, ain't you?

HARRIS

All right, all right I took 'em. But I haven't got 'em now.

FLETCHER

Well, what are you doing here then?

HARRIS

I heard you'd got a bit of a problem. You've got to find some pills and I think I know where I can lay me hands on some.

FLETCHER

(*Getting up*) Well flaming 'eck, Harris, why didn't you tell Grouty this in the first place?

HARRIS

Wouldn't dare. See, er . . . today wasn't the first day I nicked some. But I never knew about Grouty's racket. And if he knew I'd taken some before – ooh dear me – too dire to contemplate, isn't it?

LENNIE

What sort of pills have you been taking?

HARRIS

Anything. Always a market in here, isn't there? Uppers, downers, twisters, benders.

FLETCHER

Let me get this straight. What you're saying is you've still got a previous theft intact, have you?

HARRIS

Could be.

FLETCHER

So you give 'em to me, and I get them to Grouty pretending I got them elsewhere.

HARRIS

'Sright. I think it's a very noble gesture on my part, don't you? Get us both out the clarts, right?

FLETCHER

Yes, yes, very noble, Harris. Let's have 'em then.

HARRIS

No, no, hold your horses.

FLETCHER

What?

HARRIS

Depends, doesn't it?

FLETCHER

Depends on what?

HARRIS

How much?

FLETCHER

How much!!!

HARRIS

Fair do's. Give you a fair price an' all.

FLETCHER

Words fail me.

He walks to the window.

LENNIE

Has it occurred to you, Harris, that there's more at stake in life than a quick quid? Such as comradeship, honour, and chivalry?

HARRIS

No.

FLETCHER

Don't try to appeal to his better nature, son, 'cause he ain't got none. There's only one language the Harrises of this world understand and that's the one I intend to use in future negotiations.

HARRIS

What's that, Fletch?

Fletcher moves toward him.

HARRIS

No, no, Fletch . . .

7. LANDING

Several prisoners are in the association area.

Barrowclough is walking along the landing. As he passes two prisoners there is a loud scream.

Barrowclough looks around.

The prisoners do not react.

Barrowclough moves on.

8. GROUT'S CELL

Grout is on his own when there is a polite knock.

GROUT

Come in.

Fletcher enters.

GROUT

Oh, it's you, Fletch.

Fletcher puts a small packet in front of Grout.

FLETCHER

There you are, then.

GROUT

Already.

FLETCHER

Yeah, well, you said it was a matter of some urgency. But just for the record, those aren't the original pills. I did not steal them. I had to get those using all my ingenuity.

GROUT

(*Significantly*) Yes, I heard you.

FLETCHER

I just hope that this puts me at the bottom of your 'favours to be done by' list.

GROUT

Certainly, Fletch.

FLETCHER

What a lunch hour. Didn't even have time to finish my cup of tea. And now I've got to get back to work.

GROUT

(*Lying on the bed*) Yes, well, no peace for the wicked.

FLETCHER

Don't you have work to go to, Grouty?

GROUT

No, I'm on light duties, Fletch. They put me in charge of the swimming pool.

FLETCHER

That's nice, we ain't got one.

GROUT

I know.

FLETCHER

Oh – clerical error, was it?

GROUT

Something like that – which is why time hangs so heavy on my hands.

FLETCHER

Oh dear me. What a shame. Well I'd best be off then. Don't want to interrupt your boredom.

He walks towards the door.

FLETCHER

Aren't those crystallised fruits over there?

GROUT

Yes.

FLETCHER

My favourite them.

GROUT

Really, mine too. Pass them over will you?

Fletcher picks up the box. Grout has opened his pyjama case and is putting the pills inside.

GROUT

Any idea what these pills are?

FLETCHER

(*Walking to Grout*) Well, you said yourself a pill is a pill.

GROUT

No, but you got to be careful with drugs. These could be highly dangerous.

FLETCHER

Well – yes, yes – best be on the safe side. Try 'em out in the Governor's cup of tea.

Grout takes the box of fruits, but Fletcher, unnoticed holds back one fruit. When Grout is not looking, Fletcher puts it in his mouth and leaves.

9. FLETCHER'S CELL

Lennie is lying on Fletcher's top bunk, reading Fletcher's grubby paperback, when the master himself enters, not in the best of moods.

FLETCHER

What are you doing on my bunk, Godber?

LENNIE

More light up here.

FLETCHER

Yeah, to read *my* book by. Give it here.

He grabs it from him.

LENNIE

I only borrowed it.

He is swinging himself round on the bunk.

FLETCHER

Lost my place, in't you?

LENNIE

(*Getting off the bunk*) That's a good scene, that is. Where the plantation owner gets hold of the nubile young slave girl behind the cotton gin –

FLETCHER

Here, shut up, will you! I haven't got that far yet. Blimey, you got that far! You've had a hard afternoon, in't you?

LENNIE

I'm entitled. Up at four, me. No joke, you know, frying five hundred eggs at dawn.

FLETCHER

You want to make one vast omelette and let 'em get on with it. You could have tidied up a bit. I mean, look at this place. Haven't even washed the mugs out.

He swishes his tea into the sink, then reacts in surprise.

FLETCHER

'Ere, what's this?

LENNIE

What's what?

FLETCHER

Look.

He holds up a small packet of pills and moves to the table. Lennie joins him.

LENNIE

Where's that come from?

FLETCHER

It was in the tea.

LENNIE

Open it then, have a look.

FLETCHER

You know what these are, don't you? These are the original pills Harris got rid of. What are they?

LENNIE

(*Picks up two*) Can't be sure. Could be amphetamines. Or maybe Bennies.

FLETCHER

Whose?

LENNIE

Benzedrine. How did they get in your tea?

FLETCHER

They must have fallen from above.

LENNIE

Oh – Bennies from heaven.

FLETCHER

What?

LENNIE

Joke.

FLETCHER

Do me a favour.

LENNIE

It's funny though, isn't it? When you think of all the trouble you went to and they was under your nose all the time.

FLETCHER

Whole thing was a storm in a teacup.

LENNIE

What?

FLETCHER

Another joke. And better than yours.

MACKAY

(*Offscreen*) Move you men!

Fletcher puts his mug down.

FLETCHER

Mackay.

He crosses to the door.

LENNIE

(*Indicating pills*) Get rid of those.

Fletcher returns to the table.

LENNIE

He'll find 'em.

FLETCHER

Where?

MACKAY

(*Offscreen*) Don't lounge around the landing.

FLETCHER

Naffing hell.

LENNIE

Swallow them?

FLETCHER

Swallow them?

They grab some pills and start to swallow them.

Mackay looks in suspiciously.

MACKAY

What's wrong with you two?

FLETCHER

Nothing, Mr Mackay.

MACKAY

I can always tell when a man is acting suspiciously. Got something to hide.

He walks in.

MACKAY

Fletcher?

FLETCHER

No, sir.

Mackay goes over to Lennie.

MACKAY

Godber?

LENNIE

No, sir.

The container that held the pills appears to pass to Fletcher's hand. Mackay's head whips round. He points to Fletcher's hand.

MACKAY

All right, Fletcher.

He lifts Fletcher's right hand and taps it. Fletcher opens it but there are no pills in it. Mackay grabs the left hand which reveals the pills.

MACKAY

What's this?

FLETCHER
What's what?

MACKAY
I repeat what's this?

FLETCHER
Oh it's a thing, sir.

MACKAY
A thing that looks like a container
for pills.
He opens it.

LENNIE
Just a couple, like – for Fletcher's . . .

FLETCHER/LENNIE
Nerves – indigestion.

FLETCHER/LENNIE
Indigestion – nerves.

FLETCHER
I gets the indigestion on account of my
nerves, and visa versa.

MACKAY
Pills are a dirty word in this prison.
Nearly caught Harris this morning.

FLETCHER
Oh well, a man like Harris, sir.

MACKAY
Since the doctor told me what was
missing, I'd like to think the wretched
fellow ate the whole lot of them.
*Fletcher and Lennie exchange
glances. Mackay walks away.*

FLETCHER
'Scuse me, Mr Mackay. Out of idle
curiosity – what was they then?

MACKAY
They were the MO's own pills. Well not
exactly his . . . (*Crossing to Fletcher*)

They were for his spaniel's bad breath.
Carry on.
*He goes out. Fletcher and Lennie
look at each other.*

LENNIE
How d'you feel, Fletch?

FLETCHER
Rough . . . ruff.

SERIES THREE

EPISODE TWO: POETIC JUSTICE

1. LANDING
Harris and Lennie are carrying a bed, supervised by Barrowclough. They start to go upstairs.

LENNIE
Fletch won't like this you know, Mr Barrowclough.

HARRIS
He naffing won't. Didn't like you moving in here, never mind a third.

BARROWCLOUGH
Fletcher will have no choice in the matter. We're running a prison not a hotel. Prisons are very overcrowded this time of year.

LENNIE
Not surprising really. It's bitter out.

They walk along the landing and into Fletcher's cell with the bed, followed by Barrowclough.

BARROWCLOUGH
Take it in and lean it up against the wall.

Fletcher is crossing the bridge, singing.

FLETCHER
Some enchanted evening,
You may see a stranger . . .

VOICE
Shut up.

FLETCHER
Naff off!
You may see a stranger,
Across a crowded room . . .

He is making his way to his cell.

2. FLETCHER'S CELL
Fletcher walks in.

FLETCHER
Hello, what's this here?
A stranger in a crowded room.

BARROWCLOUGH
I'm just off, Fletcher.

FLETCHER
Oh no you're not.

BARROWCLOUGH
Pardon?

FLETCHER

What is that?

BARROWCLOUGH

What is what?

FLETCHER

That bed – what is it?

BARROWCLOUGH

It's a bed.

FLETCHER

What is that bed doing across
my already overcrowded cell?

BARROWCLOUGH

Well . . .

FLETCHER

And why is Harris here? I hope there's
no connection between that bed and
'orrible Harris.

HARRIS

'Ere, I only brung it 'ere.

FLETCHER

Oh good, then you can just brung it
out again.

BARROWCLOUGH

Fletcher, an alarming rise in crime
rates in this country has caused
an extra burden on an already
overworked penal system.

FLETCHER

Oh yes?

BARROWCLOUGH

That in turn has meant that prisons
have had to stretch their already limited
resources to try and accommodate the
extra influx of convicted felons.

FLETCHER

Oh yes I see, of course.

BARROWCLOUGH

Well, as long as you appreciate our
difficult position.

FLETCHER

I do yes. We've all got to make the
best of a difficult situation. Now shift
that bed out of here.

BARROWCLOUGH

Fletcher, a new arrival is moving in
here and that's that, so you may as
well accept it as a fait accompli.

*He leaves. Fletcher crosses to
the door.*

HARRIS

I'll be off too then, Fletch. Bit crowded
in here. I hope the three of you will be
very happy.

FLETCHER

Naff off, Harris.

HARRIS

Naff off yourself, Fletch. With knobs on.

He leaves. Fletcher closes the door.

LENNIE

I'm afraid the whole rhythm of our lives
is in some jeopardy, Fletch.

FLETCHER

Flaming outrage. Where's my shirt?

He goes to his bunk.

FLETCHER
What's the word then?

LENNIE
Well I had a word with Davey Greener who works in reception. He says there's three come in today. And one of them's a bit of a mystery. Name's Rawley. He was never documented.

FLETCHER
How d'you mean?

LENNIE
The screw just whipped him off some place. No documentation, no mug shots.

FLETCHER
Really?

LENNIE
I think they whipped him straight up to the Guvnor.

FLETCHER
Maybe he's a celebrity. Maybe a rock star on a drug bust and they took him off for a press conference.

LENNIE
He was no rock star. Kind of small and bald and flat-footed.

FLETCHER
Might be Elton John.

LENNIE
No, no, he walked like a pregnant duck.

FLETCHER
'Ere, 'ere, stop that.

LENNIE
Stop what?

FLETCHER
That. Drawing attention to people's physical peculiarities. I've noticed that about you recently. I was saying to Jacky, young people today are always taking the mick out of folk because they're too tall or too fat or walk with bow legs.

LENNIE
Who's Jacky?

FLETCHER
You know – bloke in the hobby shop. Fat guy with ears like jug handles.

3. GOVERNOR'S OFFICE
Prison Officer Collinson at the door. Rawley walks in.

COLLINSON
All right, Rawley, step in front of the Governor. Stand still, straighten up. Rawley, sir.

GOVERNOR
Thank you, Mr Collinson, that will be all.

COLLINSON
Excuse me, sir – you want me to leave you alone? With a prisoner?

GOVERNOR
(*Standing up*) It will be all right I think in this case.

COLLINSON
If you say so, sir.
He leaves. They wait for him to go.

GOVERNOR

Steven . . .

RAWLEY

Hello, Geoffrey.

GOVERNOR

I thought we should have a little
chat before we document you.
But . . . what can I say?

RAWLEY

Perhaps the less said, the better.

GOVERNOR

Tragic . . . how's Marjorie taking
all of this?

RAWLEY

As well as can be expected. And how
are you, Geoffrey?

GOVERNOR

Oh I'm all right.

RAWLEY

And – Muriel?

GOVERNOR

Busy as ever. She has her committees,
I have my prison.

Offers Rawley a cigarette.

RAWLEY

Haven't seen you both for such a
long time.

GOVERNOR

You must come round for dinner.
Oh no, of course, you won't be
able to. Silly me.

RAWLEY

Not unless my appeal comes
through, no.

GOVERNOR

This whole thing is most embarrassing
for me.

He sits down.

RAWLEY

It's a little worse than that for me.
The entire fabric of my life has collapsed.

GOVERNOR

Yes, but see it from my point of view.
We were at Winchester together.
In the Guards together. We're in
the same Club.

RAWLEY

We won't be for much longer – they've
asked for my resignation.

GOVERNOR

Nevertheless, our relationship is going
to create a bit of a problem.

RAWLEY

Is there any reason why people should
become aware of it?

GOVERNOR

Perhaps not. There isn't anyone from
the old school here, thank God.

RAWLEY

There's everything else though –
officers, Clubmen, Rotarians. In the
shower an embezzler came up to me
and gave me a Masonic handshake.

GOVERNOR

There you are, you see.

RAWLEY

I don't want to plead special treatment of course, but couldn't you separate me in a single cell with a few books?

GOVERNOR

Fatal. Can't have secrets in here. Cause speculation. Resentment. Best thing is to slip you into a cell with other men.

RAWLEY

But I'd be with a bunch of common criminals.

GOVERNOR

With due respect, Steven, since the verdict you are a common criminal.

There is a knock at the door.

GOVERNOR

Come in.

Mackay enters.

MACKAY

You sent for me, sir.

GOVERNOR

Ah Mr Mackay, I want to discuss a delicate situation with you. Please close the door.

Mackay shuts the door.

GOVERNOR

This is an old friend of mine, Steven Rawley, who will be with us for a while.

MACKAY

(*Shaking hands*) How do you do, sir? Will you be staying for lunch?

RAWLEY

If my appeal fails, I'll be staying for three years.

Mackay starts to laugh, then checks himself.

4. ASSOCIATION AREA

Fletcher is sitting at a table with Lennie, Warren and McLaren. Mackay walks through the gates with Rawley. Rawley is not in prison uniform.

LENNIE

Hey, that's him – the mystery man. Him with Mackay.

MACKAY

All right, you men. This is Rawley who's moving in with Fletcher and Godber. I don't know what you've heard about him already, but I want you to treat him just like any other prisoner – understand?

ALL

Yes, Mr Mackay.

MACKAY

Carry on.

He leaves.

RAWLEY

Good afternoon.

LENNIE

Afternoon. I'm Godber . . . you're in with us.

RAWLEY

Oh.

Fletcher has been staring at Rawley in amazement.

FLETCHER
God preserve us!

RAWLEY
I'm sorry?

LENNIE
Oh, this is Fletch. He's in with
us an' all.

RAWLEY
Really.

FLETCHER
You don't remember me, do you?

RAWLEY
Your face is vaguely familiar, but I
can't quite . . .

FLETCHER
Middlesex Assizes? Three years ago?

WARREN
Oh, did you two do a job together
or something?

FLETCHER
Do a job? He's the judge who bleeding
sent me here!

*Rawley peers at Fletcher anxiously.
The others stare at Rawley.*

FLETCHER
The Honourable Judge Steven Rawley!
In person! How are the mighty fallen!

RAWLEY
I'm sorry, I still don't recall you . . .

FLETCHER
Why should you? I am merely one of
a thousand faces who come before
you, while you weigh our lives in the
balance of what you call justice!

RAWLEY
(*Instantly*) It's Fletcher, isn't it?

FLETCHER
Oh, you remember now?

RAWLEY
I remember your rhetoric. I remember
your endless protestations of innocence.

FLETCHER
Which you were deaf to.

LENNIE
But you were guilty, Fletch. You've told
us that.

FLETCHER
That is beside the point, Godber.

RAWLEY
It did seem relevant when
I passed sentence.

FLETCHER
The point is the man was not fit
to sentence me, as his presence
here indicates.

WARREN
He's still a judge. Or he were at
the time.

MCLAREN
Yeah, but obviously a bent one.
When you're sent up it's one thing
knowing it's by an upright pillar of
society. But Fletcher's been sent
down by a fellow con.

FLETCHER
Thank you, Jock. He is the same as
me. How d'you think I feel being sent
down by a crook like me?

LENNIE
A judge inside!

MCLAREN
What d'they bust you for then?

RAWLEY

Bust?

MCLAREN

What were the charges against you?

RAWLEY

I was indicted on three counts for corruption at common low – party to a criminal conspiracy; forgery of legal documents under the Forgery Acts of 1913–48; and accepting an illicit –

FLETCHER

(*Joining in with Rawley*) – payment as an officer of the crown.

FLETCHER

That's bribery and corruption, don't camouflage it behind that legal mumbo jumbo.

RAWLEY

I have no wish to camouflage anything. As I instructed my counsel, 'Let light be shed on this whole sorry affair. Let's bring it out into the open, let there be no half truths or evasions.'

LENNIE

Well, that's refreshingly honest. So you're saying you're guilty then.

RAWLEY

I refuse to discuss the matter, pending my appeal.

MCLAREN

You're bound to get off. Old school tie, top lawyers.

RAWLEY

If they were that good, I'd be out on bail now.

FLETCHER

Listen, it's a token stretch. Most of what you call us common folk never get the chance of bail. Some blokes are inside for months pending appeal.

LENNIE

The same law sent him down what sent us down, Fletcher.

FLETCHER

What are you saying, Godber?

LENNIE

What I'm saying is, I think his presence here is very reassuring. It's a vindication of our legal system. It proves that no one is beyond the reach of the law.

FLETCHER

I just ask myself for every one of his kind they nobble, how many's getting away with it? The bloke who sent him up is probably worse than he is.

MCLAREN

Hear, hear!

FLETCHER

Why, do you know him?

RAWLEY

(*Making an emotional appeal*)

Don't you think I have a conscience? Can you imagine what it's been like, to live a lie?

FLETCHER

'Course we can, we're criminals.
does it all the time.

Barrowclough walks in.

BARROWCLOUGH

(*Approaching the table*) How are you
lads improving the sunshine hour?

*Rawley stands, pauses, then sits
down again.*

FLETCHER

We was just getting acquainted with
our learned friend.

BARROWCLOUGH

Oh you know who he is then?

FLETCHER

We met professionally, so to speak.

BARROWCLOUGH

I see. Well you men must treat Rawley
no different from any other prisoner.

MCLAREN

We will if you will.

BARROWCLOUGH

What's that supposed to
mean, McLaren?

MCLAREN

Dinna show no favours.

BARROWCLOUGH

Rawley will get no favours from me.
Whatever you were before, you're just
a number now. A statistic. A set of
fingerprints. A mug shot, like the
rest of these men. You'll pay your
dues the same way they do – is
that understood?

RAWLEY

Yes.

BARROWCLOUGH

Yes, what?

LENNIE

(*Prompting*) Yes, Mr Barrowclough.

RAWLEY

Yes, Mr Barrowclough.

BARROWCLOUGH

That's better. Now we must see about
getting you a job. Could you come this
way please, your honour.

*The others react as Barrowclough
leads Rawley away.*

5. CELL

*It is night time. Lennie is in his
pyjamas and is making up Rawley's
bed when Fletcher comes in from
the showers.*

FLETCHER

What are you doing, Godber?

LENNIE

Oh, just making his bed up.
He couldn't do it himself.

FLETCHER

Well, I suggest you let him bleeding
learn. Either that, or roll your trousers
up and wear a little frilly apron.

LENNIE

Oh come on Fletch, go easy on him.
He's lonely, he's afraid. Just like I was,
me first night.

FLETCHER

He's the enemy within. Within my cell, what's more.

LENNIE

No, he ain't, Fletch. He *was* a judge. But now he's a con like the rest of us.

FLETCHER

Don't you believe it. He's the establishment, he is. And I don't fancy the establishment breathing down my neck all day and all night. I mean you must admit it's a bit unusual, Godber.

LENNIE

What is?

FLETCHER

Well, when a judge sentences you to five years, you don't expect him to come in with you.

Rawley comes in, having just returned from the showers.

RAWLEY

Oh you've made my bed up, Godber, that's most kind.

FLETCHER

Ovaltine or Horlicks, is it?

RAWLEY

Excuse me?

FLETCHER

And what colour do you want your brown shoes polished?

LENNIE

Leave it off, Fletch.

FLETCHER

Where you been – having a nightcap with the Chief Warders?

RAWLEY

Look, I have no influence in here. If I had I'd be in a single cell with a few books instead of sharing with people like . . .

FLETCHER

Go on say it, people (*Crossing to the table*) like us, say it. Listen, let me tell you something about people like us. We don't make no alibis. We deserve to be here. But compared to you lot, there's something very honest about our dishonesty. Some people like us had no way of getting things, except to take them. People like you, you had it all, but you wanted more.

LENNIE

Look, he's a criminal now. Are you saying that right is only open to the poor? Don't you think the rich have a right to be criminals as well?

FLETCHER

They better not try it. The unions will be on to them straight away.

LENNIE

Don't be stupid.

FLETCHER

I'm not being stupid. You're being stupid.

LENNIE

I'm not being stupid.

FLETCHER

Well one of us is being stupid.

FLETCHER/LENNIE TOGETHER

Well, it's not me.

LENNIE

I'm just annoyed 'cause you're so inconsistent, Fletch.

FLETCHER

I'm not inconsistent.

LENNIE

Don't start that again. You are, you're inconsistent in your attitude. Inside is not out there. Inside's another world it is. We're all equal. We only have one enemy, that's the screws. And we only have one purpose in life, that's screwing the system.

RAWLEY

(*Sitting down on the bed*) Godber is right. I know we've always been on opposite sides of the fence. You're the sort of people I'd normally cross the street to avoid. But the fence is down now.

FLETCHER

I still think the gulf between us is immeasurably wide. I mean him and me, and most of the lads in here, we come from the same background, ran the same streets. They're a little different from your streets. Your streets have rich kids riding round on bicycles waving tennis racquets. Rows of elm trees and hand-carved privet hedges. Don't have no problems on your streets.

RAWLEY

Yes we do. I had to spend fifteen hundred pounds last year on Dutch Elm disease.

FLETCHER

Yeah? And I bet you went to a private doctor with it though, didn't you?

RAWLEY

Look, I know you're bound to feel cynical, I understand your attitude, but we all have one thing in common – we're in trouble.

LENNIE

He's right, Fletch.

FLETCHER

I'm just clearing the air, letting you know my feelings.

RAWLEY

I shall do my best to be as unobtrusive as possible.

FLETCHER

Unobtrusive, I see yes. Well get yourself a hammock then.

He crosses to the bunk.

FLETCHER

Shift your barrow.

Lennie moves. Fletcher climbs on to the top bunk.

LENNIE

He's a miserable old scroat. Listen, rules of the house. Top bunk's his. Seniority, like. No one reads the paper till he's through with it. It's best to speak only when spoken to, and his is the toothpaste with the marked tube.

RAWLEY

I have my own toilet requisites.

FLETCHER

Just as well.

LENNIE

Never borrow anything of Fletcher's without express permission.

FLETCHER

I am not mean, Godber, if that's what you're saying. It's just that I never give anybody anything. What one has one keeps.

LENNIE

Oh come on, Fletch. You are mean.

FLETCHER

No, I'm not. Thrifty perhaps. Frugal.

LENNIE

He unwraps Bounty Bars under water so I can't hear he's got one.

RAWLEY

I'll be only too willing to share any of the few things they've allowed me.

FLETCHER

Bribery and corruption, he's at it again!

RAWLEY

I only meant . . .

FLETCHER

Just get yourself to bye-byes, Judge Jeffreys.

RAWLEY

Well, let me say that whatever rules you make, I will go along with them.

LENNIE

Oh we're very democratic in here – Fletcher decides and we agree.

6. LANDING

Camera shows Prison Officers locking up.

6A. CELL

It is night time. Fletcher is on the top bunk. Lennie is lying on his bunk. Rawley is sitting reading in his bed. A Prison Officer looks in and closes and locks the door.

LENNIE

(*To Rawley*) Want some snout?

RAWLEY

Oh I don't, thank you. Only very occasionally.

LENNIE

Currency in here, snout.

RAWLEY

Really?

He looks very depressed.

LENNIE

You all right?

RAWLEY

Since that door slammed shut, I've realised what prison is all about.

LENNIE

I know the feeling. This is my first stretch, you know. But stir's a state of mind and survival's in your own head. His Highness taught me that. (*Jerking a thumb upwards to Fletcher*) It's only the first twelve months that are the worst . . . ha, ha, ha . . .

He registers that his joke has gone down like a lead balloon.

LENNIE

. . . Sorry.

RAWLEY

Don't feel sorry for me.

LENNIE

Oh, but I do. I mean, you've had so
much more to lose than the rest of us.
Position, respect. It's the classic story
of a man who had it all and blew it all
away in a moment of weakness.

FLETCHER

This is life, not *Peyton Place*.

RAWLEY

My weakness was a younger woman.
An avaricious, grasping nineteen-year-
old go-go dancer.

LENNIE

Oh, the younger woman, yes, typical.

RAWLEY

Yes, one sees it happen so many
times to colleagues. What is it,
some middle-aged madness that
affects us all? She was a sweet young
thing when I first met her. Then over
the years she demanded more and
more. Trinkets, trips abroad, a car,
a maisonette in South Kensington.

FLETCHER

I was wrong, this is *Peyton Place*.

LENNIE

How did you meet her?

The lights go out.

RAWLEY

Oh.

LENNIE

Half-past ten.

Rawley looks at his watch.

LENNIE

How did you meet her?

RAWLEY

At our regional reunion.

FLETCHER

Oh, nice. She was in your regiment,
was she?

RAWLEY

She was part of the cabaret. She was
assisting a magician called the Great
Alfredo. While he was making cockatoos
disappear, my eyes never left Sandra's
long shapely legs.

LENNIE

Long and shapely, were they?

FLETCHER

Look, where are those legs now?
One glimpse of a young thigh through
a fishnet stocking and look at you.

LENNIE

Well, human weakness takes many
forms. Desire, greed, lust – we're all
here for different reasons, aren't we?

FLETCHER

With respect, Godber, we're all here
for the same reason – we got caught.

7. LANDING

Barrowclough is on the
upper landing.

BARROWCLOUGH

B 3–76 all correct.

MACKAY

B 3 unlock.

A Prison Officer is in the
association area.

PO

B 1–83 all correct.

MACKAY

B 1 unlock.

A Prison Officer is on the landing
by the stairs.

PO

B 2–96 all correct.

MACKAY

B 2 unlock.

Barrowclough and the two Prison
Officers are opening up.

7A. CELL

It is morning. Fletcher is brushing
his teeth. He looks at the range of
toiletries on the judge's table.

FLETCHER

You can tell we have the upper
echelons in here. Have you seen
these toiletries? Mustang talc for
men, Rave D'Amour shaving cream
by Jean Marie of Paris, and exhibit

C, a badger's hair shaving brush.
My God, no wonder you never
see a badger these days.

LENNIE

(*Cleaning teeth*) Nocturnal animal,
the badger.

FLETCHER

Pardon, Godber?

LENNIE

Nocturnal. Only comes out at night.

FLETCHER

'Course they do. They've learnt their
lesson, haven't they? If they comes out
during the day, people keep making
shaving brushes out of them.

RAWLEY

You're more than welcome to use any
of my things.

FLETCHER

No, thank you. And you better not,
if you know what's good for you.

RAWLEY

Why?

FLETCHER

Any idea what effect Mustang will have
on the fairies in here? They'd all come
up from the bottom of the garden.

The door is unlocked and Mackay
walks in.

MACKAY

Good morning, Rawley. How did
you sleep?

FLETCHER

(*Poking his head round the door*) Oh
listen to this. Oh dear! All this time I been
inside, you never asked me how I slept.

MACKAY

I know how you sleep, Fletcher.
You sleep soundly because you have
no conscience, no shame, no guilt.

FLETCHER

True.

He returns to the washbasin.

RAWLEY

All the things which explain my
sleepless night.

MACKAY

You'll have the weekend to settle in.
Saturday today, you will stop work
at noon. Then the rest of the day
is your own.

LENNIE

I'll take you to the football match
if you like.

RAWLEY

I'm quite prepared to work on. Help kill
time, that sort of thing.

FLETCHER

'Ere – if you wants to be one of
us now, you knocks off when we
knocks off.

MACKAY

Typical prison mentality.

FLETCHER

No. Just a working-class mentality.

MACKAY

You see yourself as working
class, Fletcher?

FLETCHER

I always used to. Till I went to
Glasgow one time. Then I realised
I was middle class.

MACKAY

Fletcher!

RAWLEY

All I meant was I rather enjoyed the
work you assigned me to.

FLETCHER

'Course you do. Central Records.
Privilege, that is.

MACKAY

No, it's not, Fletcher.

FLETCHER

You'll have to admit it's one of the
cushiest numbers in this nick.

MACKAY

That's perfectly true, but that does not
mean it's a privilege.

FLETCHER

No, but which would you rather do,
Mackay? Central Records or Latrine
duty? Can't sit and read the paper in
there, can you? Well you can, but it
gets very repetitive. 'Now wash your
hands, now wash your hands, now
wash your hands.' One day inside,
he scores a job must trusties don't get.

MACKAY

He's an educated man. Isn't it logical
we should give him a job which
requires a clerical aptitude?

FLETCHER

If you don't mind my saying, so, Mr Mackay, leave it off. Since when has logic had anything to do with job allocation round here? Who was making our raspberry blancmange in the canteen yesterday? Riggs – and he's in here for poisoning.

LENNIE

Is he really?

FLETCHER

Certainly. Cause célèbre he was in his home town of Newcastle-under-Lyme. In fact, all his in-laws are under lime now.

LENNIE

Is that why they call him Arsenic Riggs?

FLETCHER

No, that's 'cos he once sat on a razor blade, you nurk.

LENNIE

He didn't, did he?

FLETCHER

Oh God preserve us.

MACKAY

I'm sorry, Rawley, that you're forced to share a cell with riff-raff.

RAWLEY

No, they've been most kind and considerate.

MACKAY

I hope so. Because I'm aware of the situation, Fletcher, between you and ex-Justice Rawley. But there will be no malice. No vindictiveness. No grudges borne from bitter memory.

FLETCHER

Grudge? How could I bear a grudge? What has this man ever done to me – except rob me of five years of my life.

8. ASSOCIATION AREA/LANDING

Camera shows a dartboard and a prisoner about to throw a dart, when Rawley enters the cell block. Rawley looks around and then moves along the landing. Harris tries to block his way. Rawley tries to get past him. He attempts to go upstairs but the way is blocked by another hefty prisoner. Finally Rawley manages to get to his cell and goes in. Fletcher is at the table reading. He looks up at Rawley. McLaren, Harris and the other prisoner follow Rawley into the cell. Fletcher shuts his book, picks it up as he stands up and leaves.

9. ANOTHER CELL

A prisoner is sitting on a bed as Rawley comes in followed by McLaren, Harris and the other prisoner.

RAWLEY

Good afternoon.

McLaren shoves the prisoner out of his cell.

RAWLEY

Seems rather quiet.

He turns to face McLaren.

MCLAREN

Oh it is. (*Taking Rawley's mug*) Everyone's at a game or visiting their loved ones. That's why we chose this moment.

RAWLEY

Moment for what?

HARRIS

Lots of blokes in here got something to settle with you. Blokes with long memories and even longer stretches.

MCLAREN

Doing you a good turn. Get it over with all at once.

He nods to the prisoner who closes the door.

MCLAREN

Then you won't have to live your life with one eye cocked over your left shoulder wondering when it's going to happen. 'Cause it's going to happen now.

Rawley tries to get up but is pushed back.

MCLAREN

Dinna fret looking for screws, there's not one in sight.

HARRIS

What do you think we are, naffing amateurs?

Rawley stands and struggles to go. Fletcher enters.

FLETCHER

Hello, hello, what's this? *Gunfight at the OK Corral*, is it?

MCLAREN

Fletcher, he's got it coming. Now you'd be the prime suspect, so we're doing you a favour. Get yourself across the yard and out of harm's way.

FLETCHER

Are you about to inflict damage on my cellmate?

HARRIS

On your what?

FLETCHER

On my cellmate. The bloke with which I share a cell.

MCLAREN

He's no friend of yours.

FLETCHER

He don't have to be a friend. But he's one of us now, and we looks after our own, don't we?

MCLAREN

What are you saying, Fletch?

FLETCHER

I'm saying if you takes him on, you takes me on an' all. Don't be misled by this bulky torso. It conceals a man of steel. On your way, Judge.

RAWLEY

On my way where?

FLETCHER

Out the yard. Go and watch the football, you need the fresh air.

Rawley pauses.

FLETCHER

Don't worry, the word'll go round. No one will touch a hair of your head.

Rawley goes.

HARRIS

Naffin 'ell, is that it?

MCLAREN

If Fletch says so, that's it. But I'd love to know why. What are you doing siding with the establishment?

FLETCHER

You knows me better than that. It's just that I uses my head. (*Holding book up*) What's this?

HARRIS

What's what?

FLETCHER

No, not what's what – *Who's Who.* I been looking up Rawley. Cross-referenced with our dear Governor. D'you know what – they only went to the same school, only went in the same regiment, belong to the same Club. They're lifelong bleedin' oppoes, those two.

HARRIS

That makes it worse!

FLETCHER

Does it? Do we quench our appetite for blood, or do we agree that what this cell block has always lacked, is a lifelong friend of the Governor? Think about it.

He drops book on Harris's toe.

10. LANDING

The Prison Officers are locking up.

10A. CELL

It is night time. Lennie is on his bunk. Rawley is sitting in his bed. Fletcher gives Rawley a mug of tea.

RAWLEY

Thank you.

FLETCHER

Comfy, your honour? Want another pillow?

He walks over to Lennie's bunk and takes his pillow. He goes back to Rawley's bed.

RAWLEY

(*Propping pillow under him*)

Oh, thank you.

FLETCHER

Extra blanket?

RAWLEY

No, thank you, I'm warm enough.

LENNIE

If you're scared of the cockroaches, we can take turns watching out for them.

RAWLEY

You're most kind. And let me say again, Fletcher, how much I appreciate what you did for me.

FLETCHER

A man in here has a right to prove himself.

LENNIE

Here – I said that first.

FLETCHER

Yeah. Well, it's hardly original, is it?

RAWLEY

You more than anyone, Fletcher, had every right to despise me.

FLETCHER

No point in that, your worship. No, let's just sit here and reminisce about happier times. Tell us about you and the Governor for example. That should while away a few hours.

RAWLEY

Myself and the Governor?

FLETCHER

Yes, well didn't I hear something somewhere that you once knew each other, was it?

He offers a biscuit.

RAWLEY

(*Taking biscuit*) Known each other for years.

LENNIE

Really, what a coincidence.

RAWLEY

I hope this doesn't explain your change of attitude, Fletcher.

FLETCHER

What?

RAWLEY

I trust you're not hoping to profit from my past relationship with Geo . . . the Governor. Because I must warn you that anything I know about him is in the strictest confidence.

FLETCHER

Oh, is it?

(*He gets up and removes the pillow*).

FLETCHER

I'll have me pillow back then.

He throws the pillow at Lennie and starts undressing.

RAWLEY

Fletcher. I am grateful. I do appreciate what you did for me today.

FLETCHER

Not all that grateful obviously.

RAWLEY

Shake?

FLETCHER

What?

RAWLEY

Shake.

FLETCHER

Shake what?

RAWLEY

Hands. No hard feelings, that sort of thing.

FLETCHER

Why should I have any hard feelings? You're only the bloke that put me in here.

RAWLEY

Fletcher, I had no choice.

FLETCHER

'Course you did. Several. Could have rejected the jury's verdict. Ordered a retrial. Given me a suspended sentence. Bound me over.

RAWLEY

Not in the face of the evidence.

LENNIE

And not with your record, Fletch.

FLETCHER

I suppose so.

LENNIE

You were guilty – you said so yourself.

FLETCHER

Yes, you're right. And seeing him in here has made me realise what a big mistake I made. My one regret is that I didn't know then what I know now.

RAWLEY

Oh, that's reassuring.

FLETCHER

What is?

RAWLEY

Remorse.

FLETCHER

Remorse! It's nothing to do with remorse! It's just that if I'd known you was crooked I could have slipped you a few bob!

SERIES THREE

EPISODE THREE: ROUGH JUSTICE

1. FLETCHER'S CELL

Fletcher is writing a letter.
Warren comes in tentatively.

FLETCHER
What d'you want, Warren?

WARREN
How did you know it was me?

FLETCHER
Rear-view mirror. What d'you want?

WARREN
I need a letter written. Home, like.

FLETCHER
Warren, how long you been inside?

WARREN
Nigh on ten months now.

FLETCHER
Don't you think you could have taken advantage of the educational facilities and got rid of your illiteracy?

WARREN
I'm not illiterate, Fletch.

FLETCHER
Forgive me, I thought that was the word what described someone who can't read or write.

WARREN
I'm not illiterate. I suffer from dyslexia.
Fletcher looks puzzled.

WARREN
You don't know what it means, do you?

FLETCHER
Dyslexia? Well, it's obviously some sort of acid stomach, isn't it? Though why that should stop you reading or writing, I can't imagine.

WARREN
You're wrong. Dyslexia is word blindness, like. I can't make out words when they're written down. They all get jumbled up in my head.

FLETCHER
Yeah, well there's plenty of room, ain't there?

WARREN
Tragic really. If they'd diagnosed it when I were a lad, I wouldn't be in here now.

FLETCHER

Oh here we go. The customary alibi.
The hard luck story.

WARREN

It's true in my case. I had a real
tough break. You see, I couldn't
read the sign.

FLETCHER

What sign was this?

WARREN

The one that said, 'Warning –
Burglar Alarm'.

Fletcher laughs.

FLETCHER

Pardon my laughing. That's much the
same excuse as Charlie Gill – he's that
burglar in B Wing.

WARREN

How?

FLETCHER

He's deaf, he didn't hear the dog.

WARREN

I didn't know he were short of hearing.

FLETCHER

That ain't all he's short of since that
Airedale got him.

WARREN

I'll come back later I think.

FLETCHER

No, hang about.

He walks over to Warren.

FLETCHER

I'll do it for you. Usual rates. Half a
snout a page.

WARREN

No, I weren't going to ask you.

FLETCHER

What?

WARREN

I were going to ask your new celly,
Judge Rawley.

FLETCHER

Why?

WARREN

Take advantage, like. He's a judge.
Educated man. Oxford. Public school.

FLETCHER

Oh I see – suddenly bowled over
by his worship's academic pedigree,
you've dispensed with my literary
services, have you?

WARREN

No offence, like. I just thought he has
to be the best person for the job.

FLETCHER

Here – letter writing is an art. A gift.
What sort of love letter is he going to
write? 'My dear Elaine, I am in receipt
of your letter of the 6th inst., wherebeit
I, the undersigned, hereforward to be
referred to as the third parly, etc. etc.'
What do you want to do, woo her or
sue her?

WARREN

Well, I just thought –

FLETCHER

You just thought wrong as usual. Letter writing is a creative art, endowed to a few of us. I mean, how many of you nurks in here have my poetic turn of phrase? For example, here's what I'm writing to my nearest and dearest – just read that. Oh you can't, can you, I'll read it. (*Reading*) 'My Darling, Though we have been driven apart by cruel fate, and an inexcusable misdirection of a jury by a biased judge, who is now sharing a cell with me, I know that our love transcends these grey, grim walls that have driven us apart. You are with me in my heart and this knowledge helps me to wring a few drops of comfort from the limp, damp towel of life. Kiss the baby for me, your own Norman . . .'

WARREN

Oh yes, that's beautiful, Fletch.

FLETCHER

Yeah, well.

WARREN

I'm sorry, Fletch. Will you do a letter for me? When you've got a moment?

FLETCHER

When I've got a moment, yes. But first I've got to finish this, get it sent off. Then after that I've got to write to the wife.

He goes back to the table and sits down. Rawley comes in.

RAWLEY

Oh, good afternoon, Warren.

WARREN

Oh, hello, Judge – your Honour.

He bows.

FLETCHER

Don't call him that. Don't smarm up to him. He is not a judge. He is a former judge, an ex-judge. He has been de-benched. De-wigged.

WARREN

He's pending appeal, and you never know . . .

RAWLEY

Oh, Warren, that matter you raised with me in the canteen. I'll give it a little thought and speak to you about it later.

WARREN

Oh thank you, Judge. See you, Fletch.

He goes.

FLETCHER

Oh – has he been raising things in the canteen again? What little matter was this then?

RAWLEY

Oh, just a legal matter. Something to do with his sister's tenancy of her council house.

FLETCHER

Oh, I see. Setting up shop, are we?

RAWLEY

Excuse me?

FLETCHER

Judge Rawley, QC, is now open for business. What you charging then?

RAWLEY

I'm not charging anything.

FLETCHER

Well, that's daft to start with. If you
have any expertise in here which
is in demand, then it's saleable.
Rule of the house. It's expected.
And any philanthropic notions will
be taken as a sign of weakness.

RAWLEY

Oh, I didn't realise . . .

FLETCHER

No, well, you ain't got the acumen.
I'll work out your fees, we'll split
'em fifty-fifty.

RAWLEY

I have no intention . . .

FLETCHER

You will do.

RAWLEY

I will not.

FLETCHER

Early days. We could clean up. I mean,
there's six hundred blokes in here,
all of whom has a legal gripe of one sort
of another. We do have an ex-solicitor
across the block, but he only knows
about mortgages and there's not a lot
of call for that in here. One thing we
are sure of is that we're always gonna
have a roof over our head – albeit with
a few slates missing here and there.
I tell you where we could score heavy.
All the poofs in here are getting a
movement together. You know,
'Equal Rights for Homosexuals'.
You're the perfect man to represent
them. Queen's Counsel, ain't you?

RAWLEY

I am not hawking my legal expertise
to the highest bidder.

FLETCHER

No need to. I do the hawking.
You just dispense.

RAWLEY

Out of the question. I would be mad
to engage in anything of that nature,
until I hear the result of my appeal.
Within a month I could be back on
the bench. One has to preserve
some sort of integrity.

FLETCHER

Oh integrity is it? I love your high
moral tone, despite the disgrace
you've wrought on your profession.
Do get it into your head, you're now
inside. Another world. It's a jungle in
here. And you just happen to be
fortunate enough to be sharing a
cage with King Kong.

2. LANDING

Harris walks along the landing.
He goes past two prisoners who
sniff the air as he walks by.

2A. CELL

Lennie is making a model aeroplane.
He looks up, sniffing the air. Harris
walks in.

LENNIE

Is that you?

HARRIS

Me what?

LENNIE

That pong.

HARRIS

There's a reason for this pong.

LENNIE

Well I hope so, Harris. Is it curable?

HARRIS

They've moved me back on the naffing farm, haven't they?

LENNIE

Nice job, farm. Lots of exercise. Fresh air.

HARRIS

Fresh air? I'm swilling out the flaming pigs. You know why, don't you?

LENNIE

Well, they try to fit people into their most appropriate function. You and pigs, that makes sense.

HARRIS

Watch your lip, Godber.

LENNIE

(*Tries to watch lip*) Can't see it from here.

HARRIS

I'll tell you why I'm on the farm. 'Cause they've been rejigging jobs round here. To accommodate your naffing VIP.

LENNIE

Judge Rawley?

HARRIS

That's him. And he only went straight into a clerk's job. Trusty's by right.

LENNIE

Has its advantages though, the farm. Don't you get outside trips, like?

HARRIS

Oh yes. Only today I went for a trip in the back of a pig truck that hadn't been cleaned for three weeks, slipping about inside. We picked up six new pigs and clipped back just in time for supper.

LENNIE

Couldn't you have had a bath?

HARRIS

This is what I smell like after a bath. Oh and I'm forgetting the highlight of the day – I caught a glimpse of a woman.

LENNIE

A female woman, really? What was she like?

HARRIS

Well, porridge does strange things to a man. It's the first time I've been turned on by a fifteen-stone pig breeder.

Fletcher and Warren walk in.

FLETCHER

What are you on, Harris?

HARRIS

Social call.

FLETCHER

(*Sniffing*) Dear me, what's that smell?

HARRIS

Put me back on the pig farm, didn't they?

FLETCHER

Yeah. I heard the pigs held a protest
march. Least it takes away the smell
of Godber's aeroplane glue.

WARREN

I quite like the smell, Harris.
Reminds me of home.

FLETCHER

Born on a farm, was you?

WARREN

No.

*Fletcher looks at Warren and shakes
his head.*

FLETCHER

Clear off, Harris, go on. It's beginning to
smell like a Turkish restaurant on a
Monday morning in here.

HARRIS

If this cell stinks, it's because of His
Worship. Don't know how you
stomach a bloke like that.

FLETCHER

We know what we can stomach.
Naff off, Harris.

HARRIS

We'll have him you know. In the end
we'll have him.

He leaves.

FLETCHER

Charmless nurk!

LENNIE

Hey, has he whipped my Aerofix?
(*Searching for it*) Oh no, here it is.

FLETCHER

You're always leaving that around,
Godber. I come back last week from
the shower and sat on it unbenknownst.
I had to be prised out me underpants
– talk about a stiff upper lip.

WARREN

Come on then, Fletch, let's have
me letter.

FLETCHER

Let's see the snout first, then.

Warren gives him a cigarette.

FLETCHER

Cor – who rolls yours? Twiggy?

*He walks across to get an envelope
from under his pillow.*

WARREN

Is it good?

FLETCHER

Fantastic, my son.

WARREN

Long as Elaine will like it.

FLETCHER

Without question. You see, last night
on the box they was showing an old
Rita Hayworth film. *Fire Down Below* it
was called. Which is exactly what your
Elaine will feel when she reads this.

LENNIE

Let's have a look.

Warren walks over to give Lennie the letter.

WARREN

Will you read it for me, please?

LENNIE

Who was Rita Hayworth?

FLETCHER

(*Sitting on the bed*) Gawd, Godber, you are ignorant.

LENNIE

No, I'm just young.

FLETCHER

Well, you missed out, my son. Your generation – what have you got? Television – Joan Bakewell and Janet Street Porter.

LENNIE

No, since the Olympics, my sexual fantasies are mostly East European gymnasts.

FLETCHER

I'm talking about women, my son. Your Rhonda Flemings, your Virginia Mayos. And at the top of that glorious pile of pulchritude was always . . . my Rita.

LENNIE

(*Peering at the letter*) Your favourite, was she?

FLETCHER

Still is.

LENNIE

Is that why you've put Dear Rita instead of Elaine?

FLETCHER

I haven't, have I? Give it to me.

He takes the letter.

FLETCHER

Where's me pen?

He gets the pen and changes the letter.

WARREN

'Ere, that's not going to look too nice. She'll think I've got a Rita on me mind. She'll get jealous.

FLETCHER

Not now she won't.

He sits down next to Warren.

FLETCHER

I've crossed it out and put Errol Flynn. Do you want me to read it to you?

WARREN

Yes, please.

FLETCHER

Dear Errol Flynn –

They all laugh. Rawley comes in carrying a towel and washing things.

RAWLEY

Fletch – oh good evening, Warren.

WARREN

Good evening.

RAWLEY

Fletch, I just bumped into that middle-aged Teddy Boy – what's his name?

LENNIE

Harris.

RAWLEY

Yes, very abusive.

FLETCHER

Don't you worry about Harris. He's all wind and water. You know what he's in for, don't you? Snatching an old-age pensioner's handbag.

WARREN

He never!

FLETCHER

At least he tried to. She pinned him down till the cops arrived. She kept hitting him over the head with the handbag.

WARREN

And that subdued him?

FLETCHER

Not half – it had a brick in it. She was just on her way to do a smash and grab.

WARREN

Oh blimey.

RAWLEY

Well, he was most abusive.

FLETCHER

Take no notice of Harris.

RAWLEY

But he threatened me.

LENNIE

Don't you worry, your Honour. If anyone comes on strong, you know we'll always back you up.

FLETCHER

Yeah, we'll see you all right.

RAWLEY

You already have. And I would like to say how grateful I am to you. You men have every right to despise me. Especially you, Fletch, since I sent you here in the first place. But you have shown me only kindness and compassion. I feel a bond with you men – I know it has been forged in adversity, but I think it will remain with me for the rest of my life.

FLETCHER

'Ere leave it off, Judge. Go on like this, you're going to make us forget our scruples and start liking you.

RAWLEY

No, I mean this. Who'd have thought a few months ago that I could so much as talk to you? Now I find that I respect – more than that – I trust you.

LENNIE

You mean that?

RAWLEY

Most sincerely.

He turns to pick up the towel.

His expression changes.

RAWLEY

Just a moment.

There is a pause.

RAWLEY

Which one of you stole my watch?

FLETCHER

You what?

RAWLEY

My watch. It was there when I went to the showers, it's not there now.

LENNIE

'Ere – hold your horses.
What's happened to this most
sincere trust you felt for us?

RAWLEY

That was before one of you
stole my watch.

FLETCHER

(*Standing up*) We don't rip each
other off. We're mates, oppoes.
We have a code.

RAWLEY

But I'm still an outsider.

FLETCHER

That's true. Give him his watch, Len.

LENNIE

That's not funny, Fletch. I'm no
petty sneak thief. Give him his
watch, Warren.

WARREN

Pardon? I haven't got his naffing
watch. I only come in here for me
letter, which I haven't had read yet.

LENNIE

See what you've done, Judge. Stirred
up mistrust among people who trust
each other implicitly. Go on, Fletch,
give him his watch.

FLETCHER

(*Waving the letter*) Talk to me like that,
Godber! You watch it, my son, or I'll
darken your outlook.

WARREN

(*Snatching the letter*) Don't scrunch it.

RAWLEY

I'm sorry, I'm sorry. I was being

stupidly hasty. One should never make
accusations without firm evidence.

WARREN

Never bothered the law in my
home town.

FLETCHER

What's that supposed to mean?

RAWLEY

But I swear to you, my watch was
there when I went to take my shower.

FLETCHER

Harris. Harris – how long was he here
before I came in?

LENNIE

Long enough. He could have palmed it
when I was glueing this aileron on.

WARREN

Come on then. (*Starting to go*) Let's
gerr'after that nurk.

FLETCHER

Hold on, hold on, you know the crafty
git will have stashed it by now.
*A bell rings. It is the prelude to
lock-up.*

LENNIE

Lock-up. Timed his exit well an' all.
Can't go nowhere now.

WARREN

I'll have to be off home, Fletch.
Should I not say nowt?

FLETCHER

Yeah, shtum, Warren. Me and
Judge will have words regarding
the possibility of further procedure.

3. PRISON

*It is night time. Prison Officers are
on their rounds.*

3A. CELL

*It is night time. Rawley and Lennie
are in bed. Fletcher is standing by
the window.*

RAWLEY

We cannot take the law into our own
hands. I shall report the theft to the
proper channels.

FLETCHER

Listen, we ain't going to set upon
Harris. We're going to conduct a
civilised investigation. We're all familiar
with the working of the law, and we're
fortunate in this instance to have a
guest Judge.

RAWLEY

What?

FLETCHER

Yes, one thing is certain, you do knows
your law.

RAWLEY

You mean, you want me to preside at
a hearing?

FLETCHER

At a trial, my son.

RAWLEY

But do we have
enough to go on?

LENNIE

Yes. Harris's reputation.

RAWLEY

I know he's objectionable, but is
he a known thief?

FLETCHER

You should know better than to ask
questions like that. We might tell you
things which would prejudice your
impartiality, know what I mean.

He gets up on his bunk.

LENNIE

Innocent till proven guilty, like.

RAWLEY

Of course, of course. Least I know
about Harris the better.

FLETCHER

'Sright. Why should you want to
know about him? A despicable
nurk like that what would sell his
Granny's Wintergreen.

He sees Rawley's look of dismay.

FLETCHER

Oh sorry, let that be stricken from the
record, your Honour.

LENNIE

Are you going to prosecute, Fletch?

FLETCHER

Certainly. Should be interesting, see
the other side of the fence, like.

RAWLEY

But do you know enough about legal procedure?

FLETCHER

Been up enough, ain't I? Look, when you chooses your living breaking the law, it pays to know the laws you're breaking. And I've had enough first-hand experience with counsels. Clever men, most of them. Although my last one weren't too bright, as my presence in this nick indicates.

RAWLEY

As the presiding Judge at your trial, Fletcher, I thought your counsel argued eloquently against – impossible odds.
Lennie laughs.

FLETCHER

(*Lifting up the mattress*) Godber! Listen, my counsel, Spence, that's him, he was a loser going in. And I ain't referring to the evidence. I'm talking about his attitude. He sent me this letter when I was on remand in Brixton. Listen I'll read it to you 'cos I kept it.
He gets it off the top of his cupboard.

FLETCHER

And you know what the pompous git says – I couldn't believe it. This was written to me while I was on remand in Brixton. 'Dear Mr Fletcher – '

LENNIE

It's good this.

FLETCHER

'I should like you to know that myself and my staff shall dispose ourselves with the utmost vigour and dedication in refuting the charges against you. Investigators will pursue a tenacious enquiry into unearthing evidence and testimony. Researchers will work into the night assembling and collating the facts at our disposal, on which I shall marshal a defence which has left no stone unturned, no avenue unexplored and which will culminate in your honourable and justifiable release. In the meantime, please proceed with your escape plan.'

4. BOILER ROOM

A table and chairs have been positioned to make a court room.

RAWLEY

This is most irregular, I cannot say I'm happy about these proceedings, Fletcher.

FLETCHER

Yeah, well happiness is relative, isn't it? I mean this is nick, who's happy – know what I mean?

WARREN

Hey up – here comes the accused.
He moves down the stairs.

FLETCHER

Under escort, is he?

WARREN

Yeah. Black Jock's got him in a half-nelson.

FLETCHER

All right your Honour, sit down. Court is convened.

A protesting Harris is propelled in by McLaren.

HARRIS

Here, here, what's going on then? You got no flaming right . . .

FLETCHER

Silence in court.

HARRIS

You what?

FLETCHER

Listen, Harris, we are here to pursue the course of justice and find you guilty.

RAWLEY

Fletcher, please. None of us heard that. Well, if we did it's stricken from our minds.

HARRIS

What is?

MCLAREN

The fact that you're guilty.

HARRIS

Guilty – guilty of what? Now listen, I'm . . .

FLETCHER

No you listen, Harris – shut up. A watch has disappeared from our flowery dell and you are the prime suspect.

HARRIS

Why me?

FLETCHER

Because otherwise it's us three and we're above suspicion. Right?

HARRIS

No, it's not flaming right.

MCLAREN

Shut up.

RAWLEY

I must protest these –

FLETCHER

Just stay out of this for the moment, your Honour, d'you mind? Thank you. Now, Harris, let me put your mind at rest. You shall get a fair trial. We have a qualified Judge with a long though slightly blemished record. We have an eye-witness.

HARRIS

Who?

LENNIE

Me.

FLETCHER

And I am going to prosecute you. But to ensure absolute fair play, you will be defended.

HARRIS

Oh.

FLETCHER

By Warren.

HARRIS

By Warren!

WARREN

What's wrong with that?

HARRIS

He's flaming illiterate, he is.

MCLAREN

Shut up.

HARRIS

Naffing hell – doesn't a man have a right to speak?

MCLAREN

In your case, only when spoken to.

FLETCHER

If you're innocent, Harris, what you in such a state about, then?

HARRIS

Wouldn't you get into a state if Warren was defending you?

WARREN

Here, Harris, I didn't volunteer for this job, I don't like you.

HARRIS

(*To Rawley*) Do you hear this, do you hear this?

FLETCHER

It's all right, Harris, he don't have to like you to defend you. You think any of our counsels liked us?

LENNIE

That's a good point, that is.

FLETCHER

Right, Harris, how do you plead . . .?

RAWLEY

Excuse me, Fletcher.

FLETCHER

What?

RAWLEY

Excuse me . . .

FLETCHER

Oh yes, be my guest.

RAWLEY

All right then, Harris, how do you plead? Guilty or Not Guilty?

HARRIS

Not Guilty.

FLETCHER

I see – a liar as well as a thief.

WARREN

(*Rising*) Objection.

RAWLEY

All right then, Warren, go on. What is your objection?

WARREN

Er – I don't know.

He sits down again.

HARRIS

Flaming heck. You were objecting to the fact that I was called a liar and a thief!

WARREN

No, I wasn't. We all know you're a liar and a thief, Harris.

RAWLEY

That remark will be struck from the record.

FLETCHER

This is all getting out of hand. I'd like to call my first and only witness, Leonard Arthur Godber. Take the stand, would you please.

Lennie moves forward.

LENNIE

I swear to tell the truth, the whole . . .

FLETCHER

Never mind all that, we've got about ten minutes before the screws tumble us. Just tell us about the events of last night, Mr Godber.

LENNIE

Well Mr Rawley took his watch off prior to going to the showers. At the time I was in our cell utilising my spare time in a constructive manner, i.e. making a model of a Flying Fortress.

RAWLEY

(*Writing*) Not so fast, Mr Godber.

Lennie looks at Fletcher.

FLETCHER

Hurry up, then.

LENNIE

Harris come in. Then Mr Fletcher and the defending counsel entered the room telling the accused to naff off.

HARRIS

Which I did.

LENNIE

Which he promptly did. Shortly afterwards the watch was found not to be there and has not been seen since.

RAWLEY

Counsel for the Defence – that's you, Warren.

Warren looks.

RAWLEY

Do you wish to cross-examine this witness.

WARREN

Pardon?

RAWLEY

Do you wish to ask him any questions?

WARREN

No, I were there, I know what happened.

Lennie goes back and sits down.

HARRIS

Flamin' heck – they're all in it together – this isn't justice.

MCLAREN

I've warned you.

RAWLEY

Let him speak. He has that right.

HARRIS

Thank you, Judge. Now you know as well as me that this is a mockery. They all know that this is flaming hearsay. No one can prove nowt. Like where's your evidence?

McLaren drags Harris back.

RAWLEY

Please, please. I have to agree with him. One man's word against another does not constitute legal evidence. This case would not stand up in a court of law, upon which these proceedings are supposedly modelling themselves. In the absence of evidence, there is no prima facie case and I am forced to dismiss the accused.

HARRIS

Thank you, your Honour.

FLETCHER

Now hang about, Judge – whose side are you on?

RAWLEY

I'm sorry, Fletcher, you insisted on a proper enquiry.

MCLAREN

Judge – your Honour – would a signed confession help?

RAWLEY

Do we have one?

MCLAREN

I could soon get one.

HARRIS

He's threatening me.

RAWLEY

Please, please, I must protest.

FLETCHER

You've had your go, Judge, it's best you stay out of this, know what I mean? McLaren, please. Now then, Harris, we don't want no unpleasantness. So wherever you stashed the watch, go git it out. All right? If you traded it, go trade it back. We just wants that watch back. If not, the consequences to your good self are too dire to contemplate.

HARRIS

Have I definitely been found Not Guilty?

FLETCHER

Yes.

HARRIS

All right – I'll go and get it.

He hurries off.

FLETCHER

See what I mean?

5. CELL

It is night time. Lennie is putting the finishing touches to his model when Fletcher comes in.

FLETCHER

Aye, aye.

LENNIE

Evening, Fletch. Look, almost finished.

FLETCHER

Oh yes, very good. How you going to get it in the bottle then?

LENNIE

Going to hang it on the ceiling. When I was a kid I had planes all over me bedroom. Me dad made them – from the war, like. Hurricanes, Spitfires, Messerschmitts. That's how I know what shape a Flying Fortress was. Me dad told me.

FLETCHER

Pity he didn't tell you about what shape Rita Hayworth and Rhonda Fleming was an' all.

LENNIE

No, he didn't talk much about women.

FLETCHER

Didn't he? Was he all right your dad? Not one of them, was he?

LENNIE

My dad – he didn't know they existed in them days.

FLETCHER

Oh yes. Your poofter just wasn't so blatant then. In my father's day they used to horsewhip them, you know. Now they've become fashionable. What worries me is they might make it compulsory.

LENNIE

Hey, seen the Judge?

FLETCHER

No, but I heard he had a call to see the Governor.

LENNIE

What'll that be about?

FLETCHER

Have to ask him, won't we?

LENNIE

Here, you don't think he'll blow the gaff do you? About our Kangaroo court?

FLETCHER

Nah. He's learned we takes care of our own. He'll respect that.

LENNIE

Specially since Harris gave him his watch back.

Rawley walks in.

RAWLEY

Hello, Fletch – Lennie.

LENNIE

Hello, your Honour.

RAWLEY

I'm glad you're both here because I want to thank you, and tell you that I now realise a lot of what you say is true. There are grave abuses of justice. There is often one law for the poor and oppressed, and another law for the rich and powerful. And the poor usually suffer while the rich get off with clever lawyers. I shall remember that lesson when I leave here.

FLETCHER

Which won't be for some time though, will it?

RAWLEY

Oh no. I'm going out tonight.

LENNIE

You're what – going out?

RAWLEY

Yes.

FLETCHER

Your appeal came through?

RAWLEY

Certainly. I'm rich and powerful. I have clever lawyers.

He goes. Fletcher and Lennie react. Fletcher sits on the table.

6. PRISON LANDING

Barrowclough comes out of Fletcher's cell followed by two prisoners carrying a bed. As they walk along the landing they pass Judge Rawley, now in civilian clothes. Barrowclough stops and says goodbye to him. The Judge then moves along the landing. He looks down to the association area and sees Fletcher. He turns and starts to go downstairs.

6A. ASSOCIATION AREA

It is night time.
The prisoners are reading and
playing cards, including Fletcher,
Lennie, Warren and McLaren.
The chatter fades away as
Rawley approaches. He is now
accompanied by Mackay.

MACKAY
All right, you men! Fletcher, Godber –
the Governor has kindly allowed
Mr Rawley to bid you a fond farewell.

FLETCHER
Oh, it's Mister now, is it?

MACKAY
Certainly. If the appeal court judges say
his nose is clean, that's good enough
for me. They are, after all, men of the
highest integrity, in the land.

FLETCHER
What are you talking about? He's *one*
of them!

MACKAY
Precisely. And he's innocent.
Which proves my point.

FLETCHER
(*Confused – thinks*) Just a minute.

LENNIE
Get out of that. You can't, can you?
Fletcher glares at him, defeated.

MACKAY
(*To Rawley*) As brief as possible,
if you wouldn't mind my laud –
the van is waiting.
He moves away from the group.

RAWLEY
(*A little uncomfortable, clears his*
throat) Er, gentlemen, it's just that I
wanted to say goodbye – and to thank
you once more; and to promise you
something. Whatever I can do to
improve the system, I shall do. This has
been a frightening experience for me
. . . but thanks to you men, a
rewarding one.
There is a moment's silence.
Their attitude is not clear.

FLETCHER
(*Gets up and shakes hands*) Listen,
you got a break. No one holds that
against anybody.
There is a murmur of agreement
with Fletcher's sentiments.
Lennie and Warren shake
Rawley's hand. Others give him
a clap on the shoulder and make
'no hard feelings' sounds.

LENNIE
(*Shaking hands*) You behave yourself
now. Don't want to see you back,
do we?

RAWLEY
Thank you, thank you . . .
He shakes hands with Warren and
McLaren.

RAWLEY
Bunny . . . Jock . . . Oh,
one more thing. Fletcher I'd
like you to have this.
He offers his watch.

FLETCHER

No, I don't want your watch. No need for that. 'Sides, only reason they allow watches in this nick is to remind us how slowly the time passes.

RAWLEY

But perhaps you could trade it. It's valuable.

FLETCHER

(*Taking it*) Oh, ta very much then.

He sits down.

MACKAY

(*Adopting the tone he reserves for visitors*) Time's up, Mr Rawley – mustn't keep the van-driver waiting, must we? He'll be wanting his tea.

RAWLEY

Once again then, goodbye . . . my friends.

He turns to leave.

LENNIE

Here, Judge. When we get out, we'll come and look you up.

FLETCHER

Yeah, talk about old times, re-establish our friendship, meet your family . . . Bring our wives round to meet *your* wife.

There is a chorus of agreement from the lads.

RAWLEY

(*His face registering the awful truth*) You will? Oh. That will be . . . awfully nice . . .

He goes.

MCLAREN

Off he goes – free as a bird.

FLETCHER

And free to go and find himself a bird, an' all.

LENNIE

While we remain behind to carry on vegetating.

FLETCHER

True, Lennie, true. But I like to think we've all learnt a little from his visit, albeit short. I think we may all have gained something as a result.

LENNIE

You have – you've gained his wristwatch.

WARREN

Needn't have bothered with that trial. Waste of time.

FLETCHER

Not In my case, Bunny. As Lennie so rightly remarks, in my case I have gained time – in the shape of this genuine gold-plated, fourteen-jewelled gents wristwatch, in full working . . . just a minute.

He rattles it to his ear. Then, with a deft movement, opens the back to the watch.

FLETCHER

Where's that Harris, I'll murder him – it's got no bleeding works in it.

He gets up and throws the watch.

SERIES THREE

EPISODE FOUR: PARDON ME

1. ASSOCIATION AREA
Prisoners are sitting at tables,
reading, playing cards, etc.
Fletcher and Blanco are playing
Monopoly. Fletcher has just rolled
the dice and picks up a 'Chance'
card. He laughs . . .

FLETCHER
Would you Adam and Eve it –
'Go to Jail, Go directly to Jail.
Do not pass go, do not collect . . .'

BLANCO
(Putting card at the bottom of pile)
I know the flaming words. Just get
on with it.

FLETCHER
All right, all right, then.

BLANCO
I could recite every card on the whole
flaming board if I wanted. Been playing
every day for donkey's years.

FLETCHER
(Giving him the shaker) No need to be
so grumpy though, Blanco, is there?
Go on, your toss.
Blanco tosses and makes
his move.

FLETCHER
Four and three. Seven.

BLANCO
I know, I can count. I may be old but
I've still got all my faculties.
He accidentally, on purpose, flicks
a hotel on to the floor.

BLANCO
Oh, I've lost a hotel – reach me it,
will you, Fletch?

FLETCHER
Leave it off, Blanco. I mean, none of
us was born yesterday. I know that
ploy of old.

BLANCO
Ploy?

FLETCHER
While I'm down there picking up your
hotel you help yourself. I lose Bond
Street and Kings Cross in the process.

BLANCO
That's a lie. Listen, Fletch, I'm not like

you lot. You take cheating as a way
of life. But I'm an older man with an
older man's sense of values, and if you
don't give a rats about my sciatic
nerve, I'll get the hotel meself!

FLETCHER

Hey, hey, hang on. I'm sorry, Blanco,
honest, I'm sorry. You're right, we're all
so corrupt in here, we forget there's
the odd honest soul.

BLANCO

Yes, you do.

FLETCHER

I'll find it for you.

*He bends down to look for
the hotel.*

*Blanco adds two more
properties to his street.*

FLETCHER

I don't see it.

BLANCO

Oh look, it's only there.

*He bends down to retrieve
the hotel from beneath his feet.
Fletcher swiftly helps himself to
some more money from the bank.
Blanco straightens up.*

BLANCO

Now, let's have no more talk of
cheating, let's just get on
with the game.

FLETCHER

Right, my son.

BLANCO

Your toss.

Fletcher throws.

FLETCHER

Odd number – three. I'm staying
in the nick.

BLANCO

My go.

FLETCHER

Come on then, seven and you'll land
on my hotels.

Blanco throws.

BLANCO

Ten! Missed you.

*With glee he moves on to 'Chance'.
Fletcher eyes Barrowclough
approaching.*

FLETCHER

Watch it, watch it, Barra.

*Blanco turns to look. Fatally, as
Fletcher takes a 'Chance' card from
his pocket and puts it on top of the
pack. Blanco turns back and goes
to pick up the card.*

FLETCHER

No, no, that's your Raquel Welch –
Community Chest. Come on, get on
with it, this one's the Chance pile.
Pick up your card.

Blanco does so.

BLANCO

'Go back three spaces.'

*Fletcher counts back, moving
Blanco's piece on to Vine Street.*

FLETCHER

Oh dear, one, two, three – that's Vine
Street with hotels. Ten hundred pounds.

BLANCO

What!?

FLETCHER

Ten hundred pounds, but I'll accept one
thousand pounds, thank you very much.

BLANCO

Oh, me back.

FLETCHER

Never mind your back, just give
us the money.

*Barrowclough approaches Lennie
who is sitting reading.*

BARROWCLOUGH

Are they still playing?

LENNIE

Four days now. Could make the
Guinness Book of Records.

BARROWCLOUGH

They're cheating each other into a
stalemate, that's why.

He walks across to Blanco.

BARROWCLOUGH

All right, you two. I think it's well nigh
time you wrapped up this marathon.
Lock-up in five minutes.

LENNIE

There's other people in here would like
to use that board. You do tend to
monopolise that game. Gerrit?

BARROWCLOUGH

What? Oh I see, yes, very
witty, Godber.

LENNIE

I thought so.

BARROWCLOUGH

Very sharp.

LENNIE

Quick as a flash, really. Do you know
what's brown, lives in the ocean and
attacks young mermaids?

BARROWCLOUGH

No, I can't say I do, Godber.

LENNIE

Jack the Kipper.

FLETCHER

Do you hear this? Palace of Varieties,
isn't it?

BARROWCLOUGH

(*Thinking*) Jack the Kipper . . .

He resumes his round.

FLETCHER

Come on then, we'd better write all
this down.

*He and Blanco start wrapping
up the game, making a plan
of where they have got to.
Lukewarm approaches them.*

LUKEWARM

Oh, here you are. Now come on,
you're a very naughty old person.
You promised me you were going to
wash your work shirt – so you'd look
presentable for the Parole Board.

BLANCO

I'm going to, aren't I? In a minute.

FLETCHER

Come off it, Lukewarm. Seventeen-year stretch, you think the Parole Board's going to be swayed by a clean shirt? It's his clean record that counts.

LUKEWARM

Silly to jeopardise it for the sake of a drop of soap and water though, isn't it?

BLANCO

Look, I've got two on Piccadilly.

He turns to Lukewarm.

BLANCO

I'll come in a minute.

LUKEWARM

See you do. I'm going to get the tea now. I've got your mug.

He leaves.

BLANCO

Worse than me daughter, nagging.

FLETCHER

I though he was your daughter.

BLANCO

Still, he does keep the cell spotless.

FLETCHER

Well, you soon won't have to worry about that. You're on your way out, ain't you?

BLANCO

No – nothing's certain. Nothing's definite.

FLETCHER

'Course it is. A doddle. A mere formality. Even Mr Barrowclough would bet on that, and you know how middle of the road he is on every flaming issue. If you ask for a yes or no, he says, 'It depends what you mean by yes or no.'

BARROWCLOUGH

What was that, Fletcher?

FLETCHER

I was saying, sir, you are unwilling to commit yourself on issues. Like to hedge your bets, sit on the fence, know what I mean?

BARROWCLOUGH

I do not. I'm as positive in my opinions as the next man!

FLETCHER

Oh well then, you'd agree Old Blanco's release is a formality this time round?

BARROWCLOUGH

Oh . . . well, I wouldn't like to say. I mean, one has to consider both sides.

FLETCHER

Oh – you sure you're not sure, are you?

BARROWCLOUGH

Oh positive.

He goes.

FLETCHER

Naffin' heck.

LENNIE

It's a disgrace he hasn't been free and clear years before now.

FLETCHER

You're on your way, Pop. Even genial Harry Grout's giving odds on.

BLANCO

I won't bank on nowt, Fletch. Too accustomed to disappointment.

FLETCHER

You know what your trouble's been? Always insisting you was innocent. You see that's where you make your mistake. For the Parole Board, it's better to be guilty and ashamed than innocent and defiant.

BLANCO

That's true. You have to show them how you've reformed.

FLETCHER

Right. In other words, you have to prove you've changed. That you ain't as despicable as what you once was. That's why parole's a piece of cake if you once was an alcoholic or a junkie, or dressed up in women's clothes.

LENNIE

So what about a bloke like me who only had the one lapse into petty crime. Who otherwise came from a decent home and had an 'O' Level in geography. What are my chances?

FLETCHER

I think your best bet is to buy yourself a cocktail dress and matching handbag. Naff all!

2. PRISON

It is night time. Prison Officers are on the prowl.

2A. FLETCHER'S CELL

It is night time. Fletcher and Lennie are lying in their beds.

LENNIE

Fletch?

FLETCHER

Huh?

LENNIE

Fletcher, do you think Blanco's a cert for parole this time?

FLETCHER

Need the beds, don't they?

LENNIE

What was he originally sent up for?

FLETCHER

Now, son, been inside long enough to know you don't ask that. Take people for what they are, not what they was.

LENNIE

I know that, Fletch, but come on.

Nothing you could say about Blanco would put me off the old boy. He's one of the nicest human beings in here. He's kind and gentle and helpful. Don't make no difference to me what he's done.

FLETCHER

He done his wife.

LENNIE

What?

FLETCHER

Done her in. Locked her in a deep freeze.

LENNIE

And we knock around with a bloodthirsty old scroat like that?

FLETCHER

See! That's why you don't ask.

LENNIE

I'm sorry, I'm sorry. That was an irrational outburst. Any roads . . . long time ago, wasn't it?

FLETCHER

Oh you mean it's okay to refrigerate your old lady as long as it's way back in 1959?

LENNIE

I mean, he's obviously changed. Had time to repent, like.

FLETCHER

The point is that he's never repented. Always claimed he never done it. Said she had a lover, and that it was the lover who killed her.

LENNIE

And was it?

FLETCHER

It's very probable 'cos he disappeared very smartish – he never hung around long enough to be asked.

LENNIE

'Spose there's no way of ever knowing now. So long ago.

FLETCHER

Right. And a wife can't testify against her old man, so there's no point calling on the wonders of modern science.

LENNIE

How do you mean?

FLETCHER

No point defrosting her and asking what really happened. Cor it's like an icebox in here.

3. CELL

Fletcher is sitting at the table doing a crossword. Lennie enters.

LENNIE

Here.

FLETCHER

What?

LENNIE

Know summat you don't for once.

FLETCHER

That'll be the day.

Lennie looks over Fletcher's right shoulder.

LENNIE

Well, I know thirteen across for a start.

FLETCHER

(*Irritably*) Look, Godber, if you wouldn't mind. Height of bad manners, that is.

LENNIE

Anyhow, it's Rook. 'Type of Bird'. R blank blank K. Rook.

FLETCHER

Not necessarily.

LENNIE

R blank blank K! What else could it be but Rook?

FLETCHER

It could just be – Rilk.

LENNIE

Rilk?

FLETCHER

Yes, Rilk.

LENNIE

No such bird.

FLETCHER

That is where you are wrong. See, Godber, you're not as smart as you thought you was.

LENNIE

What's a flaming Rilk, then?

FLETCHER

The Rilk is a migratory bird from the Baltic shores of North Finland. Its most distinguishable feature is that it flies

backwards to keep the snow out of its eyes . . . ask me another, Magnus?

LENNIE

I bet it's Rook.

FLETCHER

Too obvious, Rook. Look it's R I L K – Rilk. So what's this piece of knowledge you're aching to tell me?

LENNIE

Oh yes. First Parole Board results are through.

FLETCHER

And?

LENNIE

They've turned down Gibson who's in for car theft – and okayed Mal Brown who's in for manslaughter. I mean, that's barmy, isn't it?

FLETCHER

Not really. Just reflects society's current sense of values.

LENNIE

How d'you mean?

FLETCHER

Takes only one minute to create a life. Takes ten to make a car. And about five minutes for it to fall to pieces.

He walks across to the door and sees Blanco and Lukewarm approaching along the landing.

FLETCHER

Hey up, Nat Mills and Bobbie.

LUKEWARM

Well the old devil did it this time.

FLETCHER

What – worked his parole?

LUKEWARM

Yes – sailed through. It was that clean shirt that did it.

FLETCHER

Told you, didn't I? Doddle. Come on in.

They all go into the cell.

FLETCHER

He did it, Len. Sit down, Blanco. We're all very glad for you, ain't we, Len?

BLANCO

Ta, Fletch.

LUKEWARM

Surprise, surprise.

Produces some Jaffa cakes. Lukewarm and Fletcher stand. Blanco and Lennie sit.

LENNIE

Been a few changes, though. Since 1959.

FLETCHER

I flogged a hot car in 1959. Ford Zodiac it was. Two-tone Ford Zodiac with wing mirrors. Took the wife to Butlins on the proceeds. We won a bronze medal in the 'Tea for Two' cha-cha.

LENNIE

I were in Junior School in 1959. Sitting next to Ann Podmore. She was left-handed.

FLETCHER

Bet you got on the right side of her then.

BLANCO

I remember 1959 only as the year I were sent away for something I didn't do.

FLETCHER

Here, listen mate, you're casting a gloom on the whole proceedings. I mean, we're only trying to be festive, which does befit, dunnit?

BLANCO

Reckon?

FLETCHER

And here, now you're going out, you can level with your mates. Was you innocent all this time?

BLANCO

I was that. Listen, Fletch, I know you'd like to think I've been screwing the system all this time. But truth is, system's screwed me for seventeen years. That's why I've come to a decision.

FLETCHER

Decision?

BLANCO

Aye. For all these years, I've stood me ground. Claiming me innocence. If I accept parole you know what I'm doing, don't you? Admitting me guilt.

FLETCHER

(*Leaning towards Blanco*) Blanco, parole wipes the slate clean. It says you're free and clear.

BLANCO

It's not a pardon. It says you've done your bird for what they sent you up for in the first place. That's not good enough.

He stands up.

BLANCO

It says we'll let you out now and don't be a bad lad again. Well, I were never the bad lad they said I were in the first place. So they can take their parole – and SHOVE IT!

He turns on his heel and leaves them.

4. PRISON ALLOTMENT

Camera shows a spade digging. Fletcher and Blanco are in the prison allotment.

FLETCHER

You haven't, have you?

BLANCO

I have.

FLETCHER

Told 'em to stuff it?

BLANCO

Aye.

FLETCHER

What did Guv'nor say, then?

BLANCO

Put the wind up his clappers, I know that.

FLETCHER

You could be on the streets now, you know. Free. Queueing up at the Labour Exchange. Standing in the rain waiting for a bus. Couldn't you?

BLANCO

Waited long enough. Bit longer won't make no difference. Fetch me the scraper, will you?

FLETCHER

Rhubarb's coming on a treat.

BLANCO

Can't wait to get your hands on my rhubarb, can you? Thought I'd bequeath that if I got out, did you? In lieu of Monopoly debts?

FLETCHER

Don't be daft.

BLANCO

And me strawberries. Well, I'm still here, right? And this is still my allotment.

FLETCHER

We'd've looked after it, you know that. Till you came back inside.

BLANCO

Reckon you would. Just like life, prison. Makes plans and do naff all about it. Look at this place. I were going to do so much. Caulies, I thought. And spring onions, and big ripe runner beans.

Maybe even raspberries and goosegogs
. . . never got round to it. In all that time.

FLETCHER

Didn't one Governor once let you
grow grapes?

BLANCO

Aye, one time. I read all about vines.
Knew I could grow grapes here, even
in this neck of the woods. I did an' all.
Bloody marvel, it were. Seeing those
ripe juicy beauties, up here . . . then
they made me pack it in.

FLETCHER

Why?

BLANCO

Grapes make wine, don't they?

FLETCHER

Do they? Always used potato peelings
and anti-freeze myself.

BLANCO

Didn't tumble till we'd got about a
dozen bottles put down.

FLETCHER

Nice drop, was it?

BLANCO

In the wine stakes, I don't suppose
it was a classic. But to a man who
hadn't had a drink for eleven years –
Chateau Slade were the finest drop
I ever supped . . .

FLETCHER

If you weren't such a stubborn old
mule, you could be out there now
supping champagne.

BLANCO

Got me pride.

FLETCHER

Freedom's pride.

BLANCO

Want both, Fletch.

FLETCHER

Have to see what we can do then.
Fletcher walks away.

5. ASSOCIATION AREA

Barrowclough comes down stairs.
He walks along the area and is
surprised to find Fletcher, Lennie
and Lukewarm sitting there.

BARROWCLOUGH

Saturday, and you're all indoors!

FLETCHER

Crow, sir.

BARROWCLOUGH

I beg your pardon?

FLETCHER

These are the central headquarters of
our campaign – Crow . . . C–R–O–W.

BARROWCLOUGH

Which stands for what?

FLETCHER

The Campaign for the Release of
Old Webb. You know – Blanco.
We wanted to make it the Campaign
for the Release and Pardon of Old
Webb, but that would've spelt Crapow

– which sounds a bit rude when
you're petitioning the Home Office.

BARROWCLOUGH
The Home Office?

FLETCHER
Well, eventually the Home Office.
The Governor first.

LENNIE
See, Old Blanco doesn't want to go out
free and guilty. So we have to make
sure he goes out free and innocent.

LUKEWARM
Which is what Crow is all about.

LENNIE
Already got three hundred signatures.

BARROWCLOUGH
But what are you petitioning for?

FLETCHER
There's two ways we can spring him.
First, we can demand a retrial.

BARROWCLOUGH
After all this time! I should think the
Judge, the jury and most of the
witnesses are nearly all dead by now.

FLETCHER
Yeah, well that may be to the old boy's
advantage, know what I mean?
Secondly, the Governor has the right to
request a pardon from the Home Office,

under Sub-section twenty-three,
Part three, Paragraph D, Penal Code
(*Giving Barrowclough the book*) as
amended by the Act of 1972.

BARROWCLOUGH
Really?

FLETCHER
Oh yes, well-known fact that is.
But we're going for the retrial.
That's what this petition's all about.

*Warren comes in with a sheet of
paper in his hand.*

WARREN
Hey, look at this, Fletch. I've done
the mailbag room and got sixty-
three signatures.

He sits down.

LUKEWARM
Oh, lovely.

LENNIE
Give 'em here, Warren.

He takes the sheet.

BARROWCLOUGH
Just a minute. Sixty-three? There's only
forty fellows work in the mailbag room.

FLETCHER
Just goes to show the strength of their
feelings, don't it?

BARROWCLOUGH
There are twenty-three Xs on this
sheet, Warren.

WARREN
Lot of folk in this nick can't write.

BARROWCLOUGH
How can you be sure that these Xs are
the genuine article?

FLETCHER

Don't be daft, Mr Barrowclough.
Look at the difference in the handwriting.
Look here – one bloke's spelt X with
a Y. I'll cross him off.

BARROWCLOUGH

Well, I have to say it's a praiseworthy
effort. My only fear is the Governor's
attitude. He has an automatic
resistance to any notion proposed
by you lot.

FLETCHER

You could maybe help us there,
Mr Barrowclough, sir. Add some
weight to our pitch, like.

LENNIE

Give us the credibility we apparently lack.

BARROWCLOUGH

How?

FLETCHER

Well, you're a humanitarian, ain'tcha?
You're no hardnose.

WARREN

You've played fair with us.

LENNIE

Always have done.

LUKEWARM

Always seen our point of view.

FLETCHER

Your example has brought reason and
compassion into a world where too
often only violence prevails.

ALL

Yes.

BARROWCLOUGH

Well, as you know, I consider you men
are in here to be helped, not punished.
I try to understand, not condemn.
I respect your rights and if you have a
just cause, I'll back it to the hilt.

FLETCHER

Never doubted it, sir, so would you just
add your Monica here.

He offers Barrowclough the sheet.

BARROWCLOUGH

What?

LENNIE

Just cause, sir.

FLETCHER

Here's a pen.

LENNIE

Here, that's my pen.

He takes it.

LENNIE

That's where it went.

FLETCHER

Shut up.

He takes the pen back.

FLETCHER

Here you are, Mr Barrowclough.

BARROWCLOUGH

Oh no, you don't. No blinking fear.
I'm up for promotion next month.
I'm not jeopardising that by being party
to a prisoners' conspiracy!

He goes.

LUKEWARM
Well, I never.

LENNIE
Hardly the humanitarian we reckoned, is he?

FLETCHER
No, but give him his dues, he's smarter than we thought.

LENNIE
Pity, though. Get his signature and a few more screws might've followed.

FLETCHER
No bother.

He reaches for the pen and starts to write.

FLETCHER
H.J. Barrowclough . . .

WARREN
Can you really forge Barra's signature?

FLETCHER
'Course I can. How d'you think we got the new requisition for ping pong balls last week?

LENNIE
You'll be for it if they trace it back to you, Fletch.

FLETCHER
They're more likely to trace it back to you, it's your pen.

He puts the pen in front of Lennie.

6. GOVERNOR'S OFFICE

The Governor and Mackay are standing by the desk.

MACKAY
It means trouble, sir, with a capital T. We've got to stamp it out from the word go.

GOVERNOR
All right, they'd better come in.

MACKAY
(*Walking over to the door*) All right, Mr Barrowclough, wheel 'em in.

Barrowclough enters with Fletcher, Lennie, Warren and Lukewarm.

BARROWCLOUGH
Left, right, left. Left, right, left.

MACKAY
Stand still in front of the Governor.

BARROWCLOUGH
The petitioners, sir.

GOVERNOR
Now listen, you men, I'm not in favour of prisoners' pressure groups.

BARROWCLOUGH
They have the right, Governor, under sub-section thirteen which clearly states that in the event of –

GOVERNOR
Don't spout the Penal Code at me, Barrowclough.

FLETCHER
Let us say straight off, sir, how much we appreciate you seeing us. May I present, sir, for your perusal and consideration (*Placing petition on the desk*) our petition for the retrial of Old Man Blanco, sir.

The Governor looks at the sheets of signatures.

GOVERNOR

Do we have this many men here?

LENNIE

The petition, sir, is a sincere expression of the feeling in Slade Prison. And the fact they have responded in this way is a tribute to your enlightened administration.

GOVERNOR

Is it?

FLETCHER

Oh most certainly, sir. All them blokes out there, burly felons, putting their names to a piece of paper. In, as the lad puts it, a less enlightened administration, they'd have torn the place apart by now.

MACKAY

Is that a threat, Fletcher!

FLETCHER

Not a threat, sir. Observation. Based on several years of first-hand experience of the mood of the incarcerated male.

GOVERNOR

The mood is this strong?

FLETCHER

Growing stronger every minute . . . and uglier, sir. Present company excepted of course.

MACKAY

Sir, what is the point of this? The authorities have been compassionate enough to offer Webb a parole. He should accept it and be grateful for it.

FLETCHER

Not enough, Mr Mackay. Had to clear his name, see?

MACKAY

Then the man's a stubborn old fool.

BARROWCLOUGH

No, no, no. Stubborn, but not foolish. Something quite heroic about all this.

He trails off catching Mackay's incensed look.

BARROWCLOUGH

But, as you say, the man's a fool.

GOVERNOR

The case was too long ago, Fletcher, for a re-trial.

FLETCHER

There's ways and means, sir. This petition's only the first step in making this a national issue.

GOVERNOR

National?

LENNIE

We want to make Old Blanco a national hero. We want to touch the conscience of the nation. We want the spotlight of the mass media on the old fella.

GOVERNOR

Mass media!

FLETCHER

Yeah, make him a corse celebre . . .
Get him on the telly, in the papers.
You might be a celebrity yourself,
Governor. Might get on the *Michael
Parkinson Show* – or if the worst
came to the worst, Esther Rantzen.

MACKAY

There's no way in the world that
this petition could escalate into a
national issue.

FLETCHER

Oh in itself, no, Mr Mackay, you're
right of course. That's why we need
the hunger strike.

GOVERNOR

Hunger strike – what hunger strike?

FLETCHER

Old Blanco's. But don't worry, Gov,
a man of his age and his state,
shouldn't last more than a week.

*There is a moment's silence while
this is digested.*

GOVERNOR

All right, you can leave this here.

FLETCHER

I think we should discuss this further.

MACKAY

On your way . . . Fletcher.

GOVERNOR

Yes, get back to your cells.

FLETCHER

Sir.

*Barrowclough escorts the prisoners
out of the office, closing the door
behind them.*

GOVERNOR

A hunger strike . . .

MACKAY

Typical of Fletcher's devious mentality,
sir. Turning the old man into some kind
of martyr.

GOVERNOR

The last thing a prison needs,
Mr Mackay, is a martyr . . .

7. LANDING

*A Prison Officer unlocks the gates.
Fletcher and Lennie come into view.*

LENNIE

What you think, Fletch?

FLETCH

Keep 'em crossed, son.

LENNIE

Did seem to cause a bit of panic, like.

FLETCHER

Which was the intended effect.
They'll just have to scratch around
for an alternative now, won't they?

LENNIE

Pardon?

FLETCHER
They'll have to scratch around for an alternative.
He moves on.
LENNIE
No – pardon.
FLETCHER
Granted.
He goes.

8. GOVERNOR'S OFFICE
The Governor is sitting at his desk.
Mackay is still standing. There is a
tentative knock on the door.
GOVERNOR
Yes?
Barrowclough walks in.
BARROWCLOUGH
Could I just have one more word, sir?
MACKAY
Have you left those men out there
without an escort?
BARROWCLOUGH
No, no, Mr Collinson's taking them
back to their cells.
MACKAY
Just as well – last week we lost
a typewriter.
He checks the outer office.
GOVERNOR
What is it, Mr Barrowclough?

BARROWCLOUGH
(*Crossing over to the desk*) There might
be a solution to this problem, sir.
Which I'm sure you're aware of, given
your knowledge of the Penal Code.
The Governor looks at Mackay
for help but Mackay looks
equally puzzled.
GOVERNOR
Er . . . refresh my memory,
Mr Barrowclough.
BARROWCLOUGH
Sub-section twenty-three, part three,
paragraph D.
GOVERNOR
Ah! Yes . . . yes . . . good old sub-
section twenty-three, paragraph G.
BARROWCLOUGH
D, sir, paragraph D.
GOVERNOR
D, yes! Of course. Er, jog my memory
again, will you, Mr Barrowclough?
BARROWCLOUGH
Well, as you know, sir, under special
circumstances the Governor of a
prison has the right, if his discretion
feels it's warranted –
GOVERNOR
Yes?
BARROWCLOUGH
To request the Home Office for a
prisoner's pardon.
GOVERNOR
A pardon?
BARROWCLOUGH
That's right, sir.

MACKAY

A pardon?

GOVERNOR

It would certainly put paid to the news of a hunger strike being splashed across the newspapers.

BARROWCLOUGH

Well, all round, by and large, it does seem a good idea.

GOVERNOR

Yes, well I'm paid to come up with ideas in situations like this. I'll submit a recommendation to the Home Office. Can we get rid of all this nonsense –

He starts to push aside the petition when something catches his eye.

GOVERNOR

Just a minute . . . your signature's on this thing, Mr Barrowclough.

BARROWCLOUGH

(*Looking for his spectacles*) Oh no, sir, some mistake, sir.

Mackay picks up the petition.

MACKAY

Look man – look at that. Is that not your signature?

BARROWCLOUGH

(*Takes the petition*) Must be a forgery, sir.

He looks at it.

BARROWCLOUGH

No, that is my signature. I must have signed it.

9. CELL

Fletcher is in his cell when Lennie walks in with an envelope.

LENNIE

So miracles do happen, then. Off out today, is he?

FLETCHER

Yes, free pardon. 'Course they're all claiming credit for it. The Governor's happily going round saying he thought of it; Barrowclough's miserable because he thinks he thought of it. Funny thing is, *we* know who really did think of it, don't we?

LENNIE

Yes, me.

FLETCHER

What you talking about, Godber?

LENNIE

Only joking.

FLETCHER

Joking – I've not got over that Jack the Kipper yet.

LENNIE

Hello – Lukewarm.

Lukewarm enters.

LUKEWARM

Gentlemen, may I present the best-dressed man in Slade Prison.

He stands aside and Blanco enters, dressed in a seventeen-year-old light grey suit now a mite too large for him.

FLETCHER

Oh yes. Very elegant. Where d'you nick that – War on Want?

BLANCO

I think it were Fifty Shilling Tailor's.

FLETCHER

You were robbed.

BLANCO

January Sale, 1959.

LENNIE

Back in fashion then.

FLETCHER

I think in '59 I wore Italian pin stripes. And a shirt with a Billy Eckstein collar.

LENNIE

I wore short grey flannel shorts.

FLETCHER

All right.

BLANCO

I wore this suit to my wife's funeral.

FLETCHER

Hardly black, is it?

BLANCO

Couldn't afford another suit. Only just finished paying for that damn freezer. Terrible to think she finished up inside it. Mind you I suppose it were fitting in a way, 'cos all her life she were a cold woman.

Barrowclough puts his head round the cell door.

BARROWCLOUGH

Don't be long, Mr Webb. Bus is waiting.

He goes.

FLETCHER

Thank you.

BLANCO

By gum, d'you know how good that sounds? Mr Webb.

FLETCHER

When you goes out there, hold your head up high, my son.

BLANCO

I will that, Fletch.

There is a pause.

BLANCO

I'm not very good, you know, at expressing gratitude. But I know what you done . . . and I'll not forget it.

He shakes Fletcher's hand.

FLETCHER

You're going out now. All that matters.

LENNIE

Got a lot of living to make up for. Don't waste your time nattering with the likes of us.

BLANCO

I don't want much from life.

FLETCHER

I know, but it's good to know that justice has been done – albeit a bit late. This pardon's for your family name, for your children and your grandchildren. That's why we done it. So's you can walk out of here and look any man in the face without shame or guilt. Life's taken a lot from you, me old mate, but all you need back from it is your pride, right?

BLANCO

Right, Fletch.

LENNIE

Tarra, Blanco. Keep your nose clean.

BLANCO

So long – same to you, son.

FLETCHER

Oh and one more thing, of course.

BLANCO

What?

FLETCHER

You sue the Government for every penny they've got.

BLANCO

Too bloody true, I will.

LUKEWARM

(*Stands up and gives him cigarettes*)
Ta, ta Blanco – I'll miss you.

BLANCO

Thanks for looking after me. I'll try and get that scented notepaper that you want.

FLETCHER

Here listen – We knows you didn't do in your old lady, which means

some other bloke did. And you paid the penance. But don't you go out there harbouring thoughts of revenge.

BLANCO

I know him what did it. It were the wife's lover. But don't you worry, I shan't waste my time looking for him – he's dead.

FLETCHER

Oh that's all right then.

BLANCO

That I do know. It were me that killed him. Cheerio.

He leaves. The others exchange looks of consternation.

SERIES THREE

EPISODE FIVE: A TEST OF CHARACTER

1. STUDIO
FLETCHER'S CELL

It is night time. Lennie is sitting at the table studying, textbooks in front of him. He is deep in concentration. Fletcher walks in singing.

FLETCHER
There's just one place for me
Near you
And forever I'll be
Near you –

He crosses the cell and puts his towel on the end of his bunk.

FLETCHER
Times when we're apart
I can't hear my heart.

LENNIE
Naff off, Fletch.

FLETCHER
(*Still singing*) Say you'll never stray
More than just one bunk away.

LENNIE
Naff off, Fletch.

FLETCHER
I beg your pardon, Godber?

LENNIE
You heard.

FLETCHER
Shall I tell you something?
Prison's coarsened you, my lad.

LENNIE
Yeah well, it's hardly finishing school, is it?

FLETCHER
Nevertheless when you first come in here, you did retain some vestiges of old world courtesy – such as respect for your elders.

LENNIE
When I first come in here, you taught me the value of peace and quiet. I'm in accordance with that now.

FLETCHER
Meaning?

LENNIE
Meaning – Do not disturb.

FLETCHER
Suit yourself. Not another word.

LENNIE
Thanks, Fletch.
He goes back to his books. There is a pause.
FLETCHER
(*Putting a shirt on*) No, not another word. Not a single, solitary word will emit from my lips forthwith . . . forthwith my lips are sealed, sealed are forthwith my lips . . . I have sealed forth my lips with . . .
LENNIE
Fletch!!
FLETCHER
What?
LENNIE
You weren't going to say nowt.
FLETCHER
I'm not, am I? Honest. Schtum, right. With a capital Scht.
Lennie goes back to reading. A few moments later, Fletcher goes over to him, cupping his hands.
FLETCHER
Here, Len.
LENNIE
Oh, naffin' heck!
FLETCHER
No, no, this won't take a minute.
LENNIE
What?
Fletcher holds his hands in front of Lennie.
FLETCHER
Guess what I've got in my hand.

LENNIE
I don't care, Fletch, go away, won't you?
FLETCHER
No, it's a good one this. Have a guess. What have I got in my hands? Go on then.
LENNIE
Okay. A cockroach.
FLETCHER
No.
LENNIE
I give up.
FLETCHER
You've got two more guesses.
LENNIE
A walnut.
FLETCHER
A walnut! Where could I get a walnut?
LENNIE
All right – it's a naffin' giraffe with a harelip wearing purple Y-fronts!
Fletcher looks at Lennie and then opens his cupped palms ever so slightly, peering. He sniffs.

FLETCHER

You've been peeping!

LENNIE

Oh God, give me strength!

FLETCHER

Didn't you like that – I thought it was funny. Maybe I told it wrong. Let's try it again.

LENNIE

Fletcher, naff off! I've asked you nicely. I have an exam and I need to study.

FLETCHER

I have no objection to that. Just go and do it somewhere else, right?

LENNIE

Where, for instance?

FLETCHER

Education Room for one. That would seem the most appropriate.

LENNIE

There's a lecture in there tonight. The Accident Prevention Officer is speaking on industrial safety.

FLETCHER

That's been cancelled.

LENNIE

Has it?

FLETCHER

Yeah. On his way here the Accident Prevention Officer fell off his bike. He's in Carlisle General now.

LENNIE

I wish you were.

FLETCHER

Listen, Godber – there are two people to a cell you know. And it's very

unsettling for a social misfit like me to have someone sat here who wants to better himself.

LENNIE

Yeah, well when I get out of here I may have another 'O' Level. What will you have to show for it? Just another stretch done!

Mackay appears.

MACKAY

Oh yes, oh yes.

FLETCHER

(*Getting on his bunk*) The Town Crier.

MACKAY

What's going on here? A heated exchange, is it? Raised voices.

FLETCHER

Oh here it is, Mother Superior.

MACKAY

Watch your lip, Fletcher.

FLETCHER

My lips are sealed, sir. Forthwith my lips are sealed.

LENNIE

If only that were true.

MACKAY

What's the problem?

He walks across to Lennie.

MACKAY

Godber?

LENNIE

I'm trying to study, Mr Mackay.
You're always encouraging education,
rehabilitation – only there's nowhere in
this naffing nick conducive to it.

MACKAY

I'm afraid that won't cut much ice with
an ageing recidivist like Fletcher.

FLETCHER

Ageing what?

MACKAY

Recidivist. A person who pays his
penance for performing a crime,
goes out and straight off performs
another one.

FLETCHER

Oh – you means a professional.

MACKAY

No – I mean an habitual criminal.
Something which you may not have
been if you'd stuck in to your
education like laddo here.

FLETCHER

Yeah, well I never finished school,
did I? Never got as far as exams.
What was it called – School
Certificate in them days.

MACKAY

I can imagine.

FLETCHER

Always playing truant.

MACKAY

Oh yes.

FLETCHER

Well it was the war. We was always on
the bomb sites, collecting shrapnel and
that. Learning about sex in the air-raid
shelters during their off-peak hours.
So eventually they sent me to a
special school with other kids who
were always playing truant. But we
never learned nothing.

MACKAY

And why not?

FLETCHER

No one ever turned up for school.

MACKAY

See me, I had to leave school at
fourteen. Help bring a living wage into
the house. Hard times in those days in
the Lanarkshire coalfields. My father
was an unemployed miner but there
were still eight children to provide for.

FLETCHER

Eight kids eh? He wasn't unemployed
the whole of the time then?

MACKAY

Did I hear you correctly, Fletcher?

FLETCHER

No you didn't, sir.

MACKAY

Let me tell you something, not one
of our family neglected education.
Not one. Even under the most difficult
circumstances like Godber here.
I've had to pass exams, you know.
(*Picking a book up*) The Aspects of

the Reformation. What's the subject you're studying, Godber?

LENNIE

History. 'O' Level like. Already got one 'O' Level before I come inside. Geography.

MACKAY

That's the spirit, laddie. You stick in. And I'm telling you, Fletcher, no I'm ordering you – you do nothing to hinder this lad's concentration, otherwise get out.

FLETCHER

I just come in from work – I'm entitled.

MACKAY

You're entitled to nothing in here except to obey the sound of my voice. When's the exam, son?

LENNIE

Two days' time.

MACKAY

Right, so make yourself scarce, Fletcher. Is that clear!

He exits.

FLETCHER

(*Calling after him*) All right, all right, I'll go out for the evening! Give us the keys, I'll let meself in. So. Can't stay in me own flowery dell in case it upsets his nibs' concentration here.

LENNIE

You can if you're quiet. It's not much to ask, Fletch. Means a lot to me, this exam does.

FLETCHER

History, is it?

LENNIE

Yes.

FLETCHER

History and geography, huh!

LENNIE

What d'you mean, huh?

FLETCHER

Well they got no application have they in real life?

LENNIE

The point is not what exam I get, the point is that I got an exam. That's what's going to impress any future employer. That I had enough diligence and application to pass an exam even under the most adverse circumstances imaginable.

FLETCHER

It's not easy studying in the nick.

LENNIE

All I'm saying is, it's worth a try and I'm trying.

FLETCHER

Oh well, far be it for me, et cetera.

He settles back with a satsuma.
Lennie studies his books.
Fletcher looks at him, there
is a pause.

FLETCHER

Quiet enough for you, then?

LENNIE

Thank you.

FLETCHER

You won't know I'm here.

A few moments of rare silence,
then Warren comes in.

WARREN

Evening, lads.

LENNIE

Oh gawd.

FLETCHER

Ssshhhh.

WARREN

What's up?

LENNIE

Naffin' heck.

FLETCHER

I didn't ask him round!

LENNIE

It's impossible.

WARREN

What's up?

FLETCHER

Seat of learning in here, this is.
Professor Godber's studying for his NBG.

WARREN

Oh he's always at that lark, is Len.

LENNIE

(*Slamming the book shut*) Cobblers
to it. I give up.

He goes across to his bunk.

WARREN

I know knowledge.

FLETCHER

You know knowledge? You can't
even read.

WARREN

Maybe not, but I get it from the telly.
Schools programmes, *University
Challenge, Sale of the Century.* I learn
things and I digest them with my
memory. Shall I give you an example?

FLETCHER

No.

WARREN

Right. Apparently. Are you listening,
Fletch? If every Chinaman in China
jumped up and down – at the same
moment, like – it would cause a tidal
wave which would engulf America.

FLETCHER

Really.

WARREN

Straight up. (*Doubtfully*) Or is
it Australia?

FLETCHER

Hey – that could be used as a secret
weapon. They could hold the threat of
that one over President Carter's head.
One jump up and down all at the same
time and whoosh! World domination.

WARREN

Yeah.

He pauses.

WARREN

But they wouldn't though, would they?

FLETCHER

Well, they might you know, knowing the Chinese. If anyone could pull it off they could. 'Cos they're regimented. Do everything by numbers. Look at the menu in a Chinese Restaurant. Never work in England.

WARREN

We could, if we put our minds to it.

FLETCHER

Not a snowball's. The British working man wouldn't demean himself by jumping in the air, in case he spilt his tea.

WARREN

Still, that is knowledge, isn't it?

FLETCHER

Oh yes. May I enquire where you got this fascinating piece of information, Warren?

WARREN

Someone read it to me once from a magazine in this chiropodist's waiting room.

FLETCHER

Oh dear. What was wrong with you – toothache?

WARREN

No, I was there with me feet, you see.

FLETCHER

Naturally.

WARREN

I've always had these feet, like. It's a good chiropodist, though. They're very quick.

FLETCHER

Do they do them while you wait?

WARREN

Eh?

FLETCHER

I mean – or do they say leave 'em with us, they'll be ready Thursday. Soled and heeled.

WARREN

Get off – you're pulling my leg, Fletch.

FLETCHER

I wouldn't dare. Your foot might come off.

WARREN

No, listen, I've got some more knowledge. Even better. It's about planets.

FLETCHER

Oh planets – that'll be nice. Even better! You should write all this down, Len.

LENNIE

I've chucked the towel in.

WARREN

Now, does anyone have a football?

LENNIE

No, we ain't gotta football.

WARREN

Never mind, we can use something else. Can I borrow one of your satsumas, Fletch?

FLETCHER
My satsumas?
WARREN
And I've got my ping-pong ball.
FLETCHER
What's all this about, Bunny?

WARREN
I'll show you, I'll show you.
Fletcher gives him a satsuma.
FLETCHER
I want that back. Unbruised.
WARREN
Yes.
He takes the chamber pot and places it on the shelf.
WARREN
Now, we don't have a football but we can use this Jerry to be the sun. 'Course it should be round like a football 'cos the sun's round.
FLETCHER
That wouldn't be any good if it was round, would it?
WARREN
Why not?
FLETCHER
You wouldn't be able to sit on it. You'd keep rolling off.
LENNIE
Just let him get on with it.

FLETCHER
It's all in the sun tomorrow – that's true. Get on with it.
WARREN
So pretend the Jerry's a football but it's really the sun.
FLETCHER
I am, I am.
WARREN
Now this ping-pong ball is supposed to be the planet Mercury, and that goes right here. Excuse me, Fletch. Because it's nearest the sun.
FLETCHER
I'll get a chair in the shade then.
He moves over and sits down.
WARREN
Now – one, two, three, four
(*Pacing steps out*)
Bumps into Fletcher.
WARREN
Oh, excuse me, Fletch, you're sitting where the Earth goes.
FLETCHER
(*Getting up*) Am I – oh dear. Have I got any on my trousers?
WARREN
Now this satsuma is the planet Earth, and that goes here. Now.
LENNIE
You left out Venus.
WARREN
You what?
LENNIE
Venus comes between Mercury and the Earth.

FLETCHER

(*Stamping foot*) Yeah, about here.

WARREN

Oh, that's right. And Venus is smaller than the Earth so we need something smaller than a satsuma.

LENNIE

Your brain.

WARREN

Fletch, you got a prune?

FLETCHER

Curiously enough I'm fresh out of prunes. They got all wrinkled, so I chucked 'em out. Why don't you skip Venus?

WARREN

If you like. (*Pointing to the three objects*) sun . . . Mercury . . . skip Venus . . . Earth. Now, on this scale, not counting the sun, how far away from this cell where we are would the nearest star be? Lennie?

LENNIE

Is this one of these trick questions?

WARREN

No, no.

LENNIE

(*Getting up*) 'Cos if it is I'll stuff you, Warren.

WARREN

No it's not – straight up.

LENNIE

All right. Let's get this straight. That's the sun, Mercury, Earth. On that scale . . .

WARREN

On that scale.

LENNIE

Where would the nearest star be . . .

LENNIE/WARREN TOGETHER

. . . to where we are now.

WARREN

That's right.

LENNIE

I would imagine, er yes, I would reckon, like, well, let's see, then . . . I'll say the recreation yard.

WARREN

Wrong. Fletch?

FLETCHER

Recreation yard must be wrong. Got to be the Married Quarters, hasn't it? Thereabouts.

WARREN

You're wrong as well.

FLETCHER

Not by much I bet.

WARREN

Johannesburg!

FLETCHER

Never – never in a thousand years.

WARREN

It is. The nearest star would be in
Johannesburg . . . (*Doubt sets in*)
Or is it Australia?

***Lennie walks to the table and picks
up his books.***

LENNIE

I don't believe it, I just don't believe
it. You lot will drive me round the
ruddy twist.

WARREN

What's wrong, that's learning that is.

LENNIE

Oh yes, and what have I learned today
then? The sun is a chamberpot which
is really a football, and America will
drown given the unlikely probability
that six hundred million Chinese jump
up and down in unison!

***He throws the ping pong ball and
gets out.***

WARREN

What have I said?

FLETCHER

(*Moving chamber pot*) Finished with
the sun have you?

WARREN

It's the exam, is it? The strain, like?

FLETCHER

Won't open no doors though.

WARREN

History?

FLETCHER

At this point in time, yeah – it happens
to be history. You know what he's like.
Been through every course in this nick
like a dose of salts.

WARREN

He gets discouraged so easy.
Look how quick he jacked in
elementary Spanish.

FLETCHER

Yeah, elementary it was an' all.
After four weeks all he knew was
the Spanish for 'bread' and 'donkey'.
That's not going to get you far in
Spain, is it? Unless you want to live
on donkey sandwiches.

WARREN

I think he gives things in 'cos you
undermine his confidence.

FLETCHER

Oh it's my fault, is it?

WARREN

Yes. It's tough enough to study inside,
but you distract him.

FLETCHER

Hold your horses, Bunny. If Godber
passes that exam it will be due in no
small part to yours truly.

WARREN

How?

FLETCHER

How? I've been tutoring him, in' I?
Up all night sometimes. Learning
him about the Second World War,
as told by someone what lived
through it – me.

WARREN

Is he studying World War II then?

FLETCHER

Does it matter? A war is a war, it's
all history, in' it?

WARREN

Just saying, Fletch – thing like this
exam means a lot to young Len.
To himself like. And if he puts a lot of
store on this exam, then fails – well –

FLETCHER

What – could turn him a bit sour,
you mean?

WARREN

Shatter his confidence, like. He'll think
stuff it – go back to thieving.

FLETCHER

Well then let us agree that you and
I and the lads should unite in the
rehabilitation of Lennie Godber.

WARREN

If we can.

FLETCHER

Before he takes this exam we'll go
over the questions with him. Make sure
he passes so he can pursue a life of
honesty and integrity.

WARREN

But how can we go over
the questions?

FLETCHER

There's only one way – you and me
have got to go down the Education
Room and nick the exam papers.

2. EDUCATION ROOM

*Like all prison rooms, it is furnished
with only the basic essentials. It has
some desks and some shelves lined
with textbooks. A wall displays a
prospectus of educational
programmes, and Ministry of Labour
courses, prison rehabilitation
schemes and the like. On another
wall there is a map of the world.
Off this room is a small, private
office with a desk, a filing cabinet
and a duplicating machine.
Barrowclough and a prisoner
(Spraggon) are in the main room.
Spraggon is sitting at a desk.*

BARROWCLOUGH

This, er, manuscript of yours, Spraggon.

SPRAGGON

Always wanted to write. Always felt
I had it in me. Literary bent, like.

BARROWCLOUGH
Yes, well, it's very interesting . . . brutal, but interesting.

SPRAGGON
It would mean a lot to me. If I become a writer. Nobody in my family's ever been famous, except for me cousin Ernie.

BARROWCLOUGH
Your cousin Ernie Spraggon was a notorious tearaway.

SPRAGGON
Still famous, though, wasn't he? He got into the top ten.

BARROWCLOUGH
(*Horrified*) Top ten most wanted men, yes!

SPRAGGON
Made a name for himself, but. Couldn't go in a post office without seeing a photo of our Ernie.

BARROWCLOUGH
(*Walking over to Spraggon*) Look, er, writing could be your escape – if you'll pardon the expression – and I would be the last one to discourage that. But I think we should start with some grammatical essentials. For example, on page one, the first paragraph – there's a 'k' in knuckleduster. And also in kneecaps.

SPRAGGON
Kneecaps?

BARROWCLOUGH
Yes, the ones you break with a cricket bat ʌt the top of page two.

SPRAGGON
Look, I know I ain't put much grammar in there. I know my spelling leaves a lot to be desired, like, but I didn't want to interrupt me stream of self-conscious, did I? See, I write with me gut.

BARROWCLOUGH
Yes, I noticed that.

3. ASSOCIATION AREA
The camera shows the association area.
McLaren, Warren and Fletcher are walking along the landing and down the stairs. They are all carrying balls. They pass Mackay at the bottom of the stairs.

MACKAY
What have you men got there?

FLETCHER
Balls, Mr Mackay.

MACKAY
Why the different sizes?

FLETCHER
That's life, sir.

They start to go. A prisoner near Mackay laughs.

MACKAY
What are you grinning at Sowerby? Get your hair cut. You too, Jones.

Jones is completely bald. He reacts. Mackay reacts and starts to go.

4. EDUCATION ROOM

The door opens and Fletcher enters, followed by Warren and McLaren. They are carrying a football, a tennis ball and a ping-pong ball.

FLETCHER

Oh 'scuse me. Hello, Spraggs, not disturbing you, am I?

SPRAGGON

No, you're all right.

FLETCHER

Wouldn't want to interrupt the literary flow. I've heard about your aspirations in that direction. All very glad to hear you're going to lay down the sword and pick up the pen. As are lot of battered nightwatchmen round your way.

BARROWCLOUGH

What is it, Fletcher? What do you men want?

FLETCHER

Looking for the Education Officer, sir. The one with the brains, you know.

BARROWCLOUGH

Mr Kingsley's taking a class. I'm just helping him out with some of his more bru – er basic pupils.

MCLAREN

We want you to settle an argument.

WARREN

An intellectual argument.

BARROWCLOUGH

Can't it wait? I'm dealing with Spraggon.

FLETCHER

Spraggs is used to waiting. Been waiting parole for four years.

BARROWCLOUGH

All right, what is it then?

FLETCHER

Well, me and the lads was sitting around our cell as one does discussing the wonders of the universe.

BARROWCLOUGH

You were what?

FLETCHER

Yeah, this great and wondrous galaxy what still enthralls man with its magnitude and mystery. Anyway, Warren has a theory what me and McLaren are disputing.

BARROWCLOUGH

What theory?

FLETCHER

Now, must get this right. I'll show you, Mr Barrowclough. You see this football, well it represents the sun.

He puts it on the desk.

WARREN

It hasn't got a handle, like the Jerry, but at least it's round.

FLETCHER

Now don't confuse things, Warren. This ping-pong ball represents the planet Mercury and goes here.

He places it on Spraggon's desk.

FLETCHER

We're going to skip Venus 'cos we ain't got a prune. Follow? Now this is the Earth. (*Holding up ball*) It doesn't bruise easily like a satsuma. It also bounces. That's gravity. McLaren, show us where this goes.

McLAREN

There's not enough room in here, Fletch.

FLETCHER

Oh. Could you step in the corridor, Mr Barrowclough. Galaxy won't fit in this room it seems.

BARROWCLOUGH

Well it will, if you will just adjust the proportions.

FLETCHER

No – it has to be on this scale.

BARROWCLOUGH

Excuse me, Spraggon. I think I can see what they're trying to do. It does seem silly not to . . .

Going out of the room.

SPRAGGON

Yeah, go on, like.

Barrowclough is followed by Fletcher and McLaren. Warren quickly goes through to the inner office and tries the filing cabinet. It is locked. He returns to Spraggon.

WARREN

Hey, Spraggs, where does the Education Officer keep the keys?

SPRAGGON

Keys for what?

WARREN

Filing cabinet through there.

SPRAGGON

Hey, hey, hey. He's my tutor, old Kingsley. And Barra. They may be the screws, but they're okay. Before I met them I didn't know a semicolon from an apostrophe. When me book's published, I might dedicate it to Barra 'cos he trusts me, and you're asking me to betray that trust, right? Well, naff off!

WARREN

Tell us where the keys are and there's an ounce of snout in it for you.

SPRAGGON

In that drawer.

Warren goes quickly to desk, then freezes as Barrowclough re-enters, followed anxiously by Fletcher.

FLETCHER

Listen, we don't need to go back in there . . .

BARROWCLOUGH

If a job's worth doing it's worth doing well. I've got just the thing.

He opens a desk drawer and takes out two large red apples.

BARROWCLOUGH

There we are – just the thing we need.

(*As he passes Spraggon*) Jupiter and Saturn.

They leave the room again. Warren quickly gets the keys from the drawer and goes into the inner office. He unlocks the filing cabinet, rifles through the documents inside until he finds a sealed official envelope. He takes it out and closes the filing cabinet. He returns the keys to the desk and puts the envelope in his pocket as the others return.

BARROWCLOUGH

I know Alpha Centauri is the nearest star. Astrology is a bit of a hobby of mine.

Fletcher looks at Warren who nods OK.

FLETCHER

Really, yeah, well . . .

BARROWCLOUGH

Now on this scale, let's see. I wouldn't have thought it was Johannesburg.

FLETCHER

Yeah, well you know where to find us if you work it out – let's face it we can't get away.

BARROWCLOUGH

Just a minute – could I have my –

Fletcher and McLaren simultaneously take large bites out of the apples.

BARROWCLOUGH

– Oh well, never mind.

MCLAREN

Sorry to take your valuable time, Mr Barrowclough.

FLETCHER

Much appreciated.

Fletcher goes out followed by Warren and McLaren. When they have left, Barrowclough shakes his head disappointedly.

BARROWCLOUGH

Do you know I think that they enacted that whole, elaborate charade . . . simply to steal my apples.

5. CELL

Lennie is studying when Fletcher enters, smug in the knowledge of his secret. He is followed by Warren, equally smug.

FLETCHER

Still hard at it, are we?

LENNIE

(*Groans*) Trying, yes.

FLETCHER

Know what they says. All work and no play makes Jack a dull beanstalk.

LENNIE

D'as a favour, Fletch.

FLETCHER

(*Winks at Warren*) Already have, my son.

LENNIE

All right, you left the cell for half an hour. But did you have to come back so soon?

FLETCHER

Knew you'd miss me, little flower.
Knew you'd be worried if I didn't come
back before nightfall.

LENNIE

Where've you been?

FLETCHER

Down the Education Room.

LENNIE

(*Surprised*) What for?

FLETCHER

Thought we'd enrol in something,
didn't we, Warren?

LENNIE

(*More surprised*) For what?

FLETCHER

Trigonometry.

WARREN

What's that?

FLETCHER

Gawd, thick as two short planks.

LENNIE

Go on then, tell him.

FLETCHER

Tell him what?

LENNIE

What trigonometry is.

FLETCHER

Well, if he doesn't know by now –

LENNIE

– then it's time someone told him,
isn't it. Go on?

FLETCHER

Don't come it with me in that sarky
tone, Godber.

LENNIE

Look, Fletch. I will be the first person
in this nick to admit I owe you a lot.
But one of the reasons I so desperately
want to pass this exam tomorrow is
so's I have a chance of not ending
up like you.

FLETCHER

I'll have to think about that a minute.
It's an insult, isn't it?

WARREN

Ungrateful, that's what. If he only
knew . . .

LENNIE

(*Back to book*) Knew what?

WARREN

Knew how much Fletch cares.

FLETCHER

(*Grieved*) No, no, don't bother him.

LENNIE

Cares about what?

WARREN

Cares about you, that's what.

FLETCHER

(*Never appreciated*) One day
perhaps . . .

WARREN

No, you tell him, Fletch. Tell him what
you just done for the benefit of his nibs
here at great personal risk to yourself.

FLETCHER

You played your small part, Warren.
And McLaren. Though it makes
you wonder why we took such
terrible risks.

LENNIE
(*Leaving book*) What terrible risks?
On my behalf? Listen, the only thing
I ask you to do on my behalf is give
me half a flaming chance to pass
the exam!

FLETCHER
Which is precisely what we have
done, Godber!

WARREN
We're only going to make sure you
passes it, aren't we?

LENNIE
How?

FLETCHER
By going over the questions with
you so you can prepare the
appropriate answers.

LENNIE
(*Patiently*) In that case, it
would be useful to have the
appropriate questions.

FLETCHER
You've got 'em.
*From inside his jacket he has taken
the envelope and throws it in front
of Lennie.*

LENNIE
(*Picks it up curiously*) What's this?

FLETCHER
(*Airily*) Tomorrow's exam paper.
Now shift yourself 'cos we gotta
get it back where it come from.

LENNIE
(*Not taking it in*) The exam paper?

WARREN
(*Chuffed*) Yeah, we did it, didn't we?
*Lennie hurls the envelope down as
if he was scalded.*

LENNIE
No!
*He stands up. Fletcher and Warren
exchange puzzled looks.*

FLETCHER
What do you mean – no?

LENNIE
I mean NO. I don't want to cheat.
I want to pass this exam honestly!

FLETCHER
Well, of course you do. But honesty is
only something you can afford once
you made it. And passing this exam
is going to help you make it.

LENNIE
Don't you understand? I've cheated
all me life. For the first time in my life
I want to do something straight.

FLETCHER
Look – once you've passed this exam,
no one's going to know *how* you
passed it.

LENNIE

I will. Look, if I fail, I fail. But I'm not going to pass through cheating.

Fletcher decides to use the persuasive rationale.

FLETCHER

Len, Len. No, no, listen, will you? Lennie, my son, cheating isn't a crime.

He says this as if it were an obvious, irrefutable truth. Lennie looks at him as if to say – what are you talking about?

FLETCHER

'Course it isn't. Cheating is – getting away with it. World of difference. I mean, everyone cheats.

WARREN

(*Going to sit beside Lennie*) Listen, Len, you know when you play draughts with Fletch and he says he thinks one fell on the floor and could you pick it up, so you bend down only when you straighten up you find the board's rearranged – that's all cheating is.

FLETCHER

That's right.

WARREN

Oh, so you admit it?

FLETCHER

Name of the game, isn't it? Getting away with it. It's not what you do in life – it's what you get caught doing.

WARREN

And if you don't get caught . . .

FLETCHER

You're away, ain'tcha? Home and dry.

LENNIE

No.

FLETCHER

Listen, Godber, you watch your favourite television programme – *Kojak* – Telly Savalas, you think he's such a great actor. Well you know why he's always opening filing cabinets and looking at his shirt cuffs? Eh? 'Cos his lines are written all over the place.

WARREN

(*Rising*) And that's cheating.

FLETCHER

Right. But who gives a rat's? Listen, son, cheating is only another word for conning. Putting one over. And if that was a crime, the whole country would be doing porridge. I tell you what would be a crime. You turning down this golden opportunity we are handing you.

WARREN

We took a big risk to get that for you, Len.

LENNIE

All right, I appreciate your efforts. You want my thanks – thanks. But I'll do it my way.

He lays down the envelope, stands, walks to his bunk and lies down.

FLETCHER

If you do it your way, you ain't honest, you're dumb. 'Cos if you do it your way – you'll fail.

LENNIE

There comes a point in everyone's life

when the only person you're cheating is yourself. It's like cheating at patience.

WARREN

Fletcher does that an' all.

FLETCHER

Come on, Warren, what's the use? Let's leave him.

He and Warren make to leave the cell. Fletcher pauses.

FLETCHER

You're at the crossroads of life, Godber. You make your own breaks, son, 'cos when you get out there, people are going to give you precious few. You can go up for a job one day with all the qualifications in the world and get pipped by some nurk who's never passed an exam in his life. But he's got the right accent, plays for the local rugby club and he ain't never been in no nick!

Fletcher throws the envelope to the floor, turns and leaves the cell with Warren.

Lennie sits at the table looking at the envelope lying there. He wrestles with his conscience. Then he glances back to the open cell door. He picks up the envelope, pauses for a moment, then slowly opens the flap.

At that moment, Warren peers into the cell through a crack in the door. He smiles.

6. ASSOCIATION AREA

Prisoners are sitting around playing cards, draughts, etc. Fletcher and Warren are sitting at a table.

WARREN

Lennie should be out of his exam soon.

FLETCHER

Yeah, I wonder how he got on? Mind you, you must never let him know that you know.

WARREN

'Course not. Guvnor will be pleased when he passes 'cos Slade Prison's got a terrible academic record, Fletch.

FLETCHER

Oh I don't know. Chap got his 'O' Level in Spanish last year – what's his name – Gomez. Hey here he comes.

Lennie comes down to them.

FLETCHER

Hello then, son. How did the exam go?

LENNIE

Some questions were a bit tough, but it weren't as bad as I thought it were going to be.

FLETCHER

No, I'll bet it wasn't.

LENNIE

I think my essay was pretty fair.
Me spelling's a bit dodgy like, but they
can't have any complaints about the
factual content and that's what counts
most, isn't it?

FLETCHER

Oh yes, that's what counts.
Anyhow, asides from your essay,
what about the more technical
questions then? The dates?

LENNIE

I'll just keep me fingers crossed. But I
will admit to being quietly confident.

FLETCHER

Quietly confident, say no more.

LENNIE

I'll tell you one thing, though. Pass or
fail, at least I have the satisfaction of
knowing I did it on me own.

FLETCHER

You what?

LENNIE

I did it on me own efforts.

WARREN

Your own efforts!!

FLETCHER

Er, Godber, would you like to rephrase
that? Bearing in mind that some of us
may know a little more than what you
thinks we do.

LENNIE

I'm just saying I did it my way. With no
help from no one.

FLETCHER

Listen, Godber, there are many sorts
of crime and we're all here for most
of them. But the one thing I can't
abide is hypocrisy!

WARREN

That's the worst offence of all in my
book an' all.

LENNIE

So?

FLETCHER

So cut out the holier-than-thou
attitude, Godber, you steaming
hypocrite. He saw you through the
crack in the door – Warren saw you
look at those papers.

LENNIE

Yeah I clocked them, but it didn't make
no difference.

FLETCHER

How can you say that!

LENNIE

Who actually lifted them?

WARREN

Me.

LENNIE

Next time, pick someone who
can read.

FLETCHER

What?

LENNIE

You nicked the Biology papers.

SERIES THREE

EPISODE SIX: FINAL STRETCH

1. VISITING ROOM

Barrowclough is walking down the rows of visitors and prisoners. Ingrid is visiting Fletcher; Mrs Godber, Lennie and Jarvis (a tough unpleasant-looking inmate) is being visited by his brother.

INGRID

I know it's only Feb, but if you book your holiday now it's ever so cheap. So me and Barbara, you don't know Barbara, she's my friend at work – we fancy going to Rimini. That's on the Adriatic. We thought Italy because your money goes much further there. That's 'cos the lira's the only European currency what's as bad off as the pound.

Fletcher has been listening with little interest. He casts dubious looks at Barrowclough, who seems to be hovering nearby.

INGRID

It's either Rimini or Portofino – which is supposed to be rather smart. I believe Rex Harrison goes there.

FLETCHER

Anyhow, the riot is set for Tuesday, we're going to barricade ourselves in with half a dozen screws as hostages with which we can bargain for better living conditions.

Barrowclough has heard this. As he was meant to. He takes the bait, whipping round on Fletcher.

FLETCHER

(*Got him*) I knew he was earwigging.

INGRID

What?

FLETCHER

Listening to every word he was, of our supposedly private conversation.

BARROWCLOUGH

I was doing no such thing, Fletcher.

FLETCHER

Yes, you were, Mr Barrowclough. Shouldn't be allowed, hovering.

BARROWCLOUGH

It wouldn't be necessary if we could

trust you people not to pass each
other contraband.

FLETCHER

Oh I see, it's contraband now, is it?
Hear that!

*He has a packet of cigarettes in
front of him.*

FLETCHER

Here, check this. She's brung me half
a pound of hashish in there, she has.

*With this, he throws the packet
across the table towards
Barrowclough, but it falls
on the floor.*

BARROWCLOUGH

There's no need to take that
attitude, Fletcher.

*He bends to pick up the packet.
As he does so, the entire row of
visitors flick contraband across
the table to their loved ones.
It disappears instantly – just
before Barrowclough straightens
up, handing over the packet.*

BARROWCLOUGH

Here you are – now just carry on.

INGRID

Where was I?

BARROWCLOUGH

Rimini or Portofino.

He moves on.

INGRID

Oh yes, well we was thinking of May
before it gets too touristy –

FLETCHER

Listen, girl, has it not occurred to you
that it's a bit tactless in front of your
old dad. This conversation about
foreign climes.

INGRID

Oh.

FLETCHER

I mean you know –

INGRID

(*Sympathetically*) You've passed the
halfway mark, Dad. Less to do than's
already done. With parole, only another
year – just under.

FLETCHER

Oh, is that all – that's nothing, just a
mere bagatelle, isn't it?

INGRID

Getting rough, is it?

FLETCHER

Oh you know me, I'll survive. It's just
every time I see you or Marion or
Raymond I realise you're all grown
up a bit more. Without me.

INGRID

I grew up before you come in, Dad.

FLETCHER

Oh you had. Grew up too soon, you
did. You somehow bypassed puberty.

INGRID

No, I didn't. You bypassed my puberty
by going into Maidstone.

FLETCHER

Nevertheless it has to be said, you
was wearing a 36D in Junior School.

INGRID

Not my fault, that's nature.

FLETCHER

All right, all right put 'em away.
forewent my parental responsibilities
during your most formative years.
Same with young Marion.

INGRID

Oh she'll be all right. Don't you worry,
Marion will always end up on her own
two feet.

FLETCHER

If she ever gets herself off her back.

Ingrid looks shocked.

FLETCHER

No, no, I didn't mean that to sound like
it did. I mean, she's a lazy little so-and-
so, that's all. She still work at Woolies?

INGRID

She don't need to, Dad. 'Cos her
boyfriend Ricky's ever so well off.
He's got three cars. He gave her
one for Christmas.

FLETCHER

I'll bet he did. Did she get a present
as well?

INGRID

Dad!

FLETCHER

Well . . .

INGRID

If she marries Ricky, she'll want
for nothing.

FLETCHER

If. What's he do, this Ricky?

INGRID

He runs these cheap charter
aeroplane trips.

FLETCHER

What's it called? Gullible's Travels?

INGRID

No – Sunset Tours. It was him what
put me and Barbara on to Rimini.

FLETCHER

What I'm trying to say is, his three cars
was bought from the deposits scraped
together by the likes of you.

INGRID

Dad! I hate to hear you talk like this.
You never give no one the benefit of
the doubt. You're getting so cynical in
your old age.

FLETCHER

Listen, it ain't no bed of roses in here.

INGRID

You've got nothing to bleat about.
You chose to live outside the law,
so you accept the consequences.
What was it you told young Lennie?
If you can't do the time, don't do
the crime!

FLETCHER

How d'you know I told young
Godber that?

INGRID

He told me in one of his letters.
She turns to look at Lennie and
waves. Lennie waves back.

FLETCHER

Oh – so you've been keeping in touch,
have you?

INGRID

Only pen pals.

FLETCHER

Yeah well, but he's going out next
week, isn't he? Won't need no stamps
on your letters then, will you?

INGRID

Subject to his parole board.

FLETCHER

Oh he'll smarm his way past that lot
with his naïve charm, his boyish smile
and his one flaming 'O' Level in
geography. Probably get lost as
soon as he's outside the gates.

INGRID

That's why you're so grumpy! He's going
out and you're going to miss him.

FLETCHER

Miss him? That's not the point.
His going out reminds me that I ain't
going out. I'm staying in. While he's
out I'll still be in, won't I?

INGRID

Won't be too long, Dad. Tell you what,

soon as your release date is set I'll get
in touch with Ricky and he can book
you some lovely holiday in the sun.

FLETCHER

Yeah, well after Marion and you, why
not me and your mam? Then apart
from young Raymond he'll have done
the whole family.

2. PRISON YARD

Barrowclough comes out followed
by several prisoners. They file out
and walk away.
Jarvis calls out to Godber.

JARVIS

Godber!
Godber waits until Jarvis catches
him up. They walk along together.
Barrowclough is watching the
prisoners. More prisoners come
out of the door, including Fletcher.
The prisoners are walking away.
Godber and Jarvis start fighting.
Barrowclough is locking the door
when he notices the fight.

BARROWCLOUGH

Stop that – just a minute!
Fletcher is walking along. He spots
the fight.
Barrowclough runs to break up
the fight.

3. MACKAY'S OFFICE

Lennie and Jarvis are standing side by side in front of Mackay. Barrowclough is in attendance.

MACKAY

What's all this about then?

LENNIE

What's all what about, Mr Mackay?

MACKAY

Brawling in the yard.

LENNIE

Weren't brawling, sir.

JARVIS

Just fooling around. Playful high spirits, sir.

LENNIE

We were just re-enacting a big moment from last Sunday's football on the telly. The bit where Peter Shilton dived at Charlie George's feet.

MACKAY

I don't recall Charlie George smashing a dustbin lid over Peter Shilton's skull. Not even in the action replay.

LENNIE

He would have done if he'd had one handy.

MACKAY

Don't be funny with me, Godber.

LENNIE

Not trying to be, sir.

MACKAY

You were brawling.

LENNIE

Wasn't sir, honest. Got me parole board next week. Daft to jeopardise that, wouldn't I?

MACKAY

You would indeed, sonny.

JARVIS

Len's my mate, sir. Him and me are like that.

He holds up two crossed fingers.

MACKAY

(*Questioningly*) Mr Barrowclough?

BARROWCLOUGH

(*Uncertain*) Well, I was some distance away, but it did seem to be a vicious altercation.

LENNIE

Oh, from a way's away it could easily have been misconstrued. If you'd been close up you could have seen we were smiling.

He smiles briefly by way of demonstration.

JARVIS

Straight up, sir.

MACKAY

You're no stranger to violence, Jarvis. Your only interest in football was supervising violence at the Stretford End. It's no coincidence that since your imprisonment football hooliganism has declined.

JARVIS

Didn't know no better then, sir.
But thanks to people like Len . . .

LENNIE

It's true, sir. Look . . .

He turns to Jarvis and says,
challengingly.

LENNIE

Manchester United are rubbish
compared to Villa.

JARVIS

(*Evenly*) You could be right, Len.

LENNIE

Doesn't that prove it, sir?

Mackay looks towards
Barrowclough, as if to say
can you believe these two?

LENNIE

I admit we got a bit boisterous
in the yard.

JARVIS

That's true. But to me, sir, Len's family.

LENNIE

(*Touched*) D'you mean that, Jarvis?

JARVIS

Cross me heart.

LENNIE

Well, I'm touched. You don't know
what that means to me.

MACKAY

I'm in two minds, Mr Barrowclough.
Should I give them solitary confinement
or announce their engagement?

4. ASSOCIATION AREA

BARROWCLOUGH

Back to your cells. And think
yourselves damned lucky!

LENNIE/JARVIS TOGETHER

Thank you, Mr Barrowclough.

They walk along the landing.
Barrowclough watches them and
then walks off.
Jarvis and Lennie are walking along.

LENNIE

Got out of that then.

JARVIS

Bloody did.

LENNIE

Did well in there, us.
Abbott and Costello.

JARVIS

Morecambe and Wise.

LENNIE

We were daft though. Having a go in
front of the screws.

JARVIS

Should have found somewhere private.

LENNIE

We will do. (*Stopping*) 'Cos I'm going to punch your lights out, musclehead! *He goes.*

5. FLETCHER'S CELL

It is night time.

FLETCHER

(*Appalled*) I thought I knew you, Godber.

LENNIE

If someone provokes you, what you s'posed to do, back off?

FLETCHER

If you're up for parole next Monday, most certainly, yes.

LENNIE

He made certain remarks.

FLETCHER

What remarks?

LENNIE

Never you mind. Suffice to say I found them insulting and offensive.

FLETCHER

If my release was in the balance here, ain't an insult in the world that would prevent me from turning the other cheek.

LENNIE

Have to draw the line somewhere.

FLETCHER

Wrong. You could bring in the question of the virtue of my old woman; call me a poof; even tell me I molest goats – water off a duck's back to me – or in this case, off a goat's back.

LENNIE

P'raps you haven't the same pride as what I do.

FLETCHER

Oh, it's the old pride stakes, is it? The old self-respect.

LENNIE

It matters.

FLETCHER

Self-respect is something you preserve on the outside. No such thing inside – you forfeited that when you were sent down. Anyhow, people's opinion in here matters naff all.

LENNIE

Not doing it for them. Doing it for me.

FLETCHER

I was talking to my daughter today.

LENNIE

Ingrid?

FLETCHER

Yeah, your pen pal. She says, you know, I don't give anyone the benefit of the doubt. Thinks I'm cynical. She's probably right. I just thought someone like you could just about make it out there but . . .

LENNIE

But what?

FLETCHER

You obviously ain't got the bottle.

LENNIE

If I hadn't got no bottle, would I be taking on Jarvis?

FLETCHER

That ain't bottle, that's stupidity. Tell you what does take bottle in life – knowing when to turn the other cheek. Like Gary Cooper in *High Noon*, Alan Ladd in *Shane*, or . . . Gregory Peck in *The Big Country*; Glenn Ford in *The Fastest Gun Alive*.

LENNIE

I've seen those pictures.

FLETCHER

Then you know what I mean.

LENNIE

Just answer me one question.

FLETCHER

Gladly.

LENNIE

How come all them films ended in the worst fights you ever seen? Teeth and whiskers all over the place.

FLETCHER

I'll tell you why, sonny Jim. Because Hollywood had to pander to the public's insatiable thirst for senseless violence.

LENNIE

No, you're wrong. Those films raised a moral question which had to be answered by the last reel. A man has to do . . .

FLETCHER

(*Joining him*) . . .what a man has to do – yes, yes, oh blimey it's Batman, is it?

LENNIE

There is a basic truth there though.

FLETCHER

Let me ask you one question.

LENNIE

Go on.

FLETCHER

(*Going over to Lennie*) Would Gary Cooper and all them others have done what they done had they been up for parole next Monday? And would they have walked into the final shoot-out so willingly had they known their adversary was Reggie, the Red Menace, Jarvis? You see, there's two sorts of violence inside. One that's born out of frustration and despair, and one that comes from the likes of Reggie Jarvis. A man full of Mancunian macho 'cos he's got five years to do and nothing to lose. You've got everything to lose. Unless freedom ain't everything. Then, well . . .

LENNIE

Listen, Fletch, I appreciate your concern but it's just something I have to do.

FLETCHER

I'll make one final appeal to your sense, Godber. Then I'll wash my hands of it.

LENNIE

Go on then.

FLETCHER

There are three good reasons why you shouldn't take on Jarvis. A – you could jeopardise your parole; and B – it offends civilised sensibilities.

LENNIE

What about C?

FLETCHER

C – it's obvious, ain't it? C – he'll bleedin' murder you!

6. RECREATION ROOM

A few prisoners are playing cards or smoking. The TV is off. Fletcher sits playing dominoes with Warren.

FLETCHER

Knock.

He puts a matchstick in the kitty.

WARREN

Four–five.

FLETCHER

Knock.

WARREN

Double five.

FLETCHER

(*With rising irritability*) Knock.

WARREN

Five–one.

Barrowclough comes in.

BARROWCLOUGH

Excuse me, Fletcher.

FLETCHER

Oh dear me, interruption – void game.
He throws all his dominoes on the table and withdraws his matchsticks.

WARREN

I only had one to play.

FLETCHER

Well, that's hard luck, me old son. But we can hardly continue playing when Mr Barrowclough has something to say, can we?

BARROWCLOUGH

There was no need to break up your game, Fletcher.

WARREN

See!

FLETCHER

(*Pity!*) Too late now. Showed me hand, ain't I?
Warren disgustedly throws his remaining domino in. Barrowclough examines their respective hands.

BARROWCLOUGH

Oh, you'd have beaten him hollow there, Warren.

FLETCHER

(*Mixing the dominoes*) Matter of opinion. So what's the problem then?

BARROWCLOUGH

Just a word in your ear.
Fletcher indicates Warren.

FLETCHER

Oh. Try this one – it's further away from *him*.

BARROWCLOUGH

Oh, Warren's all right, he's a friend.

FLETCHER
Friend of whose?

BARROWCLOUGH
Godber's.

FLETCHER
What *about* Godber?

BARROWCLOUGH
Him and Jarvis –

FLETCHER
What about Jarvis?

BARROWCLOUGH
You know.

FLETCHER
Do I?

BARROWCLOUGH
You were there – after visiting –
in the yard.

FLETCHER
Was I? Where was this then?

BARROWCLOUGH
I must say, you're not much of a
conversationalist, Fletcher.

FLETCHER
What's you on about,
Mr Barrowclough?

BARROWCLOUGH
(*Darkly*) Something's brewing.

FLETCHER
Oh good. Two sugars.

BARROWCLOUGH
You know very well what I mean.

FLETCHER
Do I? Oh good.

BARROWCLOUGH
I'll say no more.

FLETCHER
Yes, I think you've said enough.

BARROWCLOUGH
As long as we understand each other.

FLETCHER
Perfectly, Mr Barrowclough.

BARROWCLOUGH
Good.
*He goes off. Fletcher starts to select
dominoes for a new game.*

WARREN
What were all that about?

FLETCHER
Godber and Jarvis had a barney in the
yard. The screws know about it – want
it stopped before it goes any further.
If it does, bad for all of us, specially
the lad. My down, double six.

WARREN
I didn't hear him say all that.

FLETCHER
Read between the lines, son. Your go.

WARREN
(*Peering at his dominoes*) Would you
believe it – I'm knocking.

FLETCHER

In the kitty. Six–two.

Lennie approaches.

WARREN

Oh, look, look, it's Lennie.

LENNIE

Hello, Fletch, Warren.

He sits down.

FLETCHER

Never mind him – have you got a two?

WARREN

No, but it's a void game, isn't it?
Interruption, like.

*He tries to gather the dominoes but
Fletcher stops him.*

FLETCHER

Naff off.

WARREN

That's what you did when Barra
came up.

FLETCHER

Barra's a screw – different, ain't it?

LENNIE

What did he want?

FLETCHER

The topic was senseless violence,
the prevention of.

LENNIE

If he wants to stop that, he should get
the telly fixed. It's been bust for a week.

WARREN

Jarvis broke that.

FLETCHER

Only because he couldn't get a good
picture of his favourite programme –
The Magic Roundabout. I tried to tell

him – I said if Florence and Zebedee
appear a little blurred, you fix it by
adjusting the fine tuner with a delicate
twist of the wrist. You don't chuck the
set against the wall – mind you, that
usually does the trick.

Jarvis enters. Only Warren notices.

WARREN

Change the subject, change the subject.

FLETCHER

What's wrong with you? Got a
sore throat?

WARREN

I said change the subject.

FLETCHER

Yeah – and I saw your lips move.

*Warren tries to warn them about
Jarvis with a subtle indication of
head but Jarvis is already upon
them. He thumps the TV set twice.*

FLETCHER

Are you knocking again?

JARVIS

Godber . . .

LENNIE

Hello, Jarvis.

JARVIS

Score to settle, right?

LENNIE

Any time.

JARVIS

Up to you.

LENNIE

Ready when you are.

JARVIS

What's wrong with now?

LENNIE

Why not? Telly's broke.

(*Getting up*) Nothing else to do.

WARREN

I think I'll go t' lavatory.

He starts to leave.

FLETCHER

(*Getting up*) You sit down – nothing's going to happen so just hold your horses. Or hold whatever you have to hold.

JARVIS

None of your business, Fletch.

FLETCHER

It's everyone's business, Jarvis.

He goes over to them.

FLETCHER

A happy nick is a placid nick. Cause a rumpus, you naff it up for all of us.

JARVIS

Listen, my gripe's with him. But I'll stuff the both of you if you want.

Fletcher, backs off to beside the TV set.

FLETCHER

Shut your face, toilet mouth.

WARREN

That's reminds me (*Getting up*) I really do have to go to the lavatory.

JARVIS

I'm going to have you for that.

Everyone in the room reacts to the tension. Jarvis walks up to Fletcher. Fletcher quickly picks up the TV set which he holds threateningly above his head. Mackay comes in.

MACKAY

(*Offscreen*) Everybody froeze!

What's going on here?

FLETCHER

Oh we was just trying to fix the telly, Mr Mackay.

MACKAY

With the set above your head?

FLETCHER

Yeah, I was just trying the vertical hold.

WARREN

(*Amazed*) Hey, look – we got a picture.

Sure enough, to everyone's astonishment, the set starts to work. All the prisoners, except Fletcher, immediately sit down, cross their legs and start watching the programme. Mackay turns up the sound. Then walks off as they all sit enjoying the TV.

7. CELL

Fletcher is in his cell darning his socks when Warren walks in.

WARREN

Fletch.

FLETCHER

What are you doing? I told you to tag Godber. To never let him out of your sight.

WARREN

That's what I've come to tell you. It's all right, he's on duty. And Jarvis is in the yard with some of his cronies.

FLETCHER

Well, we'd better tail Godber when he comes out of the cookhouse. It's the weekend now. This is when it's going to happen, in' it?

WARREN

I had 'opes you'd've talked Len out of it. If anyone could, you could.

FLETCHER

Well, I ain't. Which is a testimony to his pigheadedness.

WARREN

Maybe we should look on the bright side. Maybe the fight won't be tumbled. And maybe Len'll do all right. I mean, he knows a bit. He made the boxing squad.

FLETCHER

The boxing squad. Oh yes, the noble art. The Queensbury Rules, the fairplay and the gumshield, and all that rubbish. While Lennie is still shaking hands Jarvis will have fractured his groin with his No. 9 prison issue boot, won't he?

WARREN

Could we nobble him? Drugs like?

FLETCHER

There is some animal tranquilliser on the farm. How much do you need to tranquillise an animal like Jarvis? Not to mention the problem of who goes and sticks a hypodermic in his backside without him noticing. No, there's only one thing for it, you know – I'll have to take on Jarvis myself.

WARREN

You? (*Laughs*) D'you think you can put Jarvis out of action?

FLETCHER

No, you nurk. But it's Saturday morning now, ain't it? If I fight him and we're discovered, it's automatically the cooler for forty-eight hours and he won't come out till after Len's been up for his parole Monday morning.

WARREN

But hang on, if you're discovered you'll go to the cooler an' all.

FLETCHER

Yeah, well.

WARREN

You're going to blot your copy book.

FLETCHER

Yeah, well. Few weeks' remission won't do me any harm. But listen, I'm going to need your help Warren, 'cos I wouldn't last two minutes with Jarvis. The moment anything happens, you fetch the screws and you move like greased lightning. Right?

WARREN

Hey, wait a minute, Fletch. If I tip off the screws that makes me a snitch.

FLETCHER

If you don't tip them off, son, that makes me a corpse.

8. PRISON YARD

*A group of prisoners are playing
pitch and toss, including Jarvis.
The Prison Officers are chatting.
Fletcher and Warren come round
the corner of the building and
see Jarvis.
They look at him, then at a
Prison Officer.
Fletcher is walking across the yard
and he sees a group approaching.
When he reaches them he speaks.*

FLETCHER
Jarvis!

JARVIS
Oh hello, Fletch. You want in?

FLETCHER
You what?

JARVIS
Want to join in, like?

FLETCHER
Jarvis? I thought you and me had
some unfinished business. From the
television room, remember?

JARVIS
Oh that, don't be daft.

FLETCHER
I mean what I said, Jarvis.

JARVIS
No, you didn't. I know what you were
doing – trying to protect the kid.
*Jarvis turns back to the game.
Fletcher moves into Jarvis.*

FLETCHER
Jarvis!

JARVIS
What?

FLETCHER
You know when I called you
toilet mouth?

JARVIS
Yeah.

FLETCHER
I ain't taking it back.

JARVIS
Well, you're right, me old mate.
My language is a bit colourful.
Me wife's always on at me about it.
I try you know, but I can do sod all
about it.
*He returns to the game.
Fletcher turns and starts to move
away. But an idea strikes him and
he turns back. Fletcher returns to
Jarvis and taps him on the shoulder.*

FLETCHER
Jarvis.

JARVIS
Now what?

FLETCHER
Talking about your wife . . .

JARVIS
What about my wife?

FLETCHER

You're luckier than most of us. I mean, when a bloke's doing a long stretch, you know, his old lady's out looking for nooky, in' she?

JARVIS

Speak for yourself.

FLETCHER

I am. That's why I'm saying you're luckier than most. I 'eard your old lady's only been unfaithful to you twice.

JARVIS

Twice?

FLETCHER

Once with the milkman and once with the Household Cavalry.

Jarvis thinks, then laughs.

JARVIS

Huh, huh, huh – good one that, Fletch.

FLETCHER

Oh gawd.

He turns and starts to leave.
Crusher walks past Jarvis who calls out to him.

JARVIS

Here, Crusher.

CRUSHER

What?

JARVIS

Listen to this.

He laughs at the group and turns back to Crusher.

JARVIS

I heard that your old lady's only been unfaithful to you twice.

Crusher says nothing.

JARVIS

Once with the milkman and once with the Household Cavalry.

The camera shows the back of Jarvis's head and Crusher's fist punching it. Jarvis falls backwards. Suddenly the whole group starts fighting.
Prison Officers start running about blowing whistles.
The fight rages on. Fletcher walks off.

FLETCHER

All right then, I owe you one.

The Prison Officers run up to the group and break the fight up.

9. CELL

Fletcher is busying himself with his back to the cell door, when Lennie walks in.
He has a smile on his face and is about to enjoy imparting some news when Fletcher, without turning around, says.

FLETCHER

Congratulations.

LENNIE

(*Taken aback*) What?

FLETCHER

Congratulations. On getting your parole.

LENNIE

I was just about to tell you that.

FLETCHER

Well, I knows, don't I?

LENNIE

How?

FLETCHER

It pays me to, don't it?

LENNIE

But I only left the board an hour ago.

FLETCHER

Son, son. I works the admin block, don't I?

LENNIE

Oh yes, of course.

FLETCHER

(*Walking over to Lennie*)

Anyhow, well done.

They shake hands.

FLETCHER

Tomorrow morning then.

LENNIE

Yeah, I'd better get packed up. It's only when you move that you realise how much stuff you got.

FLETCHER

Yeah.

LENNIE

'Ere, the Governor was ever so nice about it. He let me ring my mum.

FLETCHER

I know.

LENNIE

How?

FLETCHER

I listened in on the extension.

LENNIE

Fletch!

FLETCHER

I wanted to share in your elation.

LENNIE

Oh I see.

FLETCHER

She was chuffed. Your mum.

LENNIE

Quite emotional really. For her. Wish I could tell me dad . . . if I only knew where the old bastard was.

FLETCHER

Well look at it another way. Your dad's absence meant he never knew you went in in the first place.

LENNIE

I suppose so. Come in handy today, he did.

FLETCHER

How?

LENNIE

Well I told the parole board that I thought my father's desertion was a contributory factor towards my temporary diversion from the straight and narrow. Not in so many words though.

FLETCHER

You're learning, ain't you?

LENNIE

(*Sitting*) Thanks to you, Fletch.

FLETCHER

Yeah, well.

LENNIE

If it hadn't been for you, I'd've messed this parole up, you know.

FLETCHER

True.

LENNIE

I mean, the fact that you risked solitary confinement and loss of your own remission . . . well, I mean . . . well, that's real friendship.

FLETCHER

Look, there was no way I was going to let you jeopardise your parole, son.

LENNIE

I realise that now. But I never realised it meant so much to you.

FLETCHER

'Course it did. I had three to one on you getting out.

Lennie thinks about this, then decides not to believe it.

LENNIE

You don't fool me, Fletch. You did that out of the kindness of your heart.

FLETCHER

If you believe that, then you are a stupid sentimental nurk.

LENNIE

No I'm not.

FLETCHER

Well, you're certainly stupid. As your behaviour over the Jarvis affair demonstrated only too clearly.

LENNIE

I promise you, Fletch, I did have a reason for reacting like I did. Jarvis came up to me and made an obscene remark.

FLETCHER

(*Putting envelope down*) Did that affront your Brummagem sensibilities then?

LENNIE

Yes, it did. 'Cos the remark concerned what he'd like to do to your daughter Ingrid.

FLETCHER

What?

LENNIE

To put it delicately, he indicated his carnal desires towards her, then reckoned that he fancied his chances, on account of her sexual proclivities.

FLETCHER

(*Licking envelope*) Well, she's always had those. Ever since she was thirteen. So – you was defending my family's honour, was it?

LENNIE

Seemed a good reason – I owe a lot to you, Fletch. I'd've never made the distance without you.

FLETCHER

(*Sitting*) Look, don't make me out to be no hero.

LENNIE

I wasn't. Father figure maybe.

FLETCHER

I ain't been no great shakes as a dad. 'Fact I ain't been no great shakes as anything.

LENNIE
You have to me. And I won't let you down, Fletch. I ain't coming back.

FLETCHER
Oh we all say that. But you'd better mean it, Godber. You've got your life before you. Out the last twenty years I've spent eleven of 'em doing porridge. That ain't life, that's marking time. I'm not moaning. What's done's done. But it's a terrible waste.

LENNIE
I won't be back. Given the breaks.

FLETCHER
Make the breaks. No alibis. No ifs and buts. You can make it. You're not stupid, and you're not evil. You're a good lad. Well, nuff said. Hope you're leaving me your snout.

LENNIE
Only right.

He gives Fletcher the tobacco from his box.

FLETCHER
Chocolate?

LENNIE
Fruit and nut.

He hands Fletcher the chocolate.

FLETCHER
(*Looking in box*) Other bit. (*Lennie gives him it*) And first thing you do when you go out, you do for me.

LENNIE
What?

FLETCHER
As soon as you get off the train at New Street, Birmingham, you go straight Into a pub and ordor a pint of best bitter and drink to your old mate.

LENNIE
I'm not going to Birmingham. I was thinking of Rimini actually, with a friend. We thought May 'cos it's not so touristy then. Or perhaps Portofino . . .

10. CELL
Fletcher is lying on his bunk reading a newspaper.

10A. PRISON LANDING
Mackay comes upstairs. He pauses and then looks around, moves on. Mackay walks along the landing and stops outside Fletcher's cell. He goes in.

10B. CELL
Mackay enters.

MACKAY
Fletcher?

FLETCHER
Good afternoon, sir.

MACKAY
Good afternoon, sir?

FLETCHER
Your title, in' it, sir?

MACKAY
True. I did not expect to hear it so readily from your lips.

FLETCHER
Why make waves, eh? Only ten months to do if I keep my nose clean.

MACKAY

Throwing in the towel, are we Fletcher?

FLETCHER

I just want to get home.

MACKAY

(*Moving nearer*) I've noticed a certain change in your attitude since laddo's release. Our customary ill-feeling seems to be missing. You seem to have lost a lot of that brash Cockney lairyness. Or are you just acknowledging that the system always wins.

FLETCHER

Nobody wins, Mr Mackay. That's what's so tragic.

MACKAY

Normally I would have hesitated about putting a sprog in here, Fletcher.

FLETCHER

Oh yes. Got some company coming in, have I?

MACKAY

In the past you have not been the healthiest of influences on first-time offenders. But now I don't think I have too much to fear. (*Crossing to the window*) Got a young lad called Nicholson moving in.

FLETCHER

Not a Scot, is he? I mean, we do draw the line somewhere.

MACKAY

(*Turning to Fletcher*) No, he's from Sunderland.

FLETCHER

Dangerously near.

MACKAY

He's a tearaway. Lashes out. Doesn't think. I have a feeling that the new quiescent Fletcher might be just what he needs.

FLETCHER

Whatever you think, Mr Mackay.

MACKAY

(*Moving nearer*) So you'll keep an eye on him?

FLETCHER

Be difficult to ignore him in a room this size.

MACKAY

No, but perhaps you'll show him the ropes, show him what you've learnt.

He walks towards the door.

FLETCHER

What have I learnt, Mr Mackay?

MACKAY

(*Crossing over to Fletcher*) That there's no point to bucking the system.

FLETCHER

Oh yes. Glad to, Mr Mackay. Sir. I'll watch out for him. I shall simply tell him three things. Bide your time (*Holds up one fingers*), keep your nose clean . . . (*Two fingers*) and don't let the bastards grind you down . . .

Fletcher puts up the third finger.

MEMORIES

Colin Farrell (Norris in 'Happy Release')

'Before being cast in "Happy Release", the fifth episode in series two, I had performed very little in front of a live TV audience. At that time I was mainly a theatre person and, in classical or modern works, considered that comedy was probably my forte. Faced with a live audience in a TV studio, however, I felt a complete plonker.

'I hated it. Should I time my lines in reaction to the audience, or totally ignore them? Should I compromise my angle to the camera in order to give the studio audience a better view? None of the stagecraft – or such camera craft as I possessed at that time – learned over the previous dozen or so years, seemed to apply and after two or three unhappy experiences, I made up my mind that TV comedy shows involving anybody other than the technicians and my fellow actors on the studio floor, were simply not my bag. Then along came Sydney Lotterby with an offer that I would have been mad to refuse.

'Nasty Norris was a character that leapt off the page at me. Instinctively, I knew how I would play him, and heard his whining tone of voice from the moment I read the first words. It was a peach. What's more, I would get the chance to work with the likes of Ronnie Barker and the wonderful Fulton Mackay, not to mention Sydney Lotterby – one of the very best of our TV comedy directors.

'Much of the action takes place in the prison sick ward because Fletcher has broken his leg. My character is across the ward complaining of an ingrowing toenail. In rehearsals, I was amazed to find that the old man in the bed opposite was being played by a friendly young chap much the same age as myself. It was, of course, David Jason. David used to come in hours before the rest of the cast to be fitted with layers of latex wrinkles and make-up, topped with a convincing grey wig. He was unrecognisable.

'Whoever had the courage and imagination to cast him in that role deserves a medal. His was a semi-regular character in the series and it gave him a marvellous kick-start to a highly successful career; but it would never happen today. Nowadays you are expected to turn up to a casting session looking exactly like the character you might be playing, and I can't imagine David would fancy travelling up to White City covered in latex!

'I think "Happy Release" must be the most repeated episode of the whole series; in fact, I've come to rely on it to pay off my overdraft at least once a year, and I need hardly say that I learned more about playing TV comedy from Ronnie and Sydney and the rest of that fantastic team, in a few short days, than almost any time before or since, so when the offer came to go into Yorkshire Television's *In Loving Memory*, where Dame Thora Hird continued my education, I felt equal to the task.'

Christopher Biggins (Lukewarm in the series)
'In 1974 I was a young actor – twenty-six years old, in fact, and terribly starstruck. When I went to visit Syd Lotterby, the director and producer of a new sitcom set in prison, I had no idea that it was written by Dick Clement and Ian La Frenais, and starred my all-time favourite comedy actor, Ronnie Barker.

'When my agent, Gillian Coffey, rang and told me I had got the part of Lukewarm, I was over the moon; I immediately rang my parents who were thrilled. So I suddenly became part of history by being involved in one of the most popular and, thank God, most repeated sitcoms ever.

'My first day was nerve-racking and yet so exciting. Ronnie was enchanting, as were the rest of the cast, and after the read-through one knew we were on to something rather special. Ronnie was incredibly generous and if during rehearsals he felt one of his lines was better off said by another actor, he would give it over with no complaints. It was so good to work with a star who was considering the whole product; it was a lesson I took on and, hopefully, have always tried to repeat in my career. I have come across the opposite in other stars I've worked with – not everyone's like Ronnie.

'One of my fondest memories was in the episode "Men Without Women". Fletcher wrote a letter on behalf of all the inmates to their respective wives telling them of their love of the fairer sex. When the wives were travelling to the prison on the bus, one of the wives started reading out aloud the contents of the letter, when suddenly all the women realised that their letters were the same. But one of the biggest laughs in a studio I've ever heard was when Lukewarm's boyfriend brought out the same letter – it was a moment of comic genius.

'After the first series had been completed, Ronnie gave all the regulars a silver tankard with the inscription, "Slade Prison 1974" together with our character's name; he gave mine an initial so it read "Lukewarm. P". I will always treasure it.

'I remember vividly the day word reached me of the tragic death of Ronnie's co-star, the multi-talented Richard Beckinsale. I was making a film, *The Tempest*, directed by Derek Jarman, on the northeast coast. It was bitterly cold and I was having a rest in my room late one afternoon when the telephone rang: it was a journalist from the *News of the World* asking whether I'd like to comment on the death of Richard. I was stunned and devastated; what a world star he would have been if he hadn't died so young, and how proud he would have been of his daughter, Kate.

'I, in turn, am very proud to be associated with one of the most glorious television sitcoms ever, starring two huge stars and a cast you would give your eye teeth to work with, written by two literary geniuses and held together by a brilliant producer. Nearly thirty years on nothing comes near its brilliance. Thank you, Syd.'

Cyril Shaps (Jackdaw in 'The Harder They Fall')
'My memories of *Porridge* are of rehearsals which demonstrated how inventive Ronnie Barker was throughout. His improvisations, his brilliant technique and, above all, his constant good humour were an inspiration.

'We shared a love of gardening and, in particular, rockeries. I mentioned this to him and he said he would like to see mine, which was in full bloom at the time. I invited him to tea after the day's rehearsal and he agreed immediately. We had a very happy session together.'

CHRISTMAS SPECIAL

NO WAY OUT

1. ASSOCIATION AREA

The camera shows a fairy on top of a Christmas tree. Lennie walks in to the association area with two mugs of cocoa. He hears prisoners singing carols.
Lennie walks round the catwalk and stops to watch the choir. One of the singers is Lukewarm. He looks up and notices Lennie. Lennie leaves.

1A. FLETCHER'S CELL

Fletcher is pasting a newspaper cutting of a topless girl on to a piece of card, on which he has written 'Merry Xmas'. Lennie enters.

LENNIE
What's that – you making a Christmas card?

FLETCHER
Yes – it's for my brother George. I cut it out the paper.

LENNIE
Not very seasonal, is it?

FLETCHER
It is for George – he's only allowed it once a year.

LENNIE
Can you hear the carols?

FLETCHER
Yeah – shut the door, will you?

LENNIE
Don't you like it?

FLETCHER
They've been at it for two hours – and they only know four carols. And the words of one of them are a bit suspect. Shepherds washed their socks by night!

LENNIE
Don't you find it rather moving? All those blokes, some of them real tearaways, united in a common exultation of this great occasion.

FLETCHER
Don't be daft. They're singing, my son, to drown the noise of Tommy Slocombe's tunnelling.

LENNIE
Tunnelling?

FLETCHER
That's the great occasion round here. Not the coming of our Lord, the going of Tommy Slocombe.

LENNIE
Nobody ever tells me nothing.

FLETCHER
It wasn't thought an event suitable for publication. It's a secret between Tommy, six baritones, twelve tenors and soprano.

LENNIE
Have we got a soprano?

FLETCHER
Oh there's lots of sopranos in here, my son. And a few of those baritones need watching an' all. Don't let those deep gruff voices fool you. 'Come over 'ere, son.'

LENNIE
Where is the tunnel?

FLETCHER
Where's the choir?

LENNIE
Just outside cell twenty-eight.

FLETCHER
About three feet under cell twenty-nine then. Give us a biscuit.

LENNIE
Well, I like the singing. At least it brings an air of festivity into our otherwise monotonous existence. There's ever such a lot to look forward to – there's the carol service, and the concert coming up. And the tree.

FLETCHER
Useful, the tree.

LENNIE
Useful?

FLETCHER
For stashing Christmas contraband. All those dingly danglies hide a multitude of sins. And even that Christmas fairy on the top has got two ounces of tobacco shoved up her tutu.

LENNIE
No wonder she looks uncomfortable. Where did that come from?

FLETCHER
The Governor's office. It was his present for Mr Mackay. Welsh George made a nifty switch when he was in there doing the floors.

LENNIE
He must have left something to take its place.

FLETCHER
He did. An identical gift-wrapped box, which Mr Mackay will doubtless open on Christmas Day.

LENNIE
What's in it?

FLETCHER
Well, I'll tell you one thing – if he uses it for putty all his windows will fall out.
He gets up.

LENNIE
What's Christmas like inside, Fletch?

FLETCHER
Slightly less 'orrible than any other day.

I mean, the Governor don't dress up as Santa Claus and give us all bottles of after-shave, you know.

LENNIE

But we get turkey, don't we – do we, do we get turkey?

FLETCHER

They call it turkey, but not seeing it carved we don't know, do we? If it is, the one we had in our block last year must have been a funny shape. Twenty-eight legs and no breast. Like Lulu and the Young Generation.

He sits down.

LENNIE

Hey, that's good – can I use that in my after-dinner speech? By the by, we get pudding as well, don't we? Xmas pudding like, with cream?

FLETCHER

Oh yes – that artificial whipped cream. You'd be better off shaving with that though. And, of course, the wheeler-dealers make a few bob at Xmas time. Slade Prison's Mister Big, genial Harry Grout, has granted a few franchises. Young Terry Maidment is making himself a fortune, flogging mistletoe to the poofters.

LENNIE

Just like the outside then. People have forgotten the real meaning of Christmas. It's just a commercial exercise.

FLETCHER

What do you expect? Goodwill to all men – what? From Mackay? As much chance of getting that as you have finding a partridge up a pear tree.

LENNIE

Still the actual day should be a bit brighter though, shouldn't it?

FLETCHER

Won't be this year.

LENNIE

Why not?

FLETCHER

Because of that flaming tunnel. That tunnel spells disaster for us all. That Tommy Slocombe's only chosen to make his break on Christmas Eve. Dear, dear never get through the traffic.

LENNIE

(*With a smile*) Oh – he's only got six more digging days to Christmas then.

FLETCHER

It's not funny, sonny Jim. We're all going to be implicated in this escape. Whether we like it or not.

He gets up.

LENNIE

But Slocombe's such a despicable nurk. I don't see why anyone would lift a finger for him.

FLETCHER

It so happens young Slocombe is the brother-in-law of a big villain in the smoke. A man who is also a colleague of genial Harry Grout. Now he's

obviously got the word to Harry – 'Get
our kid away for Christmas.' So Harry's
running this caper. Which means if any
of us are asked to assist we are in no
position to refuse. Otherwise, one
morning we might find something else
hanging on the Xmas tree. Us.

LENNIE
I'm not going down no tunnel, I suffer
from claustrophobia.

FLETCHER
Do you?

LENNIE
It dates back to the time when I was
stuck in a chimney for
two hours.

FLETCHER
Oh dear, how was that?

LENNIE
I was going to turn over this big house
in Sutton Coldfield. The chimney was
my only means of access.

FLETCHER
Oh yeah, and you got stuck,
did you?

LENNIE
Yes, it was terrifying. What made it
worse was my intended victims came
home from the pictures, and saw my
legs sticking out of the fireplace.
I managed to run off though.

FLETCHER
Did they give the police a description?

LENNIE
Yeah, luckily I was covered in soot.
They're still looking for a tall, blue-eyed
Negro in a black suit.

FLETCHER
Yeah – well that might excuse you
tunnelling duties. But when
Slocombe's well out of it we'll all be
well in it. You, just as much
as anybody else. The point is,
it's disturbing the equilibrium of
prison life.

LENNIE
The equilibrium?

FLETCHER
Yeah, them and us, it'll tilt the balance
of power which exists between the law
and the villain. With this escape we
shall have pushed the system too far.

LENNIE
There's nothing we can do though, is
there? I mean, what can we do?

FLETCHER
I know what I'm going to do. I intend
to be well out of it.

LENNIE
How?

FLETCHER
I'm going away for Christmas.

LENNIE
Where to, Majorca?

FLETCHER
No – everyone goes to Majorca,
don't they? No, I thought I'd try

the prison hospital this year for a change. A, because it's the nearest thing to a holiday in here, and B, because I shall be far removed from any retaliations by the screws over this escape fiasco.

LENNIE

You'll never get in the infirmary, not with that doctor. What's supposed to be wrong with you?

FLETCHER

It's my knee, isn't it?

LENNIE

I never knew there was anything wrong with your knee.

FLETCHER

No, well I've been keeping it up my sleeve. Or more precisely, my trouser leg.

LENNIE

What's the matter with it?

FLETCHER

Cartilage. I've lived with the pain for years. But recently, being on my feet all day in the damp weather, it has escalated the pain to an unbearable degree.

LENNIE

Which knee is it?

FLETCHER

Eh?

LENNIE

Which knee is it?

FLETCHER

This one . . . or is it this one?

2. PRISON CLINIC

DOCTOR

Am I hurting you?

WARREN

(*Happily*) Yup.

DOCTOR

Sorry.

WARREN

You got your job to do.

DOCTOR

It's a pretty bad burn.

WARREN

(*Still happily*) Yeah, I know.

The Doctor looks up at Warren.

DOCTOR

What are you so pleased about?

WARREN

Well, Doc, if you're going to hurt yourself in here, might as well make sure it's nothing trivial. I mean there's no way I can go back to work with this hand, is there?

DOCTOR

I'm reluctantly forced to admit there isn't.

WARREN

I think I could just about make it to the infirmary though, if somebody opens the door for me.

DOCTOR

(*Resolutely*) You're not going to the infirmary. You're confined to your cell for three days.

WARREN

You can't manage in a cell on your own with your hand tied up like this.

I know it seems silly to lie in the infirmary with a bandaged hand. But, on the other hand . . .

DOCTOR
Neither of your hands is going to find its way into the sick-bay, is that understood?

WARREN
You don't like people getting in your infirmary, do you?

DOCTOR
And mess up all those crisp white sheets, certainly not. Next! (*To Warren*) Now just hold this dressing in place for a few moments, then I'll get you bandaged up.

Fletcher enters, limping and wincing. Just the quickest of looks from the Doctor, then –

DOCTOR
Out of here, Fletcher.

FLETCHER
I got my white card.

DOCTOR
Out, out, out.

FLETCHER
I'm sick!

DOCTOR
Out!

FLETCHER
I'm entitled.

DOCTOR
Years of medical practice have enabled me to tell at a glance if a man's sick or not. You're a perfect specimen of manhood, Fletcher.

FLETCHER
It's not that I've come about, it's my knee.

DOCTOR
What's wrong with your knee?

FLETCHER
Just ask me to stand on one leg.

DOCTOR
What?

FLETCHER
Ask me to stand on one leg.

WARREN
Go on, ask him. No harm in that.
The Doctor's curiosity gets the better of him.

DOCTOR
All right, stand on one leg.
Fletcher raises a leg and then collapses on the floor as the other one buckles beneath him. He looks at the Doctor accusingly.

FLETCHER
And you call yourself a doctor!

DOCTOR
Get up, Fletcher.

FLETCHER
I don't know if I can.
He raises himself with difficulty, keeping the weight off one foot.

DOCTOR
Sit in the chair. What is it?

FLETCHER
I'll show you.
Dramatically and carefully he rolls up his trouser leg. The Doctor watches. Warren cranes forward to

*see. Fletcher uncovers a knee . . .
a perfectly normal knee . . . and
gestures towards it.*

FLETCHER

There then!

DOCTOR

There what?

FLETCHER

It's a knee.

DOCTOR

I know it's a knee, Fletcher. I learned
that in medical school.

FLETCHER

But you didn't learn about this kind of
knee. You see the old trouble has
flared up again.

DOCTOR

What old trouble? Laziness?

FLETCHER

Cartilage. And before you say anything,
it's all on my medical records.

He points towards a filing cabinet.

FLETCHER

You check your files, you'll see I have
an official history of knee trouble.

DOCTOR

I don't believe you.

FLETCHER

Have to check though, won't you?

*The Doctor turns towards the file
shaking his head.*

DOCTOR

I don't know why I'm doing this.

FLETCHER

You're doing it because you know that
there's one chance in a million that one

day one of us will be telling the truth.

*The Doctor opens the filing
cabinet and first of all removes a
Christmas cake.*

FLETCHER

What's that then?

DOCTOR

It's a Christmas cake. I get one
every year.

FLETCHER

What for?

DOCTOR

The patients in the infirmary.

WARREN

But you never *allow* any patients in
your infirmary.

DOCTOR

That's true. I always take it home for
the wife.

*The Doctor goes through the files as
Fletcher turns to Warren.*

FLETCHER

Hey, that's a turn-up for the book, ain't
it – in prison.

WARREN

What?

FLETCHER

A file with a cake in it – get it, get it?

WARREN

Oh, yes. You're a very witty
man, Fletch.

FLETCHER

Here, are you a mason?

The Doctor has found Fletcher's record and is reading it.

DOCTOR

My God, it's true – Maidstone Jail 1967. Cartilage.

WARREN

Very common with footballers that. That and groin strain.

FLETCHER

Little chance of groin strain in here.

DOCTOR

All right, I accept you have an official record of surgery on your left knee. But this was years ago.

FLETCHER

Yeah, and I've lived with the pain ever since. Now I don't complain, do I, Bunny?

WARREN

No, he don't complain. Even though we've seen him crawl in from work some days like a wounded bloodhound on his hands and knee.

FLETCHER

(*Heroically*) Please – I'm not after sympathy.

DOCTOR

What is it you are after?

FLETCHER

Well . . . every so often, when the pain becomes unbearable, I have to lie down with my leg up – just for a week or two.

DOCTOR

(*Playing along*) You think a week in the infirmary would do the trick?

FLETCHER

Maybe a week.

DOCTOR

Let me tell you something, Fletcher. Of all the penal institutions in the north of England, my infirmary has the lowest record of admissions. Donaldson, who's doing a five stretch for grand larceny and embezzlement, has more chance of getting a Barclaycard than you have of getting in my infirmary.

FLETCHER

On your head be it.

The Doctor makes up his mind. He starts to fill out a form.

DOCTOR

Fletcher, I know you, and I know you're going to make an issue out of this, and waste a lot of my valuable time with your stupid nonsense, so here's what I'm going to do. I'm going to cut it out before it goes any further.

FLETCHER

Amputate? Now, hang on . . .

WARREN

That should get you in the infirmary.

DOCTOR

I'm sending you to a civilian hospital. For X-ray and specialist examination. You'll be there and back in a day. Then the matter will be irrevocably closed.

Fletcher realises he is losing the battle.

FLETCHER

Why waste the taxpayers' money? I tell you, I know my knee. All I need is to rest up for a day or two.

DOCTOR

(*Giving Fletcher the card*) On your way, Fletcher. You're a liar and a malingerer.

FLETCHER

Harsh words, Doctor. In this season of peace and goodwill to all men. I hope your conscience pricks you, that's all.

DOCTOR

You can say a little prayer for me on Christmas morning. Next.

FLETCHER

Yeah, I will. You don't mind if I say it standing up, do you? I can't kneel down, I've got a bad knee.

He walks across to leave and shakes Warren's hand.

FLETCHER

All the best.

WARREN

Aaaagh!

3. CELL

Fletcher is in his cell. Lennie walks in. In the distance we hear the choir, now singing 'O Come All Ye Faithful'.

LENNIE

Hey, Fletch –

FLETCHER

Shut the door!

LENNIE

Harry Grout's coming to see you.

FLETCHER

(*Surprised*) What?

LENNIE

Straight up. Grouty. On his way.

FLETCHER

What did I tell you? Gawd blimey, I knew it. This will be some little favour pertaining to Slocombe's moonlight flit – hello, Harry!

Fletcher's change of expression is explained by Grout's arrival.

GROUT

Hello, Fletcher.

FLETCHER

This is a rare privilege. You don't often drop in on people. Usually you get people to drop in on you. And if they don't you get other people to drop things on them.

Lennie laughs.

GROUT

You always were a bit of a joker, Fletch.

FLETCHER

Yes, I was. Up to now. What brings you to my humble abode, Grouty?

GROUT

I wanted to get out of my cell just for a while.

FLETCHER

Change of air?

GROUT

No, a couple of warders are putting up my Christmas decorations.

Lennie laughs. Grout takes a coin from his pocket and flicks it to Lennie.

GROUT

There you are, son. Go to the pictures or something.

Lennie gets the point.

LENNIE

Oh – thank you.

He goes.

GROUT

Shut the door.

Door crashes heavily.

GROUT

Sit down, Fletch.

FLETCHER

(*Sitting down*) Oh, thank you very much. Like the smell of a nice cigar. Wish I had something festive to offer you, Grouty.

GROUT

Not in the festive mood, Fletch. There's a tunnel being dug. You've heard, I suppose?

FLETCHER

Only when they leave off singing.

GROUT

Slocombe's a relative of friends of mine on the outside, and they want him sprung.

FLETCHER

Oh, isn't his dad Billy the Ponce

Slocombe? Yes, the one that got out of Brixton in '72. Where did he end up?

GROUT

Apparently he emerged on some Caribbean Island where the authorities took advantage of his criminal experience.

FLETCHER

How?

GROUT

Made him Chief of Police.

FLETCHER

Well, he did have a bit of style, the old man.

GROUT

Trouble is, it's beholden to me to accomplish the disappearance of his idiot offspring.

FLETCHER

Delicate, Grouty.

GROUT

Extremely.

FLETCHER

If only I could help in some way.

GROUT

You can, my son.

FLETCHER

Oh gawd.

GROUT

You're having a little day trip tomorrow, aren't you?

FLETCHER
Only to get my knee X-rayed.

GROUT
Still you'll be on the outside. And we have friends on the outside who could take advantage of that.

FLETCHER
How?

GROUT
There'll be a package. Someone. Somewhere. Sometime. No sweat.

FLETCHER
I'll be under escort, Grouty. I'm not just getting the bus down there and doing a bit of last-minute Christmas shopping at the same time, you know.

GROUT
It's only a small package. A blank passport. Inky Stevens needs one to give Slocombe a more acceptable identity.

FLETCHER
Wouldn't it be safer for him to pick up his new passport on the outside?

GROUT
Normally, yes. But the finest forger in the country's Inky Stevens, and he's on the inside, isn't he?

FLETCHER
Yes, yes . . .

GROUTY
I won't be ungrateful, Fletch.
He stands up.

FLETCHER
Oh good.

GROUT
Be something extra in your Christmas stocking for this. Besides your bad knee, that is.
He laughs at his own joke. When he opens the door, the choir can be heard again. They are now halfway through 'God Rest Ye Merry Gentlemen'.
Grout reacts with pleasure.

GROUT
Oh, I like this one.
He joins in.

GROUT
'Great tidings of comfort and joy, comfort and joy . . .'
He gestures to Fletcher to join him. Fletcher does so, his expression conveying anything but comfort and joy.

FLETCHER
'Great tidings of comfort and joy . . .'

4. PRISON YARD
Barrowclough and Mackay walk up to a waiting minibus and Barrowclough gets in. Fletcher approaches with a warder.

MACKAY
Haven't you forgotten something, Fletcher?

FLETCHER
What?

MACKAY
Your limp – ha, ha . . .

FLETCHER

Oh, yes, mock the afflicted.

MACKAY

You're not sick, as the X-rays will soon prove.

FLETCHER

Well look, let's call the whole thing off then. Seriously. I can live with pain a few years longer. Hospitals is busy enough this time of year. Yeah, I'll just hobble back to my cell.

He turns and limps away.

MACKAY

Get in, Fletcher. Mr Barrowclough has his Christmas shopping to finish.

Fletcher gets in the bus and Mackay shuts the door. The bus starts to move.

5. HOSPITAL BUILDING

The camera shows the sign 'X-ray', then the hospital building.

FLETCHER

(*Voiceover*) All right, doc, you're the expert. I can take it. Give it to me straight . . .

DOCTOR

(*Voiceover*) (*Gravely*) I am afraid I have bad news for you, Mr Fletcher.

FLETCHER

(*Voiceover*) You have?

DOCTOR

(*Voiceover*) Yes . . . you have a perfectly healthy knee.

6. HOSPITAL ANTE-ROOM

It is a bare room, with a few tables, chairs and magazines. Fletcher and Barrowclough are sitting on chairs with cups of coffee. On the chair beside Barrowclough are several gift-wrapped packages. The camera shows a young Nurse holding up an X-ray photograph of a healthy knee.

NURSE

You've really got quite an attractive knee, Mr Fletcher.

FLETCHER

Not as attractive as yours, nurse. Yeah, I bet *they're* going to have a happy Christmas, ain't they?

BARROWCLOUGH

Now, that will do, Fletcher. You're old enough to be the girl's father.

FLETCHER

No, impossible, I never been round this way before.

NURSE

The main thing is, it's a healthy knee.

FLETCHER

Those X-rays prove nothing, you cannot photograph pain.

NURSE
When did your knee trouble start?
BARROWCLOUGH
Two days ago, when he
thought he'd wangle the infirmary for
Christmas.
FLETCHER
No, it does not. Goes back ten years.
As the Nurse leaves Hospital
Porter passes by pushing a trolley.
Another girl, dressed in civilian
clothes but wearing a hospital
white coat over them comes up
to the men.
SANDRA
Can I get you gentlemen some more
coffee?
FLETCHER
No, no, let's just get back to where we
come from.
BARROWCLOUGH
(*Rising*) Well, I'd like another cup of
coffee. It's all milk, isn't it? I only get
half and half at home.
FLETCHER
Half and half?
BARROWCLOUGH
Milk and water.
FLETCHER
Oh yeah.
BARROWCLOUGH
If it's not too much trouble, Miss. Very
sweet of you to ask.
SANDRA
(*To Fletcher*) You sure you don't
fancy some?

FLETCHER
Not coffee, no thank you.
She gives them a dazzling smile and
leaves.
BARROWCLOUGH
Charming girl.
He sits down.
FLETCHER
Look at you. Chapel hat pegs,
ain't it? More sex-starved than
me. How much longer are we going to
sit around this draughty corridor, then?
BARROWCLOUGH
What's the matter with you, Fletcher?
You seem very ill-at-ease. Relax.
Enjoy yourself, it's Christmas. Have
a biscuit.
FLETCHER
It's your attitude that's unsettling me.
'Have a biscuit' – God Almighty. Next
thing we know we'll have Mr Mackay
tucking us up in bed at night.
BARROWCLOUGH
Now, Fletcher! Mr Mackay's no
different from anyone else. Outside
the grey grim walls of our institution
you'll find that he can be an
amiable man.
FLETCHER
(*Incredulously*) Amiable?
BARROWCLOUGH
On Tuesday he stroked a dog. He did.
I saw it with my own eyes. The
Governor's boxer.
FLETCHER
What happened?

BARROWCLOUGH

It bit him.

FLETCHER

(*Amused*) Oh dear.

BARROWCLOUGH

Oh yes. He had to have an injection in case he caught rabies.

FLETCHER

What, the dog did – yes, he would.

BARROWCLOUGH

It's nothing to laugh at.

FLETCHER

Depends on your sense of humour, doesn't it? Look, I'm like the Governor's dog, ain't I? Conditioned to mistrust in an atmosphere of mutual contempt. I'm relaxed when we get back to the nick, you lock me up and we go back to hurling insults at each other.

BARROWCLOUGH

You're spoiling my day out, Fletcher.

FLETCHER

Oh, forgive me.

BARROWCLOUGH

Don't you think I sometimes get as sick of Slade Prison as you do? Today's been a break for me.

FLETCHER

Why? What would you have been doing today back at the prison, Mr Barrowclough?

BARROWCLOUGH

I was off duty today. I just volunteered for this trip.

FLETCHER

You could have stayed at home. Spent the day with your lady wife.

BARROWCLOUGH

That's really why I volunteered.

Sandra returns carrying a tray with coffee. Barrowclough is instantly on his feet.

BARROWCLOUGH

Here, let me take that.

SANDRA

I brought an extra cup just in case.

FLETCHER

Ta very much.

BARROWCLOUGH

You must forgive our friend here. He's a little morose. Not his usual self.

SANDRA

May I say something to your friend here?

BARROWCLOUGH

Certainly, my dear, by all means. The young lady wishes to address you, Fletcher.

SANDRA

It's just that . . . well, we're all very well aware in here of . . . what you are. And we realise it can't be a very happy time of year for you. So – with your permission (*To Barrowclough*) the radiologists and me have just got a little something here.

She produces a package the size of a large, stiff Christmas card.

SANDRA

It's not very much but I think it's the thought that counts.

BARROWCLOUGH

What a very nice thought. Isn't that nice, Fletcher?

Fletcher gets up and takes the package.

FLETCHER

Oh . . . oh, very nice of you, Miss. I can't say I'm not touched. In fact I'm deeply moved. Should I open it now?

SANDRA

(*Grabbing his arm*) No!! Not before Christmas Day.

She winks at Fletcher.

FLETCHER

Oh yes. Yes, of course.

SANDRA

Spoil the surprise, wouldn't it?

FLETCHER

(*Nervously*) Oh yes . . . oh no . . . Oh.

7. CELL

It is night time. Inside Fletcher's cell Grout is tearing open the envelope which contains a Christmas card and inside that a passport.

GROUT

Well done, my son.

FLETCHER

Give me palpitations I can tell you. Right under Barrowclough's nose!

Fortunately he was put off his guard by the day out, her legs and a couple of large Johnny Walkers.

GROUT

Smart bird that Sandra.

FLETCHER

Who is she, does she work there?

GROUT

'Course not. Come up from the smoke. All it took was a bit of nerve and a white coat.

FLETCHER

My nerve nearly went.

GROUT

Not you, Fletch, you're a dab hand. I'm only sorry your knee got a clean bill of health, Fletch. But p'raps I could do you a favour in that direction.

FLETCHER

How?

GROUT

Couple of my lads could have a go at it. Damage it beyond medical dispute.

FLETCHER

Er, I think I'll pass on that one, Grouty. Much as I appreciate your kind consideration.

GROUT

Please yourself. I just thought I'd mention it, because you see I would like to elicit the help of you and the lad a little further.

FLETCHER

Ain't I done my bit, Grouty?

GROUT

You see, it's the tunnel.

FLETCHER

Hang on a bit. The kid's got claustrophobia. And look at the size of me. A ferret I ain't.

GROUT

Nothing physical. Just want you to join the choir. They've come up against a very stoney bit, and we need all the fortissimo we can get.

FLETCHER

Oh, my pleasure, Grouty. Enjoy a good sing. Used to do a lot of it down in Maidstone when we worked on the prison farm. Church hymns mostly. Favourite one with the boys was 'We plough the fields and scatter'. A lot of 'em did, an' all. Right, that's everything then, is it?

GROUT

Not quite. Just one tiny thing.

FLETCHER

Oh, please, Harry, aren't I doing my share? Smuggling, singing . . .

GROUT

It's essential to the success of our venture.

FLETCHER

Well?

GROUT

We need a bicycle.

FLETCHER

Oh certainly, what colour?

8. PRISON LANDING

Barrowclough waits for Warren, then walks along the catwalk behind him. Lukewarm sees Barrowclough and moves to the radiator. He taps it. The radiator answers (it replies to taps). Lukewarm moves towards the tables and starts singing 'The First Noel'. Other prisoners start to join in.Barrowclough and Warren walk round the catwalk as the men are singing. As he sings, Lukewarm is watching Barrowclough.

9. CELL

Fletcher and Lennie are about to leave the cell when Warren and Barrowclough walk in.

FLETCHER

What's this, Mr Barrowclough? Lunchtime, in' it?

BARROWCLOUGH

Lunch can wait. I have something very serious to say to you three.

LENNIE

Why us three?

BARROWCLOUGH

Because it was you three who were in

the yard today when I arrived at work –
you three who involved me in a
pointless discussion on the outcome
of the Cup Final in 1962. That's why
I'm asking you three one pertinent
question . . . Where-is-my-bicycle?!!
*There is a pause while the three
prisoners look at each other in
outraged innocence.*

FLETCHER
What bicycle was this, then?

BARROWCLOUGH
The one I cycled to work on.

LENNIE
You got a bicycle, then?

BARROWCLOUGH
I've had one for a month or so. Ever
since the medical officer advised me to
take more exercise.

WARREN
I had a bike once.

BARROWCLOUGH
So did I! And I want to know what's
become of it.
*Lennie frowns as if trying to
understand.*

LENNIE
Let me get this straight, Mr
Barrowclough. You are saying that
prior to our conversation you were
the owner of a bicycle?

BARROWCLOUGH
That's right, yes.

LENNIE
And that since our conversation you are
the former owner of a bicycle?

BARROWCLOUGH
That's what I'm saying, yes.
*Fletcher sits down at the table. He
tries hard to get to the nub of
the matter.*

FLETCHER
Let me get this straight,
Mr Barrowclough. You are saying that
you arrived at work as a cyclist and
you'll be leaving as a pedestrian?

BARROWCLOUGH
Yes, yes, yes!

FLETCHER
Are you assuming there's a connection
between our discussion on the '62
Cup Final and the disappearance of
your alleged bicycle?

BARROWCLOUGH
There's nothing alleged about it. Green
it was.

WARREN
When did you last see your bicycle?

BARROWCLOUGH
When I got off it.

FLETCHER
You sure you had it with you when you
got off it?
*Barrowclough produces his
cycle clips.*

BARROWCLOUGH
Why do you think I wear these?

WARREN

To stop things falling out of
your trousers?

LENNIE

If we were talking to you, how could
we have palmed your bike?

BARROWCLOUGH

It was a well-known diversionary tactic.

FLETCHER

If you ask me, lads, this whole thing
sounds very dodgy.

BARROWCLOUGH

Dodgy?

FLETCHER

It has all the classic elements of an
insurance swindle.

BARROWCLOUGH

How dare you!

FLETCHER

(*Rising*) How dare you accuse us of
being bicycle thieves.

LENNIE

I saw that film. It was a beautiful
example of early Italian neo-realism.

BARROWCLOUGH

You're as impossible as ever. I thought
at this time of year . . . oh well, that's
just my naïve trust in human nature.
I should have known better. Warren –
follow me.

WARREN

Where to?

BARROWCLOUGH

Back to your cell. I'm going to
conduct a thorough search. And
if I find anything resembling a

bicycle pump in your trousers, you're
for it!

Fletcher reacts as they exit.

10. MACKAY'S OFFICE

*It is a tiny office with a gas fire,
racks of keys and a grubby
calendar. Barrowclough, clipboard
in hand, faces Mackay who is sitting
behind his desk.*

MACKAY

Pull yourself together, Barrowclough.
It's your own fault. You should never
turn your back on them, not for a
minute.

BARROWCLOUGH

I've always thought that the best way
to encourage trust was to show them
trust.

MACKAY

They're criminals, man.

BARROWCLOUGH

They're also human beings.

MACKAY

All right – but criminal human beings.
And they too often take advantage of
your lack of control. You lack
discipline. You're gullible.

BARROWCLOUGH

I sometimes give the men the benefit
of the doubt.

MACKAY

Never do that! It's rule one! Any time a
prisoner makes a request, a prison
officer must ask himself – 'What is he up
to?' Even the simplest request must be

treated with deep mistrust and suspicion. A prisoner ties his shoelace – question! What is he concealing in his sock?

BARROWCLOUGH

I know all that of course – but I never thought they'd steal a bicycle. They can't conceal that in their sock.

MACKAY

Oh come on, man! You know what these people are like! Did we ever find any trace of our billiard table?

BARROWCLOUGH

We found the red ball.

MACKAY

They'll have dismantled your bike in an instant. If we have as much luck as we did with the billiard table, maybe you'll get back your rear light.

BARROWCLOUGH

It seems so pointless.

MACKAY

There's always a point. My antennae tell me there's something going on. Think – have they asked you anything, any seemingly innocent favours?

BARROWCLOUGH

No, no, no. Well, they asked me one thing, but it was completely innocent.

MACKAY

(*Suspiciously*) What?

BARROWCLOUGH

They asked me to help with their choir at the carol service. There can't be any harm in that.

MACKAY

And you trusted them? Haven't I just told you – once you turn your back on them, you're finished.

BARROWCLOUGH

Oh, I won't do. I'll be conducting.

MACKAY

I think I'll conduct a little enquiry. Who's running this Glee Club?

They exit.

11. ASSOCIATION AREA

The prisoners' choir, including Fletcher, Lennie, Warren and Lukewarm, are grouped round singing.

CHOIR

'Good King Wencelas looked out
On the feast of Stephen
When the snow lay round about,
Deep and crisp and even.
Brightly shone the moon that night. . .'
Mackay and Barrowclough come from the office doorway and along the catwalk.

CHOIR

'Though the frost was cruel.'

MACKAY

Silence.

FLETCHER

'When a Scotsman came in
sight, hollering . . .'

MACKAY

That will do, Fletcher.

*Lukewarm looks towards radiator
from which can be heard 'clink, clink,
clink'. Lukewarm starts to move
towards the radiator.*

MACKAY

Stand still.

Lukewarm freezes.

*Mackay walks to the centre
of the room.*

MACKAY

What's that noise?

FLETCHER

Central heating, sir.

*Mackay moves to the radiator and
kicks it twice.*

The radiator replies.

FLETCHER

Oh – didn't know you was a plumber,
Mr Mackay. Think you've mended it.

MACKAY

All right – come on, back to your cells.

WARREN

We need more rehearsal, don't we?

MACKAY

There won't be any more.

LENNIE

Christmas, isn't it?

MACKAY

You've forfeited your right
to Christmas.

LENNIE

How?

MACKAY

Through a series of incidents,
culminating in the disappearance of Mr
Barrowclough's bicycle.

He walks among the prisoners.

MACKAY

I can't prove anything of course, but
don't think that technicality will affect
my judgement in the least. You were
put in here to keep crime off the
streets. But I'm not having you
bringing it into my prison. You will be
advised to remember that we have a
solitary confinement area, with which
you will become only too familiar if you
continue to practise the contemptible
habits which brought you here in the
first place. Clear? Right – back to your
cells the lot of you. Move!

*Prisoners file past Barrowclough
and Mackay.*

FLETCHER

I suppose you realise you've stifled at
birth what could have been the start of
a religious revival in here.

MACKAY

Out, Fletcher.

*Lukewarm stops to shake
Barrowclough's hand.*

LUKEWARM

In spite of all, Merry Christmas, sir. (*Taking his hand again*) And a very happy Christmas to Mrs Barrowclough.

BARROWCLOUGH

Right, now come on – move it along . . . (*Hesitantly*) Lukewarm . . .

MACKAY

(*To Barrowclough*) That is the only attitude they respect. The only attitude that will wipe out this wave of insubordination and petty theft.

BARROWCLOUGH

I suppose you're right . . . d'you think you could countersign my report?

He hands Mackay the clipboard.

MACKAY

Very well . . . (*Feeling for his pen*) That's funny, I seem to have mislaid my pen. (*Feeling other pocket*) Where's my wallet . . . Mr Barrowclough, I've been mugged!

BARROWCLOUGH

But that's not possible, sir. We've only been here a minute. We came in here at . . . (*Automatically checks his watch*) . . . Where's my watch!

12. CELL

Lennie is making a paper chain, when an indignant Fletcher enters.

FLETCHER

It's on the bulletin board, it's official.

LENNIE

What is?

FLETCHER

Christmas is cancelled. It says on the board, 'There'll be no Xmas Eve, Xmas Day or Boxing Day. Just the 24th, 25th and 26th December.'

LENNIE

Oh well, no point in finishing this chain.

He puts down the paper chain.

FLETCHER

I told you, didn't I?

LENNIE

About the equilibrium being disturbed?

FLETCHER

Disturbed, it's upside down, my son. Marvellous, isn't it? Tick along all year, keeping your nose clean, and through sheer intimidation we all get dropped in the yuletide clarts. And then that bleeding Lukewarm, talk about daylight robbery!

LENNIE

Not his fault, Fletch, be fair. He was under Grouty's instructions like the rest of us. They needed Mackay's wallet to keep topping up the getaway car.

FLETCHER

They didn't need Barrowclough's Timex though, did they? Force of flaming habit that was. The whole thing's been a mockery. Ill-conceived, badly organised and doomed to fail –

Grout enters, Fletcher does not miss a beat.

FLETCHER

– oh hello, Grouty. I was just saying what a shame your brilliant strategy should come to naught.

GROUT

Know what they say, the best-laid plans . . .

LENNIE

Should I – er, go to the pictures?

GROUT

No, sit down, sonny – no secrets now. Bad business. My friends in the smoke are bound to bear malice.

FLETCHER

Oh no – they'd never be so heartless, Grouty.

GROUT

Why not? I would.

LENNIE

Excuse me, Mr Grout, but couldn't you reactivate the tunnel at a later date?

GROUT

No, it was off course anyhow. He's an idiot that Slocombe. He nearly come up in the laundry last week.

FLETCHER

So the tunnel's now defunct then?

GROUT

Except for storing contraband, yes.

FLETCHER

I have a glimmer of an idea, Grouty. Which may solve all our problems.

GROUT

Oh yes?

FLETCHER

If the screws was to find that tunnel, it would do two things. One, it would tilt the balance of power back in their favour, 'cos they'd be chuffed at their own perspicacity. And two, they'd think that was the intended escape route.

LENNIE

But it was.

FLETCHER

It was, but it ain't now. It's a red herring. Then while the screws are still full of self-congratulatory ardour, you get Tommy away in a dustcart or something. That should please your pals in London.

GROUT

Here, here, you have had a thought, haven't you, Fletch.

FLETCHER

Save your face, Grouty.

GROUT

That it would.

LENNIE

It'll appear to be a perfectly executed plan.

GROUT

You're not wrong, son. Tip the Governor off?

FLETCHER

No – I think Mackay should find it. In fact if you give me the blueprints I might arrange for him to drop right in it.

13. PRISON YARD

Mackay is walking down the steps to the prison yard.

MACKAY

Fletcher, I'm told you wanted a word with me.

Fletcher moves to the foot of the steps.

FLETCHER

Just a seemingly innocent stroll, Mr Mackay. Away from prying ears. Know what I mean.

MACKAY

Oh yes.

They move away together.

FLETCHER

I know you see me in the role of adversary, Mr Mackay, but we're both old hands at this game – there's you and us. But we both know that neither of us must push the other too far.

MACKAY

That's true.

FLETCHER

Thereby we maintain a tolerable rhythm of life. We must season our mutual contempt with mutual respect.

MACKAY

What are you getting at, Fletcher?

They stop.

FLETCHER

Over this way, Mr Mackay, don't want to get too near the eavesdropping nurks.

They move on.

MACKAY

You were about to say?

FLETCHER

I was about to say I don't like to see your authority undermined.

Mackay stops.

MACKAY

And?

FLETCHER

Nothing specific. I just wanted to articulate these views. Can we go a bit further?

MACKAY

If there's any point.

FLETCHER

It would be a step in the right direction.

They move on again.

MACKAY

I wish you could be a little more specific, Fletcher.

FLETCHER

Oh I've gone far enough.

He stops and stamps his feet.

FLETCHER

Getting a bit parky, isn't it?

MACKAY

I'm a very busy man, Fletcher. I didn't come out here to discuss the weather.

FLETCHER

Nor did I, Mr Mackay.

MACKAY

I don't think this conversation's having any useful purpose at all.

FLETCHER

Well, hang about and we might discover something to your advantage.

MACKAY

Fletcher, I think you're trying to divert my attention. I'm not falling for it.

FLETCHER

No, you're not, are you?

Mackay turns and moves away.

FLETCHER

I'm only trying to explain my position.

He moves and falls through a gaping hole.

Mackay turns and walks back to the hole. He looks down in amazement.

14. PRISON INFIRMARY

Fletcher is lying in bed with his knee bandaged up, eating his Christmas lunch.

The door is unlocked by a prison officer and Lennie enters, carrying a box of cigars and a package.

LENNIE

Morning, Fletch.

FLETCHER

Morning, my son.

LENNIE

They've reinstated Christmas.

FLETCHER

I know, I'm eating it.

LENNIE

Here you are. Merry Christmas.

FLETCHER

Cuban cigars!

LENNIE

They're from Grouty.

FLETCHER

Where did he get these?

LENNIE

Some things we never know, Fletch. Where did B Block get their goose? That's one from me. Bit mundane after cigars, but I knitted them myself.

Fletcher finishes unwrapping the package.

FLETCHER

Oh very nice . . . I'll wear the other one when I get the bandages off.

LENNIE

They're mittens. Grouty says he's very sorry that his directions were eighteen inches out, but that's typical of Slocombe's prowess as a surveyor.

FLETCHER

I'm not bothered. What I set out to do's all come to roost, in' it?

LENNIE

Ensconced in the hospital, right. The screws are so chuffed with finding the tunnel – you should see them out there wha-hey . . .

Mackay walks in.

MACKAY

Compliments of the
season, Fletcher.

LENNIE

See what I mean?

MACKAY

Pardon?

LENNIE

Nothing.

MACKAY

All right, Godber, cut along. Don't want
to miss your Christmas lunch.

LENNIE

See you, Fletch.

FLETCHER

In due course, son.

LENNIE

Yeah. I'll send you a get-well-
slowly card.

Mackay laughs. Lennie leaves.

FLETCHER

Well, Mr Mackay, you look a little . . .
flushed – is that the word?

MACKAY

Just been to the Governor's sherry
party. Everyone was in high spirits.
Except the doctor . . . you've got
his cake.

Fletcher reacts.

Mackay holds up a package.

MACKAY

Look at this – a present from the
Governor. Pipe tobacco, I imagine.

FLETCHER

I'd open that when you get home
if I was you, when you're on
your own.

MACKAY

Oh, I will.

FLETCHER

Yeah, I shall look forward to that.

MACKAY

Fletcher, I wanted to say that
I appreciate what you were up to
in the yard.

FLETCHER

Oh?

MACKAY

(*Laughing*) All right, Fletcher. Just
between you and me.

FLETCHER

I don't know what you're inferring, Mr
Mackay.

MACKAY

Of course you don't, officially. But as
you said we're both old hands at the
game. Like to ask you just one
question. What became of the soil that
was excavated from the tunnel?

FLETCHER

No, wait a moment. Whatever you're
assuming about our relationship,
do not assume that you have a
new informer in your back pocket.
There's you and us, and I'm still
on the side of us.

MACKAY

It's a harmless question, for future reference. I just want to know how they disposed of the soil.

FLETCHER

Can't help you.

Mackay produces a bottle of Scotch.

MACKAY

Scotland's finest.

FLETCHER

With a couple of nips out of it, I see.

MACKAY

Still an unexpected treat.

FLETCHER

Bribe, is it?

MACKAY

Christmas present.

Fletcher looks at the bottle.

MACKAY

Come along, Fletcher. Just between you and me.

FLETCHER

Is that door closed?

MACKAY

And there's no one out there.

FLETCHER

Christmas present.

MACKAY

Christmas present.

FLETCHER

You want to know where they put the soil?

MACKAY

Simple as that.

FLETCHER

I'll tell you then.

MACKAY

I thought you might.

FLETCHER

They dug another tunnel and put it down there.

Mackay laughs with satisfaction and starts to go. Then he realises he has been done. He looks back to Fletcher who is about to have a drink.

FLETCHER

Happy Christmas.

He drinks.

CHRISTMAS SPECIAL

CHRISTMAS TRAILER

FLETCHER'S CELL

Lennie and Fletcher are sitting at the table.

LENNIE

I'm looking forward to it. There's the carol service, and the concert coming up. And the tree.

FLETCHER

Useful, the tree.

LENNIE

Useful?

FLETCHER

For stashing Xmas contraband. Even the fairy on the top has got two ounces of tobacco stuffed up her skirt.

Barrowclough enters.

FLETCHER

Hello, Mr B., what brings you here?

BARROWCLOUGH

Important message from the Governor. Christmas is cancelled.

FLETCHER

You what?

LENNIE

You what?

Mackay enters behind Barrowclough.

MACKAY

Oh yes. It's official. There will be no Xmas Eve, Xmas Day, or Boxing Day. Just the 24th, 25th and 26th December.

LENNIE

He can't do that – it's traditional.

BARROWCLOUGH

He's done it.

MACKAY

It's on the bulletin board. It's just not going to *happen.*

He chuckles.

MACKAY

Carry on!

He and Barrowclough continue on their rounds.

FLETCHER

That's rubbish, that is. Take no notice. We shall be here, shan't we, Lennie?

LENNIE

Yeah.

FLETCHER

I mean – where can we go?

CHRISTMAS SPECIAL

THE DESPERATE HOURS

1. ASSOCIATION AREA

*Camera shows the well area
and the prisoners. A warder
walks across.
McLaren and Tulip are watching.
The warder walks past a prisoner,
who watches and then nods to
McLaren. He receives the nod, in
turn nods to Tulip and moves away.
Tulip is sitting reading a newspaper.
He receives the nod and, in turn,
nods to the prisoner at the end of
the table. The prisoner receives the
nod. He then nods to Warren.
Warren receives the nod and
leaves. McLaren comes to the gates
and nods.
Fletcher receives the nod and
shakes his head. The camera
reveals that he is standing outside
the door marked 'WC'. The door
opens and Mackay comes out. He
reacts to Fletcher and then leaves.
Fletcher then nods, gets a label from
his pocket and sticks on the door
'Gentlemen only'. He then goes in.
McLaren, Warder unlocking gate.
Warren joins McLaren*

*and they walk through the
gate and depart.
McLaren and Warren go in through
the WC door.*

2. SHOWER ROOM

*Fletcher and Tulip are near the sink.
Lennie is near the second cubicle.
McLaren and Warren walk in.*

FLETCHER

McLaren, Warren . . . I have gathered
you here as representatives of your
respective cell blocks.

WARREN

What's this all about, Fletch?

FLETCHER

A minute, please. As you know, the
festive season is almost upon us.

MCLAREN

With all the high spirits and jollity which
that entails.

FLETCHER

Now come on, Jock, that's the wrong
attitude going in, that is. Let me ask you
all what is the real meaning of
Christmas? Aside from the shepherds
and the swaddling an' that. What
comes to mind then?

LENNIE

Chestnuts roasting on an open fire.

FLETCHER

What? Oh yes, very good.

MCLAREN

What about Mackay roasting on an open fire?

FLETCHER

No, that's Guy Fawkes night.

WARREN

Crackers. Holly.

LENNIE

Treetops glistening and children listening –

FLETCHER

That will do, Godber. You can leave out the Perry Como. I'm talking about what the likes of us associate with Christmas. Aside from robbing a postman.

They look at each other.

TULIP

What?

FLETCHER

Drink.

WARREN

Drink?

FLETCHER

Drink, yes. That's what everyone does at Christmas, gets drunk. Bombed. Plastered. Elephant's trunk. Legless. Brahms and Liszt as the proverbial newt.

LENNIE

(*To McLaren*) I've never understood the derivation of that expression myself.

Are newts known to be heavy drinkers?

FLETCHER

(*Irritated by the interruption*) Time is somewhat precious. We are running a security risk. Time is somewhat precious.

LENNIE

Sorry, Fletch, I was just saying . . .

FLETCHER

Yuh, well.

TULIP

What are we here for, Fletch?

FLETCHER

Wine tasting.

TULIP

Wine tasting?

FLETCHER

Yes, unbeknownst to all and sundry and out of charity to our fellow inmates, young Godber and me have been fermenting illicit liquor since last July. We done this so it would reach its peak maturity at this festive season.

MCLAREN

Fletch, you're a marvel, you're a naffing marvel, you know that?

FLETCHER

Yuh, well.

LENNIE

I helped him as well.

WARREN

And are you dishing this stuff out, like?

FLETCHER

I knew I shouldn't have used that word,

charity, Warren. This is a business transaction. You are here to obtain a free sample – sip – and place an order for your fellow felons. Godber . . .

Lennie moves to the second cubicle, stands on the toilet bowl and takes from the cistern two bottles of colourless fluid.

FLETCHER

We are offering two selections. We have five-star in the white bottle and the two-star in the blue bottle.

PRISONER

(*Putting his head round the door*) Oi!

Tulip, Fletcher, Warren and McLaren rush to the urinals. Lennie goes to the second cubicle and sits down. The warder enters and walks round looking at them. He leaves.

The prisoners return to their original places and the conversation continues.

FLETCHER

Now as I was saying, the two-star is the Vin Ordinaire, though let me tell you it ain't that ordinaire. The five-star is our special reserve, we'll sample that first.

Lennie is carefully pouring some of the five-star into a bottle cap.

LENNIE

I'd like to warn you gentlemen, that this should be sipped delicately, like a fine liqueur. It should not be smashed down the throat by the mugful, all right.

Lennie passes the cap first to Tulip.

He takes a cautious sip and passes it to Warren.

He sips and passes it to McLaren who also sips for a moment. Then they react with anguished gasps.

FLETCHER

I thought they'd like it, Len.

WARREN

You ought to have washed the bottle out first.

MCLAREN

Fletcher, are you sure this stuff is fit for human consumption?

FLETCHER

No, I'm not. That's why you three nurks is testing it for me.

TULIP

This stuff's evil, Fletcher.

FLETCHER

Don't forget it's got another week to mature. Lennie, the two-star. I should warn you gentlemen that this one isn't quite so smooth. Be careful otherwise not only will you lose the flavour and the bouquet, you will probably lose your power of speech as well.

Lennie has given them the cap of the two-star. Warren holds it. They sniff it cautiously.

MCLAREN

(*Sniffing it*) Smells like embrocation.

FLETCHER

There is a hint of that, yes.

TULIP

You could poison the whole prison, Fletcher.

FLETCHER

It's not very easy to get the right
ingredients in here you know. I got the
potato peelings, and the orange pips.
No bother. But normally I would never
have used boot polish.

*There are howls of protest from the
others.*

FLETCHER

Only a joke, only a joke.

WARREN

(With the cap near his lips)
You sure?

FLETCHER

'Course I am.

Warren drinks.

FLETCHER

It was anti-freeze.

Warren splutters it out.

3. PRISON GOVERNOR'S OFFICE

*Venables is checking the morning
mail when there is a knock at the
door.*

VENABLES

Come in.

*A trusty enters carrying a tray of
coffee and biscuits. He is a small,
inoffensive man named Keegan with
a Yorkshire accent.*

KEEGAN

Morning, Guv'nor.

VENABLES

Morning, er, er . . .

KEEGAN

Keegan, sir . . .

VENABLES

You're new aren't you, Keegan?

KEEGAN

I'm not new to prison, sir, I'm
just a new trusty. Mr Mackay's
Christmas box 'cause I'm going
out soon, like.

VENABLES

Good, good. Well, don't fall back into
your old ways.

KEEGAN

No chance of that, sir. Not since t' wife
passed away.

VENABLES

Oh I'm sorry. When was this?

KEEGAN

A few weeks before I came inside.

VENABLES

Poor woman, what happened?

KEEGAN

I murdered her.

Venables is slightly taken aback.

VENABLES

Well, see that it doesn't
happen again.

Keegan leaves as Mackay comes in.

MACKAY

Morning, sir.

VENABLES

Close the door, Mr Mackay.

MACKAY

Sir?

Closes the door.

VENABLES

This new trusty – what's his name . . . Keegan?

MACKAY

No complaints, I hope, sir.

VENABLES

The man's a murderer.

MACKAY

Oh. Yes, sir. But crime of passion. Crime passionelle – that's French. Not a criminal type. His sort of murderer makes a model prisoner. Do their porridge, no bother, full remission. According to Home Office figures, seventy-five per cent . . .

VENABLES

I'm not interested in statistics, Mr Mackay. Just don't want my morning coffee served to me by a wife murderer. All right?

MACKAY

Very good, sir.

Venables crosses to the desk.

MACKAY

Replace him, sir.

VENABLES

Now to the business in hand. I have always found Christmas to be a very difficult time.

MACKAY

Yes, sir. So open to abuse. Contraband, bartering, smuggling. There isn't a Christmas cake comes

inside that isn't laced with marijuana.

VENABLES

What are we doing about that?

MACKAY

I've taken precautions, sir. I've put Mr Barrowclough on to sampling all food parcels.

VENABLES

Has he anything to report?

MACKAY

He's still too stoned to tell me, sir.

VENABLES

What about drink?

MACKAY

Always a problem, sir. They're so ingenious at hiding it, as you know, sir. I remember once they concealed it in a fire extinguisher. A fact we only discovered because a fire broke out in the education room. It was only a small fire, but after we used that particular extinguisher, it became a raging inferno.

VENABLES

Disgraceful. Well, as you know, Mr Mackay, I am a staunch teetotaller, and I am strongly opposed to drinking, legal or illegal.

MACKAY

Yes, sir.

VENABLES

So let us be especially vigilant this Christmas and hope that we get through it with a minimum of incident.

MACKAY

I'll drink to that, sir.

VENABLES

Hardly an appropriate remark, Mr Mackay.

MACKAY

Sorry, sir.

VENABLES

All right, carry on.

Mackay starts to go.

VENABLES

Oh, and you'll see about replacing er . . .

MACKAY

Keegan, sir. Yes, sir.

VENABLES

(*Drinking his coffee*) Incidentally, how did he kill his poor wife?

MACKAY

Poison, sir.

Venables looks at his coffee cup with grave misgivings.

4. ASSOCIATION AREA

As the gate is unlocked by the warder, two prisoners come out and Fletcher and Lennie go in. They stop.

FLETCHER

Hello, hello,

Camera reveals a Prison Officer searching through the bedclothes in Fletcher's cell.

FLETCHER

I think we've got burglars.

LENNIE

Who hasn't?

They move on.

4A. FLETCHER'S CELL

Fletcher and Lennie enter to discover Barrowclough in the process of turning over their cell.

FLETCHER

(*Indignantly*) What's this then?

BARROWCLOUGH

You're not being singled out, Fletcher, we're doing the whole block.

LENNIE

Harassment. Despicable infringement of civil liberties.

FLETCHER

If you told us what you was looking for, we might be able to save you all this bother.

BARROWCLOUGH

Drink.

FLETCHER

Drink? You mean alcohol? The demon rum, mother's ruin?

BARROWCLOUGH

That's what I mean, yes.

FLETCHER

I'm a strict teetotaller, Mr Barrowclough.

BARROWCLOUGH

(*Sceptically*) Really, Fletcher.

He walks across the cell.

FLETCHER

(*Following him*) Oh yes. Never touch tea, never have. I tell you something, the pathetic state of this country today has got more to do with tea than alcohol.

BARROWCLOUGH

How?

FLETCHER

Because we invented the tea break, that's where the rot set in.

BARROWCLOUGH

You're in no position to point the finger, Fletcher, when you've never done an honest day's work in your life.

FLETCHER

Oh that's very nice. He's added slander now to breaking and entering.

LENNIE

They've been turning us over all week. D'you know what they did last night? They come in the Hobby Shop where we was making soft toys for orphan children. I saw Mr Barrowclough with me own eyes, disembowelling my panda.

BARROWCLOUGH

Don't you think I felt bad about that? Just as I felt bad about sampling your food parcels.

FLETCHER

I heard you felt pretty good afterwards, though. (*To Lennie*) They found him standing in a bucket of sand and singing the 'Desert Song'.

BARROWCLOUGH

(*Embarrassed*) Yes, well, I suggest you men get this cell tidied up.

He leaves. Fletcher raises his voice for the departing Barrowclough's benefit.

FLETCHER

Oh very nice, exit the red shadow. (*Crossing to the door*) That's charming, ain't it? You don't find nothing, but no apologies, no retraction. As you say, Len, a total infringement of civil liberties. An unjustifiable act of mistrust and suspicion.

LENNIE

They didn't find nowt, though.

FLETCHER

'Course not, we hid it too well. Shut the door and fetch your mug.

Lennie does so. Fletcher, plays barman, fetching a mug and putting a towel across his arm. He moves to the right of his bunk.

FLETCHER

Good evening, sir. And what will it be?

LENNIE

The usual.

FLETCHER

Care for a drink first?

LENNIE

Why not.

FLETCHER

Large one?

LENNIE

Mind your own business.

FLETCHER

Thank you.

He unscrews screw from bedstead and pours from it into the mug. Lennie puts a finger over the hole.

LENNIE

Have one yourself.

FLETCHER

(*Taking drink*) Oh thank you, sir. When.

Lennie puts his finger back over the hole.

They drink.

FLETCHER

(*Putting screw back on*) Prisoners one, system nil.

Mackay enters.

MACKAY

Not necessarily, Fletcher.

FLETCHER

Oh my gawd . . . time gentlemen please. Haven't you got no cells to go to?

5. GOVERNOR'S OUTER OFFICE

Mrs Jamieson, the Governor's secretary, sits at her desk. Barrowclough is sitting on a bench, waiting to see Venables. He is holding a cake. Mackay opens the

door and marches Fletcher and Lennie in.

MACKAY

Left, right, halt, face the front.

Good morning, Mrs Jamieson, Mr Barrowclough . . .

MRS JAMIESON

Good morning, Mr Mackay.

FLETCHER

Good morning, Mrs Jamieson – you're looking very . . .

MACKAY

Quiet, Fletcher. Is the Governor in?

BARROWCLOUGH

I'm waiting to see him, he's indisposed.

He indicates the corridor.

FLETCHER

In the where?

MRS JAMIESON

He's not feeling too well. Ever since he sampled the Christmas pudding.

LENNIE

(*Offended*) Here, I made that. Nothing wrong with it.

FLETCHER

That's what you said about your Hungarian gluelash.

MACKAY

The word Fletcher is 'goulash'.

FLETCHER

I chose the word advisedly,
Mr Mackay. Seeing as most of us were
stuck in the bog.

*Venables walks in. He looks wan
and pale and walks cautiously
towards his office.*

MACKAY

Attention.

FLETCHER

Bless you.

MACKAY

Morning, Governor.

VENABLES

Morning, Mr Mackay.

MACKAY

Not too good I hear, sir. Sorry to
hear it.

VENABLES

Not too good at all. That prisoner we
replaced, Keegan – you didn't put him
in the kitchen, did you?

MACKAY

No, sir.

VENABLES

I wondered if he was extracting
some terrible revenge. I'd better
have some more of that vile
stuff, Mrs Jamieson. Right,
Mr Barrowclough, you can
come through, but I warn you,
I've not got long.

*He goes through into his office,
followed by Barrowclough.*

*Mrs J. gets a bottle of medicine and
starts to pour it into a glass.*

FLETCHER

(*To Lennie*) See what you done?
A stricken Governor. What sort of
Christmas is he going to have then?

MACKAY

What sort of Christmas are you two
going to have?

FLETCHER

Chuffed, aren't you?

MACKAY

Your own fault, Fletcher. You know the
penalties for brewing illicit hooch.

FLETCHER

Wasn't illicit hooch. It was a
health drink.

MACKAY

Poppycock!

FLETCHER

No, it is not poppycock. We couldn't
get the poppies. Mind you in here
there's no shortage of . . .

MACKAY

Fletcher!

FLETCHER

Just saying, health drink. Me and four
hundred of the lads saved up a wine
gum each. Then we crushed them in a
press in the woodwork shop. The
resultant extract is a remedy for all
known ills.

LENNIE

You should give the Governor some,
Mrs Jamieson.

MACKAY

I think the Governor's sick enough.

Mrs J. stands up, crosses to the

door and goes into the office.
All look at her legs appraisingly.
Mackay notices Fletcher
and Lennie.

MACKAY
Stop it, you two.

LENNIE
I've always been attracted to older women. When I was a lad, I always wanted to be seduced by my aunty Pauline. She was very sophisticated. Worked in a dress shop in Smethwick and wore Evening in Paris behind her ears.

FLETCHER
Oh, behind the ears, yes, sure sign.

LENNIE
I nearly was once.

FLETCHER
What?

LENNIE
Seduced. I went round her house and the radio was on and she said, 'Lennie, it's time you learned how to do the foxtrot.' Well, even at the naïve age of fourteen, I thought to myself, 'Foxtrot? In the middle of the day? Yum, yum.'

Mackay, despite himself, is fascinated by the story. Fletcher notices this.

FLETCHER
Should you go on in front of Mr Mackay? Edinburgh Presbyterian you know. Sex is only allowed when Hearts beat Celtic.

MACKAY
I am not interested in Godber's carnal reminiscences.

He walks over and sits down.

FLETCHER
Well I am, so what happened, Len?

LENNIE
Nothing.

FLETCHER
What?

LENNIE
Nothing happened. I mean, she held me very close like, but for an hour we just danced round the living room floor accompanied by the Northern Dance Orchestra.

FLETCHER
Big room, is it? Godber, your stories have a habit of tailing off like that. You are the master of the anti-climax.

LENNIE
I can't half foxtrot though.

Mrs Jamieson returns and sits at her desk. There is a knock on the door.

MACKAY
Come in.

The door opens and a trusty enters carrying a tray with coffee and biscuits. It is Reg Urwin. He seems a little disconcerted to see the room so full.

URWIN
Oh . . . hello, lads.

FLETCHER
Hello, Reg.

Urwin indicates his left arm.

FLETCHER

Something wrong with your arm?

Urwin indicates the red band.

FLETCHER

Oh, trusty now, are we?

URWIN

Er, yes. Replaced Keegan, thanks to Mr Mackay.

MACKAY

If a man keeps his nose clean, I don't forget.

URWIN

Should I come back later?

MACKAY

(*Rising*) Not at all, lad – don't be thick. Take the Governor his coffee. Chop, chop.

Urwin goes through into the other office.

6. GOVERNOR'S OFFICE

Barrowclough is standing by the desk while Venables signs papers. Urwin moves towards the desk with the coffee.

URWIN

Your coffee, sir.

VENABLES

Oh, thank you, er . . .

URWIN

Urwin, sir. With a 'U'. I'm the new trusty.

VENABLES

That's a privileged position, Urwin.

URWIN

I know it is, sir. That's why I've been so well behaved the last few months. So that I could get this job. So that I could get ahead with my plan.

But a look of anguish has crossed over Venables' face.

VENABLES

(*Standing*) I'm afraid your plan will have to wait, Urwin.

He makes a dash for the door.

7. OUTER OFFICE

Fletcher and Lennie react with interest as Venables dashes through.

MRS JAMIESON

Oh, Mr Venables – have you got time to sign . . .

VENABLES

No!

He leaves. Then he comes back.

VENABLES

I'll take it with me.

FLETCHER

Pity it wasn't in triplicate.

Venables goes.

8. GOVERNOR'S OFFICE

Barrowclough and a puzzled Urwin wait.

URWIN

Where's he gone?

He moves to the door.

BARROWCLOUGH

It's just that he has a bit of an upset tummy.

URWIN

Yes, but he was instrumental in my plan, he was.

BARROWCLOUGH

What plan is this, Urwin?

URWIN

(*Distractedly*) I suppose a screw's just as good. Yeah, I don't see why not.

BARROWCLOUGH

I said, what is your plan?

URWIN

I want to get out of here.

BARROWCLOUGH

That's what we all want, Urwin.

URWIN

Yes, but you don't want me to get out as soon as what I do. That's why I'm taking you hostage.

He produces a home-made gun from his pocket and points it at Barrowclough's back. Barrowclough turns and stares incredulously.

URWIN

It's a gun. And it works. And it's loaded.

BARROWCLOUGH

Now just a moment, er . . .

URWIN

Urwin. With a 'U'.

BARROWCLOUGH

Urwin, why don't you put that gun down?

URWIN

What, so you can pick it up?

BARROWCLOUGH

You should think very carefully about what you're doing.

URWIN

Oh I have done. Now here's what I'd like you to do. First, would you draw them blinds. Second off, would you get me an 'elicopter.

Barrowclough stares at him in astonishment.

URWIN

Well go on.

Barrowclough walks across to the window.

9. OUTER OFFICE

Mackay, Fletcher and Lennie are waiting.

FLETCHER

Listen, the Governor's obviously got other things on his mind, why don't we all come back in the New Year, Mr Mackay, round about April.

MACKAY

Fletcher, I'm in no hurry. I've waited long enough for this moment.

FLETCHER

Well, in that case, let's take a seat.

They move to the bench.

MACKAY

Fletcher – how dare you?

LENNIE

I don't mind waiting. It's almost worth getting busted these days, just for a glimpse of Mrs Jamieson's lovely . . .

MACKAY

Godber.

LENNIE

Smile.

MACKAY

(*Crossing to Mrs J.*) I apologise for these two.

MRS JAMIESON

That's all right, Mr Mackay, working in prison I've learnt to turn the other cheek.

LENNIE

And a very attractive cheek, too.

The connecting door opens and a pale-looking Barrowclough pokes his head through.

BARROWCLOUGH

Eh, Mrs Jamieson, I want to get in touch with the nearest RAF station.

MRS JAMIESON

I don't know where that is.

BARROWCLOUGH

Well, the Fleet Air Arm or Air Sea Rescue. Anyone who can get me a helicopter.

FLETCHER

My word, you're being a bit lavish with your Christmas presents, aren't you, Mr Barrowclough?

BARROWCLOUGH

What?

FLETCHER

You'll need a lot of coloured paper to wrap that up.

MACKAY

Quiet, Fletcher. Is there a problem, Mr Barrowclough?

BARROWCLOUGH

Yes, Mr Mackay, something's come up.

MACKAY

Come up?

BARROWCLOUGH

Yes, I'm being held at gunpoint by Urwin here.

He gestures over his shoulder.

MACKAY

You're what?

Urwin appears behind Barrowclough, brandishing the gun.

URWIN

It's true, look.

Mrs Jamieson gives a little scream.

URWIN

Don't panic, missis. Just get on the blower.

FLETCHER

Here, Reg, you gone off your rocker?

URWIN

Shut up, Fletch.

FLETCHER

As you say, my son.

*Mackay decides the time has come
for him to take charge.*

MACKAY

All right, Urwin. Give me that gun.

He starts to move.

URWIN

You make a move and Barrowclough
gets it.

Mackay advances slowly.

MACKAY

I said, give me that gun.

BARROWCLOUGH

Shut up, Mackay! This is no time for
stupid heroics.

MACKAY

We can't let these people
intimidate us.

BARROWCLOUGH

That's all very well for you to say, but it's
my head the gun is pointing at.

URWIN

You just naff off, Mackay. I've got two
hostages, him and her, so put the
word out right?

*Mackay looks at Mrs Jamieson, then
at Barrowclough.*

BARROWCLOUGH

Go on man, do as he says.

*Mackay moves reluctantly towards
the door.*

MACKAY

Very well. Don't panic, Mrs Jamieson,

soon have you out of this. And don't
you panic, Mr Barrowclough.

FLETCHER

(*Crossing to the centre of the room*)
Mr Mackay?

MACKAY

Yes?

FLETCHER

Can we panic?

MACKAY

You two come along with me.

*Fletcher and Lennie move quickly to
the door.*

URWIN

No – they stay. I can use them. Now
naff off, Mackay.

*Mackay leaves.
Mrs Jamieson looks up from the
phone directory.*

MRS JAMIESON

I've found the number for RAF Topcliff.

URWIN

Get them then.

*She starts to dial. Fletcher and
Lennie exchange glances.*

FLETCHER

Listen, Reg, you don't really need us.
We're only littering up the place. We'll
just be getting back to our cells if it's all
the same to you. Busy day ahead.

URWIN

No, I need you two. Lock that door, Godber.

Lennie locks the door.

URWIN

Now both of you, move that filing cabinet up against it.

They start to move towards the cabinet.

MRS JAMIESON

I have them on the line, Mr Barrowclough.

BARROWCLOUGH

Er . . . should I . . . talk to them in there?

He indicates the inner office.

URWIN

Yeah, go on.

Barrowclough goes through into the other office. Urwin stays in the doorway covering both rooms.

LENNIE

Er . . . is that all you wanted us for, Reg. To move the cabinet?

URWIN

Yeah.

LENNIE

Oh well . . . we'll be getting off then.

FLETCHER

Yeah, give us a hand to shift this, Len.

They start moving the cabinet but Urwin stops them.

URWIN

Hey, hey! Think I'm crackers or something?

FLETCHER

Possibly, Reg. Your behaviour ain't exactly that of a rational man.

URWIN

I know what I'm doing. Give me that key.

Lennie gives him the key. He goes to the doorway.

URWIN

We'll just sit tight and wait.

There is a pause.

MRS JAMIESON

I have a dental appointment in half an hour.

URWIN

Then you'll have to bleedin' cancel it.

10. INNER OFFICE

Barrowclough is standing at the desk, talking on the phone. Urwin watches him.

BARROWCLOUGH

Hello? Yes, this is Prison Officer Barrowclough from Slade Prison . . . well, thank you Flight Sergeant, but don't you think I ought to speak to the Commanding Officer . . . yes, I know there's only two shopping days left till Christmas, but there is some urgency here.

Urwin crosses to the desk and grabs the phone from Barrowclough.

URWIN

Here. This is Reg Urwin. I'm in charge.

I've got the gun. Listen, I'm holding a man and a woman as hostage. I don't care how you do it, but I want a chopper here in half an hour. And wait a minute –

Fletcher and Lennie are standing in the doorway listening.

URWIN

– I also want ten thousand quid in used notes. Otherwise I'm not responsible for my actions.

He puts the phone down and turns to Barrowclough.

URWIN

That's the way to talk to those people. If they ring back and they're still stalling, make believe I'm going to kill you.

BARROWCLOUGH

I'll try to remember that.

11. OUTER OFFICE

Lennie is standing by the window. Mrs Jamieson gets up from her desk and goes to the cabinet. She opens a drawer.

LENNIE

Bearing up?

MRS JAMIESON

Pardon?

LENNIE

Under the strain, like.

MRS JAMIESON

Oh I'm keeping myself busy.

Both move towards the desk.

MRS JAMIESON

Doing some of those jobs one's always putting off. Helps keep my mind occupied otherwise I might go to pieces.

LENNIE

Not you, Mrs Jamieson.

He sits on the edge of the desk.

LENNIE

I think you're holding up extremely well. Typically British, if I may say so. Stiff upper lip. Calm under crisis, that sort of thing.

MRS JAMIESON

That's sweet of you to say so.

LENNIE

To be quite honest, it doesn't surprise me. I've always admired you, Mrs Jamieson. From afar, like.

MRS JAMIESON

Oh why?

LENNIE

You remind me of my aunty Pauline.

Fletcher comes through into the room and reacts to Lennie's line.

FLETCHER
(*At door*) Oh yes. Do I really?

LENNIE
(*Crossing to the bench and sitting down*) Oh, I was just –

FLETCHER
(*Walking over to Lennie*) I know just what you was justing. (*Quietly to Lennie*) You horny little beast.

MRS JAMIESON
He was trying to keep my spirits up.

There is a knock at the door.

FLETCHER
Come in. Oh, of course, you can't, can you? Give us a hand to shift this, Lennie.

Urwin comes to the doorway.

URWIN
'Ere, wait a minute, wait a minute, who is it?

FLETCHER
Wait a minute, wait a minute, who is it?

MACKAY
(*Offscreen*) It's Mr Mackay. I've brought the coffee you asked for.

FLETCHER
(*To Urwin*) It's Mr Mackay with the coffee we asked for.

URWIN
All right, let him in. But watch it.

FLETCHER
All right, you can come in. But watch it.

They move the filing cabinet away from the door and open the door.

Mackay is there with a tray of coffee mugs. He passes it through and Mrs Jamieson takes it.

MACKAY
Is everything all right in there, Fletcher?

URWIN
Everything's all right, so naff off, Mackay.

Mrs Jamieson takes the tray to the inner office.

MACKAY
I can't believe a thing like this is happening in my prison. And at Christmastime.

FLETCHER
All right for you lot out there. Just remember it's us what are going through this terrifying ordeal.

URWIN
That'll do, Fletch. Lock the door, give me the key and put the cabinet back.

FLETCHER
Mr Mackay, one last thing. Could you do me a favour?

MACKAY
What, Fletcher?

FLETCHER
I left my socks soaking in the basin, could you wring them out for me?

Mackay glares and closes the door.

Fletcher locks it and gives the key to Urwin. They start moving the cabinet back.

12. INNER OFFICE

Barrowclough and Mrs Jamieson are serving the coffee.

BARROWCLOUGH

Here we are, Urwin.

Urwin crosses to the desk, sits down and puts his feet up.

URWIN

Ta.

He takes the coffee. Fletcher and Lonnie walk in.

BARROWCLOUGH

Fletcher, Godber, help yourself to sugar.

FLETCHER

(*Picking mug up*) Well, I must say this is nice, very nice. Never thought I'd be served coffee by a screw.

LENNIE

(*Crossing from the desk to the chair*) In the Governor's office, too.

BARROWCLOUGH

Barriers tend to come down in situations like this.

FLETCHER

You don't mind if I sit then.

BARROWCLOUGH/URWIN (TOGETHER)

No, that's all right.

BARROWCLOUGH

Urwin?

URWIN

Go ahead.

Fletcher sits down. Lennie invites Mrs Jamieson to sit and then does so himself on the arm of the chair. Barrowclough remains standing.

FLETCHER

Thanks, Reg. Here's to you. Wherever you ends up.

LENNIE

Where will you go, Reg?

URWIN

Somewhere a long way away where they don't ask too many questions and don't care who I am as long as I can pay for it.

LENNIE

Oh you mean somewhere corrupt where they turn a blind eye if you grease their palm.

FLETCHER

Isle of Wight?

URWIN

I was thinking of South America or Mexico, somewhere like that.

FLETCHER

Oh yeah, funny country Mexico. Very . . . Mexican. Apparently all the dogs limp.

MRS JAMIESON

I didn't know that.

FLETCHER

Oh yes, well-known fact. It's something to do with the food.

LENNIE

Food?

FLETCHER

Bloke gets up in the morning,
contemplates his hideous breakfast
and kicks the dog.

URWIN

Really? And I'd always rather fancied
Mexico.

FLETCHER

Contrary to travel brochure myth,
they're not a happy people you know.
I suppose any country which has
tequila as its national drink is bent on
self-destruction.

Urwin finishes his coffee.

URWIN

I appreciate your advice, Fletch.
Maybe I'll think of somewhere else.

BARROWCLOUGH

You won't be going
anywhere, Urwin.

He picks up Urwin's mug.

URWIN

What?

BARROWCLOUGH

Don't you think we have well-
rehearsed precautions for emergencies
like this? Don't you worry, Mrs
Jamieson, you and I will not be going
South of the Border down Mexico way.

URWIN

What you on about?

BARROWCLOUGH

Didn't it puzzle you that I was being so
polite, handing out the coffee? That
was because one of those mugs was
laced with a powerful tranquilliser which

acts very swiftly, and in a few
moments, Urwin, in a few moments
you will be happily asleep in the
land of nod.

*There is a loud snore from Fletcher
who is now fast asleep, an empty
mug of coffee in his hand.*

13. ASSOCIATION AREA/LANDING

*Camera shows feet walking on the
landing. A senior Police Officer is
marching along. He meets up with
the Governor. They cross the
bridge together and walk along the
landing, round a corner and in
through a door.*

14A. MACKAY'S OFFICE

*Mackay is brewing tea as Venables
enters with the Senior Police Officer.*

VENABLES

Any word yet?

MACKAY

Not yet, no, sir. But everything's
under control. The rest of the prison
is quiet – all in the cells locked up.
Cup of tea, sir?

VENABLES

No, no. So they've no idea what's
going on?

MACKAY

(*Crossing to desk*) They know
something's up. They probably think
someone's gone over the wall.

VENABLES

As long as we keep the lid on
this thing.

MACKAY

(*Looking at his watch*) That stuff should
have worked by now. I put enough in
to knock out a rhinoceros.

VENABLES

I still can't believe that this is
happening here. Where did he get the
gun?

MACKAY

Probably made it. He's spent a lot of
time in the machine shop has Urwin,
and now one can see why.

The phone rings.

MACKAY

Aha!

He picks up the receiver.

MACKAY

Everything all right, Barrowclough . . .

His expression changes.

MACKAY

I see . . . yes, Urwin. Mr Urwin. Very
well. I'll remember that.

He puts the phone down.

VENABLES

What's happened?

MACKAY

Urwin says thank you for the coffee, it
perked him up. Fletcher on the other
hand is sleeping like a rhinoceros.

14B. INNER OFFICE

*Fletcher's head is on one side,
facing a stuffed trout which is
mounted on the wall. He is
still asleep.*

*The phone rings in the
outer office.*

MRS JAMIESON

Hello . . . Just one moment.

Urwin moves to the door.

URWIN

Is that for me?

MRS JAMIESON

(*At her desk*) I'm afraid not.

She walks to the door.

MRS JAMIESON

It's your wife, Mr Barrowclough.

BARROWCLOUGH

Oh dear. How does she sound?

MRS JAMIESON

Same as usual.

BARROWCLOUGH

Oh dear. (*To Urwin*) May I?

URWIN

Be my guest.

*Barrowclough goes across to the
phone.*

BARROWCLOUGH

Perhaps she hasn't heard yet.

He stands at the desk and picks up the phone.

BARROWCLOUGH

Hello, dear . . . what? No, I haven't forgotten but I think I should tell you there's a chance I may be late this evening . . . Now just a minute, Alice . . . Alice, if you'd give me a moment to explain . . . I know I've been late three times this week already, but I'm being held at gunpoint as a hostage . . . I *know* we're supposed to be going round to Mrs Wainwright's at eight . . . yes, yes, it's rude and inconsiderate, but I may be going abroad in a helicopter . . . Alice, I don't believe you've heard a word . . . at gunpoint, yes! There's Mrs Jamieson, two prisoners and myself . . .

He sits down and turns away.

BARROWCLOUGH

What do you mean, 'Oh is that woman with you!' . . .

Mrs Jamieson goes back to the outer office.

BARROWCLOUGH

Well, of course she's going too, neither of us has much say in the matter. Of *course* I'm not glad! Alice, this is pointless. I'll try and call again, but if I don't I suggest you watch the six o'clock news.

He replaces the phone and is suddenly aware that Lennie and Urwin have taken this all in and have put two and two together.

URWIN

(*Crossing and sitting on the arm of Lennie's chair*) Here Barra, your old lady reckons that you and Mrs Jamieson have got a little thing going, does she?

BARROWCLOUGH

Certainly not.

URWIN

I bet she didn't believe all those late shifts you've been working.

LENNIE

Now, Reg, this thing between Mr Barrowclough and Mrs Jamieson is sheer speculation.

BARROWCLOUGH

(*Getting up*) There is no 'thing' Godber. Our relationship is purely professional.

Mrs Jamieson comes in and walks across to the desk.

MRS JAMIESON

Should I clear these cups up, Mr Barrowclough?

URWIN

(*Crossing over to her*) No need to be so formal, love. We know all about you and him.

Mrs Jamieson blanches and bristles towards Barrowclough.

MRS JAMIESON

Henry, how could you!

BARROWCLOUGH

Dorothy, I never said a word.

MRS JAMIESON

Well, it never came from my lips!

She storms out, taking the tray.
Fletcher wakes up, stretching
himself, unaware at first of his
whereabouts. He starts on seeing
the fish, then looks around him, and
notices Lennie.

FLETCHER
Where am I?

LENNIE
(*Getting up and going over to Fletcher*)
We're in the Governor's office,
remember?
Fletcher gets to his feet
and launches straight into
his defence.

FLETCHER
Oh yes, sir, about Mr Mackay's
allegations, Godber and me weren't
drunk, we never drink. Sometimes we
chew on the occasional sock, but . . .
Lennie is trying to stop him.

LENNIE
Fletch, Fletch . . . The Governor isn't
here! Don't you remember?
He points to Urwin.

FLETCHER
Hello, Reg, you the new Governor?
What are you doing here?

URWIN
I'm hijacking Barrowclough, don't you
remember?

FLETCHER
How could I nod off in the middle
of that?

BARROWCLOUGH
The coffee you drank was drugged.

FLETCHER
Drugged?

LENNIE
It was meant for Reg, but
Barrowclough messed it up.

FLETCHER
I do feel a bit queer.
He sits down.

LENNIE
Could be dangerous, Fletch. Those
drugs on top of all the booze
we had.

BARROWCLOUGH
Thank you, Godber, I'll
remember that.

FLETCHER
So will I, my son.
Suddenly Mrs Jamieson comes
back with a transistor radio.

MRS JAMIESON
Listen, we're on *The World at One.*
Urwin stands up and Lennie moves
to the radio. They all listen.

VOICE
(*Offscreen*) A government spokesman
said that the Home Secretary
could not be reached for comment
regarding the situation at Slade Prison.

Details are still confused, but it appears that the Governor's secretary, Mrs Dorothy Jamieson . . .

Despite the situation, she is pleased at hearing her name on the radio, and Lennie gives her a little 'that's you' look.

VOICE
(*Offscreen*) and a Prison Officer . . . are being held at gunpoint by three desperate prisoners.

FLETCHER
Three!

He stands up, holds his head and sits down again.

VOICE
(*Offscreen*) They are demanding transportation and a large sum of money. In the City today, shares suffered a further decline when . . .

Urwin turns the radio off.
Mrs Jamieson takes it back into the outer office.

FLETCHER
(*Walking to the desk*) Here, what's this about three desperate men?

BARROWCLOUGH
They said that details were confused.
He sits down.

FLETCHER
Oh, yes, but next thing, they'll be issuing names.

LENNIE
What's my family going to think?

FLETCHER
What's my wife going to think?

BARROWCLOUGH
I hope she shows a little more consideration than mine.

URWIN
(*Getting up*) Hey, hey, hey. Never mind your naffing families, what about me? It's on the wireless so everybody knows about it. So why am I still stuck here, where's my helicopter?

Fletcher takes charge, the pacifier.

FLETCHER
Reg, Reg . . . a word of caution. I don't want you to build your hopes too high, my son.

URWIN
What d'you mean?

FLETCHER
I think you should get used to the idea that they may not play ball. Put yourself in their shoes. They have to demonstrate to an anxious public that they ain't going to bow down to every nutter with a gun and fly him off to sunnier climes.

URWIN
Here, I'm no nutter.

FLETCHER
I'm taking the Establishment viewpoint, Reg. Nothing personal.

LENNIE
'Nother thing – ten thou's a lot of money.

BARROWCLOUGH
Doesn't seem an excessive amount for a Prison Officer with twenty-three years' unblemished service.

URWIN

(*Sitting at the desk*) Let me get this straight. What you're saying like, is they're calling my bluff. They haven't been taking me seriously?

BARROWCLOUGH

(*Triumphantly*) Right. And there's nothing you can do about it now.

URWIN

There is one thing I could do.

BARROWCLOUGH

What?

URWIN

I could always shoot you.

He points the gun at Barrowclough.

BARROWCLOUGH

Yes, yes, I suppose you could do that.

FLETCHER

Wouldn't advise it, Reg. Any wave of public sympathy you might attract would go right out of the window if you was to maim a screw.

LENNIE

Listen to Fletch, and just keep cool.

FLETCHER

That's the ticket, son. 'Cause I have been through this before, you see.

URWIN

Have you?

BARROWCLOUGH

(*Disbelievingly*) Really, Fletcher?

FLETCHER

Yeah. First nick I was in. There was this bloke called Popplewell. He was a trusty like you, Reg. That's how he come to be on an outside work party. Repainting the Governor's house. Well, the next thing we knew he was barricaded in there with Mrs Bailey.

BARROWCLOUGH

Mrs Bailey?

FLETCHER

Yeah. Mrs Bailey, the Governor's wife, Mrs Bailey. That was her name. The Governor's name was Bailey, and she was married to him so she was Mrs Bailey. Follow all that, so far?

He looks round at Lennie and raises his eyes.

LENNIE

I suppose you called him Old Bailey?

FLETCHER

(*To Lennie*) Do you want to tell the story, Godber?

LENNIE

I'm sorry, I was just . . .

FLETCHER

(*Moving back to Urwin*) Yeah well.

LENNIE

Please go on, Fletch.

FLETCHER

Don't know if I can now. I've lost the thread.

URWIN

(*Pointing gun*) Get on with it.

FLETCHER

All right, all right. Well now, before you could say Jack Robinson the house was surrounded by the screws, and the law, and of course there was newspapers and television cameras. If I remember rightly, even Fyfe Robertson turned up but he soon cleared off. Anyhow, for three days all sorts of people made appeals to Popplewell, like the Chaplain, and the psychiatrist. But there was never a word from him or Mrs Bailey. Remember Mrs Bailey?

BARROWCLOUGH

What happened?

FLETCHER

On the fourth day Mrs Bailey let him go.

He sits down.

LENNIE

You mean she was holding him. Why?

FLETCHER

Why? Well, I think to use a catchphrase what was prevalent at the time, Len . . . she'd never had it so good.

15. OUTER OFFICE

The camera shows the clock on the wall which says half-past four. Mrs Jamieson is putting files in the filing cabinet. Fletcher and Lennie walk in from the Inner Office.

FLETCHER

You all right, Mrs Jamieson?

MRS JAMIESON

What is happening in there?

LENNIE

Oh, we've won a little victory. He's extended his deadline till five o'clock.

MRS JAMIESON

Oh good, then I'll probably have time

to finish this before he shoots us all. Or must I expect a fate worse than death?

FLETCHER

Is there a fate worse than death?

Mrs Jamieson thinks about it for a moment.

MRS JAMIESON

No, I don't suppose there is.

FLETCHER

That's the spirit. Here listen, are those prisoners' files?

MRS JAMIESON

Yes.

FLETCHER

Fish Urwin's out for me, would you?

MRS JAMIESON

Why?

FLETCHER

Might help, who knows? Have a quick shifty, Len.

He goes back into the inner office, while Lennie and Mrs Jamieson move to the filing cabinet.

16. INNER OFFICE

Urwin is sitting in the chair and Barrowclough is sitting at the desk.

URWIN

Listen, I'm getting bloody angry, now. When are we going to get some action around here?!

BARROWCLOUGH

I'm still waiting to hear from the Governor.

URWIN

Well, I can't wait much longer, remember that.

Fletcher feels the onus is on him to cool Urwin down.

FLETCHER

Here, Reg, you seem kind of tense.

URWIN

I got to get out, Fletch. Can't take any more.

BARROWCLOUGH

That's exactly how I feel.

URWIN

You feel like that after half a day. I've been in stir half me life.

BARROWCLOUGH

But you're up for parole soon, Urwin.

URWIN

Parole – they won't give it to me. Not a snowball's. They never have and they never will. And I just got to get out of here.

FLETCHER

But why this way, Reg?

URWIN

Because if I stay inside much longer, I'm going to top myself.

FLETCHER

Suicide. You wouldn't do that, would you?

URWIN

Tried it once before.

FLETCHER

Oh yes? How d'you make out?

Urwin stares at Fletcher for a moment.

URWIN

I failed, didn't I? Typical. I was in a supermarket. Trying to steal a tin of pork luncheon meat. Suddenly I thought, 'Is this what my life has come to? Stealing luncheon meat?'

FLETCHER

You tried to kill yourself in a supermarket. How?

URWIN

I just put me head down and charged towards the glass doors.

FLETCHER

What went wrong?

URWIN

(*Motions doors opening*) Electric. I ran head first into an off-duty cop . . . he booked me for nicking a tin of pork luncheon meat.

FLETCHER

Always one about when you don't want one. What you should realise, Reg, is you're one of those people who doesn't get the breaks. Not even with glass doors. Today's typical. Obviously you've been planning to

hijack the Governor for months. The
day you choose he gets the runs.

LENNIE

(*Offscreen*) Er, Fletch . . .

*Fletcher goes through to the
outer office.*

17. OUTER OFFICE

*As Fletcher comes in, Lennie hands
him Urwin's file.*

LENNIE

Look at this.

FLETCHER

(*Reading the file*) Would you Christmas
Eve it.

LENNIE

Three times in the past two years,
Urwin's been recommended for
psychiatric treatment.

FLETCHER

Only he never got it, did he? The
system did this to Reg. I've got to talk
to him. Mrs Jamieson, would you
come through here a minute, please.

He opens the door for her.

18. INNER OFFICE

*Fletcher walks in, holding the file,
followed by Mrs Jamieson.*

FLETCHER

Sit down, love. Reg, can you come
through and have a word with me and
Godber? Private, like.

Urwin looks a little doubtful.

URWIN

I dunno.

LENNIE

Come on, Reg. These two can't get up
to nowt.

He casts a look in their direction.

LENNIE

Well, they can, but I don't think they'd
want to with us in the
next room.

URWIN

Okay then.

*Lennie goes across to the desk with
the file.*

LENNIE

Read this, Mr Barrowclough. It should
interest you.

Lennie returns to the Outer Office.

19. OUTER OFFICE

*Fletcher escorts Urwin to
the bench.*

FLETCHER

Here, Reg, sit down. You trust me,
don't you?

URWIN

Maybe.

He sits.

FLETCHER

Well, I got to tell you, son. You ain't
going to make it.

Lennie moves in behind Fletcher.

URWIN

Got to make it, Fletch. I'm a three-time loser.

FLETCHER

I swear to you there ain't no way. They got all the arguments on their side. Worst thing that could happen is if they say okay.

He sits.

FLETCHER

'Cause you know you'd never make it to that helicopter. They've got blokes out there could shoot a fly's eyebrows off at four hundred yards. And if flies had anything else they could shoot them off an' all. Know what I mean? And say you got to Mexico. Where next? Look at you. You think you're going to check into the Acapulco Hilton looking like that?

LENNIE

They'd never let you in without a tie.

FLETCHER

Reg . . . me and lad could have jumped you over the last few hours. But we didn't. You know why?

URWIN

Why?

FLETCHER

Because that would have dropped you in even further than what you is now. They have to see that you chucked in the towel yourself. Voluntary, like. Look, I won't lie to you. They're going to throw the book at

you. But I've been reading your file. You've got some kind of case . . . if you give yourself up.

Urwin considers, then shakes his head negatively.

URWIN

No, Fletch. I'm going through with it.

FLETCHER

Think, Reg.

URWIN

No . . .

He stands up.

URWIN

I'm going the distance.

Fletcher stands up.

FLETCHER

In that case, you leaves me no choice. I'm going to have to take that gun off of you.

URWIN

You're what?

He backs off, brandishing the gun. Lennie stares at Fletcher astonished. He holds out his hand.

FLETCHER

Give me the gun.

URWIN

Stay where you are, Fletch.

Fletcher starts to walk towards him – John Wayne never did it better.

FLETCHER

Reg, you're my mucker, you ain't going to shoot me.

URWIN

Don't bank on it!

LENNIE

Hey, Fletch, give over. He's serious.

FLETCHER

Not to worry. Reg and me is mates.

URWIN

Don't push it – mate!

Fletcher reaches out a hand. The gun is in Urwin's hand. Fletcher very deliberately pushes a finger into the barrel of the gun.

Fletcher gently takes the gun from Urwin and puts it in the desk drawer. Urwin crumples into the chair.

FLETCHER

(*Arm round Urwin*) Now, Reg, on your feet, son. Don't let go. Don't pack it in. Now's the time you have to be in control.

URWIN

What's the point?

FLETCHER

Every point. Mustn't let Barra think we overcame you. You go in there and tell him this was your decision. And Len and me will back you up.

LENNIE

He's right, Reg. It's your only chance.

URWIN

You'd back me up?

FLETCHER

'Course we will, like I said we're still on the side of us. There's still them and us.

URWIN

But you two could be heroes. For what you two have just done you could probably get a free pardon.

Fletcher stands up and looks at Lennie.

FLETCHER

Well – what d'you think, Len?

LENNIE

'Tis Christmas after all.

FLETCHER

Goodwill to all men and all that swaddling. (*To Urwin*) On your way, son.

URWIN

Maybe you're right.

He gets up and starts to go, then stops and turns.

URWIN

But I'm still calling the shots, aren't I?

FLETCHER

'Course you are. Main thing is, you didn't shoot the shots.

Urwin walks through to the inner office.

URWIN

(*Offscreen*) Mr Barrowclough . . .

Lennie walks over to the door and shuts it.

LENNIE

Fletch, you are a ruddy marvel. I've never seen anything like it.

FLETCHER

What – oh, the gun, yes well . . .

He gets the gun from the drawer.

LENNIE

No, no, don't denigrate what you just done. I never seen anything like it. Not even in *Kojak*.

FLETCHER

Yeah well, I had an advantage over Lollipop head, didn't I, I knew the gun weren't loaded.

LENNIE

Wasn't it?

FLETCHER

No . . . I been working in the machine shop with Reg. He's been making that gun for months, it's only a toy.

Lennie takes the gun.

LENNIE

You knew that all along?

FLETCHER

Yes, but as I just said, if I'd mentioned it I'd've dropped him deeper in the clarts.

He takes the gun.

LENNIE

Looks very authentic to me – are you sure it's a toy?

FLETCHER

'Course I am. Look.

He points the gun towards the ceiling and pulls the trigger. There is a bang followed by a shower of plaster falling on their heads.

20. CELL

Fletcher is putting up a pathetic paper chain when Barrowclough enters. He clears his throat.

BARROWCLOUGH

Evening, Fletcher.

He walks over to the bunk.

FLETCHER

Oh hello, Mr Barrowclough.

BARROWCLOUGH

This is very nice. Is Godber about?

FLETCHER

No, he wanted to prove that his Christmas pudding was not the cause of the Governor's indisposition. So he ate three helpings to vindicate his reputation.

BARROWCLOUGH

Three!!! Oh I see, where is he then?

FLETCHER

Still in the bog. Two more to go.

He moves to the table and picks up the paper chain.

BARROWCLOUGH

How are you feeling then, after our terrible ordeal?

FLETCHER

I'm all right, Mr Barrowclough. But me and the lads are still a bit concerned about Reg Urwin.

He stands on the chair to pin up the paper chain.

BARROWCLOUGH

I have been assured that Urwin will be undergoing psychiatric treatment. He will not be punished so much as helped.

FLETCHER

(*On chair*) Yeah well, not before time.

BARROWCLOUGH

And I had a word with the Governor and in appreciation of your conduct the charges against you and Godber will be dropped.

FLETCHER

(*Getting down from chair*) Charges! Oh you mean those unfounded allegations about us making booze. Well good, only right and proper.

BARROWCLOUGH

'Nough said.

FLETCHER

Yeah, we don't get our booze back though, do we? (*Picking up the paper chain*) Hold this.

He moves the chair.

BARROWCLOUGH

In . . . in . . . in return, of course, I would like to think that you could forget certain things that may have been revealed during those desperate hours.

He moves towards Fletcher.

FLETCHER

(*On chair*) Like what?

BARROWCLOUGH

The rather delicate matter of Mrs Jamieson and myself. I'd like it to go no further.

FLETCHER

(*Getting down*) I don't know what you're on about, Mr Barrowclough.

BARROWCLOUGH

That's the spirit, Fletcher.

FLETCHER

If you're trying to tell me there's something I'm supposed to forget, I think you're overlooking the fact I was asleep most of the time. I didn't hear anything.

BARROWCLOUGH

You mean . . . you didn't know about myself and Mrs Jamieson?

FLETCHER

No, sir. Just don't worry . . . I do now, Henry . . .